ArtScroll Judaiscope Series®

Rabbi Nosson Scherman / Rabbi Meir Zlotowitz

General Editors

Collected from the pages of
The Jewish Observer
Rabbi Nisson Wolpin, Editor

THE
ETHICAL
IMPERATIVE

TORAH PERSPECTIVES
ON ETHICS AND VALUES

Published by

Mesorah Publications, ltd

FIRST EDITION
First Impression … June 2000

Published and Distributed by
MESORAH PUBLICATIONS, LTD.
4401 Second Avenue / Brooklyn, N.Y 11232

Distributed in Europe by
LEHMANNS
Unit E, Viking Industrial Park
Rolling Mill Road NE32 3DP
Jarow, Tyne & Wear,
England

Distributed in Israel by
SIFRIATI / A. GITLER
10 Hashomer Street
Bnei Brak 51361

Distributed in Australia and New Zealand by
GOLDS BOOK & GIFT SHOP
36 William Street
Balaclava 3183, Vic., Australia

Distributed in South Africa by
KOLLEL BOOKSHOP
Shop 8A Norwood Hypermarket
Norwood 2196, Johannesburg, South Africa

ARTSCROLL JUDAISCOPE SERIES®
THE ETHICAL IMPERATIVE
© *Copyright 2000, by* MESORAH PUBLICATIONS, Ltd.
4401 Second Avenue / Brooklyn, N.Y. 11232 / (718) 921-9000 / www.artscroll.com

ISBN:
1-57819-508-X (hard cover)
1-57819-509-8 (paperback)

Typography by CompuScribe at ArtScroll Studios, Ltd.

Printed in the United States of America by Noble Book Press Corp.
Bound by Sefercraft, Quality Bookbinders, Ltd., Brooklyn N.Y. 11232

This volume is dedicated
in loving memory of

Mr. Emanuel M. Ray ז"ל

An ardent supporter of Jewish education, he led
by example, understanding full well that the future of
Klal Yisrael rests in the hands of our children.
He believed that as parents and educators, we had the
sacred duty to instill in our children uncompromised
values, especially in matters of honesty and integrity.

It is our fervent hope that works such as this volume
will help inspire "our people" toward a better understanding of what the Creator expects of us and how
we must approach our daily lives. This indeed, would
be a most fitting tribute to his memory.

Barry and Harriet Ray and Family
Chicago, Illinois

The Center for Halacha and American Law

The Center for Halacha and American Law, a part of the Miami-based Aleph Institute, was established in mid-1998. The Aleph Institute is a tax-exempt, 501(c)(3), not-for-profit organization that was originally founded in 1981 primarily to provide Jewish inmates and their families with educational, humanitarian and religious advocacy and social support. Since that time, the Aleph Institute has significantly expanded its scope of activities through a variety of endeavors and projects such as the creation of The Center.

The Center's goals and objectives are:

1) to enhance the Jewish community's appreciation of the requirements of Halacha to conduct all business and personal transactions in accordance with Torah principles, ethics and values, including the obligation under the Halacha to abide by the law of the civil authority;

2) to educate the Jewish community about the seriousness of secular law and financial ethics, and the need for Jews to be examples of proper business and financial behavior;

3) to forge a better understanding within the Jewish community of the interaction between Halacha, civil authority and secular law (including both civil and criminal law);

4) to increase the Jewish community's understanding of American statutory and regulatory law, particularly in areas of application to the community; and

5) to assist Jewish businessmen and professionals in ways that will encourage and enable them to abide by the dictates of Halacha and comply with the law of the civil authority.

For more information about The Aleph Institute and The Center for Halacha and American Law, please visit http://www.aleph-institute.org, and http://jlaw.com/LawPolicy/CenterforHalacha.html, send an e-mail to Isaac Jaroslowicz, Esq. Aleph's Legal Director, at imj@aleph-institute.org or write to, or call, The Aleph Institute: 9540 Collins, Avenue, Surfside, FL 33154. Tel.: (305) 864-5553; fax: (305) 864-5675.

מכתב ברכה

Rabbi S. Kamenetsky

2018 Upland Way
Philadelphia, Pa 19131

Home: 215-473-2798
Study: 215-473-1212

בס"ד יום שלישי מן פרשת וילך

הנני להכיר טובה אוירא שוב לידי ר' יצחק קרלין
ועל יפותיו ועוזרת לצד ב' כלומר כלל שתף לגדולי הלאשונים דלינן
בפירול רב הפתגמ מאנמ ומן וכל דיני מאנט הנ ולעמים דין
יצא לתחרו דמאנין ידוד הטיד מאסולול התרום שוף שלא
לוגן חם ולמא דליו אשר כל לאוצר דלינים עלו.
ר' יצחק הנ"ל מאויץ לגבית ערב חווזק ועשה
לולאצורים רגויר לגריו דו גם ז גלאשונים לצקר
דינים צבז ועין ובגלוטרטן ועולם. כדי כתב הפאון הפפוד
שבן ג' שלה פיזואשן 93' איך אלון מאולוריא לגדרה דרה
ובקבם במאין ומ לקואת צלולמ אסר מאלוריות לחפב
ילומרה. כן כלון פך לחתויד הפדלות ולגליל ברוך
מין, אולאצריא אולאמל הרעים לעצבר דינים אלו
מצות צמלה, לחתענקו ולעובבו רצת אולן שות
ולדלולי וגברה כאלו צאים גינו וכל התאבעק ובנה
להתמיר מאצב התורה צבקבת ולאחת לצ.

דצל הכימו ודפרפם

(signature)

Table of Contents

III. The Beis Din Process

IV. Legislative Concerns

V. Public Posture and Policies

VI. Introspection / Self Improvement

Contributors to this volume*
(In alphabetical order)

Yaakov Astor is a published author whose article appeared in *The Jewish Observer,* January 1997.

Dr. Judith Bleich is a professor of Judaic Studies at Touro College, New York. Her article appeared in *The Jewish Observer,* Summer 1997.

Rabbi Aaron Brafman is *menahel* of Yeshiva Derech Ayson of Far Rockaway. His essay "The Crisis is Now - II" appeared in *The Jewish Observer,* Summer 1997; his essay "Where Are We Heading?", appeared in *The Jewish Observer,* October 1998.

Yoseph M. Braunfeld is currently a practicing accountant. He learned in the *kollel* of Yeshiva Rabbi Samson Raphael Hirsch. His article appeared in *The Jewish Observer,* May 1997.

Abba Cohen heads the Washington office of Agudath Israel of America. His article, based on an address at a convention of Agudath Israel of America, appeared in *The Jewish Observer,* February 1997.

Eliezer Cohen studies in a *kollel* in the New York area. His article appeared in *The Jewish Observer,* February 1985.

Judah Dick is an attorney in private practice in Brooklyn, New York and served as Vice President of COLPA. His article appeared in *The Jewish Observer,* March 1972.

Rabbi Avrohom Chaim Feuer is *Rav* of Kehillas Bais Avrohom in Monsey, New York and has authored numerous books. His article appeared in *The Jewish Observer,* June 1972.

Rabbi Yissocher Frand, a popular lecturer and author, is a *maggid shiur* at Yeshiva Ner Israel in Baltimore and gives a weekly *shiur* in the Agudath Israel of Baltimore. His "Fighting Assimilation From Within", based on an address at a convention of Agudath Israel of America, appeared in *The Jewish Observer,* February 1992; his, "The Invasive Spirit of Modern Values", appeared in *The Jewish Observer,* May 1994.

Rabbi Moshe Yechiel Friedman is Program Supervisor of Torah Umesorah's Counterforce program and served as Associate Editor of the *Jewish Parent* magazine. His article appeared in *The Jewish Observer,* October 1973.

---

* Most of the biographical information was culled from the original articles in *The Jewish Observer.*

Rabbi Mordechai Gifter is *Rosh HaYeshivah* in Telshe Yeshiva in Wickliffe, Ohio. His article is based on an address given at a symposium on *Law in a Troubled World,* sponsored by Western Reserve University in Cleveland, Ohio. It appeared in *The Jewish Observer,* June 1965.

Rabbi Yisroel Greenwald is a member of Kollel Beis HaTalmud — Yehudah Fishman Institute in Melbourne, Australia. His article appeared in *The Jewish Observer,* September 1981.

Rabbi Heshy Grossman, a *musmach* of the Yeshiva of Far Rockaway, New York, is a *rebbi* at Y.U.L.A. High School in Los Angeles, California. His article appeared in *The Jewish Observer,* December 1990.

Rabbi Shmuel Halberstadt is *Rosh Chaburah* of *Kollel Boker* of Flatbush. His article appeared in *The Jewish Observer,* Summer 1995.

Yosi Heber is a *musmach* of Mesivta Torah Vodaath, and is vice president of marketing at Dannon/Lea & Perrins. His article appeared in *The Jewish Observer,* November 1996.

Rabbi Levi Yitzchok Horowitz, The Bostoner Rebbe, divides his year between Boston and Har Nof, Jerusalem. He is a member of the *Moetzes Gedolei HaTorah* of Agudath Israel of *Eretz Yisrael.* His article is based on an address at a National Convention of Agudath Israel of America. It appeared in *The Jewish Observer,* February 1995.

Harold Jacobs ל"ז was president of Precisionware, Inc. in Queens, New York, and Chairman of the Board of the Union of Orthodox Jewish Congregations of America. He was active in many Orthodox organizations and Torah institutions. His article appeared in *The Jewish Observer,* April 1967.

Dr. Yoel Jakobovits, M.D. maintains his medical practice on the Yeshiva Ner Israel campus, where he was a *talmid.* He also practices at Sinai Hospital and is on the faculty of Johns Hopkins University. His article, "A Matter of Life and Death - Revisited" appeared in *The Jewish Observer,* October 1991; his article, "Kiddush Hashem in the House of Lords," appeared in *The Jewish Observer,* April 1988.

Yitzchak Kasdan, Esq. is a graduate of Yeshiva College in New York City and of the Georgetown Law Center in Washington, D.C., where he served as an editor of the *Georgetown Law Journal.* He has practiced law in Washington, D.C. for more than twenty years. Mr. Kasdan also is the founder and editor of the "Jewish Law" web site located at http://www.jlaw.com. His article, "A Proposal for P'sharah: A Jewish Mediation/Arbitration Service," appeared in *Jewish Action,* published by the Orthodox Union, in Spring, 1990.

Rabbi Chaim Dov Keller is the *Rosh HaYeshivah* of the Telshe Yeshiva in Chicago. His article is based on an address at a convention of Agudath Israel of America. It appeared in *The Jewish Observer,* June 1988.

Yisroel Mayer Kirzner is an Assistant Professor of Economics in New York University. He studied at the University of Capetown and received his doctorate from NYU. His article appeared in *The Jewish Observer,* September 1968

Rabbi Eliyahu Meir Klugman is a Maggid Shiur in a Yeshiva for Americans in Jerusalem. He is also the author of a biography of Rabbi Samson Raphael Hirsch (ArtScroll/Mesorah Publications). His article "The *Ish Ha'Emes:* The Man of Unimpeachable Integrity, Rabbi Shimon Schwab," appeared in *The Jewish Observer,* September 1995; his article, "Integrity: Rabbi Moshe Sherer," appeared in *The Jewish Observer,* Summer 1998.

Shlomo Kohn, a broker in New York City, specializes in matching Yissachars and Zevuluns. His article appeared in *The Jewish Observer,* May 1985.

Dr. Gershon Kranzler ז"ל was a professor of Sociology at Towson College, near Baltimore. His article appeared in *The Jewish Observer,* April 1978.

Rabbi Noach Issac Oelbaum, a *talmid* of the late Rabbi Moshe Bick, is *Rav* of Congregation Nachlas Yitzchok in Kew Garden Hills. His article appeared in *The Jewish Observer,* October 1999.

Rabbi Noach Orlowek serves as *Mashgiach* in several yeshivos in Yerushalayim and is the author numerous books. His article, based on a chapter in one of his books, appeared in *The Jewish Observer,* December 1995.

Rabbi Avrohom Pam is the *Rosh HaYeshivah* of Mesivta Torah Vodaath, Brooklyn and a member of the *Moetzes Gedolei HaTorah.* His article, "The Yeshiva Graduate's Obligation," based on an address to an alumni gathering of Mesivta Torah Vodaath, originally appeared in *The Jewish Observer,* May-June 1979. It was prepared for publication by Rabbis Yonah Blumenfrucht and Matis Blum. His article "The Exalted Status of the Beis Din Process," based on a *shiur* in Torah Vodaath, appeared in *The Jewish Observer,* May 1998, and was prepared by Rabbi Avrohom Liss. Rabbi Pam's "Did You Conduct Your Affairs With Faith?" is based on an address to Mesivta Torah Vodaath alumni. It was prepared for publication by Rabbi Matis Blum and appeared in *The Jewish Observer,* May 1978.

Rabbi Yaakov Perlow, Novominsker Rebbe, is Rosh of Agudath Israel of America, *Rosh HaYeshivah* of Yeshivas Novominsk and a member of the *Moetzes Gedolei HaTorah*. His article appeared in *The Jewish Observer*, February 1993.

Rabbi Yisroel Reisman is *Rav* of Agudath Israel of Madison . He is a popular lecturer whose weekly series on topics in *Tanach* attracts hundreds of participants. His article, "Minimizing the Risks of Exposure," based on a presentation at a convention of Agudath Israel of America, appeared in *The Jewish Observer*, February 1995; his article, "Our Mandate to Generate Kiddush Shem Shamayim: A Private Matter," appeared in March 1994.

Professor Steven H. Resnicoff, a Professor at DePaul University College of Law, is a *Yoreh Yoreh, Yadin Yadin musmach* of Rabbi Moshe Feinstein, זצ"ל, and learned in the Lakewood Yeshiva. A graduate of Yale Law School and Princeton College, Prof. Resnicoff has widely published and lectured regarding the interaction of *halachah* and secular law. He is a member of the Executive Committee — and former Chair — of the Association of American Law Schools Section on Jewish Law, and he has been selected by DePaul to hold its Wicklander Chair for Professional Ethics. His article, "The Secular Enforceability of a *Beis Din* Judgment," appeared in *The Jewish Observer*, October 1999.

Rabbi Matis Roberts is the *Mashgiach Ruchani* of Yeshiva Shaar HaTorah of Queens, New York. His article appeared in *The Jewish Observer*, April 1998.

Rabbi Yaakov Yitzchok Ruderman, זצ"ל was the founding *Rosh HaYeshivah* of Yeshiva Ner Israel, Baltimore, Maryland. He was a member of the *Moetzes Gedolei HaTorah* of Agudath Israel of America.

David Schaps is an American-born member of a *Kollel* in Bnei Brak. His article, "A Nation of Devourers," appeared in *The Jewish Observer*, Summer 1987; his article, "Learning From a Computer," appeared in *The Jewish Observer*, October 1987.

Rabbi Nosson Scherman is general editor of ArtScroll/Mesorah Publications, edits *Olomeinu* (Torah Umesorah's magazine for children), and serves on the Editorial Board of *The Jewish Observer*. His article, based on an address given at a convention of Agudath Israel of America, appeared in *The Jewish Observer*, March 1994.

Rabbi Shimon Schwab זצ״ל was *Rav* of Khal Adath Jeshurun (Washington Heights, N.Y.). His article, "Integrity and Faith in the Marketplace," based on an address presented to a conference for accountants sponsored by Agudath Israel of America and the Cheshbonot Society, originally appeared in *The Jewish Observer,* April 1989; his "The Jew in Galus: How High a Profile?," based on an address delivered at a convention of Agudath Israel of America, originally appeared in *The Jewish Observer,* February 1988.

Rabbi Moshe Silberberg of Monsey, New York, is an author of *sefarim* and frequent lecturer on the subject of *ribbis*. His article appeared in *The Jewish Observer,* October 1999.

Rabbi Elya Svei is *Rosh HaYeshivah* of the Yeshiva of Philadelphia and a member of the *Moetzes Gedolei HaTorah*. His article is based on an address at a convention of Agudath Israel of America and appeared in *The Jewish Observer,* December 1988.

Rabbi Ezriel Tauber, author of a number of books on Jewish themes, is the founder of Mechon HaHoyroa and Shalhevet. He lives in Monsey, N.Y. where he is active in communal affairs. His article, based on an address at a convention of Agudath Israel of America, appeared in *The Jewish Observer,* February 1995, and was prepared for publication by Yaakov Astor.

Rabbi Moshe D. Tendler is a professor of Biology and Medical Ethics in Yeshiva University. He is also the *Rav* of the Community Synagogue of Monsey, New York. His article appeared in *The Jewish Observer,* October 1991.

Professor Aaron Twerski is a professor of law in Brooklyn Law School and serves as chairman of Agudath Israel of America's Commission of Legislation and Civic Action. His articles, based on presentations at various conventions of Agudath Israel of America, originally appeared in *The Jewish Observer.* "Standing Up for Torah Principles: Battles on the Personal Front," in May 1994; "The Time for Tikkun Has come. Are We Ready?," in February 1996; and "Discordant Notes: An Essay on *Galus* and Egalitarianism," in January 1992.

Rabbi Berel Wein, a popular lecturer and author, served as Dean of Shaarei Torah of Rockland County and the Bas Torah Academy, as well as *Rav* of the Congregation Bais Torah, all in Monsey, NY. He now resides in Israel. His article appeared in *The Jewish Observer,* April 1998.

Rabbi Nisson Wolpin is a prolific writer and is Editor of *The Jewish Observer*. His "In Search of Simplicity," appeared in *The Jewish Observer*, February 1996; "When Fashion Is Eloquent, What Does It Say?," in *The Jewish Observer*, April 1991; "Some Thoughts on 'Selling' Tzenius," in *The Jewish Observer*,February 1992; and "News Clippings," in *The Jewish Observer*, April 1986.

Chaim Dovid Zwiebel, Esq., an attorney, is the Director of Government Affairs and General Counsel of Agudath Israel of America. His articles "Using Secular Government to Promote Religious Interests," appeared in *The Jewish Observer*, February 1987; his "The 'Halachic Health Care Proxy,'" in *The Jewish Observer*, September 1990; his "A Matter of Life and Death," in *The Jewish Observer*, Summer 1991; his "Rejoinder," in *The Jewish Observer*, October 1991; his "Batei Din vs. Secular Courts," in *The Jewish Observer*, January 1993; and his "Poison Ivy: Lessons of the Yale Five," in *Coalition*, 1997.

Most essays in this book first appeared,
over the course of thirty years,
as articles in *The Jewish Observer*,
a monthly journal of thought and opinion
published by Agudath Israel of America.

Rabbi Nisson Wolpin, Editor

Editorial Board
Dr. Ernst L. Bodenheimer, Chairman
Rabbi Abba Brudny
Rabbi Joseph Elias
Joseph Friedenson
Rabbi Yisroel Meir Kirzner
Rabbi Nosson Scherman
Prof. Aaron Twerski

Rabbi Yosef C. Golding, Managing Editor

Introduction

Rabbi Nisson Wolpin, Editor
The Jewish Observer

W hen the famed *mussar* figure Reb Simcha Zissel Ziv, known as the *Alter* of Kelm, returned from visiting his son Reb Daniel, he was asked by a member of his yeshivah how the young man was doing. The fact that Reb Daniel had left the yeshivah and was involved in the lumber business seemed to have cast a shadow on his loyalty to his father's teachings. "I was truly pleased by what I found," said Reb Simcha Zissel. "There was Reb Daniel supervising the business, with *Mesillas Yesharim* always at hand" — figuratively, of course; not literally.

In Germany of the mid-19th century, the motto was "*Zie ein Jude zur Hause and ein Mensch in der Strasse* — Be a Jew at home, but be a person in the street," as if the two were mutually exclusive ... as if to say: If you must be a Jew, do it privately. Don't let it interfere with your public persona as a *mensch*.

Into this environment stepped Rabbi Samson Raphael

Hirsch, to teach — and demonstrate — that in truth, the two are interdependent. In fact, they are inseparable. One cannot be a *mensch* in defiance of *halachah*, nor can one be a Jew in a non-*menschlich*, inconsiderate or unethical manner. Torah, as an all-embracing source of guidance, in fact defines the highest standards of ethical conduct, and in Rabbi Hirsch's formulation, one must strive to be a *Jude-Mensch*, wherein each component defines the other.

The scene was Budapest, in 1869. In a public debate with the *Ksav Sofer* (Rabbi Avrohom Shmuel Binyomin Schreiber), a Reform spokesman ridiculed the Orthodox for being involved in what he characterized as obsessive involvement in trivial rituals, to the degree of even having laws governing how one uses the lavatory.

To this, the Ksav Sofer replied, "Absolutely. To the Torah Jew, there is no phase of human existence *not* addressed by Torah Law. Every aspect of life has the potential for spiritualization, even bodily functions. In fact," he added, "I challenge you to name one phase of human activity not governed by Torah Law. I guarantee that it would only be a matter of your lack of awareness."

As it always was, so it is today: With the exciting progress taking place in technology — in manufacturing, communication, medicine and commerce — we are all a party to sweeping changes in how we conduct our businesses and professions, in our manner of expressing ourselves, even in our mode of thinking.

Halachah, of course, has comments and directives on all of these. It is our task to see to it that our own awareness of *halachah's* instructions keeps pace with these changes.

Part of the mandate of *The Jewish Observer* is to address current concerns from a Torah point of view — or as the late Rabbi Moshe Sherer was fond of saying, "to discuss the timely from the perspective of timeless values."

The Jewish Observer has continually made an effort to publish essays and discussions by leading Torah authorities and thinkers on pressing issues that would concern business leaders and professionals who use our sacred literature as their moral compass, their navigational guide, and their map of the ethical universe they inhabit.

We are deeply gratified that The Aleph Institute • Center for Halacha and American Law has taken upon itself to help make available a collection of such articles from our pages. This volume is an expanded version of a compilation which the Center distributed at the **Halachah Conference for Business Leaders and Professionals** dedicated to the theme: "The Interface of Ethics and *Halachah* in the Business & Professional World," sponsored by the Agudath Israel of America Torah Projects Division, held in New York City in 1999.

May we all be worthy of having the *Shechinah* rest on our handiwork.

Rabbi Nisson Wolpin, Editor
The Jewish Observer

Sivan 5760 / June 2000

✣ Business Ethics/ Workplace Issues

Integrity and Faith in the Marketplace

Did You Conduct Your Business Affairs With Faith?

Standing Up for Torah Principles: Battles on the
Personal Front

Making It in the Workplace, and Creating a
Kiddush Hashem in the Process

Challenge and Commitment

Torah Ethics in Business

Employer/Employee Relationships in *Halachah*

Modern Business and the Prohibition against *Ribbis*

A Proposal for a High School Course in Torah Ethics

Integrity and Faith in the Marketplace

Adapted from an address
by Rabbi Shimon Schwab

✦ *A Profession of Integrity*

Accounting is considered a highly dignified profession, based as it is on public trust in the integrity of men and women who apply a strict code of ethics to their activities. After all, the public relies on the financial statements and judgments of these professionals in many areas.

The conscientious CPA may encounter difficult problems, which might affect his own livelihood. At times, he might be forced to give up a well-paying client because his sense of right and wrong does not permit him to put his name to a financial statement that he considers fraudulent. For the Orthodox CPA, there might be more than one occasion when he must jeopardize his relationship with a client if the *halachah* does not permit him to be a party to financial deals that are prohibited. Even a CPA who is not merely attesting to financial statements or situations, but is acting in his capacity as advisor to his client as to how to best invest his money, or performing other such financial services, may encounter challenging situations. There are times when one must put his foot down and warn his client gently but firmly that a particular approach is shady or outright dishonest, something that is not only forbidden by the law of the land — *dina d'malchusa* — but that is directly *assur min haTorah*, and in some cases involves the possibility of *chillul Hashem*. For example, there is a very fine line that separates legitimate tax avoidance from prohibited tax evasion.

Your client may not always appreciate your ethical stringency, which prevents you from becoming a party to any wrongdoings, with the result that he ח"ו may not want to retain your services any further, which might spell a loss of *parnasah* (sustenance). Following these guidelines calls for genuine *mesiras nefesh*, a commodity that is rather rare in our generation. It therefore may be in order to define briefly the Torah concept of *parnasah*, and our attitude of *massa u'mattan b'emunah* — doing business in good faith; and at the same time, to elaborate a bit on *gezel* — thievery — in general, and *gezel akum*, in particular. All of these are closely aligned with the worst of all transgressions, *chillul Hashem* — or, on the other hand, with the *zechus* and distinction of an opportunity for *kiddush Hashem*.

✦ A Background of Limited Aspirations

Permit me here to inject a personal note. I was brought up as a child of parents, grandparents and great-grandparents who all were businessmen — *yerei'im u'sheleimim*, G–d fearing, upright people. Until the age of 27, I was so naive as to believe that running a business for the sake of *parnasah* meant no more than to strive to make a decent living, to pay all debts on time, to put some funds aside for various contingencies, and to give generously to *tzedakah*. As for the monthly *tefillah* for "*osher v'chavod* — riches and honor," it was never aimed at acquiring great wealth and public honor. Rather, wealth was defined in *Bircas HaMazon* (Grace After Meals) — "*lo lidei matnas basar va'dam, v'lo lidei hal'vaasam*" — not to be in need of any gifts, handouts, charitable loans; not to be beholden to anyone for assistance. Pursuing my business or profession was in keeping with the guidelines of *"Eizehu ashir, hasame'ach b'chelko* — Who is wealthy? He who is satisfied with his lot"(*Avos* 4:1). This is the philosophy that I inherited from my parents and grandparents.

And what type of *kavod* does one pray for? That I not suffer *bizyonos*, not do anything shameful that will spoil my character or sully my reputation, but to remain all my life a decent righteous and straight individual ... to be generous, a *baal tzedakah*, and not be the object of insult and embarrassment. This was the *kavod* I sought, and nothing more.

Then, when I got older and I came to these shores, I learned that I was wrong: As a newly arrived rabbi, I was asked to officiate at a funeral of a wealthy person who was unknown to me. Before the *hesped*, I inquired about the *niftar*, and was told by his relatives that this man was a *shomer Torah u'mitzvos*, an *ish tam v'yashar* — wholesome and straight. But I was cautioned not to overemphasize the last word because he was a businessman.

I, in my naivete, asked: *What does that mean?*

It was then revealed to me that, in this country, a businessman is somebody who works very hard, day and night, to make as much money as possible, to earn much more than he or his children will ever need. Then, observing the world around me, I came to realize that the harmless, legitimate pursuit of *parnasah* could escalate until it becomes an *avodah zarah*, a deity that one worships to the extent that eventually one identifies himself with one's financial enterprises; and without worldly possessions, life loses all meaning.

It is clear that the Torah concept of *parnasah* is quite different. In *parshas Vayechi*, both *Midrash Rabbah* and *Tanchuma* tell us: *"Gedolah haparnasah yoser min hageulah"* — In terms of our relationship to *HaKadosh Baruch Hu*, *parnasah* is even greater than *geulah*. Making a living involves a greater intimacy with G–d than redemption from danger, because *geulah* is effected through a *malach*, in keeping with *"Hamalach hagoel osi mikol ra."* That is, G–d dispatches a *malach* to redeem us from all evil. But *parnasah* is delivered by *HaKadosh Baruch Hu*, the money I earn is given directly from His hands, without the intervention of a *malach*: When I obtain a job, whenever I earn money or I am successful in my profession or my business, I am having a direct encounter with the *Ribbono Shel Olam*. And if I become wealthy, it is His doing .... Everybody is familiar with the *Gemara*: "A person's entire income is decided on Rosh Hashanah and confirmed on Yom Kippur" (*Beitzah* 16a). And we refer to this in *Bircas HaMazon*, when we request that our *parnasah* come directly from *HaKadosh Baruch Hu*'s hand. "Your full hand, [Your] open, holy, generous [hand] ...." In fact, the *Gemara* (*Pesachim* 118) characterizes Chapter 136 in *Tehillim* as "*Hallel HaGadol* — the Great *Hallel*," because of one verse: "He gives food to all flesh, His kindness is eternal." And the *Gemara* goes on to describe the Divine throne as hovering above the world, from where He apportions food and sustenance to all His creatures.

❖ Business as Usual, With "Emunah"

On that awesome day when we will each be called upon to give a personal accounting to the Heavenly Tribunal, the first question will be: "*Nasasa v'nasata b'emunah*? Did you conduct your business dealings with *emunah*?" The word "*emunah*" has two meanings: "Were your dealings done honestly?" — and "When you were engaged in business, did you possess *emunah* in *HaKadosh Baruch Hu*?" In other words, did you believe that G–d "feeds and provides for all" — that *hashgachah pratis* (Providence) rules? — that there is Someone observing you? — listening to what you are saying and thinking, and that all that you do is being recorded for future reference?

Following these guidelines of accountability, one may conclude that if I have the *zechus* to enjoy a *parnasah* that is free from all possible infractions, no *chillul Shabbos v'Yom Tov*, no *chillul Hashem*, no *sheker*, no *gezel*, no *ona'ah*, no *osheck*, no *ribbis* — no cheating, robbing, swindling or duplicity — and I am not lazy in my *hishtadlus*, my honest efforts to make a decent living, then I have every right to have *bitachon* (faith) that, "He who gives me life, will give me sustenance." And if I succeed in my efforts, then I know it was not *kochi v'otzem yadi* — not my know-how, not my intelligence, not my energy, not my hard work. Any success that I achieve is to be attributed to "It is He who grants you the *prowess* to amass a fortune" (*Devarim* 8:7), as He said so clearly: "Mine is the silver; Mine is the gold" (*Chaggai*).

Indeed, He alone gives us the intelligence, the strength to labor, the astuteness to determine what is good in the long run, for as the *Targum Onkelos* explains "prowess" in the above passage in *Devarim*: "G–d gave you the counsel to amass holdings." We cannot take credit for our ingenuity or intelligence. It all comes directly from G–d.

And should I fail in spite of all this, I must accept the loss with *emunah* because all comes from Him. And throughout, I maintain the firm *bitachon* that He will not let me down, and that my financial difficulties are temporary; I have a right to be *mispallel* — to pray — to have *bitachon* that my trust in *HaKadosh Baruch Hu* will not go unrewarded. Shlomo HaMelech says it clearly: "He who has trust in G–d deserves much blessing, but he who rushes to get rich [unscrupulously] cannot remain blameless" (*Mishlei*).

From this discussion, we must draw the conclusion that those who resort to cheating, trickery, dishonesty, and fraud — *gezel, sheker*, and *ona'ah* — while they sometimes may have the outward appearance of being G–d-fearing Jews, in fact they are irreligious. They lack *emunah*, for they do not believe that G–d "feeds and provides for all." They may well be strict in their observance of certain mitzvos, but in their business dealings they reveal that they are *kofrim* in *hashgachah pratis*: They certainly do not believe that G–d wants them to lie and cheat and take what is not rightfully theirs so as to obtain their sustenance, their great wealth, from Him. This would be blasphemy. What they are actually doing, then, is conducting their business affairs as though He does not exist חלילה!

We are required to say the song of praise "*Ashrei*" three times a day because it includes the *pasuk*: "*Posei'ach es yadecha u'masbia l'chol chai ratzon*" (*Tehillim* 145:16). If we fail to say it with *kavanah* — proper concentration — we must repeat it, to hammer into our consciousness that *HaKodosh Baruch Hu* opens His hands to satiate all living creatures, according to His will. Permit me to expand on this.

Exactly 57 years ago, at my *Sheva Berachos*, an elderly man who was a grandson of Rav Samson Raphael Hirsch, recounted an incident from his youth. As he was taking his grandfather for a walk, his grandfather asked him the meaning of the phrase *"masbia l'chol chai ratzon."* It should read, *"masbia ratzon l'chol chai* — He satiates the desire of all living creatures," or *"masbia chol chai b'ratzon* — He willingly satiates all living creatures." Rav Hirsch then explained that the word *"ratzon"* here was related to the expression *"yehi ratzon"* — that the matter be *ratzui lecha,* pleasing to You. It is in this spirit that *ratzon* is to be understood in our prayers for sustenance. In fact, this phrase from *"Ashrei"* contains the quintessence of *parnasah* — why some obtain it and others do not: G–d grants *ratzon* — favor — to those whom He chooses to grace with it. This applies to the beggar at the door, the professor lecturing in college, the merchant selling his product and the professional selling his services; if the individual is not liked and does not find *chein* and *ratzon* in the eyes of others, he will remain poor. Many a famous painter whose works of art sell for millions of dollars today, starved to death because during his lifetime his paintings simply did not find *ratzon.* The public did not respond to them.

Parnasah, then, represents direct intervention of G–d, granting the individual *ratzon.* It is a response that cannot be forced, or gained through manipulation. And if I am liked or appreciated, it is *"miyadcha hamele'ah, hapesuchah, harechavah* — from Your full, open, broad hand." It comes directly from G–d.

→ *Holy Money or Unholy Profits*

In regard to funds given to *tzedakah,* we paraphrase an expression from the Torah: *"shekel hakodesh,* sacred money." This is based on a *Gemara* that states: "Some *tzaddikim* consider their money more precious than their body, than their life, because they did not ever extend their hands to take anything that was not rightfully theirs" (*Sotah*). Now, the Torah defines *shekel hakodesh* as *esrim geirah hashekel.* In the vernacular, we say 20 shillings to the pound, a 100 cents to the dollar, meaning that every cent in that dollar belongs to me *al pi din*, in accordance with Torah law. It is clean, pure money, and that is what is meant when the Torah tells us that G–d wants *shekel hakodesh* to construct the Sanctuary.

People often ask, if *emunah* dictates that everything comes from the hand of G–d, why do people who are involved in shady business practices — people who steal and lie and commit all kinds of thievery — become wealthy and successful, and most of the time go undetected? Don't they also get their *parnasah* from the *Ribbono Shel Olam*? The answer is "No!" Emphatically *NO!* They receive it from the *Sitra Achra.* That is to say, every sin that a person commits creates forces of evil — *kochos hatumah*, which is called *Sitra Achra*, the other-world order which exists only to test us, to tempt us, and ח"ו eventually to punish the evil-doers. The magnificent mansion that was built with money tainted by dishonesty, or the good times that are paid for by tax fraud or other forms of *gezel* and *ona'ah,* all come from *kochos hatumah*, which turn eventually into forces of destruction — *hu hasatan hu malach hamaves* — either in this world or in the World to Come — which is far worse.

The guilty party may contribute vast sums to *tzedakah* and perform certain mitzvos very rigorously, but these will not help him, for the Torah tells us *lo yikach shochad*, that G–d does not accept bribes. This, *Chazal* explain, even includes the bribery of mitzvos. As for his wealth, it does not come from G–d. It comes from an unseen Mafia, so to speak, from the *kochos hatumah*. There is no reason to envy the dishonest and fraudulent, for — as the passage from *Mishlei* states: "*Bircas Hashem hi sis'asher* — Only the blessings of G–d make one truly rich."

✦ *"Gezel": The Parameters*

"Gezel" is defined loosely as "theft" or "loot." The *Choshen Mishpat* includes under this rubric all monies that do not belong to a person *al pi din*. In a case where Reuven does not know the *din*, and a *beis din* that is empowered by the Torah *paskens* that Reuven must give a contested sum of money to

Shimon, and Reuven does not follow the *psak* of the *beis din*, then his money is *gezel*. In other words, one must avoid any property held without justification as though it were outright stolen funds.

The late Brisker Rav, Reb Velvel, asked, "What prompted Yosef to give the money back to his brothers, and put it into their sacks?" He answered, "Because he wanted to make sure that they would come back." Someone present at the *shiur* asked him, "They would have come back anyway — considering the famine, their need for food would drive them back. And besides, their brother Shimon was taken hostage. They had to return to redeem him. Why did he find it necessary to put money in their sacks to make sure they'd come back?"

The Brisker Rav answered, "The ten brothers were *Shivtei Kah*, the forebears of the Ten Tribes. We cannot fathom the depths of their *bitachon*, their trust in G–d. Perhaps, thought Yosef, they would decide to ride out the famine: G–d would not forsake them and they would not die of hunger. Nor would He forsake Shimon; G–d would eventually cause him to be released from prison. But Yosef knew that should his brothers have in their possession money that was not theirs, they would certainly come back. *Shivtei Kah* would not want to keep any money that does not belong to them *al pi din*.

✣ An Overlooked Opinion

Many of our business dealings are carried on with non-Jews. Since some *poskim* are of the opinion that halachic guidelines for business dealings with Jews are much more stringent than the norm, some business people are less than scrupulous when dealing with the general public. I often wonder why people who are so *machmir* (stringent) in regard to a *yesh omrim* (a differing opinion) in *Orach Chaim* and *Yoreh Deah* (sections of Codes dealing with ritual law) simply ignore the *yesh omrim* in *Choshen Mishpat* (business law) regarding *gezel akum*. Indeed, the *Choshen Mishpat paskens* clearly that it is forbidden, based on the *Gemara* in *Bava Kamma*. Furthermore, the *Shulchan Aruch* says that if a person evades payment of his taxes for which he is liable, he has transgressed *lo sigzol* (Ch. 369). As to *ta'us akum*, taking advantage of mistakes made by non-Jews, the *Be'er HaGolah* (Ch. 266) says, that returning money to a gentile if he makes a mistake in my favor is praiseworthy, for then non-Jews will come to admire Jews for their integrity.

This decision was written in the Middle Ages, a primitive time when many non-Jews were illiterate and could not calculate properly, and it was very easy to take advantage of them. In this context, the *Be'er HaGolah* writes in an uncharacteristic manner:

> I am writing this down for future generations, for I have seen many who have become wealthy through errors that gentiles have made. But I have also seen how they have lost their money again, and have left nothing for their heirs, as is recorded in *Sefer Chassidim*. Those that sanctified G–d's Name by returning gains made through the error of others became wealthy and left much of their riches to their children.

(This applies, of course, to mistakes made by the computer, as well.)

How rewarding it must be to live a life of integrity and inspire recognition from others in regard to the sanctity of His Name!

Webster's Dictionary lists a verb "to jew," which is defined as "to cheat, to be engaged in sharp practices." Of course this is an anti-Semitic response to conduct that constitutes a *chillul Hashem* — but the bottom line is incontestably a *chillul Hashem*. I live with the hope that there will be a new edition of *Webster's Dictionary* that will say, "to jew: to be scrupulously honest, to be decent" — that would be a literal *kiddush Hashem*. We must bear in mind that when one has *chillul Hashem* on his hands, neither *teshuvah* (repentance), nor Yom Kippur, nor *yesurim* (suffering) help to achieve full atonement *ad yom moso*, until the day of his death. To this, the *Gemara* says, "No credit is given for good deeds [to counteract the effects of] *chillul Hashem*, even if it occurs by mistake" (*Kiddushin*). The *Sifri* in *Haazinu* says, "Eventually, G–d forgives all sins, but — by contrast — He exacts immediate punishment for *chillul Hashem*."

In this context, I feel duty-bound to mention that there are ה"ב a great many cases of *kiddush Hashem* in the field of business dealings between Jews and non-Jews, and between irreligious Jews and devout Jews. Quite a number of such cases are known to me, and I stand up in reverence for those who are *mekadesh Shem Hashem* in our times, which otherwise are full of cases of colossal *chillul Hashem*. A recent article in *The New York Times* dealing with the owners of a particularly large real-estate firm stated that "because they are strictly Orthodox Jews, their word is their bond." And they are trusted universally. Now that family's legendary *tzedakah* is, indeed, *shekel hakodesh*. It is a model of *nasasa v'nasata b'emunah* for all of us to emulate. And if their example will find many followers, it might deflate the scourge of worldwide anti-Semitism.

In *parshas Ki Seitzei* we read, "False measurements, false weights, cheating in business, is an abomination in the eyes of G–d" (*Devarim* 25:13-19). Following immediately is: "Remember what Amalek did to you."

Rashi tells us that this grouping of mitzvos teaches us: "He who cheats with measurements and weights has cause to worry over the onslaught of enemies." On the other hand, *kiddush Hashem* by honest Jews, by Torah Jews, such as the CPAs who have assembled in respect for Torah and its teachings, gives us the right to hold our heads high in the presence of our enemies.

Did You Conduct
Your Business Affairs
With Faith?

Rabbi Avrohom Pam

*An eminent Rosh Yeshivah examines the
implications of the question that every man
must ultimately answer.*

✦ The Questions

*A*fter a person has lived his years on earth, he must appear before
the Beis Din Shel Maalah (Heavenly Tribunal) and answer,
*among other questions: "*הנשאת ונתת באמונה*" — Did you conduct
your business affairs with faith? (usually taken to mean "with integrity");* קבעת עתים לתורה *— Did you establish set times for studying
Torah?...; "*צפית לישועה*" — Did you anticipate the Redemption?"
(Shabbos 31a). Interestingly, another source in the Talmud (Kiddushin
40b, Sanhedrin 7a) says that a person is first judged in regard to Torah,
which, as Tosafos points out, is an apparent contradiction. Tosafos then
explains that while in judgment, business conduct takes precedence
over Torah study, retribution is in a different sequence: Punishment for*

neglecting Torah study comes first. The reason? The cause of a person's misconduct in business is a lack of proper knowledge of Torah and a lack of loyalty to its teachings. All else is built upon that foundation .... The questioning starts with a man's integrity in personal relationships with others — but punishment begins at the source — laxity in Torah study.

→ *Why This Topic*

At first glance, a discussion of honesty and correct business practices may appear to be out of order, since such fundamental principles of Torah could well be taken for granted. It is interesting to note, however, that the *Gemara* uses the term "באמונה" — "Did you conduct your affairs with emunah — with faith?" — instead of *"tzedek,"* or *"mishpat,"* or *"din"* — Were you *righteous,* or *just* in your business affairs? The reason might be because *emunah* has a twofold meaning: integrity, and faith in G–d. Complete trust in G–d would prompt one to act even לפנים משורת הדין — beyond the letter of the law, and imbue him with a higher sense of ethics; his faith dispels any apprehensions about loss of income resulting from ethical conduct.

The Chofetz Chaim declared that a G–d-fearing man entering the field of commerce is obliged to study carefully the second section of *Choshen Mishpat* (the section of the Codes dealing with monetary matters), especially those *halachos* dealing with cheating, and the possibility of an error in sale (§227-238); just as a *shochet* is obligated to learn the laws of ritual slaughter, and a *sofer* must be an expert in the field of Torah script, so, too, must a merchant be equally proficient in the *halachos* pertinent to his profession. It would be wonderful if just as ordination is granted to rabbis to permit them to enter the rabbinate, so, too, would some form of *semichah* in הלכות מקח וממכר (Laws of Commerce) be instituted for people entering the business field.

> *A shochet once told Reb Yisrael Salanter, "I'm giving up my position because I find the responsibility of slaughtering properly too much for my conscience to bear. If I make but*

one mistake, imagine how many people would be eating unkosher meat because of me!"

Asked Reb Yisrael: "What will you do for a living?"

Replied the man, "I'll open up a small business."

To which Reb Yisrael said: "Do you really think that's preferable? As a shochet you have one responsibility — people should not transgress 'You shall not eat any meat improperly slaughtered' (Devarim 14:2), and that makes you tremble. If you'd be involved in business, do you know how many positive and negative commands you'd be dealing with, how careful you'd have to be not to violate any of them?"

The Chofetz Chaim cites a few examples of *halachos* that are of extreme import to those engaged in business.

→ *Some Common Examples*

Defects in Sales

When selling an item, a person must be very careful that it does not have any flaw in it, or that it is lacking in any way. And should it be flawed, he must notify the would-be purchaser in advance, for if he does not, the sale may be invalid. If it is a defect that would cause a person to reconsider the purchase, not informing the purchaser would be deemed deception. This consideration applies whether the purchaser is a Jew or a gentile, for one may not take their money under a false pretext — *gezel akum* is forbidden. (The Chofetz Chaim cites various sources, the *Rambam, Hilchos Geneivah* 7:8, among others.) Should a person have made this kind of invalid sale, he must return the money.

Similarly, a person is not permitted to cheat anybody — Jew and non-Jew alike — in any manner, in keeping with the passage: "Do not commit an injustice in measures, weights, or volume" (*Vayikra* 19:38). You must make an exact accounting with the person who buys. "Committing such an injustice is an abomination before G–d" (*Devarim* 25:16).

Defective Merchandise

The Chofetz Chaim also cites examples dealing with the purchaser: When a person who has discovered that an item he purchased has a defect, and uses it anyway, he may not bring it back for a refund, for use implies acceptance (*Choshen Mishpat* 232:3). Of course, if the defect is discovered after the item is used, it is a different matter, and a refund is in order. But the purchaser *must* be certain that he did not cause the flaw. (A person may feel that the shopkeeper will return the item to the manufacturer, and the manufacturer has thousands of such items; what difference does one more make? This type of rationalization is, of course, invalid and self-deceiving.)

Similarly, when examining an article one must be careful not to damage it in any way. When people purchase a *lulav*, and they examine it for defects, such as a split down the spine, they may well cause the split by examining it carelessly, and then say: "I don't want this one. Let me see another one, please." This is a common occurrence, and one should be exceptionally careful about it.

The Chofetz Chaim's son, Reb Leib, wrote that when the *sefer Chofetz Chaim* was being printed, his father spent weeks on end in the print shop in Warsaw to make certain that there should be no error in the printing or the binding; he was truly frightened that perhaps someone would purchase a faulty copy which might constitute *gezel* (unintentionally defrauding the purchaser).

> *In 1906, when the Chofetz Chaim was publishing his Mishnah Berurah, he asked Reb Leib, who had moved to Warsaw, to supervise the production of the sefer. Later, somebody purchased a set of Mishnah Berurah with one section printed incorrectly. The man sent a complaint to the Chofetz Chaim, who immediately wrote to his son, protesting: "What have you done to me, my son? All my days I was concerned that I be spared from even the remotest likeness to gezel. Never did I think I'd be caught up in outright gezel! And now, because of you, I fell into the trap of full-fledged gezel." He commanded his son to print a number of extra copies of this section without the inversion in it, for fear that others were similarly*

"defrauded," and put a notice in the newspaper to the effect that: "Whoever purchased the sefer Mishnah Berurah containing a misplaced section should please write me, and I'll send you a corrected section." Which he did.

Reb Avraham Horowitz, a true tzaddik, ran a bedding supplies store in the East New York section of Brooklyn. When someone would ask: "Do you have a nice mattress?" he would say: "Nice? I don't know. Maybe others have better merchandise. I can only show you what I have."

If he was in the back room of the store, and he overheard his wife showing a particular mattress to a purchaser, he called out to her: "Did you show the customer the damage on that? Please show her."

He was always wary of defrauding the customer or misleading him in any way. (Offering a person advice that is to his disadvantage is a transgression of the Torah command: "Do not place a stumbling block before a blind person" (Vayikra 19:14).

If someone asks a salesman for an item, specifying a desired color or fabric, and that particular item is not in stock, the salesman may not say: "They stopped making those. But I can show you something else that's much better."

Specifying Details of Agreement Beforehand

The Chofetz Chaim stresses (in *Sfas Tamim*, and also at the end of *Ahavas Chesed*, Section I) that when two people enter an agreement for some contracted work, it is extremely important that they both spell out precisely what they expect from each other in terms of work and payment. Frequently people say: *Start now. When the job's done we'll get together.* Then, upon completion of the job, disputes arise regarding payment, or how well the job was done; and when they part company, each one claims that he was shortchanged by the other party .... Worse yet, some people prefer not to argue and let things go — but one party does not really forgive the other for the money withheld or overpaid, and thus the matter ends up with possibilities of *gezel*.

Should such a dispute arise, the *Shulchan Aruch* rules that payment should be determined by the prevailing custom of the locality in regard to such work. If someone pays one cent less than required, then "The Torah considers this man dishonest, and guilty of withholding the wages of his worker."

However, it is usually difficult to ascertain the prevailing customs which govern a particular type of work. Therefore, it is best that the two parties spell out precisely what each expects from the other before entering into a contract.

→ *The Deep-Seated Attributes*

Charity and Justice

In his introduction to *Ahavas Chesed*, the Chofetz Chaim comments on G–d's reference to Avraham Avinu: "I love him because he will command his children and his household after him, that they will keep the way of G–d, to do charity and justice" (*Bereishis* 18:19). "Justice" refers to doing things correctly, in keeping with the law. "Charity" involves yielding to somebody else's needs beyond the requirements of the law. How are these two expressions to apply simultaneously?

The Chofetz Chaim explains that in dealing with somebody else, one must not say: *He won't mind if I pay him a little less for the item*. Or when sending out an order: *He won't mind if I short-supply him slightly*. With regard to fulfilling one's obligation to somebody else, the rule should be *mishpat* — justice — adhering to the letter of the law, no matter how insignificant the amount. On the other hand, in your expectations from others, the rule should be *tzedakah* — tend to be generous and waive your rights in minor matters. Thus, *tzedakah* and *mishpat* can both reside within the same person.

In the *Chut HaMeshulash*, the children of the K'sav Sofer (Rabbi Shmuel Binyamin Schreiber) recorded how their father was so cautious in regard to other people's money that he would not rely on seventy reasons for *heter* (permission) against one reason for *issur* (prohibition).

The Extra Measure of Caution

> In 1872, when Reb Yisrael Meir HaKohen was ready to print the sefer bearing the name by which he eventually became known, Chofetz Chaim, he traveled to various communities neighboring his own Radin for advance orders. Normally, people make some payment, but he refused to accept any money. When his son, Reb Leib, asked him why he had so refused, the Chofetz Chaim explained: "Perhaps some of these people will move, or even die by the time the sefer is finished. How will I be able to trace their heirs, or find them if they're alive in other cities? It is better that I take orders without money." So his son asked: "Then tell me, why do you go to the trouble of getting orders altogether? Print the sefarim and then travel around and sell them." His father replied, "I have to borrow from others to finance this undertaking. What right do I have to ask others to lend me money on a risk, unless I have some idea of how many sefarim I am going to sell?"

When two people verbally enter a business agreement, without any exchange of money or merchandise, either of the principals could change his mind, but it is contrary to the wishes of the sages (*Bava Metzia* 48a). There is a difference of opinion between two authorities, however, whether or not this type of conduct renders a person מחוסר אמונה — "lacking in integrity," and halachic authorities decide according to the more stringent view (Rav Yochanan). Thus, if two people enter into an agreement — no money was taken, no contract was signed, no deposit was made — and later one changes his mind, he is not acting contrary to the strict requirements of *halachah*. The situation often arises when someone selects merchandise but has no money, and says: "I'm going to buy it," and the proprietor says: "Okay, it's yours. Come back tomorrow with the money." He returns the next day and the item is gone; or *he* is guilty of not returning the next day. Such practices are frowned upon by our Sages. (Some authorities say that these restrictions do not apply when the price of the item has changed [*Choshen Mishpat* end of Ch. 202], but it is a minority view.) Integrity means being faithful to your word. When a person fails to do this, he is not "conducting his affairs with *emunah.*"

Faithful in Thought

There is yet another, higher degree of *emunah*, of faithfulness in transactions: Rav Safra fulfilled "speaking truth in his heart" (*Tehillim* 15:2).

> *In addition to "not going back on his word," Rav Safra never went back on his thoughts: A customer once entered Rav Safra's store to make a purchase. He offered a price, but Rav Safra was saying Krias Shema and did not answer. The customer raised the offer several times and Rav Safra still did not comment. When Rav Safra completed the Shema, he said: "I'll accept the first price." Said the man: "But I'm willing to pay the last." Rav Safra replied: "Yes, but I was willing to accept the first. And since in my heart I said 'yes' — although I could not speak — I will not change my mind" (She'iltos D'Rav Achai, Vayechi, 36). "Speaking honestly in one's heart" is an extremely high level of integrity.*

The same *She'iltos* quotes a *midrash* that comments on the passage: "My [i.e., G–d's] eyes are on the trusted, that they dwell together with Me" (*Tehillim* 101:10). In this regard, the *Midrash* (on *Shmuel*) relates how the celebrated *Amora* Shmuel was named:

> *Shmuel's father had been a merchant. Rabbi Yehudah ben Beseira asked him to put aside for him a measure of silk, but he did not pay for it, nor give a deposit. A long period of time transpired, until Shmuel's father had occasion to bring it to Rabbi Yehudah. Rabbi Yehudah was surprised: "Why did you keep this merchandise for me?" he asked. "After all, we only*

exchanged words. I didn't pick up the silk, nor did I give you money." Answered the merchant: *"An honorable man's word is as good as money."* Reb Yehudah marveled at this man's concept of integrity, and he blessed him: *"Because you trusted in me, may you be worthy of begetting a son like the prophet Shmuel, about whom the Scripture testifies, 'And all Israel from Dan to Beer Sheva knew that Shmuel was a trusted prophet of G–d'"* (I Shmuel 3:20). *When his son was born, the merchant named him Shmuel.*

Perhaps that is what is meant by "dwelling within the boundaries of G–d." Being worthy of bringing Shmuel into the world is the equivalent of dwelling with G–d.

The Blessings of Trust

"A man of trust is many times blessed, but the man anxious for wealth is never clean" (*Mishlei* 28:20). While the first part of the passage is an obvious truth, the second part is more subtle, referring to someone who is impatient for G–d's blessings, and wants to become rich immediately; he will never emerge clean from the stain of sin.

"The man of trust many-times blessed" refers to Moshe Rabbeinu. Indeed, every endeavor that he undertook, or for which he served as treasurer, was blessed. To demonstrate his trustworthiness, Moshe called together *Klal Yisrael* for an accounting when the building of the *Mishkan* (portable sanctuary) was completed. This was surely unnecessary, for G–d Himself testified that "My servant Moshe ... is trusted throughout My house" (*Bamidbar* 12:7). The *Midrash* explains that Moshe did this to avoid the suspicion that he had become wealthy from handling the funds used for building the *Mishkan*.

It seems strange that someone trusted by G–d still was not satisfied until he had proven himself clean in the eyes of man. Yet, this is of extreme importance. The Talmud reports that the proceeds of the *shekalim* tax were stored in huge vats, and periodically an official would remove some of the coins to make purchases for the *Beis HaMikdash*. He was not permitted to wear a hemmed garment, shoes, or an amulet around his neck, because it would offer an opportunity for him to smuggle out some coins for himself. Then, should he become poor, people would say: "Do you know why he became poor? He was punished because he stole from the treasury." And in case he becomes wealthy, people would say: "Do you know how he became rich? Because he stole from the treasury" (*Shekalim* 3:2). He must ascertain that his actions are beyond suspicion. In this regard it says: "And you shall be clean before G–d and Israel" (*Bamidbar* 32:22). Then, the *Mishnah* cites an additional passage: "And you should find favor and good understanding in the eyes of G–d and man" (*Mishlei* 3:4).

Tiferes Yisrael explains that both passages are needed. The first one ("*And you shall be clean ...*") teaches us that we must avoid acting in a manner which could cause suspicion. But it is insufficient to clarify our actions after they are done. We must "find favor and good understanding" in everyone's eyes, so that people have no reason to question our actions before or after they occur. This is what we learn from the second verse.

A Twofold Obligation

The Chasam Sofer (Rabbi Moshe Schreiber) writes (*Collected Responsa* 59):

> All my days I was in anguish over the passage: "And you shall be clean before G–d and Israel." These two obligations are like two millstones weighing on my neck. It is possible to absolve oneself of the first — that is, to be clean in the eyes of G–d — much more easily than it is to satisfy people, for they imagine bizarre plots; and the punishment for failing to satisfy others is far more severe than for not satisfying G–d י"ח. Indeed, the *Gemara* (end of *Yoma*) tells us that there is no atonement for *chillul Hashem*, desecration of G–d's Name (which results from misrepresenting the high standards demanded by the Torah). Unfortunately, too

often we hear people say: "Imagine that a Torah scholar such as he should be guilty of such-and-such!" even though it is pure speculation that leads them to judge him so. I often wonder whether any man has actually fulfilled this obligation to his fullest. Perhaps this is what King Solomon had in mind when he said: "There is no fully righteous man on earth, who has done right and not sinned" — meaning that even though a man has done only good it is impossible that he should not have "sinned" in somehow falling short of having his actions understood by others.

The Chasam Sofer adds that while the tribes of Reuven and Gad more than fulfilled their obligation of "And you shall be clean ..." by fighting on the front lines of *Bnei Yisrael* when they conquered Canaan, it is unlikely that they could completely clean themselves in the eyes of their brethren. It may well be for this reason that these two tribes were later exiled before the remaining 10 tribes.

A Peaceful Hereafter

The Chofetz Chaim points out that when Yisro advised Moshe in regard to setting up a judiciary system, he concluded his words with: "If you follow this approach, then you will be able to withstand the pressures. All these people will return to their place *b'shalom* — in peace" (*Shemos* 18:23). It is strange that Yisro spoke of the people returning *"in peace,"* when this is terminology usually reserved for the ultimate peace wished to a person when he dies [as opposed to *l'shalom*] (*Berachos* 64a). The Chofetz Chaim explains that when somebody is guilty of some type of cheating and dies without returning the money to its original owner, he has no rest in the World to Come until somehow the monies are restored to the original owners or their heirs. Thus, Yisro assured Moshe that if he sets up a proper judiciary system, justice will prevail. Then when the people ultimately die, they will find eternal rest and not be troubled by unfulfilled financial obligations.

Pleasing to the Eye ... Acceptable to the Heart

In spelling out the exact details of the construction of the *Mishkan*, G–d gave Moshe precise instructions on how to drape the material used in covering the Sanctuary (*Shemos* 23:13); to which *Rashi* comments: "The Torah here teaches us proper conduct — that a man should be concerned with the aesthetic."

A yeshivah student who has absorbed the light of Torah within himself radiates a special beauty of his own. It is this beauty that he should preserve with the utmost care. Even a small stain can mar it. Especially in our times, when people are so quick to find fault with the Torah and its students, *bnei yeshivah* must endeavor all the more to present the beauty of the Torah in all its aspects.

Thus it is insufficient to simply meet the requirements of *din* (Torah law), but one must strive for ever higher levels in faith, until one can respond positively to the query: "Did you conduct your business affairs with faith?" in all its possible implications *... Were you among the faithful of the earth upon whom "the eyes of G–d gaze"?* Thus, the judgment of the rabbis, that a scholar with a stain on his garment is among those who "cause disenchantment with religion" (*Shabbos* 114a; *Rambam, Dei'os* 5:9) certainly applies to misconduct in human relations and general unethical behavior.

Upon completion of the *Mishkan*, Moshe blessed the people (*Shemos* 39:43); according to *Rashi*, he said, "May it be the will of G–d that the *Shechinah* (Divine Presence) rest on all your activities," implying that the *Shechinah* not be limited to the Sanctuary but be found everywhere, in all their endeavors. This fulfills the command: "And you shall love G–d," which refers to being so exemplary in conduct that it inspires love and appreciation for G–d; people will say, "How graceful are the ways, how perfect are the acts of So-and-so who has studied Torah!" (*Yoma* 86a).

Fortunate is he who inspires others to the love of G–d and enhances Torah in their eyes.

Standing Up for Torah Principles: Battles on the Personal Front

Professor Aaron Twerski

✢ *My Enemy, My Brother*

M̲ost of us inhabit a world where modernity and eternal values are in constant confrontation. Each of us will approach this clash from his own perspective, drawing upon his own feelings. To me, the topic is not a philosophical one; it is a conflict of immediate, emotional impact that I feel in my bones, for I live it every day. I believe that, as with most of us, I am part of the problem. And while I do not have any fool-proof solutions to the dilemma, I would suggest that understanding the problem is an extremely important first step in solving it.

The tension inherent to living in a world that is hostile, yet terribly friendly, is aptly expressed by Yaakov Avinu in his prayer to G–d to save him *"miyad ochi miyad Eisav* — from the hands of my brother ... Eisav."* In his words, the situation is grave enough as a threat emanating from Eisav, but the enemy is also *"ochi* — my brother."* And that additional factor only intensifies the problem.

It was the fourth week of the semester in the law school. A student in my torts class came in to see me with a pack of books on his back. He slipped off the pack and said, "Professor, I'd like to talk to you, but it has nothing to do with torts. Can I close the door?" (Here it comes, I thought.) He took a seat — a fine boy with a knitted *yarmulke* on his head. His mouth began to grimace and his eyes welled up with tears as he struggled to get the words out. Finally he mumbled, "Professor, I can't handle it. I'm in this environment. I want to be able to get along. I want to be friends. I want to be a part of this society. And my *Yiddishkeit* is slipping away."

With that, he began to shed tears. This was just four weeks into the semester! The first thing I told him was, "*Yididi*, you don't have a problem. There are lots of other *frum* kids in the class who are not in here crying. *They're* the ones who have a problem."

He pressed on, "Look! I have a thousand *nisyonos* a day! A thousand decisions to make. I can't handle it. I'm going crazy!"

I offered some advice to the young student, which will wait for the end of this discussion. First, however, I would like to impress on the reader that this young man's situation is far from unique, and it is in this broader context that I would like to discuss the problem that his experience personifies.

→ *Beyond the Halls of Law School*

Brooklyn Law School is not different from a law office, nor is it different from an accounting office, from the offices of Smith Barney on Wall Street, or from the situations encountered by any of us who are involved in any kind of complex business undertakings. We do not, in our day and age, go forth merely to seek *parnasah* — a livelihood. When we leave our homes — and this, I feel, is the most serious aspect of the clash between the forces of modernity and eternal values — and we venture out, we enter a different world. It has its own system of rewards and punishments. It has a complete culture of its own. People in a large corporate office live in a closed world in which people talk to each other and consult each other in a self-contained environment, a situation that blinds them to the most obvious mistakes.

People inhabiting these sealed worlds are subject to the impact of four forces.

•First of these is that of financial reward. Money in this country is not merely a means for purchase and security. It is the equivalent of self-esteem: *What is he worth? What are you worth?* As one climbs the corporate ladder, financial rewards involve the entirety of the human ego. We are out there with somebody else telling us what we are worth.

That is only one small part of the situation. In both the business world and the professions, one has access to all kinds of "perks" — ways in which people are made to feel important. In law school, it is appointments to positions like assistant professor, associate professor, full professor. In a stock-brokerage house, one becomes a senior advisor, a senior consultant, vice-president, or executive vice-president. All of those are enormously meaningful in terms of shaping a person's self-image.

•And then there is the *chavrusa* — the companionship. The people one works with are not evil; as a matter of fact, they are quite bright, and can be extremely pleasant. One *yungerman* told me recently, "I knew it was time to leave my law firm on Wall Street when I realized that my closest friend was a fellow named John McHenry."

We all have these professional relationships. They're meaningful to us, we internalize them, they become part of us.

•The most potent force that we upwardly-mobile professionals and business people must contend with is the way the work we engage in — putting together deals, litigating, doing whatever our professions or businesses demand of us — has become enormously challenging. It's exciting. It's demanding. It's rewarding. I am now a Reporter of the Restatement of Torts for the American Law Institute. It is a thrilling experience! I sit with sixty of the finest legal minds in the country who critique my work. And if you think it does not penetrate my innermost senses, you're wrong. Anyone who is deeply involved in business or a profession is part of the same phenomenon. We share a common spiritual ailment. So we're not yuppies; then we're "fruppies" — *frum* yuppies.

→ *The Fruppy Syndrome*

What does this up-to-the-nose involvement do to us? First of all, we are involved in a relationship with a world alien to Torah. More significant than that, we are not working on a machine, and then coming home, as our grandfathers may have done. When I come home, my vitality is drained from me. I can barely breathe. At that point, how meaningful can my *davening* be?

You've probably had the experience of hitting the *beis midrash* Friday night, and in the midst of *"L'cho Dodi"* you're somewhere in China, not in the *beis midrash*. You're as connected with ecstatic clapping for *"L'cho Dodi"* as I am with the moon! And it's not only Friday night. It's still that way Shabbos morning, at *"Shochein Ad."* By *Minchah*, when we say *"Atta echad,"* we're a bit thawed out, although by that time, Shabbos is all but over.

I recently underwent an experience that many a reader has probably shared. I had put a year's work into a project, and it was submitted for evaluation to an expert who would be reporting to my co-author on Shabbos. My stomach was churning all Shabbos. I dutifully waited the requisite 72 minutes after sunset, I *davened Maariv*, and then picked up the phone to call my partner. It turned out that it was all right. But what kind of Jew am I, sitting and impatiently counting the minutes for Shabbos to come to an end? If you live in my world, you've had that experience, and it's devastating.

•Once we are talking honestly and candidly, there is another topic that must be addressed, as indelicate as it may be. As *bnei Torah, kedushas am Yisrael* — the sanctity of our people — is of prime value to us. How do we relate to the commercial and professional world in which 50 percent of the workforce is comprised of women? And how does the 50 percent who are women relate to a world of co-equal male workers? And it is not only a matter of dealing with co-equals of the opposite sex; one also deals with superiors — the vice-president above you who is a female, and vice versa, when women work under male supervisors. The light talk, the friendly banter and occasional teasing that takes place under such conditions do not take into account *Chazal*'s warnings against excessive talk between men and women. *Rabbanim* have informed me that they counsel their congregants in regard to how they relate to their female colleagues, who work alongside them as equals, and are indeed their intellectual equals: These women do not carry the draining burden that their wives at home have, caring for six or seven children. Yet in a world of keen competition and intellectual stimulation, comparisons loom before these men, and can put the wife at unfair disadvantage, and themselves at moral risk. Unfortunately, this continues to occur, with tragic results to erstwhile solid marriages.

✦ Advice to a Student on the Edge

Permit me to return to what I told my student, what I should tell myself, and what — in essence — all of us should be telling ourselves.

The first point I raised with the student seeking counsel was: "You have too many *nisyonos*. No human being can live with a thousand challenges a day. You have got to remove some items from the table. Your colleagues want you to join them at the local bar for a beer after the study group .... *You don't go to a bar*. They want you to join them in the cafeteria downstairs to socialize after a session.... *No, thanks*. You study only in the study room, *and that's it for the day*. And so on. You've got to take things off the table."

Chazal understood the need for protective ordinances, which are absolutely essential as the first component in a survival kit, if we are to survive in a world in which we have that kind of collegial relationship with people distant from our *weltanschauung*. We must draw the line beyond which we do not tread: *This I will not do*.

Secondly, it seems obvious that *limud haTorah* — involvement with Torah study — and maintaining *chavrusos* (study partners) are a must. But even more important, constant check-in with *rebbe'im* is vital. Throughout the generations, venerable Jews who had no apparent need for it, hired for themselves a *mussar zogger* to point out their "faults" and chastise them for them. We truly need someone to whom we can talk honestly and openly, who will tell us in response to our queries what to do and what to avoid.

The third point is something that I personally find very difficult, but which I deem absolutely necessary: finding some ways to curb ambition. Several years ago, I called my *Rosh Yeshivah*, Rabbi Yaakov Weinberg, about a *she'eilah* on an opportunity presented to me. He told me that the *she'eilah* that I had posed was not a halachic concern. He did ask me, however, "Who told you that you are permitted to do it? By what right should you grab this so-called opportunity at the expense of your family, your Torah study, your peace of mind?"

We must find ways to curb ambition. Whether we are business people, driven by the maxim, "He who has a hundred [thousand] wants two hundred [thousand]," or professional people who seek professional advancement, we must put a cap on our drive. Because if there is no cap on it, the pursuit is endless. During our yeshivah years, we absorbed the lessons of the *beis midrash* well. We are highly motivated, highly driven, highly successful, and we can push ourselves very, very far. Transferring this lesson to the corporate scene, however, can push us so far, nothing will remain of our *Yiddishkeit*.

Finally, I offered my young petitioner one piece of practical advice. He — we — cannot permit other aspects of our lives to be so exciting and stimulating that they leave Torah to be humdrum by comparison. A regular commitment to *Daf Yomi* is very important. But learning with passion is even more important. And being involved in a mitzvah project that excites you, and energizes you, is "living in Torah." Should we become excited in our professional affairs, and engage in Torah in a manner of "paying our dues," it will be a dim echo of a declaration that says, "*Na'aseh v'nishma*."

Rabbi Yechiel Perr (*Rosh Yeshivah*, Derech Ayson) told me a short while ago that he had run into a *talmid* who had gone off to school, and now seemed to be on the brink of leaving *Yiddishkeit*. Rabbi Perr advised him, "Organize a *Minchah minyan* on campus."

The fellow responded to the suggestion, founded a *Minchah minyan*, and in a short time became a different person. Because he was the head of the *minyan*, he gained a new vitality in mitzvah performance, his identity became more spiritual and he began to grow in Torah, as well.

I view the clash between modernity and eternity as a fight for the essence of our souls. Do we belong to them? Or do we belong to the *olam haTorah*?

No easy answers. The questions I have posed are truthful. They affect all of us in our daily lives. And now I can only ask, teach us, *Rabbeinu*: How do we handle them?

Making It in the Workplace, and Creating a Kiddush Hashem in the Process

Yosi Heber

T*rue kiddush Shem Shamayim — sanctifying the Heavenly Name — is achieved when an individual is alone within the four walls of his room; faced with the opportunity to violate a Torah command, he refrains from doing so because he realizes that his every action is scrutinized by G–d. When others are also aware of his respect for G–d's wishes, the kiddush Hashem grows; the wider the awareness, the greater the kiddush Hashem. But the starting place is in the privacy of the heart of that single Jew.*

Widespread kiddush Hashem will prompt observers to comment: "How wonderful are the deeds of So-and-so. How fortunate are his parents for having taught him Torah!" (See Yoma 86a.)

The Orthodox Jew in the marketplace faces frequent challenges to his fidelity to Torah values and mitzvah observance. At the same time, he may be struggling to make his mark in his particular field of endeavor, which may appear to be threatened as a result of his open adherence to Torah guidelines. In the article that follows, Yosi Heber, an executive at Dannon/Lea & Perrins, describes his effort to succeed in his corner of the corporate world, while remaining faithful to Torah, and hoping to generate a kiddush Hashem at the same time.

❖ ❖ ❖

I'll never forget the first week of my "career." Here I was, a newly-minted Wharton MBA, ready to plunge into the corporate world and make my mark. At the end of my first week at General Foods, I called my mother and told her how worried I was about my future prospects. There was a "class" of six of us who started at the same time in the Desserts Division. Spence and Carol were best friends from Harvard. Matt was one of the boys who played golf with the big boss on Saturdays. Mary really looked the part of junior executive. And then there was me, Yosi. I overheard one of the secretaries ask, "What's a Yosi?" One of my new roles was to create new Jello recipes. I couldn't even eat the Jello! "I'll never make it," I told my mother. I couldn't possibly be one of them or fit in with them. How would I survive in this "jungle"?

After a year on the job, I came to the following conclusion: If an employee is a non-Jew, he or she can be perceived in the eyes of an employer in one of three ways: liked by people, disliked by people, or middle of the road ("one of the boys").

If a person is a *frum* Jew, however, there are only two possibilities: Either you will be *respected* because you are a *frum* Jew (and you create a *kiddush Hashem*), or you'll be *disliked* because you are a *frum* Jew (and that can lead to *chillul Hashem*). You cannot and will not ever be accepted as "one of the boys." There is simply no middle ground for you in a corporate environment.

Therefore, when faced with the prospects of working in this type of setting, you would want to be sure to land on the right side. In fact, the possibility of creating a *chillul Hashem* cannot be taken lightly. As the *Gemara* says: "If a person creates a *chillul Hashem*, even doing *teshuvah* on Yom Kippur does not achieve atonement for him" (*Yoma* 86a). The question is — how can one insure that he or she will create a positive impression, be properly respected, and make a *kiddush Hashem* in such a difficult environment? One must work hard at it. I have consulted with people who are in similar situations, and we have come up with six rules that have been found to be helpful in achieving success.

→ *Six Rules of Thumb*

Bend over backwards to be nice to people. Did you ever notice that when something goes wrong, people are always "Johnny on the spot" to complain and blame? Be the one to speak up when things go right! Offer compliments to people who deserve them. Send greeting cards on appropriate occasions and verbally express thanks to the people who have been of help to you. And if you move up the corporate ladder and become other people's boss, aim at being an "easygoing" boss. The bottom line is, if you treat people well, they'll both respect you and like you as a person.

Do outstanding quality work. Don't just do your job, do it with a high degree of excellence. Know your field inside out, and be creative with new ideas. Become recognized as the resident expert on chosen subjects. Offer help and give guidance to anyone who needs it, at any level. By giving the job your absolute best, you'll be highly valued for your contributions to the organization.

Be consistent in your religious conduct. Never waffle. They'll respect you for it. If they perceive that you are only religious when it's convenient for you (e.g., leaving early on Fridays), then you're in trouble.

> *David, a successful systems analyst in a large firm, knew that he was on the right track when a peer said to him, "If only I were as consistent with my diet as you are with your religion, I would've lost 30 pounds by now."*

Be _frum_, but show them that you are a "normal" person. Begin by being "professionally" friendly. Demonstrate that you have a sense of humor, talk about politics, and ask your co-workers about their families. They'll appreciate your worldliness and your interest in them personally. This type of professional friendliness can be more powerful than conforming to the "social" friendliness stereotype that people think one needs to succeed (e.g., having drinks together after work).

Although it can be a bit tricky, one should actively look for ways to demonstrate "normality" to them. Use common sense. While there are a number of _halachic_ issues that you cannot compromise on, there are other things that can be done well within the boundaries of _halachah_.

> Josh, a finance director at a well-known New York bank, remembers having been "required" to go to the company's annual picnic and baseball game. He felt uncomfortable playing in the field, so he grabbed the microphone and announced the proceedings play by play, and enthusiastically cheered the hits and catches. To his colleagues, it demonstrated that he was "normal."

Be someone whom people enjoy being around. Have a positive attitude and project yourself as a happy person. As the _Gemara_ (_Succah_ 49) says: "If a person projects happiness and _chein_, it becomes clear to people that he is a _yerei Shamayim_."

Strengthen your _ruchnius_ level at home. This, in truth, is the core of all _kiddush Hashem_. Being exposed to the added _nisyonos_ (temptations) of the outside world requires that extra attention be paid to your _frumkeit_ level when you're not at work. Make certain that you have a _Rav_ to whom you can present _she'eilos_ and can consult for advice, and always maintain a _k'vius_ (set time) to study Torah every day without fail. _Daf Yomi_ is an excellent vehicle for this because even if you travel on business, the daily _daf_ is exactly the same whether you're in Los Angeles, London or Lawrence.

It may seem improbable, but I have met many prominent people in the corporate world over the years, who say that by merely following these types of guidelines, they have never really had a negative experience. Even in seemingly difficult situations (e.g., late Friday meetings, business trips abroad, etc.), many comment that they have always felt that they were respected for their religious beliefs, and not thought of as "odd" because they were so different from everyone else in their respective companies.

→ The Importance of Being an Ambassador

One might ask, why is it so important to bear in mind that one is representing the Jewish people, so to speak, in the marketplace — the *kiddush Hashem* factor, if you will? Isn't it sufficient to just do your job positively, deliver faithfully, and hope for the best? The answer is simple. First of all, as one is always a Jew — 24 hours a day — so too, is one always viewed as a Jew. *Kiddush Hashem* and the opposite are always on the agenda.

In addition, it is worthwhile to bear in mind the bigger picture. One can never know which person one works with today will be in a position of major influence for *Klal Yisrael* in 20 years. The lawyer next door may someday be sitting on the Supreme Court. If he's deciding a case important to the Jewish community, and you were his "Jewish" friend, the impression one leaves today could have a profound impact on vast numbers of people.

An excellent example of this is President Harry Truman's Jewish connection. While a young man, Truman's business partner and closest friend happened to be Eddie Jacobson — a Jew. Most likely, back in Independence, Missouri, young Harry did not meet many Jews. But when it came time for the U.N. to vote on the partitioning of Palestine when Israel had declared its independence in 1948, Jacobson's influence as President Truman's "Jewish" friend was pivotal to Truman's pro-Israel policy (against the wishes of many of his advisors in the State Department). Always tell yourself, "If I'm one of the only Jews they ever really get to know, I'd better be sure that they have a positive impression of us all."

✦ Taking the Show Home

Until now, we've discussed the subject of what I would call "external" *kiddush Hashem* — a passive sort of projection of *kiddush Hashem*, as it relates to people we work with outside of the Jewish community. Of even greater importance is an additional aspect that I would call "internal" *kiddush Hashem*, the positive impact one should make on others *within* the Jewish community.

To begin with, each person has certain talents, and everyone has an obligation to give of some of those talents back to his own community. One can easily find ways to channel his or her strengths toward "internal" growth and improvement, creating a *kiddush Hashem* in the process. For example, if you are a computer programmer, volunteer a few hours a month to the local yeshivah to computerize the yeshivah's financial and academic records, or to teach computer skills to the students. If you're a lawyer, offer to help the *shul* draft its real-estate contract. If you're a yeshivah *rebbe*, counsel those considering a career in *chinuch*. These opportunities, however, must be actively sought out. Often, they do not just come to you by themselves.

At times, one can use one's strengths in surprising ways. While working in England a few years ago, I had developed a cordial relationship with my boss, who was chairman of the company, and in fact the only other Jew in the firm. He was not religiously observant, but since we met once a week to discuss business matters, I summoned up the guts to ask him if he would be interested in beginning our weekly meetings with a 10-minute session in *Mishnayos*. To my surprise, he was thrilled to do so. And so we began doing this every week. As time progressed, he came to the *shiur* every week not only to learn *Mishnayos*, but to ask questions on the *parshah* and *halachah*, as well.

✦ The Constant Question

As I just indicated, many of the points highlighted in this discussion apply not only to those who work in a non-Jewish environment, but to those who work in a Jewish environment, as well. Being nice to people and doing outstanding work can actually create a *kiddush Hashem,* and at the same time have the not-insignificant result of helping build a person's reputation in his and her place of work. This is true whether you're a stock broker, a *rebbe* or learning in a *kollel.* In fact, the Rambam in *Hilchos Yesodei Hatorah* (5:11) delineates the prescription for successful *kiddush Hashem.* This includes treating people well, dealing honestly in business, and keeping a positive attitude. And the notion of "internal" *kiddush Hashem* via volunteering some of one's talents and time is something everyone has an obligation to do. Hashem gave each of us special abilities and talents. It is certainly expected that we share a portion of these *berachos* with others.

Sometimes the potential *kiddush Hashem* opportunity is right before you, other times you must look hard to find it. The key is to always be asking yourself, "How can I do my best to be *mekadesh Shem Shamayim* both externally and internally?"

Challenge and Commitment

Dr. Gershon Kranzler

*An orthodox sociology professor
examines the role of the ben Torah
in the professional world*

✧ *The Way It Was*

A growing number of Orthodox young men and women about to enter the job market are facing serious challenges to their strength of commitment as *shomrei Torah u'mitzvos*.

Essentially these challenges are the same that *galus* Jews have faced whenever their host countries offered them the chance to enter their socio-economic mainstream, between periods of oppression, persecution, and expulsion. In some respects it is also the same test of commitment that faced the masses of earlier Jewish immigrants when they arrived in the *goldene medineh*, this land of unlimited opportunities. Most had come with a baggage of Torah knowledge and Jewish culture from their *cheder* education, and from the informal socialization of the *shtetl* milieu. Unfortunately, even many who passed the first assimilation test of *bitul Yiddishkeit* at Ellis Island and at Orchard

and Hester Streets, and who continued their study in the synagogues and *shtieblach* before and after sweatshop hours, paid
their due respect to the idols of public education and acculturation. They sacrificed their children to the *Molochs* of social, economic, and cultural mobility, and paid homage to the *Ashtaros* of
success in the relatively open marketplace. Each yard of their
uptown trek was paved with jettisoned ballast of their Jewish
heritage and Old World tradition. As the Yosseles, Yankeles, and
Moisheles became Joes, Jakes, and Mortons, many of their parents watched proudly from the sidelines. This all-too-familiar
story cost Jewry hundreds of thousands from the masses that
came to the U.S. since the 1880's, as they moved from the sweat-
shops and grocery stores to the textile, garment, and fur centers;
and as their gilded-ghetto children entered into the professional
and managerial classes in upper middle-class communities.

✣ Today: More of the Same and Then Some

The challenge today is the same, and the test of commitment
is equally as grave as the one that made Sammy run *yarmulke*-
less, head-over-heels into the social ritualism of the greener fields
and the increasing immorality of the new mores — only to face
the self-righteous rebellion of his freaked-out kids searching for
a genuine commitment. No need to further belabor the tragedies
of the leaping interfaith marriage statistics on one end of the
Jewish spectrum, while at the other end, ever increasing numbers of earnest youngsters are flocking to encounters with
Chassidism and *baal-teshuvah* yeshivos, or challenging their elders for more observance and a better Jewish education.

But unlike the Orthodox Jewish community that was built by
the earlier waves of Jewish immigrants, the largely native
American *bnei* and *bnos Torah* of the third and fourth generations
of today have been nurtured by the wellsprings of a new, vibrant
Orthodoxy, reshaping the realities and the dimensions of the
American Jewish community beyond the keenest hopes of the
great educators and leaders — the *Rabbe'im* and *Rebbes* who had

initiated and engineered this transformation. The products of the expanding day schools and yeshivos, and of the intensively Jewish new communities, are the core of a strong, positive Jewish future that belies the Vanishing Jew myth. They dispel the gloom of the projections of demographers who point up the serious population implosion, the growing outmarriage of the college generation, and who have little faith in the 85 percent of the national sample that proclaim their Jewish identity as something of a value.

In terms of absolute numbers the Orthodox Jewish Community is not large. In fact, as the older immigrant generation becomes smaller, those who identify with Orthodoxy in the communal and national studies are decreasing. But ours was never a number game. And the demographer's studies do not reflect the large family size of the chassidic households and of the Torah communities. They do not show the new Orthodox Jewish image that is surprisingly as "American" in its self-assurance and communal involvement as any of the former "allrightniks" who led the secularization of the Jewish community so close to the point of no return.

Even some of the formerly severe critics of the Torah world are now looking enviously at the Day-School movement in view of the bankruptcy of the Afternoon Hebrew School and Sunday School education. They are proclaiming the Orthodox Community as "the only hope of American Jewry." Bona fide social researchers such as Marshall Sklare state that "in less than three decades Orthodoxy has transformed its image from that of a dying movement to one whose strength and opinions must be reckoned within any realistic appraisal of the Jewish community" (*The Jewish Community in America*, '74, p. 131).

✦ Challenge in Three Dimensions

Because the vigorous Orthodox Jewish community is gaining recognition, it is all the more important to confront the serious challenge that faces our youth as it enters into old and newly opening avenues of professional life. The non-observant Jew, like the typical American middle-class suburbanite in general, has but two considerations in this situation: First, he worries about a professional career, chances for growth, and advancement. On the second, deeper level of the American dream, channeled into the vaunted middle-class achievement syndrome, he is concerned with "making it." This goes beyond the Horatio Alger approach of pulling oneself up by one's own bootstraps, for the more current, rigid structures of the managerial society have tied the soaring wings of the young man entering its hierarchy to degrees, test scores, and differential access to the openings in the corporate system.

The Sabbath and mitzvah observer faces an added dimension to his/her future scope which can challenge his religious commitment. For him, his choice of a profession is more than a matter of finding a livelihood with a future. He must select an occupation or profession that on one hand minimizes the head-on collision between values acquired in the years of intensive education and the requirements of making it in the rough and tumble of the "real" world. On the other hand, he seeks an opportunity to optimize his professional aptitude and interests, especially those he has cultivated and refined in the intellectual and social milieu of the Torah community, which allowed him to develop his personality and gifts in the ideology of *Torah im Derech Eretz* (unless he is one of the select whose extraordinary faculties and dedication qualify him for exclusive devotion to *limud haTorah* as a vocation). The realization of this professional aspiration is fraught with *nisyonos* (temptations and pitfalls) from the moment the committed Torah Jew enters his vocational or professional apprenticeship until the day he retires.

→ *The Girls, Too*

Not so long ago this was mainly a matter of concern for boys, for the ideal of Jewish parents was always to prepare their girls for "the proper *shidduch*," setting up and maintaining the ideal setting for raising a family. This has changed considerably even in chassidic circles that had once been totally averse to any education for girls beyond minimal requirements. Today the discussion of the *shomer mitzvos* in the professional world must also include the *shomeres mitzvos*, the product of a Bais Yaakov type of intensive Jewish education. In fact, the challenge for the girl in the demoralizing realities of the job market is so much more fraught with *nisyonos* if one only considers matters of *tzenius* (modesty), besides all the other risks.

The average young man's successful transition from the controlled atmosphere of his school days to the harsh requirements of his actualization on the outside concerns mainly him, his family, and his close associates. When the *ben* and *bas Torah* venture forth, the degree and manner in which they face up to the challenges of the world involves *kiddush Hashem* or (*chas vechalilah*) *chillul Hashem*. The boy with the *yarmulke* on the college campus, in the government office, in a research laboratory, or in the business world cannot afford to think only of himself, his career, his personal needs and ambitions. He must also prove whether he actually absorbed "*lilmod, ulelamed, lishmor, v'laasos* — to teach, learn, keep and perform ...."

Obviously we are not here concerned with the ideal young *talmid chacham* whose dedication and intellectual and emotional gifts qualify him for the *kollel* and post-*kollel* level from which our future spiritual leaders, teachers, and vital *klei kodesh* come. They are foregoing the mundane rewards the average vocation or profession offers its successful members. They have their own crises and *nisyonos* of an order and type that require more than the ordinary measure of stamina and self-limitation for the higher and greater good.

✦ Grappling With the Factors

Focusing on some of the problems and limitations, as well as the opportunities the *shomer mitzvos* must consider as he prepares himself for his career choice, four factors or conditions are dominant:

First, economic and political changes are limiting or totally eliminating many heretofore promising careers in the academic, government, and business world.

Second, one must confront the basic stance one will take in one's interaction and association with, or isolation from, the people with whom one works. Here, of course, the problems vary for the *ben* or *bas Torah*, and for the single or married person — particularly for the married woman.

Third, one must consider the degree of commitment one will have to one's career: as merely a way of making a living/ as a vocation/ as an avocation/ as a life calling to which one gives one's all and best, to the neglect of other aspects of life.

Last, we must face the corollary degree of "success," of material and nonmaterial status symbols, of social and professional prestige to which the young *ben Torah* aspires.

The first of these points — the changing face of the career market — has been discussed at length in a number of other articles, including several in *The Jewish Observer* (June 1976, September 1976).

✢ *The Social Ground Rules*

Let us, then, deal with the second of these considerations — the basic stance which the young man or woman must take, and the underlying values that will enable him or her to cope with the social problems. It is simple to say that this is strictly a matter of *halachah*, of knowing what is permissible and what is not in the associational requirements of the job. But, there are a number of open or gray areas beyond the limits of the *halachah*. One need only refer to the interpretations of *Rashi* or *Ramban* on "*Kedoshim tiheyu*, You shall be holy" to realize the potential dangers of the *naval b'reshus haTorah* — violating the very spirit if not the exact definitions of the Law — and the value of *kadesh atzmecho bemutar lach* — self-restraint beyond the limits of the Do's and Don't's. As a result, the young *ben Torah* about to enter a profession must be aware of these possible positions:

That there are a number of broad areas where one must apply the principles of a life of *kedushah* (sanctity) within the confines of the *halachah*; that one might take a flexible attitude — the degree of flexibility defined not by whim or want, but by the latitude of the *halachah*; that there are various formats or lifestyles of *chumros* (stringent rulings) or limitations, ranging from rigid observance of all *issurim* (prohibitions) and the exacting observance of all commandments to simply trying to get by without violating blatant prohibitions, such as eating *tereifah*.

That one may avoid being conspicuous at all times and under any condition; that one may try to limit being or acting different to the very minimum — not wearing a *yarmulke* on the job, putting it on only when saying a *berachah*; that one may insist on wearing it at all times; that one may try from the very outset to be separate and act as differently as the *halachah* requires, without totally isolating oneself from one's work- or business-associates; that there is the extreme position taken by chassidim, who in garb and appearance, on their job as well as off it, emphasize their deliberate otherness as a form of protection against even the slightest level of assimilation.

✦ Making Crucial Choices

Having defined the implications of his personal commitment — hopefully after consultation with a Torah mentor — the *ben Torah* must next lay down the mandatory ground rules for his choice of a job. Above all else, these ground rules must allow him scrupulous observance of Shabbos and Yom Tov, with flexible hours for *erev* Shabbos and Yom Tov. Similarly, it would seem to me that the wearing of a *yarmulke* must be acceptable in his place of employment. The consequences are obvious: The more restrictive one is in his social interaction on the job, the more limited will the opportunities be for entering and successfully functioning in some realms of professional life — though by no means in all. But this condition should be a *sine qua non*, regardless of the degree of one's commitment to his chosen profession and of one's chances for success and self-realization. *This will surely put some jobs or vocations out of bounds.*

Other fields of endeavor are more fraught with serious *nisyonos* — such as certain areas of art, sculpture, sex counseling, and physical therapy — as much as the Orthodox community needs qualified personnel to service these areas. In addition, there is a great need for qualified *bnei Torah* in mental-health fields, but the crucial vocations of psychologists, psychiatrists, and psychoanalysts are particularly dangerous for the committed young man and woman, unless they have a strong foundation in *halachah*, are ideologically schooled in *hashkafah* (Torah philosophy), and continue their *limud Torah* — their general and relevant Torah studies under qualified *rebbe'im*.

✦ The Detailed Decisions

Beyond the basic problems, there are a number of other secondary decisions for which one must be prepared — secondary in terms of choice of work, but primary in terms of one's commitment to Torah. Besides the relative question of wearing a *yarmulke* on the job all the time, sometimes, or not at all, or showing one's *tzitzis*, there is for example, the lunch problem: to eat in total isolation out of a sandwich bag / to go to lunch with co-workers while eating one's own food / or to go out with others and eat only salads, fruit-plates, and similar types of food, where the questions of *kashrus* are limited, but nonetheless real.

One must decide whether one will go on business trips with co-workers or the boss; whether to take out clients for dinner, or to a nightclub, as is customary in some businesses. This, in turn, involves the question of social drinking, and similar popular expectations of professional association and success.

The problems are even more serious for a woman who is determined to maintain Orthodox standards in terms of *tzenius*, *yichud* (laws prohibiting isolation of a man and woman under certain conditions), wearing a *sheitel*, and other restrictions that are bound to affect human relations on the job. Even more than the male, she has to set her ground rules as to the type of social distance she imposes in her relations with co-workers, supervisors, subordinates, and customers or clients. If she is an office secretary, for example, will she insist on keeping the office door ajar to avoid *yichud* problems? Will she participate in office parties, with the accompanying problems of social drinking and the related musts of professional and social success? Only few jobs permit total isolation of the sort required by the strict standards of *halachah*. And from the very outset, the *shomer mitzvos* must decide on the *modus operandi* that behooves his Orthodox commitment on the continuum from being maligned as "*farchnockt*," to being flexible or liberal in the interpretation and application of the letter and the spirit of the Law. The inherent threats and *nisyonos* are obvious.

✦ The Ethical Problems

Equally — if not more — serious are ethical considerations, that can limit one's chances of success by rejecting common, yet questionable business practices in mark-up, advertising, sales techniques, and in tax and political customs, which seem woven into the very fabric of our commercial life — as evidenced in prominent court cases against well-known businesses, and legal or political figures. To make an "honest buck" is sometimes so impossible as to seem almost immoral. Posing questions of *halachah* concerning manufacturing, packaging, and other areas that beg the question of *geneivas daas* (false representation) often provoke little more than incredulous smiles, scorn, or outright ridicule. One need not allude to recent widely publicized problems in institutional and political life to dramatize the gravity of the *nisyonos* which confront the Orthodox Jew as he enters professional life within the Jewish community, and even more so on the outside.

✦ The Search For Alternatives

Obviously, candid confrontation with blatant and subtle pitfalls in all levels of the professional life severely limit chances of higher advancement, and greater success of the All-American variety for the *ben/bas Torah* in many fields. Then the only option is to search for viable alternatives that allow for maximum independence or freedom of behavior and the sort of self-assurance and intrinsic pride in one's heritage that has gained more acceptance in our age of assertive self- and collective-expression and freedom. Sincerity and morality, religious consistency and genuine decency, when coupled with a willingness to try harder, will open many avenues of professional advancement traditionally closed to Jews in general, and to observant Jews in particular.

Fortunately, as the result of recent changes in government regulations and greater open-mindedness in some vocations, there are areas in government work, corporate structures, and business that meet the above suggested ground rules. They allow for more flexible work schedules, accommodating *tefillah bizmano*, and Shabbos and Yom Tov observance; that do not depend on a high degree of close personal association, thus avoiding crises or alienation; that offer a relatively high degree of independence; that do not impinge on conscience questions of ethics and legality of various practices. The rapidly expanding use of computer technology in government, banking, and private industry, for example, offer the yeshivah graduates excellent opportunities, if they dedicate but a little time to specialized training. Their intellectuality usually makes them highly suited for computer logic on many levels.

Similarly, the increasing acceptance of careers in selling and business in middle-class Jewish circles points to these as attractive opportunities for greater flexibility of hours, independence, and self-limitation. One may point with pride to the striking business acumen and resulting success of many chassidim in printing, manufacturing — even in fashions — without their yielding an inch in their chassidic lifestyle. Many crafts and skilled trades have been too long neglected by our youth, yet they are ideally suited for the requirements of mitzvah observance.

In addition, numerous government, administration, and research jobs depend mainly on objective test scores rather than on social intimacy — although advancement to higher levels is frequently bound up with vital "personal connections." And of course the standard jobs "for a Jewish boy," like accountancy, law, medicine, engineering, consulting work, and the expanding paraprofessional fields grant a high degree of independence and flexibility in scheduling and working conditions, without seriously impeding growth, advancement, and success.

→ *The Price*

Mesiras nefesh — the willingness to sacrifice — to be satisfied with less rather than to pay the price for greater success, and other status symbols of the middle-class culture — are the essential ingredients ... above and beyond a thorough Torah *chinuch*, a strong, viable, intelligent *hashkafah*, and strong involvement and bonds in the Torah community. These offer the *ben Torah* the best chances to maintain his integrity in the professions.

It is incumbent on parents, educators, and concerned members of the Torah world to guide American Orthodox Jewish young men and women; to produce in them the high degree of commitment needed in their confrontation with the challenges and risks of a world fraught with tests and temptations on their way to professional success.

Torah Ethics in Business

Harold Jacobs

✦ *Is Honesty Really "the Best Policy"?*

An article in the *Harvard Business Review* a number of years ago, asked the question: "How Ethical Are Businessmen?" In the last decades, businessmen themselves — and the public at large — have been raising this question, and arguing it. More recently, the advertising industry has been subject to careful scrutiny in newspaper and magazine articles, and in a number of popular books.

For some idea of the scope of the questioning, here are some of the norms employed by the Advertising Federation of America in a book prepared by their associate general counsel. He suggests that the businessman can easily judge the honesty of his sales message by asking himself a few direct questions:

Is it *really* honest?

Is it *clear* to the people who hear it or read it?

Can I *prove* all this?

Would *I* approve, if my *competitor* used this sales approach?

Would I want *my* wife to spend *my* money, because of this ad?

Of course, honesty in business goes far beyond the advertising or sales-approach a business firm may use. It goes to the heart of every aspect of business: It relates to management practices; relationships with government; personnel practices, and, to a growing degree, the influence of business as a political and social force.

Let's take a brief look at some of these areas.

It has been said, with a good deal of truth, that every businessman is in partnership with government. It is also almost axiomatic that business partners frequently don't get along, and tend to keep things from each other. But, the government is one partner who insists that we get along with him, and has the machinery and the police-power to assure that we "get along." Yet, there are loopholes; there are ways in which one can deceive the government in providing tax information, in padding expense accounts, and in ways that are too numerous to mention.

Business and businessmen today are not simply merchants; they are not simply engaged in creating products and services for sale to the public. Business today is a social and political force which has great influence in the affairs of men, and carries a great responsibility to the buying public, beyond the commodities and services it offers to the public.

Of course, the power that business exercises, and abuses of this power, are not often called to the attention of the public, until, that is, some scandal breaks in the newspapers. In 1959, the famous TV payola scandal rocked the country, followed in 1961 by the indictment and sentencing of G.E. and Westinghouse officials for illegal price-fixing. Both these incidents had one thing in common: *No one would accept the responsibility*. Higher officials blamed it on lower officials, and lower officials blamed it on their superiors. And both these incidents have much in common with a moral problem of much greater proportions: the responsibility for the destruction of European Jewry in the Holocaust. Hardened criminals guilty of the most horrible crimes paraded to the witness stand and told their accusers that they were simply cogs in a big wheel, *"kleine mentschen,"* and the defense, "Everybody was doing it, we had no choice," continues to be heard in defense of all sorts of immorality and criminal acts.

When scandals become public, there is a quick rash of discussion, and then, as quickly, the discussion stops; it becomes dead as yesterday's newspaper. But businessmen, who must live with these problems constantly, do discuss them, very often in the pages of various business journals. And one theme recurs and recurs: "GOOD ETHICS IS GOOD BUSINESS." Now, one may agree or disagree with this formulation, but it brings us to the question: How is a Jew, who has committed himself to obedience to Torah and *halachah,* to react to this morass of ethical confusion, and refusal to accept responsibility?

One of the myths of American life — you probably were taught this at school in your earliest years — is embodied in the expression: *"Honesty is the best policy."*

But what do we mean when we say it's "the best policy"? Perhaps what we really mean is illustrated by the story of the two women who boarded a bus and sat down together. One of them said, "Oh, I forgot to pay my fare." The other shrugged her shoulders: "Listen, the company has plenty of money, forget about it." "Oh no," her companion said, "honesty is the best policy." She walked down to the driver and returned with a big smile on her face. "See, I told you 'honesty is the best policy' — I gave the driver a quarter and he gave me change for half-a-dollar."

Honesty works — it "pays off"... good ethics is good business ... it pays off in the long run. But this is not what the Torah demands of us. Does eating only kosher food "pay off" — hardly, it's usually more expensive. Does observing Shabbos "pay off" — it may involve a serious financial loss. Does any mitzvah "pay off" ... except of course in a spiritual sense. And one *may* seriously question whether good ethics "pays off"; whether it really is "good business"; whether it will ultimately show up on the black side of the ledger. Good ethics is a Torah imperative — the Torah demands it of us, even at the expense of losing money which will never be recouped. We might ask just as well, does *tzedakah* "pay off" — if it does, there may be something wrong.

An entire section of the *Shulchan Aruch* concerns itself with business ethics and procedures. It is interesting to note that in order to pass judgment on such matters, a rabbi must have a higher *semichah, Yadin Yadin,* than the general *semichah* given to rabbis. We can here only underline the simple fact that the *Shulchan Aruch* is concerned with what happens at the office, or at the plant, as much as it is concerned with Shabbos and *kashrus,* with our *tefillos* and our *tefillin.* But even the text of the *Shulchan Aruch* itself does not have all the answers. Just as modern technology and food chemistry, for example, have created new problems which require technological data and a deeper understanding of *halachah,* so too, the complexities of modern business and finance require new insights and in-depth understanding of both sides of the coin.

Yet, this is not to say that the average Jew, anxious and willing to be guided by *halachah,* is left completely in the dark. There are some basic guidelines in Torah tradition which can serve as rules-of-thumb in basic business problems.

1. The Torah deems personal property to be inviolate. Any act which seeks to secure ownership of property without the clear will and understanding of the person who is transferring the property, is a violation of one or more basic laws of the Torah. Of course, our zealousness to protect the rights of private property must work both ways. Reb Yisrael Salanter, the great *mussar* teacher, put it this way: *Yenems mili d'alma, zeinen meine mili d'Shemaya.* That is, something which for my fellow Jew is simply a physical or material need, is for me a spiritual responsibility. Or, to put it in more concrete terms, for someone to provide bread for himself and his family, is a material problem (*mili d'alma*); but for me to help him to meet these needs, is a spiritual obligation (*mili d'Shemaya*). Bearing this in mind will help to solve many ethical, or halachic problems that arise in the business world. A great *tzaddik* and *talmid chacham* offered this example: If a man runs a winery and underpays his employees because they are off from work on Shabbos, then he is producing the worst kind of *yayin nesech.*

2. *Dina d'malchusa dina*, the Sages tell us; the law of the land in which we live is as binding as a *din* of the Torah (unless, of course, the law would force us to violate Torah law, a circumstance which we, in democratic lands, fortunately do not face). This means, very simply, that our obligations to our government are to be viewed in the same light as we view our obligations in the religious sphere. If we are opposed to compromise in the realm of Shabbos, for example, then to be consistent, we must avoid compromise in meeting our obligations to the state, as well.

3. In our relationships with people, Jews and non-Jews, we must carry with us the basic teaching of our Torah: "*Choviv odom, she'nivra b'tzelem elokim* — Man is especially dear, because he has been created in the image of G–d." While many problems may arise in dealing with personnel on all levels which are of a more specific nature and may require specific consideration and consultation with a rabbi, nevertheless, this rule-of-thumb can serve as a faithful guide in most instances.

Above all, the most basic rule-of-thumb that must guide the businessman is this: The *halachos* which govern business ethics and business procedures require at least as much competence as the vast body of *halachos* for which we usually turn to the rabbi as the expert. We live in an age of specialization; the good businessman confronted with a problem which takes him out of his depth in a particular area, will seek out expert advice from someone who has mastered this specific area. So too in the area of *halachah*, if we would be true to our G–d, and true to ourselves, we must seek out the rabbi whose competence in Talmudic scholarship qualifies him to give us the most expert guidance in this area.

A recent writer on the subject of business ethics proposes a test of your "integrity quotient" and here are some of the questions he asks:

- Do you pad your business expense accounts by overstating mileage, hotel, food, and other expenses?
- Do you place the blame on someone else for your own mistakes?

- If you are an employee, do you use company time or facilities for personal business?
- Do you try to "beat" traffic laws, or try to avoid the consequences when you have been caught violating them?

There are other questions he asks, questions we might all ask ourselves, but his jackpot question is most revealing:

HAVE YOU ANSWERED ANY OF THE ABOVE
QUESTIONS WITH A "NO," WHEN IN YOUR
HEART YOU KNOW IT SHOULD BE A "YES"?

There is a familiar story told of the Chofetz Chaim — he had hitched a ride with a *baal agalah*. The driver, seeing a field of fresh hay, stopped his wagon and asked his passenger to stand guard while he snitched a few bales. Within minutes, the Chofetz Chaim began shouting, *"Me' kukt, Me' kukt"* (we're being watched). The driver rushed back to his wagon, and hurried off. "Who was watching?" he asked his passenger, and the Chofetz Chaim pointed his finger upward.

We may fool others; we may succeed in fooling the government; and someone may even find a way to beat the computers, but the Jew must always remember: We are being watched.

Employer – Employee Relationships in Halachah

Rabbi Noach Isaac Oelbaum

❖ *In the Footsteps of Yaakov Avinu*

A t first glance, it would appear that many of the directives discussed at this conference are no more than admirable, ethical practices. The unavoidable truth, however, is that most of the guidelines presented are basic *halachah*.

It is truly sad when we realize how far we have strayed: today, one gets the impression that a person who makes an honest living, who does not cheat, and is *oveid b'emunah* (faithfully serves his employer) must be a *tzaddik v'chassid*. When the integrity of an employee is called into question, it is quite common to hear a retort, "My employer doesn't deserve any better. He doesn't treat me with respect. He isn't fair with me, either." The *Shulchan Aruch* (*Choshen Mishpat* 337:20), however, states that an employee must work "*b'chol kocho* — with all the power he possesses," as we learn from Yaakov Avinu, who said, "*Ki b'chol kochi ovadeti es avichen* — With all my might, I served your father [Lavan]" (*Bereishis* 31:6). And he later tells Lavan: "By day, scorching heat consumed me, and frost by night, my sleep drifts from my eyes … And you changed my wage a hundred times" (ibid. vs. 40-41).

Let us take into account that Yaakov Avinu's employer was Lavan HaArami, who went down in history as the eternal symbol of dishonesty and chicanery, who continuously cheated Yaakov Avinu. Every employee should thus ask himself: "Was I ever treated more unfairly than Yaakov Avinu? Was I also cheated one hundred times, as was Yaakov Avinu?" And yet, Lavan's treatment of Yaakov did not influence him to deviate even minutely from the path of honesty and faithful service. Yaakov could not be deterred from fulfilling his duties to his employer with all his energy and all his might. He acted as if nothing happened.

Today's employee might attempt to justify himself, and say, "How can I compare myself with Yaakov Avinu? Who can reach his *madreigah*?" We must bear in mind, however, that every episode recorded in the Torah is there to instruct us. *Chazal* derive hundreds of *halachos* from every extra letter. The Torah went to such great length to record Yaakov Avinu's behavior in such specific detail, to instruct us to learn from Yaakov Avinu and to try to emulate him, by serving our employers with honesty and integrity. This source is even mentioned in Codes of Hebrew Law (see *Rambam* and *Shulchan Aruch*).

✧ Employers' Obligations

The *halachah* clearly underscores the importance of paying one's debts. Even if one has limited funds and finds it difficult to pay money owed, it is clearly stated in *Choshen Mishpat* (*Siman* 97) that paying one's debts even comes before supporting one's wife and children.

The time for payment of wages, for example, depends on the arrangement made at the time of employment (*Choshen Mishpat* 339:1). In the absence of an agreement, one would need to follow the accepted practice of that place, i.e., whether to pay at the end of the week or the month, etc.

These laws apply also to rental fees. When the rental period is over, payment must be made by the end of that day or night (*Choshen Mishpat* ibid.).

Payment for work contracted by the job is also included in this commandment. Thus, when an item is taken in for repair, cleaning, or adjustment, or if a plumber or an electrician is contracted to perform a service in one's home, payment must be made "on the day" that the item is picked up, or the job completed. (*Beur Halachah, Orach Chaim* 245; *Choshen Mishpat* 339:6). Payment must be made on time to a minor, as well. Therefore, when a babysitter is hired, she must be paid before the day or night is over (*Ahavas Chesed* 89:5; *Nesiv HaChesed* 16). One is allowed to make a pre-condition with his worker that he will not be paid on time. This condition, however, must be made before the worker agrees to the job (see *Shach, Choshen Mishpat* 339:2; also *Ahavas Chesed* 10:13). Not having the exact change on hand is no excuse to delay payment (*Ahavas Chesed* 89:7; *Nesiv HaChesed* 21).

Paying with a post-dated check is not considered paying on time. It is permitted only on the condition that the worker says that he does not mind (*Teshuvos VeHanhagos* I *Siman* 899).

Payment of wages precedes one's personal needs; thus if by paying wages, the employer will not have sufficient funds to purchase *lechem mishneh* (two *challah* loaves) for Shabbos, or he will not be able to buy *tefillin*, he nevertheless must pay the wages first (*Beur Halachah Orach Chaim* 242).

The Chofetz Chaim's daughter recalled an incident that took place in the middle of a cold winter night in her youth: Her father asked her to accompany him to a tailor's house. That evening, the tailor had finished some work that the Chofetz Chaim had given him, and he had not been paid. The tailor's house was at the other end of the town, and it was freezing cold outside. The Chofetz Chaim told his daughter that the effort was worthwhile in order to pay the tailor on time (*Michtevei Chofetz Chaim*, p. 38).

Modern Business and the Prohibition Against Ribbis

Rabbi Moshe Silberberg

The topic of *ribbis* (usury) is broad and complex, thus this presentation is limited to a few of the critical areas of concern.

The direct charging of interest by the lender is prohibited by the Torah many times. In fact, the lender is transgressing six distinct prohibitions as spelled out in *Rambam* (*Laws of Lenders and Borrowers* 4:2). The borrower is transgressing two distinct prohibitions. Even the witnesses, the preparer of the documents, and the guarantors are all prohibited expressly from involvement in a loan with interest between a Jewish lender and a Jewish borrower.

✢ Helping a Friend With a Poor Credit Rating

There exists a very common practice that seems perfectly permissible — in fact, many consider it very praiseworthy for it is done only for altruistic purposes and not for personal gain;

and yet, in the Divine plan of our Torah lives, it is prohibited. We will not attempt to give the philosophical underpinnings or logic behind this prohibition; time and space do not allow for this. We will only clearly state the *halachah* pertaining to this practice.

A borrower would like to borrow money from a non-Jewish bank (with interest) on a credit card, credit line, or a mortgage on the house he is buying. This is definitely permissible. The borrower, however, has poor credit and cannot qualify for the loan. A friend or relative is willing and able to take the loan on his own name, the loan money will go directly to the borrower (by making the purchase using the friend's credit card), and the borrower will pay principal and interest directly to the lending bank. The friend will not touch the money (neither loan money nor repayment money), and our own logic would say that the loan with interest is only between the borrower and the non-Jewish bank.

This practice, however, is severely prohibited by the Torah as a transgression of *ribbis*. The Torah identifies the cardholder or signer of responsibility as the real borrower from the bank. Touching the money or purchase is irrelevant; responsibility to the lender to repay the loan is the criterion for determining who is the real borrower.

Therefore, by the criteria of *halachah*, the facts are as follows: The friend has borrowed $1000 at 10 percent from the non-Jewish bank, and the friend has then lent to the borrower the same $1000 at 10 percent in order to repay the friend's debts to the bank. Two Jews are engaged in a loan transaction with an interest obligation from Jew to Jew, and therefore an appalling transgression of Torah law has taken place.

At the close of this short presentation, we will suggest the way to correctly structure this debt to make it permissible and praiseworthy.

✦ *Corporations*

The vast majority of *poskim* (*halachic* decisors) have ruled that corporations are to be treated as partnerships, owned jointly by the partners, with the singular distinction of limited liability and no personal liability. Therefore, almost everything that an individual Jew is prohibited from doing, is also prohibited to the Jewish corporation. A Jewish corporation (entirely owned by Jews or one with majority ownership in Jewish hands) is therefore prohibited from lending money with interest to another Jew.

A difference of opinion has arisen concerning corporate borrowing. One opinion holds that a loan with no personal liability is not categorized as a loan in Torah law. This opinion holds that although the agreement to have the limited liability is contractually and legally binding, nonetheless it has left the legal boundaries of being a loan and is consequently not included in the prohibitions of interest.[1] This opinion was promulgated by one of the *gedolei hador*.

A second opinion holds that since it is legally binding, and fits into the parameters of the lender getting the borrower to repay more than the amount of money received, it is definitely included in the prohibition. To accommodate this view, the author has a remedy spelled out at the close of this short presentation.[2]

→ Involvement With Non-Religious Jews in Ribbis

Lawyers and legal secretaries prepare interest-bearing loan documents between two non-religious Jews — lender and borrower. This is definitely prohibited, as mentioned before in the first paragraph of this discussion. The prohibition even applies to notarizing such documents, since the notarization finalizes the validity of the document. There is no real remedy for this problem, except to get a non-Jewish lawyer and secretary to handle this work. A competent rabbinical authority should be consulted to ensure that the non-Jew should not become an agent of the first lawyer and secretary.

---

1. Editor's Note: At the same session of the conference, Rabbi Yisroel Reisman presented this *psak*, which was issued by Rabbi Moshe Feinstein, as being widely accepted.

2. In the opinion of this presenter, it would seem obligatory to follow the majority who prohibit this type of loan.

→ A Fee for Cashing Checks

A common practice, especially when sending checks to children living in *Eretz Yisrael*, is to have the checks cashed by a private person for a fee of 1½ percent of the face value of check. The check casher gives $985 to the presenter of the check and approximately a week later receives $1000 when the check has cleared. A loan has transpired by giving the cash and waiting for repayment. The $15 is either interest, or a fee for services rendered.

The majority rules to permit this — that is, to consider the $15 a fee for services. They cite the fact that the check casher would charge the same $15 even if the presenter of the check would wait for the cash and not have the week's use of the money, which proves that the $15 is not interest on the loan.

The minority rules to prohibit; they cite many early *poskim* who say that fees for services are usually determined by an hourly rate or by a flat fee. Any fee that is determined by the amount of money transferred ($15 for $1000, $150 for $10,000) cannot be a fee and must be viewed as interest, which is always charged according to the amount of the loan.

The majority answers that this is no longer the case; today we find many service industries that determine the fees charged by the total dollar amounts handled — brokerage of real estate, stock sales, etc. This majority view is the ruling followed by most, and this writer also agrees that it is indeed permissible.

(Many more areas were presented at the lecture; however, we cannot summarize them in the space allowed in this article.)

In conclusion, we must stress that the important and vital factor in dealing with this sensitive area is an ongoing relationship with a *halachah* authority with whom to discuss *ribbis* questions in business. Most times, that *Rav* will be able to structure the deal in a substantively different manner to make the transaction permissible.

For instance, in case #1, if both sides agree before the deal that the purchase made with a friend's credit card or mortgage will indeed belong to the friend (and not to the borrower), then whatever the friend charges the "borrower" will not be interest; rather it will be a permissible rental charge. For instance, in case #2 a *heter iska* can easily be drawn up by a rabbinical authority, which will allow the corporation to utilize the funds as an investment and not as a loan. The remedy is usually available; the needed ingredient is forethought and communication with the *rabbanim*.

A Proposal for a High School Course in Torah Ethics

Professor Steven H. (Shlomo Chaim) Resnicoff, Esq.
and Ira (Yitzchak) Kasdan, Esq.

in conjunction with the

Aleph Institute • Center for Halacha and American Law

*R*ecently, one of the authors was contacted by his local
yeshivah high school. Would he be willing to coach the
Yeshiva moot court team? Agreeable, he was sent and
reviewed the materials — prepared by the state agency that
was overseeing the competition — that the students used in
the program. To say the least, he was keenly disappointed.
Highly professional in appearance and well organized, the
materials left much to be desired, in his opinion. The case
that the yeshivah team would "litigate" revolved around a
drug deal gone awry and the sentencing of the youthful
offender. Real world issues to be sure, but hopefully foreign
events for the typical yeshivah boy and girl.

Why not, he thought, take this secular program and
infuse it with elements of kedushah (holiness)? Why not
reshape the moot court competition as an advocacy program
that teaches the interaction between halachah and secular law
— that teaches students about the issur of arkaos (the general

*prohibition against secular court litigation) and the
importance of dina d'malchusa dina (the need to abide by the
laws of the secular authority)? One that introduces students
to various halachos from that oft-disregarded and forgotten
part of Shulchan Aruch — Choshen Mishpat (dealing with
contract, tort and similar interpersonal and business-related
issues)? A program that allows the students to argue not
only before a "civil" court but also to a beis din (Jewish
court)? The possibilities and permutations
abounded….*

Deceit, fraud and injustice increasingly pervade the secular world in which we live. Unethical behavior has become so commonplace that even when it is clearly perceived, relatively few witnesses are surprised. An ethical callus develops, preventing the expression of any moral outrage and making it continuously easier for individuals to misbehave. Indeed, white collar crimes and other forms of deceit have become so routine that some who previously comported themselves with scruples have openly reevaluated whether they, too, should get their "share" of the dishonest dollars that others seem to harvest so painlessly.

Individual Orthodox Jews sometimes are influenced by the corrupted standards of the secular society that surrounds them. When such Jews succumb, *rachmanah l'tzelan* (Heaven forbid), to such influences, the result may not only be tragic for them personally but may also involve *chillul Hashem* (the desecration of the Name of Heaven).

The secular world has recently begun to respond to the lapse in ethical standards. Increasing numbers of professional schools require ethics courses. Government regulatory bodies in many states require practicing professionals to fulfill continuing education requirements with mandatory ethics education components. It is time for the Orthodox community to respond in kind. The Aleph Institute's Center for Halacha and American Law (the "Center"), with which the authors are associated, proposes that the battle begin much earlier than professional school. The Center suggests that one step that can be taken to inculcate halachic-guided behavior early on is the development of a Jewish high school course on Torah ethics in the business world. Herein, we briefly describe the course the Center envisions and explain why we think it should work. We invite our reader's comments and suggestions.

⤳ *Course Goals*

The goals of the course are manifold: The intent is to contextualize the study of Torah ethics, to sensitize students to the myriad halachic issues that can arise in common commercial transactions (such as the rental of an apartment or the purchase of a home) or business settings (such as the relationship between an employer and employee), and to force students to evaluate their halachic rights and responsibilities with reference to specific fact patterns and hypothetical cases. Two additional over-riding purposes of the course are: 1) to make students aware of the secular law's pervasive regulation of commercial practices including, for instance, the reporting requirements for cash transactions, and 2) to ensure that students are cognizant of the consequences, often quite serious and sometimes tragic, of failing to comply with the law.

⤳ *Course Methodology*

In order to approach ethical and legal issues, students would first study primary sources (Talmud, *Shulchan Aruch, Rambam* and Responsa) about the interrelationships between *halachah,* on the one hand, and secular law and commercial practices, on the other. They will be introduced to doctrines such as *dina d'malchusa dina* ("the law of the land is the law") and *minhag hasocharim* ("commercial practices"). Then they will be presented with hypothetical cases detailing a particular transaction or business deal. Examples of such hypothetical cases are found in the "Preliminary Torah Ethics Course Outline" appended at the end of this piece. With each hypothetical fact pattern, students would be provided not only with with primary halachic materials, but also secular legal materials as well, including copies of federal and state statutes and case law.

This contextual — if you will, "case study"— approach and methodology is designed to breathe life into the classroom and to force students to integrate theory and reality. Reading ethical aphorisms in a vacuum may just not sink in. It is essential that students see how these principles apply in concrete cases.

✈ Course Training for the Teachers

We understand that many high school *rebbe'im* and teachers are not trained to teach such a course, but we hope to address this problem in several ways.

First, the Center expects to develop a clear and comprehensive teacher's manual, which will set out all the materials and case studies. *Second,* the Center would provide live and video-taped training classes for those who undertake to teach the course. *Third,* the Center intends to provide ongoing support for *Rebbeim* and teachers by making available, via phone, e-mail and/or the Web, experts on the halachic and legal issues raised in the hypotheticals cases. *Fourth,* the Center would encourage, and assist, schools to establish links between their *rebbe'im* and teachers and various local, qualified lawyers who have intimate knowledge of *halachah* who would be able and willing to provide substantive guidance to the teachers. *Finally,* rebbe'im and teachers do not have to be prepared to provide precise and unambiguous answers to every question that is raised in the course. The reality is that *poskim* ("decisors") often differ on many issues. The objective is to cultivate the students' ability to perceive the existence of halachic and ethical questions and to train them as to how to go about trying to resolve them.

✈ Educational Returns

We believe that a high school Torah ethics course structured in this way offers many educational returns and benefits, particularly from a halachic perspective. One benefit is that in studying about the relationship between *halachah* and secular law, students will be apprised of the importance of resolving disputes (that cannot otherwise be settled) in front of rabbinic tribunals, before they become programmed to think only of resorting to secular processes and institutions. At the same time, students also will gain valuable and necessary knowledge about the structure of secular law and the relationship between the state and federal legal systems. Additionally, by focusing on hypotheticals, the course will enable *rebbe'im* and teachers to utilize a variety of engaging and interactive exercises, such as the conducting of mock rabbinic or secular trials (in which students could play various roles), the preparation of written briefs, the rendition of oral argument, or the conducting of a moot court. Consequently, the Center's course could easily replace — or serve as an alternative to — the various moot court "courses" that many Jewish high schools offer, while providing the opportunity to sensitize students to Torah ethics. Of course, each school would have to determine how the Center's course would best fit into its curriculum, e.g., whether it should be designated as an "English" course — potentially for college credit — or a "Hebrew" course, or whether it should be offered daily, once a week or on some other basis. However, regardless whether the course is offered as an "English" or "Hebrew" class, it would have to be staffed by pre-trained, competent *rebbe'im* and teachers.

✦ Concluding Thought — Why Start on a High School Level?

High school students are sufficiently mature and experienced to appreciate the types of ethical issues that arise in business. But why begin teaching law and proper business conduct in high school rather than in some post-high school setting?

Within certain Orthodox communities, it is not uncommon for some students directly to enter the business world without any post-high school secular education. Thus, in some instances, high school is the only opportunity to sensitize these individuals to important legal issues in a formal educational setting. Even students who go on to "higher" secular education will benefit from a high school course. As these students get older, they are increasingly likely to take part-time jobs, summer jobs or internships where they may observe the unethical realities of the secular marketplace. A high school course could teach them Torah ethics before they become cynical about or, worse yet, habituated to blindly imitating the misdeeds of those with whom they may work. In addition, even if students would not become jaded after high school and would take required "ethics" courses in some professional school, they would still need a course — which the professional schools cannot or will not effectively offer — in Torah ethics.

The proposed course is still in the planning stages. The authors and the Center would be grateful for any suggestions or other support to bring the vision of a Torah ethics course within the yeshivah high school world to reality.

To comment upon, or for further information about the proposed course, please send an e-mail to Professor Steven Resnicoff at sresnico@condor.depaul.edu or Yitzchak Kasdan at ikasdan@erols.com.

✦ Postscript

Since this article was originally drafted, the proposed Torah Ethics course has become a reality in yeshivos on each coast. Rabbi Yitzchok Adlerstein teaches one "pilot" course to 12th - graders at Yeshiva of Los Angeles High School (Rabbi Sholom Tendler, *Rosh HaYeshivah*; Rabbi Dovid Landesman, Principal), while Rav Sholom Kamenetsky teaches the other to seniors at The Sol Sved Boys High School Division of Torah Academy of Greater Philadelphia (Rabbi Ari Medetsky, Principal). Classes at both schools are conducted twice a week — each class lasts an hour or more — and are based on "case studies" and sources prepared by one of the authors of this article, Professor Resnicoff, and by Rav Kamenetsky himself. Rabbis Adlerstein and Kamenetsky present the materials in their own unique style and at a pace suitable for their respective students. So far, topics that have been covered in one or both of the schools include: breach of contracts and keeping one's word in business (the *sugyah* of *"m'chusrei emunah"*); money laundering and *dina d'malchusa dina*; *arkaos* (the prohibition generally of litigating against a fellow Jew in secular court); misrepresentations in the sale of real estate; and the halachic status of corporations. Other issues that the *rebbe'im* intend to cover in the coming months include: copyright (in secular law and *halachah)*, and mediation, arbitration and *p'sharah*. For further information about their classes, Rabbi Adlerstein may be contacted at (310) 552-4595 and Rav Kamenetsky at skam4@juno.com.

✷ About the Center for Halacha and American Law:

The authors are independent consultants to The Center for Halacha and American Law ("Center"), a part of the Miami-based Aleph Institute, which was established in mid-1998. The Aleph Institute is a tax-exempt, 501(c)(3), not-for-profit organization that was originally founded in 1981 primarily to provide Jewish inmates and their families with educational, humanitarian and religious advocacy and social support. Since that time, the Aleph Institute has significantly expanded its scope of activities through a variety of endeavors and projects such as the creation of the Center.

The Center's goals and objectives are:

• to enhance the Jewish community's appreciation of the requirements of *halachah* to conduct all business and personal transactions in accordance with Torah principles, ethics and values, including the obligation under the *halachah* to abide by the law of the civil authority;

• to educate the Jewish community about the seriousness of secular law and financial ethics, and the need for Jews to be examples of proper business and financial behavior;

• to forge a better understanding within the Jewish community of the interaction between *halachah*, civil authority and secular law (including both civil and criminal law);

• to increase the Jewish community's understanding of American statutory and regulatory law, particularly in areas of application to the community; and

• to assist Jewish businessmen and professionals in ways that will encourage and enable them to abide by the dictates of *halachah* and comply with the law of the civil authority.

For more information about the Aleph Institute and the Center, please visit http://www.aleph-institute.org and http://jlaw.com/lawpolicy/centerforhalacha.html, send an e-mail to Isaac Jaroslawicz, Esq., Aleph's Legal Director, at imj@aleph-institute.org or write to, or call, the Aleph Institute: 9540 Collins Avenue, Surfside, FL 33154. Tel.: (305) 864-5553; fax: (305) 864-5675.

✦ *Appendix*

Preliminary Torah Ethics Course Outline

Copyright © 1999
The Aleph Institute • Center for Halacha and American Law
and Steven H. Resnicoff

The course will initially employ a lecture framework that will introduce students to the following concepts:

- The halachic responsibility to resolve disputes among Jews without resort to secular courts (the *issur arkaos*)
- The structure and practice of *batei din* in the United States
- Exceptions to the general prohibition against using secular courts

- When the exceptions arise
- Limits as to what one may collect in secular court in reliance on an exception
- The structure of secular law in the United States
  - Federal law
  - State law
- The interrelationship between Jewish law and secular law
  - "The law of the kingdom is law" — *dina d'malchusa dina*
    - Application of this principle to matters involving civil law
    - Application of this principle to matters involving criminal law
  - The effect of commercial custom — *minhag hasocharim*
  - The effect of an agreement — *tenai she'b'mamon*

The course will then introduce students to a variety of halachic and secular legal selections and will require students to apply the concepts raised by such authorities to specific hypothetical fact patterns.

The teaching materials will provide teachers with a variety of hypotheticals from which to choose, based on various factors. Some issues may arise in connection with the hypothetical sale and purchase of a house, with the relationship between an employer and an employee, with the filing of questionable insurance claims or tax returns.

The following partial list of issues arising from the sale of a house may not represent the most cogent issues. Nevertheless, these examples illustrate the breadth of possibilities.

Stage #1 — Soliciting Someone to Sell His House

Assume that Reuven has a rich father-in-law who wants to purchase a house for him near the yeshivah, where real estate values are very high. Shimon, who is relatively poor, has such a house only because he bought it many years ago when the price was low. Shimon is not thinking of selling his house. May Reuven offer to buy the house from Shimon — or is there a problem with the prohibition against coveting another person's property (*lo sachmod*)? If Shimon initially rejects Reuven's offer, would it be permissible for Reuven to ask the head of the yeshivah to suggest to Shimon that he accept the offer? Would it be permissible for Reuven to ask his friends to ask Shimon to sell?

Stage #2 — Negotiating for the Sale of a House

For purposes of this issue, assume that Shimon wanted to sell his house and put it up for sale before Reuven ever approached Shimon. Negotiations for the sale of the house give rise to various halachic and secular law issues, including:

• Suppose Reuven is really willing to pay $250,000 for the house. May he tell Shimon that "There is no way that I will pay more than $225,000 for the house," or would such a statement involve fraud (*geneivas daas*)?

• May Shimon say that he has already received an offer to sell the house for $260,000 (even though he has not) and that he would therefore only consider selling it to Reuven if Reuven offers more than $260,000? Suppose Reuven believes Shimon and, based on this belief, offers Shimon more than $260,000 and the sale is consummated. If Reuven later finds out that Shimon had lied to him, may Reuven undo the deal?

• Suppose that during the negotiations over price, Reuven tells Shimon that Levi's house is just as good as Shimon's and Levi's is available for $200,000. May Shimon tell Reuven about defects in Levi's house (assuming, of course, that there are, in fact, such defects) or is Shimon limited to describing the advantages of his own house?

• In describing the "advantages" of his own house, to what extent, if any, may Shimon engage in "puffery"?

• Suppose Shimon knows about certain problems with his house (e.g., the basement floods, the plumbing is problematic, there are termites). May Shimon take any action to "cover up" such problems? Assuming that Shimon may not actively cover up problems, must he affirmatively disclose them or may he remain silent about them?

• Suppose Shimon has lied to Reuven about certain defects

in Shimon's house and that Yehudah, a friend of Shimon's, knows about the lie. If Yehudah cannot convince Shimon to tell Reuven the truth, should Yehudah tell Reuven because of the obligation not to stand by while another Jew suffers a financial loss (*lo sa'amod al dam rei'echa*)? Would it make any difference if Yehudah's knowledge is based on information given to him by Shimon "confidentially"? Would it make any difference if Yehudah were Shimon's lawyer?

• What if Dan owns the property next to Shimon's and Dan wants to buy Shimon's house: Must Shimon sell the house to Dan? Must Shimon give Dan an opportunity to purchase the house on the same terms that Reuven has offered? Do the answers to these questions depend on any particular facts?

• Suppose Reuven and Shimon have orally agreed on terms for the sale of Shimon's house, but they have not signed a written contract. Suppose Naftali would also like to buy a house within two blocks of the *beis midrash*. May Naftali go to Shimon and offer him more money than Reuven offered or would such conduct violate the rule against interfering with another person's rights (e.g., *ani mehafech bi'chararah*)? Would the answer be any different if Reuven and Shimon had signed a written contract? Why or why not?

• Suppose Reuven and Shimon have orally agreed on terms for the sale of Shimon's house, but they have not signed a written contract. May either Reuven or Shimon change his mind and refuse to go through with the sale? If one of them did change his mind, would this indicate that he was not trustworthy (*mechusrah amanah*)? Would the one who backed out receive a "curse" in *beis din* (a *mi sheparah*)? Are there any circumstances that might change the answers to these questions?

Stage #3 — The Contractual Terms

• Suppose Reuven does not really want to live in Shimon's house. Instead, he only wants to purchase the house if he first finds someone who will buy the house from him at a higher price than he pays Shimon. Of course, he does not explain this to Shimon. Instead, he asks Shimon to put a clause in the contract allowing Reuven to have the house inspected within a certain number of days and providing Reuven the right to cancel the contract should he be dissatisfied with the results of the inspection. Reuven knows from experience that a house inspection will always reveal some problems and he is relying on this contractual provision as a way out. Has Reuven acted properly? Why or why not?

A similar question would arise if Reuven asked for the contract to be contingent on his ability to obtain a mortgage from a bank. In fact, Reuven, who is unemployed, knows that he does not qualify for a mortgage. Instead, to the extent Reuven may need some cash to buy the property before reselling it, Reuven is really relying on his rich father-in-law. Has Reuven acted properly in asking for the mortgage contingency clause?

• What does the contract say about the *mezuzos* on the house? May the seller replace the present *mezuzos* with ones that, although still kosher, are of a lesser quality?

Stage #4 — Financing the Purchase

• Does the financing of the purchase involve problems regarding the prohibitions against the giving or taking of "interest" (*ribbis*)?

Consider, for example:
• If the down payment is being held in an interest bearing account, who gets the benefit of any *ribbis*?
• May a borrower pay a "finder's fee" to a Jew who arranges a loan for him?
• May someone pay interest to a "Jewish" bank or mortgage company?
• May someone serve as a guarantor in an interest-bearing loan?
• If someone obtains cash by borrowing someone else's credit card, may the borrower pay directly to the credit card company any interest that accrues on the money borrowed?

- What halachic or secular rules might a purchaser violate if he includes false information in a mortgage application?

Stage #5 — The Closing Itself

Assume that the buyer pays part of the purchase price in cash:

- Does secular law require that such a cash transaction be reported? If so, does *halachah* allow (or require) such reporting?
- Suppose that the seller or one of the lawyers knows that the purchaser wants to use cash in order to "launder" money. Does this affect the parties' halachic or secular obligations?
- What if Reuven is willing to pay $300,000, but only wants the documents to reflect a purchase price of $250,000. Reuven agrees to pay the other $50,000 in cash. What halachic, legal and practical problems may arise? If the cash turns out to be counterfeit, what could the seller do?

Other Possible "Cases":

Civil

Dispute between former employer and employee: The latter had signed a two-year term agreement with a two year "non-compete" and non-solicitation provision, but nevertheless left his employer to join another Jewish-owned business that directly competes with the first. Based on these actions, the employer accuses the former employee of breaching the contract and of *hasagas g'vul*. In addition, the employer claims that the employee hired away a non-Jewish worker and stole company secrets. Without admitting or denying the allegations against him, the employee claims that he desperately needed the new job (which doubled his old salary) and that, in any case, he was mistreated by his former boss who cheated him and his co-workers from certain promised (but never delivered) bonuses and benefits.

Civil/Criminal

Property dispute between Jewish and non-Jewish neighbors: A Jew with a large and growing family erects an extension to his house that arguably is prohibited under zoning ordinances, but not necessarily under *halachah*. He funds the construction with a bank loan. In applying for the loan, the person omits possibly relevant information requested on the application form. A Jew who davens in the same *shul* as the homeowner and is his neighbor but not a friend (indeed, he lives on the same street where the allegedly illegal construction took place and is not happy with the "monstrous" addition) finds out about the possible fraud because he is a bank auditor. The *frum* auditor must decide whether to aid the community members who want the city to force the homeowner to tear down the addition by revealing the alleged fraud to bank officials. When confronted by the *frum* auditor in a private conversation, the homeowner admits that he knew that he possibly was committing fraud. In any case, as things develop, other bank officials discover the alleged crime and the homeowner is prosecuted. The authorities seek to compel the auditor to testify against his fellow Jew.

Based on this fact pattern, this case can actually have three simultaneous "proceedings": an administrative proceeding before the Zoning Board; a *beis din* action; and the criminal investigation and proceeding — with all their attendant legal and ethical issues and problems.

Business Negotiation

Another case study could start out with "negotiations" involving a business takeover or similar transaction. The deal can either: (i) close but later go sour, leading to claims and a lawsuit and/or *beis din* case, or (ii) can break down before it is completed, leading to litigation in that instance as well. The "negotiations" will be designed to raise ethical/moral/halachic issues concerning *emes* and *sheker*, etc.

✢ Combating Societal Influences

More Than Mitzvah Observance: A Matter of Values

Based on remarks by
Rabbi Yaakov Yitzchok Ruderman

→ In Lavan's Domain but not Under His Influence

We are all familiar with the *midrash* that expands on Yaakov Avinu's message to his brother Eisav approaching him for their first encounter in over 30 years: "I lived with Lavan — *I lived with Lavan (גרתי), I kept the 613 mitzvos (תריג), and I did not learn from his evil deeds.*"

Several questions arise: If Yaakov had observed all the mitzvos, it should be apparent that he did not emulate Lavan. What need was there for Yaakov to say the obvious — "I did not learn from his evil deeds"? Furthermore, what need was there for Yaakov to tell any of this to Eisav? And, generally, how did Eisav have the audacity to arm himself for battle with Yaakov? He surely did not forget their father's blessing to Yaakov: "You shall reign supreme over your brother" (*Bereishes* 27:29). He did not have a chance to be victorious over him in combat.

The answers to these questions are interlocked with each other. While Yaakov was blessed with supremacy over Eisav, this power was conditional, dependent upon his strict loyalty to Yitzchak's standards of purity of belief and mitzvah performance. This, thought Eisav, was an attainment impossible for Yaakov after living under Lavan's influence for so many years. For sure, Yaakov weakened somewhat in his observance; didn't their father assure him: "When your brother descends, you (Eisav) will rise in control over him"? Thus, Yaakov, realizing his ambitions, informed Eisav that his assumption was false. Even while "I lived with Lavan … I kept the 613 mitzvos."

But more — even a person who is most fastidious in the performance of mitzvos and in avoidance of transgressions can hardly help but be influenced to some degree by his environment. While this may not affect his actual mitzvah observance, it can erode his value system in extremely dangerous ways. To be impervious to the influences of the environment calls for an extra vigilance and an unusual perception. In my experience with Lavan, Yaakov told his bloodthirsty brother, I preserved my vigilance. I did not learn in the least from Lavan's evil deeds. My values remained intact.

Similarly, we find that Moshe Rabbeinu is praised for his wisdom when he sidestepped the opportunity to amass personal wealth from the booty of the Sea (following the Egyptian debacle on the shores of the Red Sea after it was split) and instead applied himself to recovering the remains of Yosef from Egypt to transport them to their eventual burial in the Holy Land. While this may not seem to be an act of wisdom, it truly was. For without special perception, Moshe would have joined the multitudes who were immersed in the mitzvah of collecting the booty, neglecting the overriding commands of honoring the dead and keeping the vow made to Yosef. Indeed, wisdom is called for in setting priorities when mutually exclusive mitzvah activities compete with each other.

✦ Suspect "the Man of His Times"

In a similar vein, the Talmud relates a judgment made by Rabbi Meir when he was traveling with several companions and, upon nightfall, was searching for lodging. They arrived at an inn, but before settling there Rabbi Meir asked the owner, "What is your name?" He replied, "KiDor." "Come," Rabbi Meir told his companions, "let us travel further and search for a different lodging." "What's wrong with this place?" they asked. Said he, "The man's name forebodes evil, as it says: '*Ki dor tahapuchos heimah* — For they are a perverse generation.' I don't want any part of him" (*Yoma* 83b).

This may strike one as a very capricious manner for refusing a place of lodging for the night. What actually took place in this exchange?

Rabbi Meir asked the innkeeper: "How do people refer to you? What is there about your conduct that singles you out?" The man answered: "KiDor — like the generation." That is, he is telling us that he conforms with the spirit of the times.

"Come," said Rabbi Meir. "The times are turbulent. 'This is a perverse generation.' People are selfish, materialistic and hedonistic. We cannot have trust in an individual who does not have the strength of purpose to stay above the current of the times."

The dangers of floating along with the spirit of the times is surely at least as dangerous today as it was 2,000 years ago in the times of Rabbi Meir. Unfortunately, too many among us who are observant Jews in every respect are swept away with the fever of the times that puts emphasis on acquisition of material wealth and amassing of personal fortunes, overlooking the spiritual treasures of our people.[1]

---

1. A student in our yeshivah was marrying the daughter of a wealthy, prominent member of the Jewish community, known as a pious individual. Just prior to the *chuppah*, the young man approached me, and asked, "Rebbi, you know that I am entering my father-in-law's business. What obligations shall I assume now to establish the right kind of household?"

I told him, "Set aside a period of 2 to 3 hours a day for intensive Torah study with a *chavrusa* (study partner). Adhere to this for the first three years of your marriage. This will establish the foundation on which to build a household we will all be proud of."

At this moment, the father-in-law entered the room and asked, "You're delaying the *chuppah* — what's happening here? Is there a problem?" "No," I replied, and reported our exchange to him. The man became furious. "What kind of nonsense are you telling my son-in-law? He is entering the business world now and he has one overriding task at hand — learn the ropes and make a fortune."

The young man heeded my advice and truly succeeded in setting up a model household,

❧ Of Mind and Muscle

The *Midrash* (*Sifri, Vayikra* 19) records differences of opinion regarding what is "כלל גדול בתורה — a fundamental principle in the Torah." One opinion is "*Shema Yisrael* ... this is כלל גדול בתורה." Another contends that, "*You shall prepare one sheep (as a sacrifice) in the morning, and a second sheep in the afternoon,* this is כלל גדול בתורה." The author of the first statement selects the first passage of *Shema*, which declares the Jew's belief in monotheism and unity of the Divinity as central to Jewish belief. The fundamental principle of Torah, according to him, is a matter of correct ideology.

The second opinion, however, focuses on the daily service in the *Beis HaMikdash*. Regular performance of Divine service — this is the fundamental principle of the Torah. Here the implication is that whereas philosophy and ideology are important, unless one translates this commitment into the world of activity as a way of life, the conviction is found lacking. First, it may not be strong enough to stand the test of temptation and challenge in the world of action. Second, thinking correctly in and of itself is simply not enough. Thought, to be meaningful, must find expression in action.

Our discussion today dealt with preserving our value system in spite of the constant assault it suffers because of the current *zeitgeist*. It is an achievement, indeed, to survive the battle in the world of ideas. But this is not enough. This ideological victory must also be translated into responsible action. This is a fundamental principle of the Torah. We are fortunate that Agudath Israel of America represents Torah ideals in both ideology and activity.

---

yet, I still do not cease to wonder at how his father-in-law, such an ostensibly religious man, could suffer from such a confusion of values .... Of course, he keeps all 613 mitzvos, but unfortunately is affected by the evil trends of society.

Sadly, this incident does not stand alone. There are others, many others, to illustrate the same dichotomy.

The Yeshivah Graduate's Obligation

Rabbi Avrohom Pam

*T*he maximal goals of the yeshivah are well known: opening
of the limitless vistas of Torah to its students and imbuing
them with the ambition to become gedolei haTorah. Not all
students succeed in realizing the yeshivah's highest goals; the
yeshivah thus also has other lesser expectations for its students
— goals that are more universally attainable. First among them
is that all who pass through the portals of the yeshivah always
reflect Torah values in their personal lives.

Two principal aims of the yeshiva are: (a) to produce
talmidim of outstanding personal character and integrity, who
will reflect in their personal lives the ethics of the Torah which
they learned in the yeshivah; and (b) to imbue its *talmidim* with
the spirit of dedication to the service of *Klal Yisrael*, and to
encourage them to devote their energies and talents to the
advancement of Torah.

These objectives were established and pursued by the founder
of Mesivta Torah Vodaath, Reb Feivel Mendlowitz, whose entire

life was dedicated to *Klal Yisrael*, thereby serving as a living inspiration to *talmidim* and *baalei batim* (laymen) alike. Let us pause to ponder these goals, however briefly, and rethink the direction of our own lives in light of these guidelines.

1. Kiddush Hashem

The *Sefer Yereim* states that although the mitzvah of *kiddush Hashem* is incumbent on every Jew, there is a very special obligation on *lomdei Torah* (Torah scholars) to be cognizant of this obligation. He writes: ואם הוא לומד תורה צריך שישמור עצמו מן הכיעור ומן הדומה לו — "One who studies Torah must take care to avoid any manner of repulsive behavior, and refrain from any action that bears any resemblance to it."

The *ben Torah* is expected to personify the teachings of the Torah, thus reflecting the image of the Torah itself. He can, on the one hand, be a living example of the beauty and sanctity of the Torah way of life, lending honor and glory to Judaism, and conveying *kiddush Hashem* to Jews and non-Jews alike. The prophet Yeshayahu in his vision of the Children of Israel in the days-to-come, depicts them in these words: "And their children will be distinguished amongst the nations, and their offspring amongst the peoples of the world, and all who behold them will know that they are the blessed children of G–d."

On the other hand, if the *ben Torah* is not meticulous in his personal conduct, and is lacking in integrity, righteousness, and refinement, he misrepresents Torah, leading people to think that the Torah approves of or condones unethical conduct. He is thereby unwittingly bearing false witness against it, for the Torah is *Toras emes* (Torah of truth) and *"D'rochehah darchei noam* — Its ways are pleasant."

We are witness today to an alarming decline in morality, both in the individual and in society. The continuous breakdown of age-old concepts of decency is shocking and causes us to wonder: What next? Where is the world headed?

There are the cynics and pessimists who say של עולם כך היא מנהגו — "This is the way of the world." Man's character is inherently corrupt and immoral; strife, greed, and lust are inevitable. That's the way it always has been, and that's the way it will always be. We Jews, however, believe that the Torah can mold the individual into a magnificent personality, instilling within him integrity, nobility, courtesy and dignity. We are persuaded that Torah can and will in the days to come create a righteous society that will reflect the glory of G–d.

But if *lomdei Torah* are found wanting in their personal ethics, they give rise to the belief that Torah does not have the capability of improving mankind and cannot cure the ills of society. אין לך בזיון כבוד התורה גדול מזה! — "There can be no greater defamation of Torah than this."

2. The Vital Obligation

There is a fascinating *psak halachah* in *Yam Shel Shlomo* (*Bava Kamma* 38a), in reference to misrepresentation of Torah. The Talmud relates that the Roman government once dispatched two officials to the Sages of Israel to make a comprehensive study of the Torah and to report their findings to the government. Upon completion of their study, they told the Sages: "We have delved into your Torah and have concluded that it is indeed a *Toras emes* — except for one *halachah*, which seems to us to discriminate against non-Jews. However, we will not report it to the government."

The *Yam Shel Shlomo* raises the question: Why did the *Chachamim* risk the safety of *Klal Yisrael* by teaching this *halachah* as it is to the Roman agents? Could they not have altered this one *halachah* for their own protection, to avoid resentment and the likely consequences of repression and persecution? He answers: מכאן שאסור לשנות דברי תורה אף במקום סכנה — "From here we may derive that it is forbidden to falsify Torah even at the risk of danger to *Klal Yisrael*." One is obligated to sacrifice his life rather than misrepresent a *din* of the Torah.

Inasmuch as Torah scholars are expected to reflect the teachings of Torah in their personal conduct, and — indeed — in the eyes of the public they do represent the Torah way of life, the responsibility they carry is a grave one. The extent of this obligation, as spelled out by the *Yam Shel Shlomo*, is awesome in its implications.

3. The Sensitivity of the Royal Guard

Torah scholars are members of the Divine militia, and as such they should be in the forefront of the *milchemes Hashem* — every battle for sacred causes. This is the essence of the second objective of yeshivah *chinuch*. Every yeshivah student should organize his life in the way that permits him to best serve *Klal Yisrael*, according to his capacity and the prevailing circumstances. There are no exemptions in this battle.

Shaul HaMelech (King Saul) once called in the members of his court and chastised them for disloyalty to him. He spoke harshly: "You have all conspired against me by not disclosing to me that my son is in league with the son of Yishai (in a plot against the Kingdom) and none of you is distressed by this threat to me" (*I Shmuel*: 22:8). As the commentaries explain, Shaul faulted his closest associates even if they did not perceive David as a threat to Shaul's rule. They should have at least shared his anguish.

By the same yardstick, our loyalty to the Divine King can be questioned if we lack concern for *kavod Shamayim*; if we are not distressed over the fact that the vast majority of our youth is totally ignorant of Torah and could not care less; if we are indifferent to continuing distortion of Torah and its misrepresentation — in the name of Judaism; if we are not disturbed by the fact that our people are degraded, despised, maligned and abused by the nations of the world, and yet the philosophy of "Let us be like all the nations" dominates the policies of the political leaders who presume to guide the destiny of the people of Israel.

The current state of affairs in Jewish life should sufficiently touch every yeshivah alumnus to impel him to orient his life to the service of *Klal Yisrael* and to make his contribution to *kevod Shamayim* in one form or another.

A well-known *rosh yeshivah* once visited a wealthy businessman — a former yeshivah student — in his office to solicit a sizable donation for the yeshivah. It was during business hours, and the man claimed that giving such a sum would require a trip to the bank, and he was much too busy for that. Whereupon the *Rosh Yeshivah* said to him: "Do you think that you were sent down from Heaven to this world just to sell *gatkes* (underwear)? You were sent here to do something for the *Ribbono Shel Olam*, His Torah, and His People."

These objectives of the yeshivah *chinuch* assume added significance as we hope, pray, and yearn for the *geulah sheleimah*, soon in our day. The vision of the *geulah sheleimah* entails the restoration of *Klal Yisrael* to its pristine dignity and its distinction as a Kingdom of Priests, a Holy Nation; the realization of the prophecy, "And all Your sons will be learned of G–d"; the transformation of the land of Israel into The Holy Land, permeated with the *Shechinah* — the Divine Presence, and radiating the glory of G–d.

Being Truly Jewish in a Society of Plenty

Rabbi Berel Wein

"There is one who waxes wealthy and possesses nothing, and one who is impoverished and has great wealth"
Mishlei 13:7 (according to the translation of the Malbim).

→ Reverse Marranos

Jewish history is replete with differing problems, paradoxes and challenges. But the basic problem that faces every generation is how to remain truly Jewish in an overwhelmingly non-Jewish world. The Torah itself addresses this problem: "How do these nations worship their gods; let me also do likewise!" And the story of the Jewish people in their long exile is again one of that struggle to remain uniquely Jewish in spite of the pressures of an alien, encroaching and different world.

As long as the world was openly hostile to the Jew, as in much of Europe during the Middle Ages, then, perversely, it was easier for Jews to remain thoroughly Jewish. As the ghetto walls began to fall in the 18th and 19th centuries, however, the problem of being Jewish became acute once again and this still is the greatest problem facing American Orthodox Jewry. We are attempting to live a life that conforms to Torah and *halachah* while living and participating in a society whose value system is completely inimical to the value system implicit in *halachah*. We lead lives that at least superficially conform to the requirements of *halachah*, but what about the ethical values of our Orthodox society and its priorities? Are we truly Jewish?

Attributed to Rabbi S. R. Hirsch, famed *Rav* of Frankfurt-am-Main until his passing 100 years ago, is a comment that still rings true in late 20th century America. "The Marranos of Spain were *goyim* on the outside and Jews on the inside. My Jews are reverse Marranos." The problem of American Orthodoxy is that no matter how *frum* we appear on the outside, our inside reflects the American way of life. We think as the general society thinks, its value system is ours, its goals are ours, and its measures of success are definitive for us as well. It is difficult to be proud of a halachic society that lives a life system that mocks halachic Jewish values.

✤ *"Religion" Without Ethics*

According to the *Midrash*, Esau fooled his father, Isaac, while mocking him by asking him *she'eilos* — halachic questions: "How does one give the tithe from straw?" That is a halachic question; it has a halachic answer and Isaac undoubtedly did so answer Esau, giving his son the benefit of the doubt. But the rabbis, from the perspective of later millennia, having seen what became of Esau and his descendants, saw in that halachic *she'eilah* a mockery of all that Jewish life stands for.

It brings to mind the story of the man about to embark on a 10-day cruise on *erev* Pesach who frantically called his *Rav*, "I've checked out the matzos and the food, and it's all *mehadrin*. But the ship will be sailing in international waters, and there will be casino gambling on board. Do they have to provide all new gambling chips for Pesach?" People ask all sorts of nitty-gritty questions regarding *kashrus,* and miss the whole point of leading a Torah life, fulfilling the awful description of the *Ramban* of "being a *naval,* a disgusting person, while remaining somehow within the parameters of Torah law."

This bitterly amusing anecdote is symptomatic of our society where the federal prisons of our country provide Jewish inmates with strictly kosher food on a regular basis. When the author headed the *kashrus* department of the OU, a warden called to review his Pesach order. After Pesach, the OU received a blistering letter of criticism from one of the inmates at that prison who demanded a particular brand of *coffee* for Pesach, and was upset by the "inadequacy" of the recommended brand.

The element of shame has disappeared from our Jewish society, just as it has disappeared from the general society. Exposure has become one of the risks of the game: If one gets caught, then one gets caught. If not, then one has won the game and successfully beaten the odds; forget about the felony. These are the rules of elements within contemporary Jewish society; it is not a question of right or wrong — or *kiddush* or *chillul Hashem;* only whether the potential gain is worth the risk. We are more concerned with *"frum"* coffee than with the true ethics of being a halachically observant person.

✦ A "Thing-Centered" Society

The *Midrash* describes the generation of the Tower of Babel in ways that bear some resemblance to ours. They were concerned with *things,* but not with people. If a brick fell from the tower and was smashed, they mourned the loss; but if a human being fell — that was all part of the risk associated with technological progress. Construction projects, space-shuttle programs, new highway techniques, all are achieved at the cost of the quality of human life. Society generally is more interested in things — furniture, objets d'art, foreign sport cars — than in people, especially people who are different from the norm. This attitude is quite prevalent in Jewish America, as well. Materialism and conspicuous consumption of goods destroy the fabric of a life consistent with Torah values and halachic principles. Many times, too much becomes too little and more is definitely less. The test of affluence is a difficult one to pass.

G–d has granted us plenty, perhaps because of the terrible tragedies of the previous generation — like a spoiled child, born after a terrible tragedy in a family. So has G–d granted us many things that we don't quite know how to deal with: great material wealth and new opportunities, a resurgence of Torah study and traditional life, a Jewish state in the Land of Israel. Our successes have overwhelmed us. We are unable to place them into historic perspective and thus deal with them in an optimum fashion.

Moreover, material abundance actually can interfere with spiritual growth. The *Mashgiach* of the yeshivah that I attended — a *baal mussar* of the highest order — once said to me, in great frustration, "*Mussar* will never succeed in America. It was very relevant in Lithuania, where people did not have extra food, a second overcoat. Their material poverty helped the people concentrate on their inner ethical self. When one owns several coats and half-a-dozen jackets, and eats in restaurants, it dulls his ability to hear talk about *middos* and *mussar*."

For many years, a Shabbos afternoon "Mishnah Club" met in my house for a number of boys aged 5 to 12. By year's end, my closet would house a collection of coats, gloves, scarves, ties — many with designer labels, costing a great deal of money. (When I was young, if I lost my coat ... there would not be a second coat.) Yet, no one called to ask about a missing coat. A child who loses his coat will, as a matter of right and course, receive another one. No wonder there is no respect for clothing among our children .... A society that values things over people, eventually respects neither.

✦ *Things Versus Substance*

This thing-centered attitude has spilled over into our observance of mitzvos to the point of measuring *hiddur mitzvah* (enhancement of mitzvah performance) primarily in terms of monetary costs. *Hiddur mitzvah* today is a thinly-disguised form of social one-upmanship. The *yeitzer hara* has entered the mitzvah business. Indoor removable-roof *succah* rooms; hundred dollar *esrogim* encased in luxurious boxes; more expensive, though not necessarily more reliable, kosher products; enormously expensive Sabbath clothes … all are the vogue. But unfortunately, the mitzvah ethic is many times lost in the *hiddur* wrapping.

> *A number of years ago, a certain Rav in Jerusalem was observed by a well-known writer purchasing an esrog before Succos. The writer then saw the Rav on Succos morning without lulav or esrog. "What happened to your esrog?" he asked.*
>
> *The Rav answered, "I'll tell you, but only if you do not write of it until after my death."*
>
> *Next door to him lived a Jew with a very short temper who frequently beat his children for minor infractions of home rules. On Succos morning, the Rav awoke early to hear weeping from the balcony next door. His neighbor's daughter had been holding her father's esrog and had inadvertently dropped it, breaking the pitum, rendering it unfit for the mitzvah. The girl was in tears, fully anticipating her father's wrath. The Rav reached over, placed his esrog in his neighbor's esrog box and told her to tell her father that he, the Rav, had examined his neighbor's esrog and had decided that the new esrog was more proper for him. And the Rav took away the broken esrog. The writer correctly titled the story, when he finally wrote it, "Hiddur Mitzvah." It reflects a unique concept, an authentic Jewish value system of how to deal with halachic problems. This concept should be applied in our society.*

✢ *The Values in Career Choices*

Living a life guided by the way things seem rather than by their inner content, stressing things over values, can lead a person to opt for an unfortunate career. Now, choice of career may seem to be a "neutral area," but it can touch on some fundamental problems of *halachah* and of basic values. Not every career is for every Jewish boy, and certainly not for every Jewish girl. Because of our success in achieving equal opportunity in the professional world and the marketplace, we are dealing with a generation that sees no limits on its horizon. One can, without undue penalty, wear a *kippah*, eat kosher food, and be fully Sabbath and Yom Tov observant in the medical centers, the boardrooms of major corporations, the legal centers, and the highest levels of government in our country. But the price of "making it" in our world is not small.

The Rabbis' admonition to engage in an *umnus kallah u'nekiyah* — a career that is light and clean — is always relevant. Today, people immediately think in terms of computers. They may be right, but one could challenge that. Basically, an *umnus kallah u'nekiyah* is one that will permit a person to come home at a reasonable hour, that will enable one to spend time with family, children, synagogue and Torah.

The archetypical Jewish mother wants her son to be (at least) a lawyer. Today, your average yeshivah graduate can make it through law school, pass the bar, and go on to the most prestigious law firms in the country, at no recognizable cost to his *Yiddishkeit*. But as a successful lawyer, he will not see his children awake from one Shabbos to the next. (I speak from experience; I was a lawyer for nine years before becoming a full-time *Rav*.) If a lawyer wants to "make it," he has to leave the house at 6 in the morning and attend appointments with clients at 10 at night. One is not paid $65,000 per year as an entering lawyer in a Park Avenue law firm to reasonably expect to work normal hours or have a normal family life. Law is not an *umnus kallah u'nekiyah*.

The yeshivah where I am *menahel*, certainly not exceptional in this regard, has a number of *yesomim* (orphans) with living parents. The father works, the mother works, and the house is empty — physically, psychologically, educationally, spiritually — deafeningly empty. The child comes home to exquisite furniture, to fine art on the walls, to air-conditioning and carpeting — but the house is empty. The child would be better served to come home to a more modest physical environment, endowed with a presence of people of tradition and warmth and care and interest and love. The largest industry in our suburban community is child-care, babysitting! No one is home.

Is it worth it? I doubt it.

✣ Of Professions, Purposes and Destiny

The individual's choice of profession and career is vital to the future of the Jewish people and the fulfillment of our cosmic purpose. The mother of one of my students complained that her son decided to study Torah in Israel for a year or two after graduation from mesivta high school. Her son would "lose a year," which he would need later in his medical education.

I dared ask her the unspeakable question, "Why must he be a doctor?"

She answered, "I don't understand you. He may discover the cure for cancer. Do you want to prevent that?"

In reply I told her an old, wry Jewish joke: A *yishuvnik* (provincial fellow), who lived in a hamlet in the Ukraine that had a general population of thirty and only six Jews, sent his son off to university, in Berlin. When the son returned years later, the father asked him, "How many Jews are there in Berlin?" Answered the son, "Thirty-five thousand."

The father rejoiced at the astronomical number. He then asked, "How many *goyim* are there in Berlin?" The reply: "Three million."

The father, in shock, responded, "Why do they need so many *goyim*?"

We should not be like that *yishuvnik*. G–d has created a great and varied world. There are over four billion non-Jews in the world. We don't have to do everything in the world by ourselves. The Jews are not obligated to supply all of the doctors, lawyers, judges, corporate raiders, real-estate developers and entrepreneurs of this world. The Jews are, however, obligated to be the Jewish people, with all of the moral and ethical obligations that this implies. We should have no objection to an Italian or an Irishman or a Black or a Hispanic discovering the cure for cancer. But Torah, *halachah*, Jewish ethics and eternal value systems are the primary Jewish agenda, both nationally and individually. What I can do, only I can do: our role in the world is therefore very exclusive. Hence, the choice of an *umnus kallah u'nekiyah* is a crucial one. If the choice is not directed at propagating Jewish values, it should at least honor those values and permit ample time for their pursuit.

✦ "Ivri anochi" — a Badge of Honor, a Way of Life

It is not my intention to write negatively about the Jewish people. In our generation, all Jews are heroes. Anyone, still standing in the shadow of Auschwitz, who proclaims that "*Ivri anochi* — I am a Jew," is to be admired, complimented and aided. We are the only Jewish people around and the L-rd apparently is still willing to deal with us on His usual exact, demanding and intimate terms. Therefore, to the extent that we can address our problems realistically and put ourselves in the proper perspective of Jewish historical tradition vis-a-vis the non-halachic society in which we live, will we be able to continue to see the supremacy of halachic thought and values in our lives and continue to be authentically Jewish in the full sense of the term.

"Thus says the L-rd: Let not the wise man glory in his wisdom, neither let the mighty man glory in his might, let not the rich man glory in his riches. But let him that glories glory in this, that he understands and knows Me, that I am the L-rd who exercises mercy, justice and righteousness, in the earth; for in these things I delight, says the L-rd" (*Yirmiyahu* 9:23).

Greater Resources, Greater Accountability

Dr. Judith Bleich

"It was the season of Light,
it was the season of Darkness,
it was the spring of hope,
it was the winter of despair ...."

✦ *A Paradoxical Duality*

P erhaps I have reached an age at which sentimentality may be condoned. I confess that when I attend a wedding and observe the garb and comportment of the assembled friends of bride and groom, when I arrive at class a bit early and come upon students *davening Shacharis*, when I note the seriousness and frequency with which young people call our house night after night until the wee hours to ask *she'eilos*, when I enter a lecture hall filled with a capacity audience gathered to listen to a *shiur*, I find myself moved beyond words, to tears, at the transformations that have taken place in our community.

As I call to mind similar weddings some 30 years ago, the

questionable *kashrus* standards of those years, the laxity of observance, the ubiquitous ignorance, and then read the words of individuals who express concern at the "shift to the right," I am simply astounded at what appears to be a severe case of amnesia. Can anyone really advocate a return to the "good old days"? Yes, now *sefarim* stores are teeming with customers, *chol hamoed* throngs reclaim the Yom Tov spirit, and despite the tens of thousands that can be accommodated in Madison Square Garden, the forthcoming *siyum haShas* is already oversubscribed. Even *The New York Times*, a staid bastion of the establishment, sits up and grudgingly takes front-page notice. And if these phenomena do indeed come at the cost of a few stringencies perceived as unnecessary by some, the benefits seem well worth the price.

But … I turn the pages of the newspapers and read of scandal after scandal in which identifiably Orthodox individuals and institutions are implicated. I note the high statistics of family breakdown in our community, the instances of abuse and dysfunction, and the staggering number of older singles — surely one of the saddest social maladies of our times. I attend conferences and dinners sponsored by venerable Orthodox organizations — and even yeshivos — and no longer wonder why far too many of those who seek spiritual satisfaction turn to new-age philosophies or to the charismatic allure of pseudo-Kabbalah. Few of our own organizational and congregational events serve as sources of either inspiration or edification. I search in vain for consistent expression in the public arena of Jewish values and integrity as befits a people who are *yirei Hashem* striving to sanctify the mundane and to be *mekadesh shem Shamayim*. I take a hard look at our community and *benistarim tivkeh nafshi*, in its hidden places my soul cries out.

✛ Beyond the Confines of Orthodoxy

This paradoxical duality is mirrored beyond the confines of the Orthodox community. The numbers lost to intermarriage are devastating. Jews with no ties whatsoever to either the religion or peoplehood of Israel abound. For ever larger numbers, Judaism is hardly more than a culinary experience with little impact upon attitudes, values or beliefs, and none at all upon religious practice.

Yet, at the same time, there are many who express a genuine thirst for knowledge and manifest an avid intellectual interest in virtually every facet of Jewish history, philosophy, theology, ritual and custom. The Anglo-Jewish press is more focused and sophisticated than heretofore. Hebraica and Judaica publications flourish. In the world at large, newspapers, radio, television and the cinema resonate with Jewish themes. There is a new resilience and vibrancy in the most unexpected of quarters. Rabbi Avraham I. Kook, in his essay *"Ha-Dor,"* depicts his own time as a wondrous age in which light and darkness mingle in confusion. Our generation is no less reflective of that phenomenon.

I. Of Wealth, Generosity, and Materialism

Within the Torah community itself there has evolved across the United Sates and Canada a network of exemplary organizations, formal and informal, dedicated to a wide variety of charitable activities, including *hachnasas kallah, bikur cholim, tomchei Shabbos* and others. Operating without fanfare or publicity, these groups and their volunteers exemplify the highest standards and the noblest teachings of Judaism.

Nevertheless, it is undeniable that, at the other end of the spectrum, a galloping materialism has engulfed significant sectors of the Orthodox community. This is evident not only in dress, home decoration and overly ostentatious private celebrations, but has spilled over into organizational and institutional events as well. In the worst manifestation of materialism, it is the need to procure the wherewithal to support such lavish lifestyles that is at least partially to blame for the erosion of probity and the emergence of various forms of financial chicanery.

But greed and materialistic competitiveness cannot in themselves serve to explain behavior that crosses the line from the socially offensive to the unethical, illegal and even criminal. Of particular concern is the fact that crass materialism has found its way into the inner sanctum of Orthodoxy as well as into the upper echelons of yeshivos and *kollelim*. There must be some terrible flaw in our communal / social / educational institutions. We extol the paramount value of *limud haTorah*. Yet families whose entire existence is patterned around sacrifice for *limud haTorah* discover that their daughters are disenfranchised in the matrimonial sweepstakes because the family is not able to promise lavish support for a sufficiently prolonged period of time.

The *Noda BiYehudah* questioned the value system of people of his time who were reluctant to enter into a marriage because of similarity in the names of a prospective groom and father-in-law for fear of trespassing the strictures of the testament of Rabbi Yehudah HaChassid, but were not concerned with seeking a *talmid chacham* as a son-in-law. One wonders what he would have made of a society in which the qualities of *bas talmid chacham* and *yichus atzmah* are disregarded unless accompanied by the requisite financial package. Our society has strayed far from the concept of *pas bamelach tochal*.

> It is related that the founder of the Novardok Yeshivah, Reb
> Yoizel Hurwitz, succeeded in obtaining an extremely generous
> sum of money for his yeshivah from a former student who had
> become a business magnate. The same businessman gave only
> a paltry sum to the head of another yeshivah, which he had
> also attended in his youth. When questioned why the Alter of
> Novardok was given so lavish a contribution while the other
> Rosh Yeshivah received so little, the businessman explained:
> "When Reb Yoizel visited my home to solicit funds for the
> yeshivah, he paid no attention whatsoever to his surroundings.
> He was oblivious to the elegant furnishings and valuable
> paintings, but was concerned totally and completely with the
> needs of the yeshivah. It was evident that my wealth and
> possessions were unimportant to Reb Yoizel. I realized that to
> him my money was only of instrumental value, of significance
> only in terms of the good it could do. When the other Rosh
> Yeshivah visited my home, however, it was obvious that he
> was extremely impressed by its grandeur and deferred to my

wealth with great respect. If my money was endowed with such intrinsic importance, how could I give it away?"

The message that we are imparting is loud and clear: Material possessions are of great value, and riches are to be both honored and courted. If riches are viewed as an intrinsic good, little wonder that there are those who are prepared to resort to any means, ethical or unethical, permissible or impermissible, in order to attain wealth.

Countering this perversion of values is no simple matter. There has been a serious failure in internalizing fundamental teachings that constitute the very core of Judaism. Perhaps a renewed emphasis on idealism and communal responsibility would also serve as an aid in reestablishing a proper sense of priorities and values.

II. Our Mandate to Save Jewish Souls

The concerns of a Torah society *must* encompass the needs of the entire Jewish community. Presumably, any hesitation in articulating those concerns is born of a fear of erosion in the quality or intensity of practice in the observance of mitzvos within the sector of the committed. But life is fraught with risk. When perception of risk is magnified, the result is paralysis. The ideal of *mesiras nefesh* includes many types of sacrificial devotion, and surely acceptance of minimal spiritual risk is among them.

During the fateful years of World War II, Rabbi Michael Dov Weissmandl wrote impassioned letters to America imploring his fellow Jews: "Now we ask: How are you able to eat, how are you able to sleep, how are you able to live … ? A holy and awesome responsibility devolves upon you. Blessed are you if you understand and fulfill it, woe unto you, if the reverse ...." (*Min HaMetzar*, pp. 189-190). Do we not now face a threat to the spiritual survival of vast numbers of Jews? Are we not confronted by a matter of *pikuach nefesh*, literally saving the souls, of fellow Jews? How can we equivocate with regard to the need for a response?

An acquaintance, a Jew born and bred in a European *shtetl*, used to recount an experience that had stood him in good stead as wise counsel throughout his life. Once, as a child in a small town in Poland, his father gave him a few *groschen* and dispatched him to purchase a loaf of bread for the evening meal. As a result of a series of misadventures, which occurred through no fault of his own, he returned home empty-handed and proceeded to deliver himself of a full account of the incidents that thwarted his mission. His father accepted his excuses, but admonished him to remember that *"Tzum teretz ken men zich nisht vaschen* — With the excuse one cannot wash [one's hands for bread]."* Yes, we have good and sufficient excuses for failure and nonfeasance. But what benefit do they bring us?

Perhaps a personal experience will serve as a graphic illustration. Several years ago, a member of our congregation became acquainted with two adolescent boys of Bukharian origin who expressed a willingness to attend a yeshivah high school. I tried to place these youngsters in a suitable school. I spent hours telephoning yeshivos and solicited the help of both local and national organizations. I pleaded, cajoled and even presumed upon personal relationships. I thought I knew the identities of the movers and shakers in our community as well as a little bit about pulling strings. Nevertheless, my efforts were to no avail. The following year I tried again, and was finally able to place one youngster (by then, the second had found other interests) in a school whose existence was somewhat precarious. (Was that why its principal was receptive? Or, to be fair and more appreciative, was the school's precarious financial situation at least partially attributable to its receptivity and openness?)

The educational background of these two boys was minimal, family support was non-existent, their academic performance was poor and their behavior could hardly be described as exemplary. Indeed, there were good reasons for each of the schools that I had approached not to welcome such youngsters as students. But, *"Tzum teretz ken men zich nisht vaschen."* These were Jewish children and even somewhat interested in learning Torah. In point of fact, the one who was admitted to a Jewish school did profit from the experience. More to the bottom line, *the public school system unhesitatingly accepted those children.* Why? Because universal education is its mandate. Is ours any different?

We do have specialized yeshivos designed to meet the needs of children with weak Jewish backgrounds, but far too many fall between the cracks. And tuition is still a hassle in virtually every institution. *Pikuach nefesh* in its literal sense demands that tuition-free *chinuch* for any Jewish child who wishes to avail himself or herself thereof must become the first priority for the entire American Jewish community.

III. Raising the Level of Our Communication

The battles of 50 and 75 years ago are not those of the present. At its inception, Agudath Israel was a unifying force bringing together the disparate sectors of Orthodoxy: Lithuanian yeshivos, chassidim and adherents of the philosophy of *Torah im Derech Eretz.* Our times demand a new coalition for Torah, one that is non-political and non-partisan. In a different, less politicized sociological context, it behooves Agudath Israel to utilize its resources, its highly effective staff and its powerful media and communications skills to project a voice of conscience, nationally and internationally.

It is distressing that the term *charedi* has all too often come to be understood as synonymous with narrow-mindedness or know-nothingism. In recent years, there has been a welcome proliferation of juvenile literature, of popular writings and of translations of Torah classics. There remains a dearth of serious works suitable for an intellectual or academic readership. If the Torah *tzibbur* is to have impact upon the community at large, it is essential that it address the concerns and interests of an intellectually oriented and secularly educated society.

Many of the salutary changes that have occurred on these shores may be attributed to success in the religious education of women in this country. At a time when feminist issues are the focus of attention, our stance should be responsive and responsible. Derision and negativism are inappropriate, unseemly and counterproductive. *Chazal* understood the importance of imparting Torah teachings in a manner that attracts and does not alienate — *"Ko somar l'beis Yaakov."* In a generation in which the level of women's education, both Jewish and general, is high, it is unfortunate that much current Orthodox programming for women remains simplistic and patronizing.

Someone once remarked to Rabbi Meir Shapiro that he had been unable to understand the speech of an *adam gadol*, one of the leaders of the Agudah movement, because that sage's delivery had been *"tzu shtil* — too quiet." The Yiddish *"hoich"* can mean either "loud" or "high." In a play on words, Rabbi Meir Shapiro quipped, *"Nisht tzu shtil — tzu hoich.* Not too quiet — too elevated." The Torah community's publications, conventions and programs in these times of crisis and opportunity must give expression to the moral conscience of Orthodoxy. We must strive to be neither quiet and ineffective nor loud and shrill, but elevated and uplifting.

IV. Ordering Our Priorities

Apart from *chinuch*, how do we order other priorities? How do we choose among the welter of competing needs? Where do we start? Well known is the response of Reb Yisrael Salanter to the query: If an individual has but one half-hour of time should he study *Chumash*, Mishnah, *Gemara*, or *halachah*? Answered Reb Yisrael Salanter: Let him study *mussar* and he will discover that he has much more than a half-hour a day for learning. How should we order our priorities? If our own community would turn aside from smug self-satisfaction to genuine soul-searching, from conspicuous consumption, headline hunting and obsession with P.R. long enough to imbibe a healthy dose of *mussar*, we would discover that we are blessed with the resources, the talents — and even the funds — to address all our priorities. We would succeed in tapping the reservoirs of learning, *chesed* and spirituality of *Klal Yisrael* and, harnessing them, turn our abundant energies toward hastening the promised time when "The earth will be filled with the knowledge of G–d as the waters cover the sea."

In Search of Simplicity

Rabbi Nisson Wolpin

I. The Emergence of a Trend

Downsizing. Voluntary Simplicity. Return to Basics. It comes by any number of descriptions. According to the Trend Research Institute of Rhinebeck, NY, Voluntary Simplicity is among the top ten trends of the 90's. Its unofficial headquarters are in Seattle, but it is subject for discussion across the country, including several feature articles in *The New York Times*.

In some cases, admittedly, simplification was adopted involuntarily, the result of corporate downscaling. But even then, the "victims" have come to appreciate their newly gained perspective on life. Similar scenarios can be found describing other formerly affluent people who have scaled down their lifestyles — not by force of circumstance, but by conscious choice.

For a variety of reasons, more Americans are working, earning and spending less in search of a life richer in other ways. Part spiritual, part practical, it's not being cheap, practitioners say, and it isn't a regimen of deprivation. It's more a matter of figuring out the difference between what you want and what you need, and realizing how the country's spend-and-charge mentality can keep you tied to a job or a life you don't want.[1]

Interestingly — and, one might add, ironically — guiding others in their pursuit of simplification has become a growth industry of sorts. Producing books and periodicals on the topic, and being featured on the lecture circuit on the theme, are some who have succeeded in this endeavor. For example, Amy and Jim Dacyczyn (pronounced decision) through frugality and belt-tightening bought their own home (a pre-1900 farmhouse in Maine) after seven years of marriage, on an annual salary of $30,000. She is editor of *The Tight-Wad Gazette* and author of two respectably-selling books on simplification, as well as a popular lecturer. (It's almost like Disney making a Walden Pond theme park to honor Henry Thoreau!) The point is not that there are hidden fortunes in the hills of simplicity, but that the goal is popular enough to spawn a growing literary output.

II. In Search of a Jewish Counterpart

One waits for the tidal wave of downscaling to wash over the religious Jewish community. Yet at first blush, the trend seems almost irrelevant to us. There are those in the *"ben Torah"* class — struggling *kollel* families and *melamdim* — who made their choices, more or less, years ago to forgo a life of affluence. And those who would qualify as middle class in general society do not have all of the same options available to them as do their non-religious counterparts. A family paying a high rental or property tax in Flatbush or Monsey can't chuck it all for a humble house in a Fort Worth suburb (as a former IBM executive in San Francisco did). They need their community and its myriad facilities to support their religious activities. The closet must sport several Shabbos & Yom Tov outfits. "Private schools" are a must. For many families with children, escaping oppressive urban summers make bungalows and/or summer camps a given. All told, the lifestyles of Orthodox Jewish families have a much heftier

---

1. "The Simplicity Pattern," by Leslie Rubinkowski, *Pittsburgh Post-Gazette*, Dec. 24, 1995.

non-negotiable core than do those of their secular neighbors.

Moreover, there is an element of *hiddur mitzvah* that, in its more liberal interpretations, can be contorted to justify an ornate sterling silver *esrog* box, quite aside from the costly *esrog* itself; similarly, a highly stylized silver Chanukah *menorah*, in addition to "a light for each member of the household" (the Talmud's starting place for *hiddur mitzvah* on Chanuka); a slew of gifts and ostentatious extras at a wedding, as part of the "basic *simchas chasan v'kallah*".... Yet this still leaves us with much non-mitzvah activity to question — the necessity for a three-figure price tag on a 13-year-old boy's fedora, the need for the suit or the outfit or the silk cravat that are "right" this particular season, the burning necessity to possess a human hair *sheitel*, styled just-so, the desired spot for a midwinter vacation without which one's life is so deprived.

III. A Human Dynamic: the Need to Nurture Ambition

Instead of dwelling further on the particular items or expenses that are perceived as bottom-line necessities, however, it may be worthwhile to examine the human dynamic that drives individuals to seek new, ever-more stimulating experiences and constantly upgrade their possessions and lifestyles. After all, as a society, people are far more comfortable and affluent than a generation ago, and yet — except for pockets of downsizers — people are as dissatisfied with the status quo as ever.

Rabbi Eliyahu Eliezer Dessler, in an essay published as part of his *Kuntres HaChessed* in *Michtav MeEliyahu*, discusses this phenomenon. His insights form the basis for all that follows:

People appear to be inherently ambitious for improvement of their circumstances. In fact, a popular European proverb had it that ambition is the substance of life; without a set of goals one is actively pursuing, one is as good as dead. Indeed, civilizations flourish as a result of the continuous growth that feeds on setting and pursuing clear, identifiable goals; moreover, their full flowering is a product of their escalating hopes and expectations.

This is troubling, because it implies that realization of a specific goal does not usher in an era of prolonged happiness. "When one has a hundred, he desires two hundred," *Chazal* say. "And when he attains two hundred, he desires four hundred." If man is destined to forever desire more than he possesses, then why bother? The promise of fulfillment that fuels the engine of productivity is only a mirage!

IV. The Image in the Psychic Mirror

Actually, man is endowed with an inner urge to grow. The chosen area of growth is only a matter of how the individual sees himself in his psychic mirror — that is, how he defines himself. At any given point, he will sense a dissatisfaction with his current status, and will then fix his ambition on a specific item or experience or achievement that at the time is beyond his immediate grasp. Once he will have acquired that elusive item (or what-have-you), he is convinced, he will be happy. And he is, for a while. But once he has become accustomed to the newly gained goal, and he has internalized that increment of growth, having incorporated it into his self-image, he begins to crave more.

The budding entrepreneur aspires to earn a net of six figures per year, and then he'll be happy … for a while. But once that's achieved, his sense of contentment gives way to an urge to buy into a yet larger firm, which eventually leads to the drive for hostile takeovers of other corporate entities on yet a grander scale.

In terms of personal experiences: After a few years, the winter getaway to Florida is not nearly calming or distracting enough. New horizons are sought. Next year, Acapulco, perhaps; and then, maybe, the Riviera …. The country bungalow becomes a summer home, and why not? In the same manner, a family that makes do with a beat-up station wagon, eventually needs a new van. And then, of course, an additional car for "personal use." Soon the Town Car is traded in for a Lexus.

The *Gemara* in *Nedarim* relates an incident involving a known philanderer. Once a man came home for his midday meal and his wife served him a course. Suddenly this suspected adulterer appeared from out of a hiding place and warned the husband not to touch his food. Unknown to the man or his wife, a snake had tasted from the food and likely deposited venom in it. He could lose his life if he eats it. "We see from this," says Rava, "that the man was innocent of having had an affair with the woman. Had he been guilty, he would not have hesitated to see the husband die, thus removing an obstacle to fulfilling his desire."

The *Gemara* asks: Isn't that obvious? No, replies the *Gemara*. Perhaps, I would think that he would rather she be married than widowed, because "stolen waters are sweeter" (*Mishlei* 19). Rava tells us that this is not the case here (*Nedarim* 91b).

Commentaries (the *Chasam Sofer*, among others) ask why he would not want to preserve the unattainability of the waters, so as to ensure their sweetness. They explain in reply that sweetness is not an actual property of stolen waters. It is merely an illusory feature of anything a person craves while it is beyond his reach. Subconsciously, he perceives himself as limited in self-definition as long as he does not possess that particular item, or does not taste that forbidden fruit. The drive to achieve personal growth endows that elusive item with an aura of excitement, sweetness, and fulfillment. But the person driven by ambition or desire or perceived need does not recognize that there is nothing intrinsically sweet about the forbidden fruit. If he would, he would abandon the pursuit. In the case of the adulterer, would he realize that it is only the unattainability of the woman that makes her company exciting, but otherwise she is quite ordinary, he would not be driven to engage in infidelity.

In much the same way, a person seeks to be in control of his future, leaving nothing to chance. Thus he not only purchases insurance policies on his life, his property and his business — which of course is rational — he feels compelled to protect future generations from the vagaries of economic vicissitudes. It's not that his children and grandchildren are so less talented than he is. It's a matter of securing their well-being even after he is gone. If he does not take care of them, he feels, no one will.

The political scene is no less fraught with illusory goals, that — when achieved — only arouse expanded ambitions which are all the more difficult to realize. Truly, "No man dies with half his desires fulfilled" (*Koheles Rabbah* 1:16).

V. Escape From the Rat Race

It is almost a truism: "Who is wealthy? He who is satisfied with his lot" (*Avos* 4:1). It follows, of course, that since a sure sign of wealth is to lack absolutely nothing, the wealthy man should naturally be satisfied. Yet, no matter what one achieves, he will soon find himself thirsting for more. It is endemic to the human condition. The only possibility for contentment, then, is to assume an attitude that says: "Enough. I don't need more. I have everything I could possibly want." Yet who doesn't lack for *something* new, improved, or as yet untasted?

The touchstone, then, is the focus, the ingredients of one's self-definition, the reflection one sees in his psychic mirror. If a person sees himself as a spiritual being, and measures his growth in spiritual terms, then Torah studied and mastered, *middos* fine-honed and enhanced, *chesed* activities assumed, realized, and expanded — these are the brush strokes that paint his self-portrait on a spiritual canvas. The economics are but the circumstances of his life, the means with which a person is meant to create *kiddush Shem Shamayim*. One person serves Hashem with an abundance of financial resources, another with a paucity of funds; much as one person is handsome, another plain; one is gifted with brilliance, another with mediocre mental resources; one has a thrillingly beautiful singing voice, and the other is tone deaf. All of them can be wealthy in the sense that they accept Hashem's edict as their non-negotiable circumstances. So they are content with their predestined lot.

Spiritually, however, the possession of one hundred whets the appetite for two hundred; the attainment of two hundred makes one crave for four hundred. The fact that "No man dies with half his desires in his hands," in this context, frees him from the rat race and places him on Yaakov's ladder of spiritual ascendancy, ever climbing, ever reaching for a higher rung. All increments of growth fire the ambition for more. And whatever has been achieved is truly the individual's possession.

Material simplicity, in such a setting, can be a spiritual blessing.

The Crisis Is Now II

Rabbi Aaron Brafman

I. The Spate of Suffering

There isn't a *frum* community in our metropolitan area that is not reeling from tragic deaths of young and middle-aged people, which are occurring with terrible frequency. The *Tehillim* and *"Mi sheberach"* lists for *cholim* just keep on getting longer and longer, with the numbers of seriously ill *frume Yidden* far out of proportion to the general population. The story has circulated several times that a health-care worker in one of the major New York hospitals said, "G–d must be angry at your people because so many of you are sick."

Part of our *mesorah* and *emunah* as Torah Jews is based on hundreds of sources, starting in the Torah when Yosef's brothers exclaimed, *"Ma zos assah Elokim lanu!* — What is this that G–d has done to us!,"* through the pages of *Nach* and Talmud, as well as in all *sifrei mussar* and chassidus, that nothing that happens to us is mere coincidence or the result of natural forces at work.

It is therefore incumbent upon us to discover why the *middas hadin* — the Divine attribute of justice — is so strong.

The Rambam at the very beginning of *Hilchos Taanis* states that the response to tragedy, as well as to all types of *tzaros*, is *teshuvah* and *tefillah* (repentance and prayer) — which includes fasting. This will cause the suffering or difficulty to be alleviated. The *Rambam* then goes on to say, "And if they will not cry out [in *teshuvah*] and merely say, 'it is just a normal occurrence or happenstance,' such a reaction is the way of cruelty, and will only cause them [the people] to continue in their evil ways, which will only result in an increase in their suffering."

We are not *Neviim* or *baalei ruach hakodesh* (prophets or spiritual visionaries) to know for sure why certain things occur. We also have no right to tell anyone who is in pain that he is suffering for his own sins (based on the *Gemara* in *Perek HaZahav* and based on recent writings and discussions I've had with *gedolei Yisrael*). In fact, the possibility is there that a righteous person suffers as a means of *kapparah* (atonement) for the entire community.

There are many other possibilities of why different people suffer and this is dealt with in numerous *sefarim*. The Chofetz Chaim, for example, has written a number of letters and published more than one *kol korei* (public proclamation) that takes note of tragic occurrences and natural catastrophes, such as devastating floods, earthquakes and pogroms. (See *Published Writings of the Chofetz Chaim*, Letters 10, 11, 12 and 40.) While he clearly declares that it is beyond us to determine why G–d has brought such calamities on mankind, he also reads these events as unmistakable calls for *teshuvah*. Rather than seek some direct linkage between sin and punishment, he calls for people to examine their private and communal affairs for areas that need correction. In his time, he pointed to *shemiras Shabbos* and adherence to family laws, which he found suffering neglect, as needing attention. His call for introspection aimed at self-improvement is no less relevant today .... Ultimately, of course, we submit to the will of Hashem, knowing that there is a just reason for all that Hashem does — a reason that we cannot fathom. I once heard from an old chassidic Jew that the Kotzker Rebbe was once asked, "*Why?*" in a tragic situation, to which he responded: "*Shain volt der Ribbono Shel Olam oisgekukt ven ich Menachem Mendel ken Im farshtein!*" (Loosely translated: "How would G–d look if I, Menachem Mendel, could understand His ways!")

Nevertheless, we as a *tzibbur* must respond to all of the tragedies we experience, so they can serve as a wake-up call to spur us to *teshuvah*. This is always painful, because it necessitates a truthful, critical self-analysis. It is a call to correct our behavior even if it cannot be directly linked to specific instances of suffering and loss.

We must also differentiate between battling for the authenticity of Torah, which necessitates our focusing on the deviationist behavior of others (i.e., Conservative and Reform), and *teshuvah*, which requires us to focus inwardly. [Ed. Note: See excerpt at end of article.]

As a *tzibbur* — as a united, cohesive community — we must examine our situation and seek to correct what may be our flaws at this juncture. We live at a time, on the one hand, of unprecedented Torah learning, certainly in the numbers of people learning full time, the number of *baalei batim* learning, and the breadth of the Torah being studied. The meticulous observance of mitzvos is much greater than ever in recent times. There is an amazing amount of *chesed* being done, both individually and through communal organizations such as *Hatzolah*, *bikur cholim* groups and *Tomchei Shabbos*.

On the other hand, aside from the tragedies befalling our communities, there is a growing spate of headlines that are being *mechallel Shem Shamayim*; though these incidents are painful, they can no longer be ignored. The crisis of the *frum* family, also, is no longer a minor problem. Neither is its spinoff, the growing teenage dropout rate from yeshivos.

II. A Pattern Noted in the Past

In a 1982 article for *The Jewish Observer* entitled *The Crisis Is Now*, I voiced some of the potential dangers developing, which unfortunately have now proven to become part of our reality. The analysis in that article was based on the *Meshech Chochmah*'s commentary in *parshas Bechukosai*. There, the *Ohr Same'ach* analyzes an underlying sociological pattern and process of change in our long history. He describes the continuous cycle of expulsion, to reset-tlement and rebuilding, to decline and to expulsion again. He offers an explanation for the spiritual, psychological and social reasons in this cycle. He points out how precisely at the apex of the cycle, when *Yiddishkeit* is thriving, danger and decline set in.

What might the sin of our day be? What could be the under-lying cause of our suffering? And more, is there anything that can be done to remedy the situation?

I submit that the new sins to be concerned about are those of *geneivah* and *gezeilah* (thievery and robbery) — dishonesty in monetary dealings. And the underlying cause is that we trans-gress one of the *Aseres HaDibros* — that of *Lo sachmod* — Do not be envious. As the *Gra* in *Even Shlomo* 3, says: *"Kol ha'aveiros v'chata'im ba'im mechemmed — kemo she'amru 'Lo sachmod' kollel kol ha'aveiros v'chol haTorah; v'histapkus, shehu hahefech, hu yesod shel kol haTorah ….* All sins and transgressions stem from envy — as they said, 'Do not covet' includes all transgressions and the entire Torah. [By contrast,] contentment, which is the polar opposite of envy, is the foundation of Torah [life]."

The *Gemara* in *Taanis* 12b teaches (and the Rambam codifies this opinion as *halachah*) regarding the order of a fast day: "From early in the morning until noon we analyze the activities of the city," which *Rashi* explains: "We thoroughly examine the activi-ties of the city to see if there is any *gezel* or *chamas* going on." This was the duty of the community leaders on a day of fasting and *teshuvah*.

While striving to live in material excess was always a prob-lem — the *Chovos HaLevavos* writes in *Shaar HaPerishus* — G–d exhorts us to live in modesty and refrain from excess. His description of the self-destruction that comes from the pursuit of luxury and wealth reads as if he were reporting the contempo-rary scene. He then says in Chapter II: "And because this *yeitzer* (drive) has infected a *majority* of the Torah people, we must stand up against it with a special emphasis on *perishus* — abstinence — until we bring the people back to the proper path [of modesty]."

This was written by the *Chovos HaLevavos* in 11th century Spain.

Today, the situation is much more complex and difficult, because the ability to achieve wealth is available to all. It is part of the American dream. It is the thrust of all the messages emanating from Madison Avenue: to arouse within you a desire to possess what you neither have nor need. This pressure has trapped a great part of our *tzibbur*, causing some to stoop to *geneivah*.

I'm not referring to the stories that make the headlines, but to the increasing number of white collar crimes that are too embarrassing to describe in a public forum. Ask any doctor, retailer, businessman or any of the *batei din*, and I guarantee that you will be astounded by their response. Can we just shrug our shoulders and go on?

Rashi at the beginning of *parshas Noach* quotes the *Chazal*: "*Lo nechtam gezar dinam ella al hagezel* — The decree of the Flood was sealed because of thievery." Whatever explanation one gives (and there are many), the fact remains fact — *gezel* is a very serious transgression.

The *Gemara* (*Bava Basra* 88b and *Yevamos* 21a) says: "*Kasheh onshan shel middos yoseir me'onshan shel arayos* — The punishment for dishonest weights and measures is more severe than for immoral conduct." The using of false measures is also a cause for the rise of *Amalek*, the arch-enemy of the Jewish people, *Rashi* points out in *parshas Ki Seitzei*.

This too is not a new phenomenon. Rabbi Yisrael Salanter in his seminal *Iggeres HaMussar* (Letter on Ethics) writes:

> In our communities, thank G–d, the *issurim* of *kashrus* are deeply embedded in the Jewish soul, to such an extent that it is not even a struggle to stay away from prohibited foods. It would not even enter anyone's mind not to ask a *she'eilah* of his *Rav* if he were concerned about the slightest question of *treifos*.
>
> Tragically, however, when it comes to business and monetary dealings, the opposite is true. Most people seem so beset with desire for money, that they seem indifferent to the *issur* of *gezeilah* or any of the other transgressions relating to money ....
>
> But in the Torah's view, they are all the same. [He proceeds to demonstrate with several examples.] Even learned and somewhat G–d-fearing people are simply

not as careful as they should be with regard to the *issurim* of *gezeilah*, even though Yom Kippur or even death cannot bring forgiveness to the perpetrator [— one needs the forgiveness of the injured party].

Reb Yisrael was decrying this tendency at a time when perhaps one could justify the lack of concern over fiscal honesty because Jews were living in terrible conditions. In Russia, Poland — in most of Eastern Europe, for that matter — poverty was rampant, the governments were extremely oppressive to Jews, and there was very little opportunity to earn an honest living.

This cannot be said today. In this country, which has given us all the avenues of opportunity, the rationalizations do not hold water!

III. What Can Be Done?

Reb Yisrael in his letter suggests an answer that should be of help to us as well, in at least working on curing the symptoms. Reb Yisrael suggests the in-depth studying of *Choshen Mishpat* — that section of *Shulchan Aruch* that deals with laws of business and other financial issues. This will slowly have an impact on people, and heighten their awareness and sensitivity to sins connected with monetary affairs.

Choshen Mishpat, which is usually relegated to the province of *dayanim* or used as a springboard for studying *Ketzos* and *Nesivos* (two classical *lomdishe sefarim* studied in yeshivos), has to be brought into our everyday world.

Just as many of the recent *sefarim* and books written on a variety of halachic subjects have brought new knowledge to a wide variety of people, we need young *talmidei chachamim* to publish on *Choshen Mishpat*. More public *shiurim* should be given on this subject matter.

Just as the campaign to increase awareness of the issue of *lashon hara* has created a sensitivity and concern for the topic among masses of *Yidden*, perhaps a campaign about this as well should be launched.

⤳ In the Ways of the Chofetz Chaim

There are dozens of stories about the Chofetz Chaim and his exemplary concern over other people's money. There are several stories of his scrupulousness, when traveling, to pay duty on his packages, rather than avoid paying such taxes to the government. Or buying stamps and ripping them up when he would send his packages with someone rather than the government mail service. His son, Reb Leib, writes (quoted in the biography about his father, and in the *Chofetz Chaim* on *Chumash*) of the many hours the Chofetz Chaim, who never wasted a minute, spent looking over the pages of his *sefarim* to ascertain that there were no errors, which would result in defrauding the buyers.

> When Reb Leib had moved to Warsaw, the Chofetz Chaim entrusted him with the assignment of looking over a certain volume of the Mishnah Berurah that was on press. Several weeks later, the Chofetz Chaim received a letter of complaint stating that the correspondent had received a sefer with misprinted pages. The Chofetz Chaim wrote to his son, "What did you do to me, my son! All my life I've worried about how to avoid avak gezel (a Rabbinic or minor form of the transgression). It never entered my mind that I would be ensnared, as I now was, in actual gezel."
>
> He instructed his son to have the pages reprinted and to place ads in the papers informing customers that they could get replacements of the misprinted pages.

There was a time when he had engaged salesmen to sell his *sefarim* for him. He recalled one of them when he heard that he was selling the *sefarim* in a small town before Yom Tov. Before Yom Tov, when people have so many expenses, explained the Chofetz Chaim, it is forbidden to bother them about buying *sefarim*.

There are many hundreds of stories about other *gedolim*, as well, whose care in fiscal matters has to be brought to the consciousness of our people.

Man's yearning for spirituality and his desire to come closer to Hashem seem easier to achieve when one is involved in activities or acts that are clearly religious and spiritual in nature, as opposed to areas of *bein adam l'chaveiro* — interpersonal affairs. But listen to *Rabbeinu Yonah*, regarding the *mishnah* at the beginning of *Avos*, where the *Anshei Knesses HaGedolah* are quoted as saying, "*Hevu mesunim badin* — Be deliberate in judgment." He says:

> The reason for this warning to be deliberate in money matters, as opposed to other areas of *psak*, is because they [*dinim*] are a major factor in knowing Hashem the Creator. As Yirmiyahu HaNavi writes: "*Haskeil veyadoa osi ki ani Hashem oseh chesed u'mishpat u'tzeddakah ba'aretz* — Give thought and know Me, for I am G-d who does kindness, and justice and charitable deeds on earth."

Thus, *Choshen Mishpat* is not just a means for society to function, but a program to reach spiritual heights and come closer to Hashem.

→ *Cutting Back*

When most Jews were living with the daily struggles to put food on their table, it was not the propitious time to talk about *perishus* or managing with less. The stature and spirit of the Orthodox community had to be lifted and raised. Now that we have, *baruch Hashem*, created communities where the norm is an upper-middle-class lifestyle, perhaps the time has come to say "Enough!" If we do not arrest the pursuit of materialism, it might devour us.

The Chofetz Chaim writes about the awesome responsibility of *rabbanim* to speak out and to try and correct the generation's problems, referring to an incident he had witnessed (*Chofetz Chaim on Torah*, p. 125):

> I was passing through a small town and saw a large crowd gathered in the marketplace surrounding a prisoner, who was in chains, being sent to Siberia for forging money. The prisoner asked that the *Rav* of the town be called, as he had something important to tell him. His

guards agreed and the *Rav* came out. The prisoner called out to him and said, "You should know that I am about to be sent to Siberia, and you — the *Rav* — are at fault! Because I'm sure you knew what was going on. Why didn't you stop me? Why didn't you warn me and tell me that one day they will catch me and send me away? It's the *Rav*'s responsibility to warn his people about their evil ways. And since you didn't warn me, I fell further and further into the trap. It's your fault!"

The Chofetz Chaim drew a powerful lesson from this incident. So should we.

Shortly after the bloody riots of 5689 (1929), the conversation at a gathering in Reb [Yosef] Chaim [Sonnenfeld]'s home turned to the question of why G–d had brought this tragedy upon the land. One of those present offered that it was in punishment for the soccer games that were being held on Shabbos. Reb Chaim stood up and protested vigorously. "I do not share your opinion," he said. "The majority of these people were drafted into the Russian army during the [First] World War where they were forced to eat non-kosher food and violate the Shabbos and other laws, as well. When they were released from the army, many returned home and saw their parents and families massacred in pogroms. Do you really think the sin of people who abandoned Torah under such conditions, is so heavy that G–d would punish the entire nation because of them? If anyone's sins are to blame for this tragedy perhaps they are ours. We were fortunate enough to live here in Jerusalem — a place where no one was forced to violate the ways of the Torah, where we were spared the sight of families being murdered, where we were constantly in the presence of great *talmidei chachamim*, from whom we could learn. Having been granted all this, we are much more to blame. Perhaps that is what G–d is calling us to account for."

(from *Guardian of Jerusalem*, by Rabbi Shlomo Zalman Sonnenfeld and Rabbi Hillel Danziger, Artscroll History series, p. 198)

The Ben-Torah's Dilemma: The Problem of the Divided Selfs

Moshe Yechiel Friedman

*The American yeshivah system has succeeded
in producing a highly developed personality.
After the ben-Torah leaves the confines of the yeshivah,
however, he may face serious stress:
While his "private self" may still seem
to have secure footing, he often finds his "public self"
without anchorage.*

M an may be viewed as possessing two selfs: one that is private and another that is social in nature. The private self exists in a secluded world of its own. In this personal enclave man is alone with his secret dreams, his secret fears, with his very own image of himself. The language of this world is man's inner speech, and with this condensed, abbreviated form of self-communication his mind engages in a reflexive dialogue. In this small kingdom each man is a sovereign, for no other mortal can enter these precincts without his acquiescence.

And each of these worlds is unique; no two are identical. It is this quality of uniqueness which impels each man to strive for his individual self-fulfillment.

The social self is public; it is a collective sort of thing. It functions only as a member of a joint enterprise, chiefly in the company of others. The social self thrives on closeness, togetherness if you will. It fulfills itself through those experiences which enable a person to transcend his private self and achieve new levels of consciousness through subordination to the group interest. In the group experience, the social self interacts, communicates, deals with the thoughts and feelings of others. Only when a person is a *part* of something larger than itself, the social self perceives, is it possible to be truly *whole*.

When the group setting is benign, the private self and the social self live in happy accord. The dreams of the private self move toward realization by virtue of the group experiences. The group is supportive: the individual belongs; he feels secure; his fears and tensions are allayed. Participation in the group is not at the expense of his private esteem; on the contrary, his feelings of worth are enhanced and ennobled through his sharing with others.

Group identification is the term that is used to indicate this sense of kinship with others. In childhood, the individual identifies first with the members of his immediate family. His identification widens as he learns to socialize with other children. Subsequently, his identification proceeds to embrace ever-broadening groups, like the concentric ripples in a pond which spread from a central point. He becomes civic-minded, patriotic, even internationalistic. In all of these dimensions, group identification signifies a progressive heightening of self-fulfillment through growth in social development.

✦ Those Who Do Not Join

There are individuals who cannot or will not fit into the accepted pattern of social growth. They do not make the identifications which help in the development of a healthy personality.

The social self finds the environment hostile rather than supportive. The private self is unable to find realization through group membership. Two alternatives lie before the individual who finds himself in this quandary. He may repress his social self and withdraw into the cocoon of his own private world. His contacts with the world outside himself will be determined by necessity only. Or he may become part of a social unit composed of individuals like himself, other persons who seek group identification compatible with their own values and beliefs. Drawn together by their common hostility to society at large, members of this atypical group may evince stronger feelings of kinship and belonging than those found in the accepted groups.

In these times, for reasons not relevant to the argument of this discussion, there is a tremendous surge in the numbers of persons, especially among the young, who experience this crisis between the two selfs. These are the alienated, the estranged, the uncommitted. A vast quantity of literature has been generated by this feature of contemporary society. It is the purpose of this writer to examine the problem of the divided self as it manifests itself in the world of Torah. It is a well-established phenomenon in Jewish history that the ills that beset the world are mirrored, through various transformations, in the life of our people. It should come as no surprise, therefore, to find that the social troubles of our own era reverberate even within the relatively cloistered compartments of Orthodox Jewry.

✦ Genesis of the Divided Selfs

In Jewish life, the incompatibility of the private and social selfs is a consequence of *galus,* exile from our homeland and dispersion among the nations of the world. To appreciate this proposition, one must first recognize the transcendental nature of the Jewish people. *Klal Yisrael* is more than a total aggregate of Jews taken individually or in groups: It is a metaphysical reality which possesses its own *formal* existence. Jewish collective life in its totality, at any point in history, is the concretization of this entity at that given moment. If this concept seems abstruse, it is nevertheless basic to a genuine understanding of the central problem of this discussion.

Before the destruction of the first *Beis HaMikdash*, when all of Israel was still settled on its homeland, it was possible for a Jew to identify spiritually with *Klal Yisrael* through an ordered sequence of intermediate identifications. Each Jew was a member of a primary family group; of a patriarchal family group; of a *sheivet* (tribal unit); of the entire people of Israel. During the *shalosh regalim* (three pilgrimage festivals) when the entire country assembled in Jerusalem, group identification was not only understood as a spiritual fact; it was also experienced on all levels as a physical reality. In the context of this dualistic thought, it is natural to conceive of the relationship between Jewish society and the metaphysical *Klal Yisrael* as being analogous to the relationship that exists between body and soul.

The social unity of the people was of course reinforced by the fact that the Jews occupied their own land. The political independence which they enjoyed was another factor that strengthened their group ties. Then came the *Churban* (the destruction of the Temple), and the virtual disintegration of Jewish social life on a national scale. The process that began when the Assyrians drove off the ten *shevatim* came to a climax with the expulsion of the remaining population by the Babylonians. In all of its facets, group identification was seriously attenuated. Although every Jew still regarded himself as belonging to the eternal *Klal Yisrael*, he was still confronted with the reality of the physical world in which Israel was seriously fragmented and stripped of its national integrity.

The *galus* that later followed the destruction of the *Bayis Sheni* (the Second Temple) persisted and intensified; dispersion following dispersion, banishment following banishment, and dissimilarities between scattered Jewish communities became more pronounced. Not only were Jewish groups separated from one another by geographical, lingual, and political barriers, but also in such religious areas as *halachah, minhagim,* and *nuscha'os.* It became increasingly difficult, therefore, for a Jew to feel part of the social totality of the Jewish people. His group identification would end, in most instances, with the community into which he was born. Of course it was known that there were other Jewish communities, and contacts were maintained with them to some extent; in terms of experience, however, there was virtually no opportunity for a Jew to actually feel part of the Jewish people in its entirety. On the other hand, although the breadth of group identification was highly localized, its intensity remained strong. Whether it was a town, a village, a *shtetl*, or a ghetto in which the Jew lived, his ties to the community were well formed. His world may have been greatly constricted, but in this world he belonged and was able to find fulfillment for the private and social selfs which he possessed.

It should be noted at this point that in Jewish life there is a form of group identification which may in a large measure be independent of the ways of a particular community. Our People boasts an impressive gallery of eminent individuals who, by virtue of their piety and learning, brought communities of devoted adherents into existence. The general religious lifestyles originated by these outstanding personages and their particular modes of conduct were imitated in a manner which crossed community lines and ignored established patterns of group behavior. At times, such figure-oriented identification groups brought about a modest reconstruction of an autonomous Jewish society.

✦ *The American Split*

Group identification that had degenerated so precipitously in Europe disintegrated much more so among the millions of Jews who migrated to the American shores. Family and community ties were severed. *Landsmanschaften* were organized along previously established community patterns, but in time they lost their vitality and withered away. The absence of a strongly organized religious establishment, due primarily to the democratic principles of freedom of religion and separation of church and state prevailing in this country, meant that religious affiliation as such could not serve as a rallying point for the formation of a closely knit group. To some degree the community was replaced by the congregation, particularly if the membership of the congregation was representative of a certain European town or county, but binding affiliation did not exist.

With the evanescence of the traditional communal and religious ties, Jewish immigrants began to identify with their new social environment. This tendency of the social self to seek fulfillment led to the rejection of religious observance, to acculturation, and ultimately to assimilation. In recent years a new dimension has entered into this progressive breakdown of Jewish identification. While families cut their ties with the past in terms of daily practice, they still subscribed to the moral and spiritual ideals that are part of their heritage. They were able to maintain this loyalty because in the past the American ethos leaned heavily on Biblical sources. The current generation, however, spurns even these ethical principles. Not only do young people refuse to identify with the community, they even turn away from their parents. Thus the social self of today's youth generates all sorts of atypical associations to allow the private self to find gratification in a sympathetic group.

✧ *American Social Units: the Yeshivah Students / the Chassidim*

The formation of yeshivos in this country was an affirmative effort to counteract the complex of influences which caused American Jewry to become absorbed into the general population and suffer religious anonymity. While the restoration of Jewish communal life did not seem feasible at the beginning of the 20th century, the yeshivah did attempt to re-establish identification with the eternity of *Klal Yisrael*. Pupils in yeshivos represented a highly diverse population. Their parents were chassidim and *misnagdim; Galitzianer* and *Litvakes;* Russian-born and American-born. What united all these children was their common descent from the People who received the Torah at Mount Sinai. For the young souls who attended these institutions, the yeshivah itself became a nucleus around which intense group identifications could be built. The emergence of the yeshivah as a quasi-community was also prompted by the fact that the American *bachur,* unlike his *shtetl* counterpart, could not count on sharing with his classmates the day-to-day religious experiences, such as praying together weekdays or on Shabbos and Yom Tov in any community outside of the yeshivah. The exclusiveness of this relationship gave the yeshivah group greater autonomy and, consequently, firm integrity.

For the yeshivah student who continued his Torah studies to high school and beyond, his identification with the yeshivah community was likely to become intensified through the personality of the *Rosh Yeshivah* who, by virtue of his stature, served as a magnetic force which unified the young *bnei Torah* who flocked around him. Out of this strong *rebbi-talmid* relationship there emerged a religiously self-contained community, following the style, the *minhag,* the *nusach,* and the *pesokim* of the *Rosh Yeshivah.* Included in the style of this group was the ideological orientation of the leader and his attitudes toward matters of contemporary concern.

The chassidic community is another illustration of a religious group organized around a central figure. Moreover, in some instances the chassidic circles have succeeded in restoring, in varying measures, the *kehillah* structure of bygone eras. The *bnei Torah* of a particular chassidic denomination not only study at the same yeshivah but also tend to concentrate in the same residential area, attending their own *beis haknesses,* and in other ways demonstrating their high degree of belongingness. Chassidic groups, too, have a distinct style, a definite ideological orientation, and specific *minhagim, nuscha'os,* and *pesokim* that they collectively follow.

Members of these two groups are fortunate in that they have been able to forge an intimate group affiliation despite the many environmental influences to the contrary. Members of these groups are able to resolve many of their day-to-day religious problems because the group as a whole already possesses decisions on these matters. This situation is true both for objective questions of Torah and *hashkafah* (personal philosophy) as it is for personal concerns of subjective nature. In case of doubt, furthermore, one always has the option of coming with his trouble to the spiritual head of the group and finding peace of mind from the counsel he offers.

✦ The Unattached "Ben Torah"

The focus of this discourse, however, is the *ben Torah* who has not established any meaningful group identification, neither within the circle of the yeshivah which he attended nor in some chassidic sect. The status of this *ben Torah* is pathetic for he is dreadfully alone. Even the Jew who lived in some outlying European *shtetl*, where only a handful of his coreligionists resided, did not feel the social isolation which is the lot of the unaffiliated Orthodox Jew who seeks vitality in his religious social life. The associations he makes through his attendance at the *beis haknesses* or his membership in professional and social organizations are unable to compensate for the vacant feelings that result from the inability of his social self to find the proper climate for the adequate public expression of the private self.

Operating apart from a structured social context, the isolated *ben Torah* is prone to follow a religious lifestyle that is confused, disintegrated, shot through with conflict and contradiction. What is even more regrettable is that large numbers of these *bnei Torah* are not conscious of the disorganized pattern that characterizes their lives, of the anomalies that result from an uncritical view of their own existence. They proceed from situation to situation, from decision to decision, without making the effort to determine whether these separate actions fit into a coherent, consistent pattern.

✦ Some Questions

It may be profitable to enumerate a few of the dilemmas that the lonely *ben Torah* must resolve for himself. Despite his unswerving loyalty to *Klal Yisrael* as a metaphysical entity, his lack of identification with any segment of the physical Jewish society means that he must, on his own, settle such questions as these:

> *Should I follow the religious style of my parents, the yeshivah where I studied, or the beis haknesses I now attend? When I learn Torah, should I study primarily to achieve depth in understanding or to broaden the scope of my knowledge? Which mefarshim on Chumash should I include? What about chassidic sources and commentaries? Is Zohar for me ... or Kabbalah? And what about mussar? Tanach? Jewish history and philosophy? Secular studies? In halachah matters whom do I follow when there is a difference of opinion? Whom shall I consult when I am in doubt?*

In addition, the unaffiliated *ben Torah* is constantly faced with countless questions less general, but perhaps with greater spiritual ramifications. How does he answer questions of lifestyle such as:

> *How and where shall I spend recreational time and vacations? What shall I read in my home, on my subway ride? What mode of dress and home furnishing is appropriate? What kind of school shall I select for my children? Where shall I direct my tzedakah dollar? My discretionary time reserved for klal work?*

✢ *Some Consequences*

These and many other questions of similar nature must be answered for the *ben Torah* who wishes to lead an examined life which has method and reason as underlying principles. Leading a solitary existence, he is unable to use group conduct as an indicator for his own behavior. In honesty to himself, therefore, he must choose some alternative to a formless and unintegrated mode of existence. Particularly in the ideological sphere, no *ben*

Torah who is true to himself can permit himself to continue in an unproductive course. *Hashkafah* is not an academic study: It has practical consequences for the total life pattern of the individual. *What happens when a person studies a mussar sefer one day, a chassidic work the next, a philosophical work on the following day, then examines a work which sees hashkafah from the standpoint of halachah? Is it possible to internalize, in a systematic fashion, these distinctively different aproaches into one's religious temperament?* More likely the response will be erratic, haphazard. *Which ben Torah, once he is conscious of the irrationality of his behavior, can tolerate such an existence?* Moreover, the absence of a calculated system of *hashkafah* may easily lead a person to thoughts and deeds that are in serious conflict with Torah precepts.

The mature *ben Torah* who has not made a conscious effort to systematize his life pattern and who falls first under one influence and then under another is not unlike the individual described by Rabbi Saadia Gaon in his preface to *Sefer HaEmunos VeDei'os*. In his discussion of different types of persons who fail to achieve truth in their faith and ideology, Rabbi Saadia concludes with a description of the person who intermittently changes from one system of beliefs to another. He is likened to a traveler who seeks to visit a city but does not know the way. He goes in one direction, strays, retraces his steps, starts out in another direction, strays once more, again retraces his steps, and goes through the same process over and over again. To this person Rabbi Saadia applies the verse: *"The toil of the fool wearies him for he does not know how to go to the city"* (*Koheles* 10:14).

✦ Alternative Solutions to the Dilemma

Joining

Once a *ben Torah* has become acutely aware of the untenability of his position as an isolate with an unstructured religious life, what course lies open before him to rectify his situation? One possibility is that the recognition of the value of group identification may in itself serve as a sufficiently strong motivation to induce him to become a member in a group. This strategy may be accomplished through socialization with members of the group and the simulation of group behaviors, or it may be achieved by establishing the appropriate relationship with the spiritual head of the group. Perhaps the new relationship may seem strained and contrived at first, but time should eventually remove the awkwardness of the first encounters. When the process of absorption into the group is completed, the new member will discover that a preponderate number of conflicts which had confronted him earlier will be resolved through his adaptation to the group pattern.

But what about the "loner," the *ben Torah* who for reasons real or imagined, selfish or unselfish, genuine or hypocritical, is unable to discover the proper unit in which his social self can find adequate anchorage? He is incapable of adopting a group style either by affiliation with members of the group or by becoming an adherent to the group's guiding spirit. While perforce he engages in certain collective activities of a religious nature, his participation is mainly mechanical, governed by the halachic requirements that certain mitzvos be performed with a *tzibbur.* Otherwise, he is adrift, completely dependent upon his own resources to steer himself toward some life port. What solutions are available to this perplexed individual?

Path of the Loner

The life of this *ben Torah* is hard indeed. With no guidance except from the lessons and experiences of his earlier life, with no assistance except from his own intellectual resources, he must thread his way through his precarious existence in a world that is steeped in evil and falsehood. He is compelled to pit his meager knowledge and wisdom against the massive assault on his senses, feelings, and thoughts that is launched against him each day, every minute of the day. In a multitude of shapes and forms the *yetzer hara* (inclination toward evil) will seek to ensnare him in his toils, taking every advantage of his weaknesses both large and small. Good will appear as evil, and evil as good. And even if he survives this ceaseless strife he will not yet gain the total fulfillment that comes about through the harmonious fusion of the private and social selfs.

There is no salvation for the socially uncommitted *ben Torah* except a life of almost fanatical self-discipline and sense of purpose. Through unremitting effort, he must develop the skill of subjecting his own life pattern to constant and merciless evaluation, to explore the source and motivation of his conduct, to set for himself a rigorous schedule of Torah study that is designed according to a systematic and rational formula. His actions must be calculated, his decisions deliberate, his judgments carefully balanced. He must be a grand strategist, a master planner, an astute scholar, and a superb man. With undeviating single-mindedness and total dedication the *ben Torah* who has to "make it on his own" must strive with every bit of energy to draft the architectonics of his own life so that it encompasses a comprehensive program of Torah study, observance of mitzvos and *halachos,* and a coherent system of ideological principles which has live pertinence for today's world.

But what about the social self? Granted that the program outlined above will give the individual a meaningful life plan, how will it reduce his loneliness? How will the private self, locked in as it is with its own particular strivings which are so highly personal in nature, harmonize with the social self which searches for communication for that which is larger than man himself? Indeed this is a difficult question to answer.

Circumventing the Group

Let it be argued that the search for group identification is essentially a striving for immortality. In its true sense, the group must be viewed holistically: The group is not merely the sum total of the individual members of the group but is rather a corporate unit which possesses an identity of its own. As such, the life of the group outlasts the life of the members who constitute the group. Members come and go, but the group lives on. Group identification, therefore, can be interpreted as a process whereby the individual escapes the limitations of his own existence by participating in an entity which has an indefinite life span. When the private self realizes itself through the activity of the social self, the individual senses that he has achieved immortality.

For the *ben Torah* there is another pathway to immortality. By living a life indissolubly bound with *Toras Yisrael* he transcends the here and now, the earthly shackles which bind him to the present. And through his identification with *Toras Yisrael* he also becomes identified with that other eternal reality known as *Klal Yisrael*. It is possible, therefore, that the road that ought not to have been taken, the long and tortuous odyssey which virtually signifies the failure of the individual to traverse the well-trod pathways formed by the collective wisdom of the ages, may yet lead the lonely but truth-seeking *ben Torah* to a haven of peace.

A Nation of Devourers

David Schaps

"Devourers" is not the term usually used; we usually call ourselves "consumers." Somehow we have gotten inured to that expression, comfortable with the idea of defining ourselves as people who consume. We consume wheat, milk, meat, potatoes. We consume oil, gas, electricity. We consume wool, cotton, silk, bulls, cows, calves, and who knows what else. That is, perhaps, the nature of the body. But it is the peculiar nature of the 20th-century American to call himself a consumer: to define himself as a hundred-and-fifty-pound machine whose purpose is to destroy what others have produced. Once consumption was the name of a disease; now we have a Consumers Union, and in some places even a Consumers Party, and nobody seems to blush at all.

There are reasons why consumption is so respectable in America. All of us, today, live by selling something. Some sell their own products and are called manufacturers; some sell other people's products and are called wholesalers or retailers; some sell their services and are called either workers or professionals, depending on the services they sell. Even the farmer no longer lives off his own land: He farms acres and acres of one or two crops, sells them, and buys what he needs with the proceeds.

In a society so organized, consumption is essential. Each of us is dependent upon there being others who need what we are selling. It matters little, indeed, whether the society is capitalist, socialist, communist, or what you will; modern economic battles center on the question of how to divide up the products, not whether or not we need them. It is vital to all of our well-being that the nation be plentifully supplied with consumers. And so to be a consumer is no longer a term of opprobrium. We wear the label with pride.

→ Who Is Rich?

It is not a pride our rabbis would share. "Who is rich?" asked ben Zoma, and we are taught the answer at the earliest age: "He who is happy with his own lot" (*Avos* 4:1). We try to teach this lesson to our own children, but deep and powerful voices are telling them the opposite.

"If you could have anything in the world, what would you wish for?" How many times is a child asked this question? Each time he is taught that the world is full of things he should want — if he only had the imagination to think of them.

"What would you like for your birthday?" The youngest children are often stumped by this one, but they soon catch on. They moon in store windows, looking at things that they can ask for for their birthday, for the *afikoman*, for Purim — for anything.

The rabbis explain that when we speak of Hashem "wanting" something, we are speaking only metaphorically; "we want something" implies a lack, and Hashem, of course, lacks nothing. When I heard this argument, I could follow it, but it was a new idea to me. For the first 20 years of my life, I had become used to the idea that a person wanted things even if he lacked nothing. When, as a child, I was told that President Roosevelt had called for "freedom from want," I could not imagine what that might mean.

"What can you give the man who has everything?" I have never heard it suggested that there is no need to give anything to a man who has everything — and indeed, such a man would probably be insulted not to be given anything.

The situation is, perhaps, more obvious to one living in Israel, where the Old World is no more than a generation or two away. I ride in taxis on occasion and listen to the driver expostulate on how terrible the situation is, how hard it is to live on what he makes. I wonder whether to be amused, angry, or just sad. I do not mean to cast aspersions on the relative justice of cabdrivers' salaries; but I know that his grandfather, in Europe, North Africa, or the Middle East, lived in a place where he traveled by donkey or by wagon, performed hard physical labor, lived in the shadow of starvation — and would never have contaminated his lips with the kind of language his grandson uses to vent his rage at not being able to afford an air-conditioner. The consumer society has given everything to the taxi driver, but it has not made him happy. It cannot make him happy.

"My father," a Moroccan acquaintance told me, "was a fuller — what would nowadays be called a dry cleaner. He had no modern chemicals, none of the new machinery that cleans a whole pile of suits in an hour. At best, he could clean about two suits a day. And yet whenever a friend walked in, he always had time to offer him a cup of coffee and talk with him. Today the dry cleaners can do in an hour more than my father could do in a week. Have you ever seen one with the time to offer you a cup of coffee?"

✦ Creating the Need

"Before the coming of the Messiah," says the Talmud, "arrogance will grow mighty ... and the truth will be absent." The need to advertise one's wares was recognized many generations ago, but it was left for the 20th century to fix the matter as a principle: The seller does not really have to produce anything for which I have any need; all he needs is for me to *think* that I need his product. He may do this in various ways: He may pretend to be selling something that he is not ("Buy Krispy Krinkles and win an all-expenses-paid tour to Bulgaria"), he may claim for his product qualities that it does not have ("New, improved"), he may pretend that your own property has lost its value ("Trade in your old 1986 model"), or — most insidious of all — he may try to arouse in you wants that you did not have ("Don't you wish you were a blonde?"). The dangerous factor in all of these is not the direct message; go ahead — buy Krispy Krinkles, if they're kosher (and if they are not, wait a few months and somebody will be selling Kosher Krinkles). The dangerous factor is the implication that the need that they can fulfill is a need that you have. It is not stated directly, it is just assumed; and there is no surer way to bypass a person's critical facilities and put foreign values into his mind.

Private consumption up in Israel

> Tel Aviv (JTA) — Private consumption in Israel rose by 12 percent per capita in 1986 although private incomes declined by 3 percent and public consumption was down by 3 percent, according to the Central Bureau of Statistics. A Bureau official said the consuming binge continued in the first four months of 1987.

✦ *Values of Consumption and Consumption of Values*

This, more than worldliness itself, is the true danger of consumerism. The books of *mussar*, it is true, are full of warnings not to spend our lives in pampering our flesh, preparing a good meal for the worms — our own ultimate consumers. The warnings are as true today as ever, but in our generation consumerism has become something much more sinister. Take the universal need to sell, add to it the trick of selling your product by changing the customer's ideas, and there follows a nation in which almost everyone is trying to influence others for his own profit. Most of the alien and negative values that threaten our own and our children's spiritual health come from somebody who is trying to sell us something. In some of them — drugs, pornography — the commercial motive is obvious; the sellers themselves are pushing their product, and their product itself is the danger. In other cases the matter is less obvious, but no less true. We may waste our days and our years worrying about distant calamities and exaggerated threats — indeed, the United States has in the past gone to war, with all the attendant death and distress — under the influence of people whose only real interest is to sell us newspapers. Daughters of Israel are taught to be "attractive" (attracting what?) by people whose interest is to sell them clothing. The problems of *kashrus* are not only a matter of "modern technology"; if it still exists, a National Pork Institute funded by pork farmers, searches day by day for new uses for its product, inventing undreamt-of ways to sell us what we may not eat. And of course, day by day, year by year, people who wish to sell us their services as public officials, sell us ideologies whose bottom line is: Now you are oppressed, and when you make us your leaders, you will be free. The biggest danger of consumerism is not epicureanism, but *apikorsus.*

My heart still cries when I remember a letter I read some years ago in an English newspaper. The writer — I have no reason to believe she was Jewish — began by saying that it seemed that no matter what parents did, they could not succeed. She and her husband had tried to give their daughter a decent upbringing, but as she began high school, she started bringing home "values that certainly weren't ours." It did not take much insight to see that the values described were those of the advertising world: be the life of the party, be attractive, be a new you. Decency does not allow me to describe in detail — as the poor girl's mother did — how daring led to debauchery, alcohol to drugs, until the girl, only 24 at the time of the letter, was so thoroughly destroyed physically and mentally that there was no hope of her ever being able to work at a job, much less get married. I do not necessarily share the values of a middleclass English woman, but I was distressed to see a young girl turned into a vegetable while her parents looked on powerlessly. I was infuriated to consider that the people who had sold her the chintzy values that ruined her life had done so in order to sell her a few pennies' worth of perfume and makeup.

There is no limit to the distortion of values that the consumer society can create. "Live, live, live modern! Smoke an L&M!" — to give just one slogan that I remember from my youth. I don't know how many L&M's it sold; but what a crime that it convinced millions of young men and women that "living" meant smoking a cigarette — or, if you were too smart for that, at least something similar.

✦ In the Consumer Society

Consumerism is not something from which we can run away. Our economy, our society, runs on it, and none of us have the resources to live without it — indeed, there would be no special merit for a Jew to become a subsistence farmer. As his grandfather told my brother-in-law when the latter toyed with the idea of taking over grandpa's farm, "I worked most of my life to pay off the mortgage to the bank. I think you can do something better with your time." The Jew can certainly do something better with his time. He can learn Torah. He can perform acts of *chesed.* He can pray. He can bring up a family of G–d-fearing Jews. He can do important and even earth-shaking (perhaps more correctly, *earth-holding*) things, if he can only keep his mind free of the idea that he is here to consume.

The Jew eats food, indeed, but he does not consume; he is never allowed to consume. To consume means to devour the item and leave nothing behind. The Jew chooses a kosher animal; slaughters it according to the Torah; blesses Hashem over the slaughtering, before he eats it, and after he eats it. The Jews does not consume; he is *metakken* the item, raising it to a higher plane. What was a mindless animal has become a praise for Hashem; what was a silicon chip has become a device to ensure that he prays on time; what was a salary check has become a source for *tzedakah;* what was an hour off has become an hour of Torah. We are not here to consume, we are here to raise the physical world to a higher plane. We consume the physical item in the process. But we must never let ourselves become a nation of devourers.

The Challenges
of Our Current Galus:
an Agenda for Greatness

based on an address by
Rabbi Elya Svei

✧ The Assignment: Perfection

E very aspect of our existence as people has its place in the
Divine scheme of mankind's spiritual ascent — certainly
the present stage of our current *galus*, as well. Somehow, the
conditions in which we are currently living must also be
designed to bring us closer to our goal of achieving *sheleimus*,
perfection. To better understand the specific role we are expected to play, we must first step back to gain a better perspective of
the general purposes of *galus* and the lessons it is meant to teach
us.

It is commonly known that Creation would have reached
its ultimate purpose had Adam HaRishon followed G–d's
command not to eat from the *Eitz HaDaas*, the Tree of
Knowledge. But, as we know, he did violate that first mitzvah.
After his fall, the task of bringing Creation to perfection was no
longer his alone; it fell upon Adam's children, all of mankind.
His descendants also followed with failures of their own, and

as a result, this task was assigned to yet narrower groups: after the corruption of the *dor haMabul* (the generation of the Deluge) and the destruction of the *Mabul* that followed, the sons of Noach remained to be charged with the task of striving for perfection; and then, with the rebellion of the builders of the Tower of Bavel, the circle of those responsible for the elevation of the world was further narrowed, placing the assignment exclusively on the shoulders of Avraham's progeny — specifically, Yaakov Avinu and his children. It was now incumbent upon them to raise the world to its ultimate level of *sheleimus*.

After the Exodus from Egypt and the 40 years of wandering in the *midbar* (wilderness), *Klal Yisrael* was on the threshold of entering the Promised Land, where it finally could have achieved its goal of *sheleimus*, once it built the *Beis HaMikdash* and the people pursued a life of *kedushah* (sanctity), as described in *Shiras Haazinu*: "He [G–d] sought them [the Jewish people] out in a desert land, in the desolation … He enclosed them [with the Clouds of Glory], instructed them [with the Torah], watched over them as the apple of His eye" (*Devarim* 32:10). In the Holy Land, Israel was expected to benefit from the fulfillment of G–d's promise: "He raised him to the lofty plateaus of earth" (Ibid., v. 13), referring to the *Beis HaMikdash*. For the *Beis HaMikdash*, the epicenter of *Klal Yisrael* in the Holy Land, represented the lofty level *Klal Yisrael* had reached when grouped around Sinai, and could have reached again. Jewry's growth to *sheleimus* was to be facilitated by *Eretz Yisrael's* crops, notably its vineyards and olive groves. Demanding minimal care and yielding bountiful harvests, they could support a populace that makes spiritual growth its major concern, requiring relatively little time or effort from them for providing sustenance.

But instead of using the special features of *Eretz Yisrael* for achieving *sheleimus*, *Klal Yisrael* endured the realization of a different, tragic prediction: "Then Yeshurun became fat and rebelled" (Ibid., v. 15). The name *"Yeshurun"* was not chosen at random to describe *Klal Yisrael* at this stage, *Sforno* tells us; it refers not to the dull, materialistic hedonists whom one would expect to reject G–d's leadership, but to those of *dakus ha'iyun* —

keen sensitivity and insight (related to *"ashurenu* — I will gaze at Him"). Even they would rebel against their Father, in the very same way that a beast kicks at its provider who feeds it.

So *sheleimus* was not Israel's in its own land. Yet, *Klal Yisrael* was still charged with the task of reaching *sheleimus* for itself, and in the process, for all mankind. To achieve this, *Klal Yisrael* was moved on to another stage of activity, another status of existence — that of *galus*. In *galus*, it was expected that the wanderings, sufferings and deprivation of exile would remove them from the numbing influence of luxurious living and materialism. *Galus* would sharpen the dulled sensitivities of those who were meant to be in the vanguard of our people's spiritual ascent, but were not, because of living a life of abundance. In *galus*, it would be different.

✧ *After the Suffering Is Over*

Looking back at two millennia of *galus*, one could well say that as a people, Jewly has been exposed to every type of persecution conceivable, climaxed by the unprecedented death and destruction suffered during World War II. Our current state of affairs in the Western lands and in *Eretz Yisrael*, however, is (thank G–d) devoid of the oppression and persecution usually associated with *galus*. In fact, we are enjoying an abundance that is a dramatic departure from our earlier experiences. Does the life of plenty that we are now enjoying actually continue the process of fine-tuning our spiritual sensitivity, preparing us for *sheleimus*, when it was the very cause of our downfall when we had been living in *Eretz Yisrael*, millennia ago?

One might suggest that our current, pre-Messianic era brings to a close the years of suffering, and our new more favorable condition is a final test of sorts, to see if, after all the grinding away at the grossness of our feelings, we can finally deal with affluence: if we can be exposed to material abundance as we once were, as a people in a land of our own, and this time not fall victim to *"vayishman Yeshurun* — and Yeshurun grew fat and rebelled," and not lose our *dakus ha'iyun,* our capacity for keen sensitivity and insight — once more.

But the struggle to gain and preserve *dakus ha'iyun* in a *galus* setting is complicated by factors of its own. True, generally speaking, *galus* does possess corrective powers, but it also has a strong liability: exposure to alien cultures; and this persists to this very day. *Dakus ha'iyun* calls for clarity of thought, unadulterated by non-Jewish ideologies, and we, in our present setting, must endeavor to keep our thoughts, our values, and our frame of reference faithful to Torah. This calls for unusual vigilance, for even the slightest distraction can be confusing.

This can be understood against the background of two exceptional experiences recorded in Scripture. On two separate occasions, the entire world was silent — not one bird sang, no leaves rustled in the wind, to insure that the impact of the event be pure, unadulterated. The first time was when G–d uttered the first two of the Ten Commandments: *"Anochi* — I am the L-rd your G–d,"* and *"Lo yihye* — You shall not have any other gods." The second time total silence pervaded the earth was when Eliyahu HaNavi called upon G–d to bring a miraculous fire onto his offering, on Mount Carmel. In each of these instances, it was essential that no trace or suspicion of a foreign element be present which might confuse the thousands of people witnessing the events: *"Anochi"* is exclusive, with no allowances for sharing of Divine sovereignty with any other power. To insure the purity of this message, no extraneous sounds could accompany the pronouncement of *"Anochi."* Similarly, the miracle of *Har HaCarmel* resulted from Divine intervention, with the presence of no other accompanying force. To make certain that the people make no mistake regarding the exclusivity of the Source of the miracle, no sound was heard.

Our hearts and minds are extremely sensitive, and are receptive to all sorts of confusing messages. In fact, *Chazal* (the rabbis of the Talmud) suggest that a person pray — before consuming food — that it not affect his mind through the material substances ingested, rendering him incapable of studying Torah without any dilution or compromise of its message. This concern is in regard to interference provoked by food, which enters the digestive tract and only reaches the brain much later, in a highly refined form, after following a circuitous route. Yet *Chazal* were fearful of the possibility of it causing some confusion in a person's cognitive capacities! Imagine the care one must exercise to avoid the direct influence of false values and ideologies!

We who are fortunate enough to bring children into the world surely hope that they will grow to be counted amongst the children of *Yeshurun*, who will possess that precious *dakus ha'iyun*. Consider, then, the conscientious parent who is highly selective in regard to the school in which he enrolls his young son, the *rebbe* who teaches him, and the companions with whom the child spends his time. Surely, even after all his probing and selecting, the child will still need *siyata d'Shemaya* to learn Torah and absorb it well in his tender mind, to become that select member of *Yeshurun*. Nevertheless, after a stimulating and strenuous day in yeshivah, many such children return home, often to turn on their television sets for entertainment and relaxation. There, within the *mezuzos* of the sanctuary of a Jewish home, an impressionable young child sits and fills his mind and heart with vivid portrayals of all sorts of blasphemy, immorality and violence. The evils and pernicious values of the marketplace do not enter his thinking and mold his attitudes by indirection, pursuing some circuitous route, but forcibly invade the seat of his intelligence and vigorously engage his emotions. Is it at all conceivable that come the next morning, he will be able to absorb Torah with any degree of purity, that he will engage in his studies with the optimum degree of success? That the clarity of his mind will not be sullied?

→ A Guide to Clarity

Contemporary life is full of crises and challenges. To be sure, we cannot rely fully on our own judgment to resolve these issues, but must be in constant consultation with *gedolei Yisrael*. They truly carry the burdens of *Klal Yisrael*, suffer its problems, and view events from a perspective of Torah. Beyond doubt, the irreplaceable losses of the last few years have left us bereft of the towering leaders of the previous generation. They were our eyes, our hearts, our guides, and we have no one else even approaching their stature. Nonetheless, bear in mind that when the Torah directs us to bring our questions to our sages, it tells us to consult *"the judge that will be in those days"* (*Devarim* 17:9), to which *Sifri* comments, "Even if he is not of the stature of his predecessors, you must listen to him, for you only have the leaders of your own time."

Fortunately, the Torah leadership has articulated its stance on many issues in public life today that cry out for intelligent responsible assessment. For instance, the Conservative and Reform movements are putting immense pressures on the powers that be to grant them recognition in *Eretz Yisrael*. While they mouth appealing slogans, calling for *"achdus,"* pluralism, and mutual respect, *gedolei Torah* have pointed out that their true agenda is to institute changes in *halachah* and corrode the *mesorah*. This calls for vigilance and a willingness to take unpopular positions …. Issues such as this are often dealt with by the lay leadership and bureaucracies of the establishment without the guidance of a Torah perspective. Such an approach cannot succeed.

Many look back at the events surrounding World War II and conclude that precious lives could have been saved if only people had taken more decisive action. Burdened by guilt for this lack of activity, they attempt to compensate for it with what often is a surfeit of action. Yet action is not always called for, and when not warranted, it can be counter-productive, even deadly destructive. And when action is warranted, it must be purposeful. Picture, if you will, a fire sweeping through a house. A passerby is desperate to do something — anything — to douse the flames. No water is available, but there is a bucket of gasoline. So he picks it up and throws it into the fire …. Obviously, "no action" would have been far more preferred to "any action, as long as *something* is done." The only way to determine if something at all should be done — and if yes, what — is by consulting with our *gedolei Yisrael*. Without their counsel, we dare not act.

As we strive for *sheleimus*, we must have some kind of vision, some sort of goal in mind. The *Ramban* (end of *Bereishis*) introduces *Chumash Shemos* as the *Sefer HaGeulah*, the Book of Redemption. This redemption process continued through the Ten Plagues and all the miracles of the Exodus, on through the encampment at the foot of Mount Sinai. But it did not reach its fulfillment until the erection of the *Mishkan* (the sanctuary that traveled with Israel through the *midbar*, into *Eretz Yisrael*). With this, the *Sefer HaGeulah* is complete. So, in our effort to scale the heights reached by the *Avos*, our Patriarchs, we strive to emulate their ultimate achievement and make the *mikdash me'at* (the miniature sanctuary of our communities), our houses of study and worship, the focal point of our lives. By studying Torah regularly and faithfully, growing in Torah, and living our lives in accordance with Torah and mitzvos, we can transform ourselves into the People of the Torah in the fullest sense of the word.

Such an agenda may sound over-ambitious, especially in view of the terrible destruction we suffered just 40, 50 years ago. Indeed, one of the leading *mussar* figures of the previous generation asked someone how severe he thought the Jewish losses of World War II were. "Six million Jews were lost" he replied.

"No," responded the questioner. "Much more. All of *Klal Yisrael* was diminished with the loss of the six million."

Such a comment might sound like a call of despair. Yet after some thought, it should inspire encouragement, a rallying cry for more ambitious planning and more decisive action. If after such a devastating loss, we succeeded to some degree in repairing our ranks, and rebuilding Torah to its present level — with more young men studying Torah today in American yeshivos than in all the yeshivos in Lithuania before the War — with our numerically greater forces, and our vastly greater financial resources, we have the capability to accomplish much, much more. Surely, Rabbi Aharon Kotler had every reason for *yi'ush* — resignation and despair — when he arrived at these shores during the early years of World War II. All that he had created and nurtured — his yeshivah in Kletsk, his role in Agudath Israel — the society in which he flourished and developed to such greatness — all of this was almost completely destroyed. Nonetheless, he started from scratch and rebuilt on American soil a Torah institution of magnitude and stature that in no way condescended to American conditions. With herculean effort, he reestablished Kletsk, and the Torah society that surrounded it, in Lakewood, in America. We, too, can look back at our own successes, realized in spite of unprecedented hardships. These should serve as an incentive to accomplish even more in the future.

✦ *"Sheleimus": Within our Grasp*

Of the three *Avos*, only Yaakov Avinu has his name associated with the *Beis HaMikdash: Beis Elokei Yaakov.* When Avraham came upon the place of the *Mikdash*, he called it *"har,"* a mountain, seeing it as a height yet to be reached. Yitzchak called it a *"sadeh,"* a field to be developed. Yaakov named it *"bayis,"* house: it was still a mountain to be climbed, a field to be cultivated, yet he envisioned the completed *Beis HaMikdash,* and was not discouraged from striving for the ultimate achievement, from the very outset. We, too, must keep our vision and our hopes on an ideal, even if it seems unattainable at the time. *Sheleimus* can be within our grasp.

It is no simple matter to rise above the spirit of the society we live in, to screen out its subversive influences, to reject its corrosive values. It is not easy to channel energies and devote finances to desperately needy Torah and *tzedakah* causes when the major emphasis today is on spending time and money on self-gratification. But then, Reb Tzaddok HaKohen of Lublin once commented that often when one engages in a number of undertakings, a specific one may prove to be exceptionally difficult as compared to the rest. At first impulse, one might be tempted to drop that one, and concentrate instead on the easier tasks on hand. But it is the most unyielding one that is the most significant one, and that is precisely why it is so heavily invested with obstacles.

This last phase of *galus,* our rehearsal for striving for *sheleimus* from a setting of affluence and freedom in our own land, is fraught with difficulties — difficulties of a sort that we never faced before, in recent history. Responding to the guidance of our Torah leaders, avoiding the pernicious influence of non-Torah values — with determination, enthusiasm, and optimism, we can be equal to the challenge.

When Fashion Is Eloquent, What Does It Say?

Rabbi Nisson Wolpin

→ *The Definitive Illusion*

F ashion is an illusion of sorts. Well-crafted phrases, using emotionally charged words — like artfully shot photographs — play an important part in projecting this illusion. From "dramatic entrance" to "this year's power tie," there is little hard-edged realism in the lexicon of fashion.

One phrase in the dressing-up dictionary, however, does have a degree of integrity to it: "fashion statement." First, and just about always, when someone's clothing reflects the latest trends, it says something about the wearer. He (or she) is willing to spend the extra dollar it takes to look *au currant* ... with it. One should pay attention to the wearer.

In addition, style and quality of clothing testify to an individual's professional standing, as well as his/her place on the social scale or the corporate ladder. There's a whole schedule of do's and don't's, ranging from color and make of fabric to size and style of buttons, which tells all about a person's status to the otherwise uninformed. Clearly, details of fashion do convey a message.

→ *Backdrop to Dignity*

A person's "fashion statement" also transmits another message — not so subtle, yet not always meant to be communicated by the wearer. But first, a step back to the beginnings of it all:

The entire concept of clothing is an after-thought of sorts to man, for until Adam and Chavah ate from the forbidden fruit, they had no need for clothing. From that point on, however, when they became aware of their nakedness, G–d Himself fashioned clothing for them. It was a Divine act of *chesed* through which He "personally" provided their exposed flesh with covering. Perhaps that is why Rabban Yochanan, in the Talmud, referred to his clothing as "*mechabdai* — my source of dignity," a perpetuation of the *chesed* that G–d had extended to the first man.

Using clothing as originally intended can go beyond dignity to *kedushah* — sanctity. And, indeed, when the mitzvah of "*kedoshim tiheyu* — and you shall be holy" was proclaimed in a gathering of the entire Jewish people — men, women and children — there was a message in the format that defined the words: Every Jew has a role, and a responsibility, in exemplifying the distinctive Jewish trait of sanctity ... each one individually, all together in composite, forming a nation of priests, a holy people.

In a conversation with the author, Rabbi Shimon Schwab (K'hal Adath Jeshurun, Manhattan) pointed out the singular opportunities for achieving *kedushah* inherent in judicious dress, especially for women: A person striving for spiritual growth might admire the Kohen, who wears his special *begadim* (raiments) *l'kavod u'l'tiferes* — for honor and glory in service of his Creator. And imagine the special standing of the Kohen Gadol — the High Priest — who had eight special garments, including the *choshen* (breastplate with twelve gems) and *tzitz hazahav* (golden plate on his brow) with G–d's name engraved on it .... By the same token, there are the men's *tefillin* containing sacred parchments, which can endow the wearer with such an aura of G–dliness that "all the nations of the earth will see the Name of G–d hovering over you, and they will be in awe over you." *Is there some way that I, too, can achieve that type of special awe?* asks the spiritually ambitious woman.

In truth, she has her own distinctive approach to this awe. And it is available to her, and only to her, on a constant basis. Not so with the Kohen Gadol, who only wore his garments when serving in the *Beis HaMikdash.* Or the ordinary Kohen, who generally was scheduled to wear his *begadim* on perhaps two days of the year. Not even men: because of their inability to be impeccable in body and pure in thought for any length of time, they generally wear *tefillin* only when they *daven* — a half hour, 40 minutes, or an hour a day.

By contrast, a woman who wears clothing in a manner consistent with *halachah* and in the spirit of *tzenius* (modesty), radiates a *kedushah* that testifies to her fulfillment of her role as a *bas Yisrael.* She inspires respect, and creates a distance from the profane, even as she sits on a bus, works at her desk in her office, pushes the kids in a carriage on the avenue, or otherwise strolls the roads of her life.

Can any man equal that achievement, any day … every day … all day long?

✧ Lost to the Winds of Fashion

Sometimes the sense of dignity meant to be endowed on a person by virtue of his or her clothing, the distinctive aura of sanctity that every Jew carries, is lost, scattered and dispersed by the winds of fashion. This is particularly the case with women — the more fashion-conscious gender, the one more charged with *tzenius.* (According to the *midrash* in *Bereishis,* woman's each and every limb is charged with a command implicit in the source from which she was fashioned, the rib: "As I was discreet, so should you be discreet.")

Thus, feminine followers of the latest fashion fad just might find their choice of clothing making statements on their behalf that they hardly knew existed; that they surely would not identify with, if they only "heard" what their clothing was saying. Fashion designers are not shy about creating clothing that, by virtue of cut, length, color and accentuation, proclaim all sorts of messages — messages regarding attraction as opposed to privacy, promiscuity versus restraint, shouts of "look at me" in contrast to an unequivocal "mind your own business."

In her very touching address at the Felt Forum gathering marking the fiftieth *yahrzeit* of Sarah Schenirer, the late Rebbitzen Vichne Kaplan, founder of the Beth Jacob High School and Seminary in America, commented on how she often had difficulty recognizing young ladies when she met them at weddings just a year after she had taught them in the Seminary. Their highly fashionable manner of dress projected a message that surely did not speak for them. They, in all innocence, were responding to the siren call of fashion, which the designers were issuing in accordance with an agenda all their own … a far cry from what these young ladies would want to say. "Don't let your mode of dress convey ideas so foreign to your true self," she pleaded.

Rebbitzen Kaplan issued this call six years ago. The seasons since then have witnessed a shifting of emphasis and a redefinition of propriety in terms of hemlines, fit, and so on. When clothing makes a "fashion statement," the wearer would do well to bear in mind that it speaks in accordance with the manufacturer's designs, not necessarily those of the purchaser. And all protests to the contrary notwithstanding, the designer has the last word. When choosing to make a fashion statement, one would be well advised to see who is saying what for whom.

Some Thoughts on "Selling" Tzenius

Rabbi Nisson Wolpin

O ne must, at times, object vociferously to *kefirah* — heresy. There may be a place for shouting *"Shabbos!"* at a deliberate violator of the Sabbath in *charedi* Jerusalem neighborhoods. And one might well publicly denounce a purveyor of *tereifah* food under a kosher label. But how does one respond to *pritzus* — brazen violation of basic decency? Is it effective to loudly berate the violators and scream *"Tzenius!"*? Is it *tzenius'dik* — in keeping with the guidelines of modesty — to do so?

This question comes to mind as one encounters incident after incident of people reacting as individuals and as spokesmen for institutions, decrying the lack of decency in the media — both entertainment and informational. Yet crying out "foul!", with elaborate documentation, is not always in full keeping with decency in expression.

The principal of a respected mesivta high school in the New York area contacted *The Jewish Observer* after he had heard Rabbi Shimon Schwab's speech condemning the pernicious influence of television on the Jewish *neshamah*, at a convention of Agudath

Israel of America. He assumed that *The Jewish Observer* would publish the speech and he offered some corroborative material: reprints of various articles decrying the immoral influence of TV and other popular entertainment. This principal has mailed copies of these articles to parents of students that own TV sets, to spell out clearly, candidly, explicitly, the situations, words, and attitudes that their children are exposed to on a daily basis. "You may want to quote them alongside Rav Schwab's article," he offered.

The enclosures were undoubtedly powerful arguments against indiscriminate radio-listening, and even owning TV sets — to those who have them. Maybe the rough language they included have a place in shaking up uninformed or indifferent parents, and alerting them to what their children hear and see. But verbatim quotations — especially on these pages — would surely prove offensive to the unsullied eye or unpolluted ear. To give the reader a very general idea of their content: On the *US News and World Report* editorial page (May 20, 1985), columnist David Gergen calls parents to arms against "X-Rated Records":

> *"We just listen to the beat, never the words,"... insisted [my 14- and 11-year-old kids]. My wife and I backed off for 24 hours and then snuck up from behind: "Have you ever heard of the song _____?" we asked sweetly. Spontaneously, they both broke into the number performed by Frankie Goes to Hollywood, a group that advocates ... [defiant behavior].*
>
> *Some sociologists say the music doesn't make an impression on teenagers. Others think nothing can be done. Nonsense.*

In *Newsweek's* "My Turn" column (Aug. 6, '85), Kandy Stroud quotes generously from the lyrics of what she calls "Pornographic Rock," and reports:

> *... My 13-year-old, rock-crazed son muttered, as he inadvertently tuned [the car radio] to [a] ... loud and crude*

song, "I hate this song." My own Mr. Cool was visibly
embarrassed. Embarrassed? I almost drove off the road.

I confess to being something of a rock freak ... since the
50's ... But innuendo has given way to the overt. And vul-
gar lyrics supported by uncomfortably provocative sound
effects result in musical pornography.

Enough said. Or perhaps too much.

Another angle: *The New York Times* featured an article in its Sunday Business Section (Dec. 6, '91), where Stuart Elliot reports on trends in TV and print advertising, which are progressing from what he terms "naughty" to the "shocking," demonstrating that America is taking its cues from Europe, where attitudes are much more "liberal." "As advertisers push the boundaries to find risks," Elliot says, "some in the industry fear, they risk polluting the entire advertising environment."

Indeed, nowadays, evening, prime-time commercial spots are far more shocking than after-11, "adult" programs were 15 years ago.

If folks think that they can be more relaxed about the content of family shows, or popular film fare, they should subscribe to the National Coalition on Television Violence's *NCTV News*. TV shows, movies, performers, songs, and videos are described and evaluated for unwholesome (a very mild term!) content. In many cases, the mere *descriptions* deserve an "X" rating.

The cautionary note being sounded here, then, is deliberately focused exclusively on descriptions of the offensive material. No direct quotations of the offensive material are offered here. We wish others would follow the same practice. In its full-page ad on the last page of the Finance Section of *The New York Times* (Jan. 7, '92), the *Wall Street Journal* touted its comparatively high standards of decency by reprinting an editorial from the previous December, decrying the sorry state of journalism, exemplified by a front page *Newsday* report on the William Smith case, which had featured verbatim quotes from the trial transcript. Samples from the *Newsday* story were quoted, to demonstrate the *Wall Street Journal's* virtue and discretion ... all on the back page of my *New York Times* (no paragon of discretion either, for that matter). Nothing like screaming expletives to restore a little peace, quiet and decency to the print media.

Perhaps we should not expect too much restraint from secular sources.

But what are we to make of a popular Orthodox rabbi who decided that the best way to campaign for a life of *kedushah* among Jewish singles and adherence to *taharas hamishpachah* in Jewish families is by appearing in a dialogue with "Dr. Ruth" on a public forum? He had wanted his message to be heard — and apparently he calculated correctly, in that they drew an overflow crowd. But he seems to have forgotten that Dr. Ruth's frank, uninhibited talk shows earned her an FCC ruling barring her coarse language and bold clinical discussions from the airwaves. To his credit, the Rabbi did admit to the audience that he could not help but blush at some of the Doctor's declarations, but otherwise he was unrepentant. When one's sensibilities rebel at being affronted with indelicate talk, one would have been well advised to have stayed home, in the first place — and thus to have spared the audience gratuitous exposure to its worse elements, rather than having them serve as an unwitting party (or witness) to a shocking breach of decency. Titillation can fill the bleachers, but it leaves the soul empty.

Tzenius is a very fragile commodity. One can teach it by talking about it. One can imbue people with it through example, by demonstrating it. But one cannot succeed in impressing others with its value by violating it.

Fighting Assimilation From Within

Rabbi Yissocher Frand

✧ *Mitzvah Observance and Evil Conduct: not Mutually Exclusive*

The theme of combating the forces of assimilation carries the implication of "us versus them." Perhaps it would be more accurate to characterize the conflict as "us versus us." This insight was pithily summarized in a comment I once heard from my late *Rosh Yeshivah,* Rabbi Yaakov Yitzchak Ruderman: *Rashi* cites Yaakov Avinu as saying: *"Im Lavan garti, v'taryag mitzvos shamarti v'lo lomadeti mi'maasav hara'im* — I lived with Lavan, I kept the 613 mitzvos, and I didn't learn from his evil deeds." The *Rosh Yeshivah* noted that the assurance that Yaakov learned no evil was not a superfluous statement; apparently one can be a *shomer Torah u'mitzvos,* and nonetheless learn from Lavan's evil ways. Let us see how this *might* describe our contemporary situation:

Without a doubt, my children are receiving a vastly superior education to that which I received in a day school, what with the proliferation of intensive *yeshivos ketanos* and Bais Yaakov schools. One might add, however, that the America I grew up in was safer than the America our children are growing up in. There was a survey done in the 1940's in regard to the discipline problems plaguing America's schools. They were noted in descending order: number one: talking; #2: chewing gum; #3: making noise; #4: getting out of turn in line; #5: wearing improper clothing; #6: not putting paper in the wastebaskets. The same study done in the 1980's, elicited the following list of problems: drug abuse, alcohol abuse, pregnancy, suicide, robbery, and assault. That should be a fair indication of what has happened to America in the last 40 years. The problem underlying all these changes, a leading sociologist wrote, is that America has lost its sense of shame, and people are no longer ashamed of what they do. If one had any doubts regarding this, then the Thomas Supreme Court hearings should have dispelled them. If foul-mouth confessionals can be uttered in our Senate, for men and women and children across the entire country to hear, is there any vestige of shame left in the national psyche?

Many years ago, when Rabbi Yaakov Kamenetsky was in Baltimore, visiting his children for the Succos holiday, a friend invited him to tour Washington, D.C. It was a miserably hot and humid day, and Reb Yaakov took off his *kapotte*. When they came to the gallery of the U.S. Senate, however, Reb Yaakov put his *kapotte* back on. He explained that the Senate represents *"shpitz malchus* — the epitome of sovereignty — of America, and we must respect the dignity of America's sovereignty."… I wonder: After the Thomas hearings, would Reb Yaakov still have put on his *kapotte* to enter the Senate?

✦ Lost: an Innate Sense of Shame

Unfortunately, we are learning from the ways of Lavan, and we, members of *Klal Yisrael*, are losing our sense of *bushah*. This loss should not be underestimated. The *Gemara* (*Yevamos* 69b) identifies the three character traits of *Klal Yisrael* as *rachmanim*, *bayshanim, v'gomlei chassadim* — they are compassionate, they are kind, and they have an innate sense of shame. The Maharal of Prague explains that we have each of these traits as a legacy from the *Avos*: Avraham imbued us with his selfless *chesed*. We are *rachmanim* thanks to Yaakov. It was Yitzchak, who represents *yirah* — awe before G–d, who gave us *bushah*, because the prelude to *yiras Shamayim* is *bushah* — the capacity to know and to feel one's utter insignificance in the presence of a Greater Being. And what is the prerequisite of *bushah*? The first *Rama* in *Shulchan Aruch* tells us that one must feel a sense of *"Shivisi Hashem l'negdi samid* — I picture G–d before me at all times." From that point of awareness, continues the *Rema*, one can embark on one's *avodah*, one's Divine service, "with awe before G–d, and a constant sense of *bushah*." Not only must we be on guard to protect our innate *bushah*, we must be wary of the alternative, which comes in its absence. The alternative? *Azus* — brazenness. And Rabbi Yehudah ben Teima says: *"Az panim l'Gehinnom* — The brazen one is destined for *Gehinnom"* (*Avos* 5:24).

The famed *mussar* personality of the previous generation, Rabbi Elya Lopian, highlighted the extra risk involved in being an *az panim*. He asked, "How can a character trait sentence someone to *Gehinnom*? Can't he recognize his failings and repent?" To which he answered: "It's not that the *az panim cannot* do *tesuvah*. He *won't* do *teshuvah*. In his view, he's always right."

In a society where people lack *bushah*, there is a tremendous amount of *azus*. And when *bushah* is replaced by *azus*, a person feels *I can do whatever I want, I can wear whatever I want, I can transgress any laws I don't agree with*. Anything — and everything — goes. Indeed, the Maharal says that a society without a sense of shame is perforce an immoral society. Its members must sin, because when there are no inhibitions and people are indifferent to society's standards of decency, a person can act on any impulse. Does "a society that can utter anything, write anything, sing anything, wear anything" sound familiar? That is a telling description of Western culture at the end of the 20th century.

Even the non-Jewish world has found the situation catastrophic. To quote the Chaplain of the U.S. Senate:

We demand freedom without restraint, rights without responsibility, choice without consequence, pleasure without pain, in our narcissistic, hedonistic, masochistic, valueless preoccupations. We are becoming a people dominated by lusts, avarice, and greed.

→ *Hitting Home*

The problem of *bushah* leading way to *azus* is cropping up in our sheltered community. There is a crisis in many of our schools, a lack of *derech eretz*. Children are insolent, disrespectful, and cynical — *mevatlim*. In some classes, everyone wants to be the comedian, the "star" that has the one-liner to tell the *rebbe* in front of the class. Schools like these become a *moshav leitzim* rather than a *makom Torah*.

We try to shut out the ubiquitous influence of the marketplace, yet children do pick up this attitude of *azus* — because they often do not have the opportunity to see us acting with *derech eretz*. In earlier, less mobile times, grandparents lived close by. There was a built-in *limud* — a vital object lesson — when a 40-year-old father listened to the *zeide* and the children witnessed that inspiring, instructive lesson in respect for elders. Today the *zeides* are distant and our children do not see us listening to our parents.

Nor do they see us listening to our *Rabbanim, Roshei Yeshivos*, and *Admorim*. Periodically, the *Rabbanim* mount the *bimah* and give us *mussar*, but we don't listen. Do our children hear us say: "We can't do this because the *Rav* told us that we shouldn't"? In many *minyanim*, the *baalei batim* say, "We don't need a *Rav*. I can look up the *halachah* myself, thank you." But we do need a *Rav* if only to enable us to tell a child — "The *Rav* says we must do this … The *Rav* forbids that"… if only to teach our children *derech eretz* by example. A gross manifestation of this loss of *bushah* is that we are suffering in our *middas hatzenius*. The lack of *tzenius* in women's fashion is not only the fault of the women. If a husband expresses disfavor over improper clothing, his wife will probably not want to displease him, and she will not pursue the latest brazen fashion. Dayan Dunner of London tells of a group that had approached Reb Moshe regarding a particular mode of dress. When Reb Moshe answered that it was unequivocally forbidden, they asked, "Why don't you write it in a *kol korei* (public proclamation)?"

Reb Moshe answered, *"Vos zei zogen in Paris iz shtarker fun mein psak* — Edicts from Paris carry more weight than my halachic decision." It is time to stand up and be counted: Who will determine our dress? Reb Moshe Feinstein, or *lehavdil* some decadent designer in Paris?

✢ *Groping for a Sense of Kedushah*

One ramification of our lack of *bushah* is that we are in danger of becoming a *Klal Yisrael* without a sense of *kedushah* — a desire for sanctity. If we cease to be the *am kadosh, perishus* (abstention from excess indulgence) will become a lost art.

The message of *"kedoshim tihiyu"* is: *Abstain.* The late *Mashgiach* of Ner Israel, Rabbi Dovid Kronglas, was keenly aware of the enormous contrast between the spartan *"Europshe"* life and lax American society. To his finely-tuned sense of *perishus*, drinking soda on *Rosh Hashanah* was totally inappropriate. Even ketchup was an indulgence. Trends in our milieu have been in the opposite direction. How far have we strayed from the sensibilities of a Reb Dovid! Indeed, as a community we are wallowing in excesses. Excess in food, cars, houses, home furnishings, vacations, just to name a few.

Unfortunately, should we not be an *am kadosh,* Hashem would not want to dwell in our midst. The Chofetz Chaim, in his introduction to *Sefer Geder Olam,* writes: "The *pasuk* says: '*Ki Hashem Elokecha mis'halech b'kerev machanecha lehatzilcha — v'lo yireh becha ervas davar.* G–d walks within your camp to save you — and He should see nothing shameful in your midst.' By the same token, when there is no *kedushah, hester panim* prevails (G–d conceals His Face from us)."

This comment of the Chofetz Chaim may offer us an insight into the reason that we might suffer *tzaros* when there is no apparent reason for us to be so afflicted. We do not have a *navi* or Kohen (prophet or priest) to explain the causes for our suffering. Yet G–d states clearly that He does not want to walk or remain within *Klal Yisrael* when it lacks *bushah* and a sense of *tzenius.*

So what can we do? Should we throw up our hands and conclude that the situation is hopeless? I suggest perhaps a two point counterattack. Firstly, let us — as Rabbi Mattisyahu Solomon pointed out — take an indelible image from the Gulf War and employ it, at least psychologically: the *cheder atum* — the sealed room. We must create our own *cheder atum* — a spiritual barrier that filters out the poisonous environment that surrounds us. We have to realize that it can be hazardous to breathe the outside air without analyzing its toxic potential.

Secondly, we must depart from our complacent acceptance of the *status quo,* and begin to yearn for the *geulah.* To be sure, these United States are a precious haven for us. My parents, for example, had nowhere to turn when they fled the Nazi onslaught in Frankfurt-am-Main in 1939 — nowhere but this blessed land. The U.S.A., indeed, has been most hospitable, but our true salvation must be one of a spiritual nature. We must feel it and we must crave it, rejecting the brazenness of a shameless, materialistic society. The next time we take *siddur* in hand to daven *Shemoneh Esrei,* and pray for *geulah,* our words should reflect an inner thirst and express our desperate need for the complete spiritual redemption.

The World Around Us: The Risks of Exposure, the Costs of Insularity

Rabbi Levi Yitzchok Horowitz, The Bostoner Rebbe

Fifty years ago we would not dream of discussing insularity versus exposure. We were weak, scared, unsure, ridiculed. Whatever gains we could realize were appreciated, and that closed the discussion. Today we can discuss the topic because we find ourselves strong and secure, with others envious of our position. What should our stance be?

→ The Need for Insularity

Without belaboring the obvious, let us first simply mention the positive advantages of living in that environment which we view as ideal. Only listen to the *pesukim* that trip off our tongues, the words of the *tefillos* that we say:

"A Jew is expected to delve into Torah, day and night." The benefits? "There is no free person, except for one immersed in Torah." And: *"V'nismach* — We will rejoice in the words of Your Torah study." A life of freedom and joy.

Then there are the negative advantages of avoiding the degenerate society of drugs and depravity, self-indulgence and violence, which is an outgrowth of the sense of purposelessness that pervades a life without Torah.

The description of our way of life in contrast to that of people not involved in Torah pursuit, as recounted at the celebration of the *siyum* of a *mesechta* (completion of a tractate of *Gemara*), sums it up well: *Anu ratzim, v'heim ratzim* — We pursue goals of eternity and they pursue goals that are void of meaning.

We make much of our cloistered protected life, but is our world truly insulated — even when not going far beyond our proverbial *daled amos*? Has not, in fact, the outside world penetrated ours? Just as pollutants invade the environment, we too are invaded by the secular world, and, like pollution, we are often totally unaware of it. The minimal exposure we undergo to maintain our financial and social agendas does reduce our isolation, and does take its toll.

For example: the 10-minute *Minchah* break for the busy lawyer is commendable, but … and then there is the speed of the *davening* to get him to his next appointment on time.

How do we handle ourselves during lunchtime — during office parties? As we sip our ginger ale, is there not a *hashpaah* (influence) on our *neshamah* from the surroundings?

Professionals and business executives travel a great deal: Is our behavior on the road, the way we comport ourselves, consistent with Torah standards?

Ignore the realm of earning a living for a moment. What is the nature of our summer vacations? For that matter, what determines our post-*Shabbos* "weekend" activities? As soon as we have made *Havdalah,* do we change instantly, from the Shabbos *Yid* — the *Yid* of *erev* Shabbos — to a *motza'ei* Shabbos mode that ignores the previous 24 hours, slipping into our leisure dress to go out, into another world? Even more important: How do we feel about the change — in which mode are we really more comfortable? Are we Torah-observant Jews who "happen" to be secular professionals for *parnasah* reasons, or do we think of ourselves chiefly as individuals living, accomplishing, and even thriving in the secular world — who also "happen" to be Torah Jews?

Even in ordinary phases of life, we are assaulted by sights and images. The media is truly invasive; one can hardly be insulated once one walks the streets, travels the subways, glances at a newspaper, or listens to a radio. Recently, someone commented that we see more *tumah* (indecent sights) on magazine covers, native dress and joggers in their athletic gear, than our *zeides* saw in an entire lifetime.

Moreover, a subtle, negative fallout of society has crept into our lives. We are virtually contaminated by the social impact of technological advances. The fax, disposable dishes, answering devices, computerized data retrieval have taught us that we need not be patient to see the results of our efforts. As a result, expectations of instantaneous gratification are no longer exclusive to the domain of machines: *If something does not work, throw it out, don't bother fixing it.* This attitude carries over to our personal lives: *If relationships don't work, they too are disposable.* Don't attempt to fix it if you don't see quick results. More frequently than ever before, we respond to crises with, "I have no more patience!" The sad results? A feeling of endless frustration in attempting to cope, adopting the strategies of the non-Jewish world in seeking to find relief through walking away from a problem, and, of course, a high and continuously growing divorce rate.

Do we ever seriously consider using the traditional support systems that we already have in place, such as a *kappit'el Tehillim*, consultation with *daas Torah*, plus a dose of old-fashioned *savlanus* (forbearance)?

✦ How Reasonable Is Insularity?

Our insularity, then, cannot be complete. But is it even a reasonable hope?

In personal terms, we are justifiably concerned about making a living. But how do we keep ourselves insulated and still have a *parnasah*?

Should our wives go to work, and then, amongst other problems, risk exposure to the evils of secular society?

On a communal level, at what point are we obligated to contribute our help to the community in which we live, and at what point must we hold back? At what point should we not even care what is going on?

We must know relevant information to identify with our brothers' plight and suffering ... even if for the purpose of *tefillah*. Total insulation puts one in the position of not knowing how to talk to others, and ultimately, even losing the ability to communicate with Hashem!

Furthermore, many individuals are temperamentally not suited to live a cloistered life. This factor should certainly be taken into account when deciding the direction one's life should take, in calculating the benefits versus the losses. In addition, some people do not have the intellectual capacity for the rigors of Talmudic study, and are ill-placed in conventional institutions of Torah study.

Both cases are included in the *Gemara's* saying: "A thousand enter to study *Chumash* and one emerges as a halachic authority."

Regarding our relationship with the non-Jewish community, even here in the United States, we are still only "tolerated." One must know the enemy. One must know how to protect his own rights.

The best example that comes to mind in this regard is the groundbreaking work done by Agudath Israel offices in New York and in Washington, D.C. How many threatening situations would have gone unnoticed if not for the efforts of those leaders of Agudath Israel? Their eyes and ears help protect the foundations of America's Torah-true Jewish community.

Another reason why we might consider not isolating ourselves within that ideal world is that it would eliminate opportunities for *kiruv*. Some very special souls would be lost, which may outweigh any insular agenda we may have.

How do we bridge the gap between our brethren who are captives in what we see as that strange secular world out there and our own value system — that which we view as the *kedushah* of our own *frum* community?

I would offer the following formula for success: To the extent that we are insular in our *kedushah*, we are effective in bringing

Yiddishkeit to the masses. We make a mistake if we think that we need to be "with it" on every subject in order to be effective in *kiruv*. If we assume that we must be sensitive to every wrinkle in the popular culture, we will sacrifice our *kedushah* and negate what we have to give. To keep up with Hollywood and Dior's latest is not the answer.

Nevertheless, I would suggest that during their years of total immersion in the Torah world, our *bnei Torah* should somehow be prepared to deal with the outside world. And parents should prepare their children concerning the problems they may encounter and how to handle them: in the workplace, as well as in marriage — and, of course, for those who send their children to institutions of higher secular education, in the university.

✛ *Overdoing Insularity*

With all the notes of caution, insularity can be overdone. Do we have the right to "protect" our children from playing with youngsters who are not exactly as *frum* as we are? Should we deprive the "less *frum*" kids of their opportunity of seeing what the other world — our world — is like? How would we feel if our children were rejected by a school that fashions itself to be "only for the learning elite"?

It is precisely the insularity — the ability to see and feel the purity of Torah, the maintaining of a sense of *kedushah,* the separation from the *tumah* all around us — that gives us the understanding that all Jews need. So somehow a balance between risk and preservation of insularity must be found.

This need for balance applies to *hachnasas orchim* (hospitality). This often means inviting college students to the *Shabbos tisch* — which, by the way, may well begin with giving *shalom* to the next person on your bench in *shul,* a part of the mitzvah of welcoming guests that we may overlook. Some frown on the idea of bringing home these students because they do not want their children to hear the "terrible" questions that may be asked. Today's university student, however, does not question to antagonize. He, or she, simply wants to know. If your child cannot hear an innocent question being posed because he is too fragile, then you are remiss in fulfilling your obligations of properly securing your family by preparing them for whatever the future may bring — whether the student guest joins you or not.

A person who has hosted many uninitiated Shabbos guests told me that only twice in 30 years was a subject broached that may have been out of bounds because of the children present. In both cases, his wife simply cut off the discussion by saying, "This topic is not for the Friday night *tisch*."

→ Risking "Out-of-Town"

The members of the Torah world are involved in subject matters of a loftiness that is beyond human comprehension, and a person given to such aspirations feels that this is where he wants to spend his entire life. Those within the walls of the *beis midrash* will naturally look at the outside world where people simply lack understanding of Torah *Yiddishkeit*, as empty of values. This makes it, at times, difficult for an "out-of-town" *kollel* (a denigrating term for those allegedly on a lower *"madreigah"* than the rest of us) to recruit candidates; after all, who wants to go to a desert where even observant Jews are not on the *madreigah* of a *ben Torah*?

> *I recall when, after my chasunah, the call came from Boston for me to return and pick up the mantle of my late father. I wouldn't hear of it. I thought of my feelings a few years earlier, when Reb Feivel Mendlowitz had confronted the four chassidishe bachurim in the beis midrash of Mesivta Torah Vodaath and said to us, "I will tell you what you shall be in the future." When he turned to me, he said, "You, Levi Yitzchok, will be a Rebbe." I dreaded that comment. Me? I'm the last person In the world to fit that position ... and, besides, who wants to go to Boston? I did not want to leave Willamsburg and Torah Vodaath. I wanted to stay in the beis midrash with my chavrusa, the late Reb Moshe Lieberman. I will do something on the side, I thought ... just to survive ... but not leave the Gan Eden in Williamsburg.*

The *Ribbono Shel Olam* had other plans. Of course, one must not take the liberty of making this type of serious decision (which world he belongs in) without consulting a *gadol*, *rebbe* or *rosh yeshivah*. Looking back at my own decision-making process, at the *Ribbono Shel Olam's* hand in the events, and the ultimate results, my youthful assessment of my mission in life was terribly wrong.

When *bnei Torah* do venture out-of-town, they discover wonderful people who are concerned with observance, are anxious to learn, and are genuinely excited about the opportunity to absorb Torah values — yes, at times, more excited than their superiors in knowledge and background.

They come to learn Torah after a hard day's work. They have to deflect the demands of their wives, who become worn down taking care of the children all day, not having grown up with the pride and sense of purpose of *bnos Torah*. Every move they make resonates with *mesiras nefesh*. The *kollel yungerman* out-of-town could well tip his hat to that *am ha'aretz* (ignoramus) sitting across the table, whom he is instructing.

A further fringe benefit that will accrue to the *ben Torah* who finds himself interacting closely with that other world is that he will develop a keener appreciation of who he is and what he is — in stark contrast to the secular world at large. His thrice-daily recitation of *"Aleinu,"* in which he thanks G–d that He has not made us like the other nations of the world, will be infused with a new measure of *kavanah*.

In sum, he has ventured into another world, with different challenges than Lakewood, Telshe, or Brisk. But what is the reward?

Neshamos!

✦ Proceed With Caution

When one makes the ultimate decision to enter the outer world — if one is required, for any reason, to be in that other world — one must know the pitfalls. One must proceed cautiously — at times, reluctantly. You're walking across minefields. Be sure to put on your protective gear, as is stated, "A *tzaddik* with his faith shall live." From a perspective of faith, the situation becomes not strictly secular, but rather a way to serve G–d.

To underscore that other world's need to meet authentic *Yiddishkeit*, as well as *our* need for girding ourselves with Torah as insulation, let me relate some incidents. These incidents should also serve to reinforce my theme that by being more involved in the Torah world, one can more effectively influence those in that other world. There is a special *siyata d'Shemaya* for helping another *Yid* join *Klal Yisrael*.

> *Several years ago a young lady sent me a note, informing me that she had become engaged to a yeshivah fellow in Jerusalem. She added, "I don't know whether you remember me. I observed my first Shabbos in your home. You asked me what I do. My answer was, 'I am a sculptress,' and you said, 'Why don't you sculpt yourself? It is more important than sculpting stone.' Those words started me off on my search for how to 'sculpt myself.'"*

I never met a sculptress before or since. The answer was extemporaneous. But these few — and seemingly Divinely-inspired — words saved a *Yiddishe neshamah*. G–d provides those persons who act *lishmah* — giving up personal gain for the sake of an ideal — with the words, the instruments, to make their endeavors a success.

This is the reason for the success story of our esteemed Reb Aaron Twerski: How many, many *neshamos* did he reach in the dark jungle of the university? This is the remarkable story of my *chassid*, Reb David Gottlieb, a star lecturer and mentor in Ohr Somayach, Jerusalem. What number of individuals did he pull from the depths of that other world, who were totally tuned out from Torah and *Yiddishkeit*?

I do not know to what degree they, and others like them, prepare for their impromptu encounters. They, themselves, are the strongest argument. Their Torah personality is both the medium and the message.

How does one protect oneself through Torah observance?

> *A woman professor of law of our acquaintance favors a*
> *tichel. She despises covering her head with a sheitel, but will*
> *not appear in class without one. In her view, it represents a*
> *greater level of Yiddishkeit than she feels she has attained.*
> *But she wants to make sure she takes the system with her.*
> *The sheitel is her protective "spacesuit" in a hazardous*
> *environment.*

Being recognized easily through dress and behavior as an observant Jew is our greatest protection in hostile surroundings, and at the same time maximizes our message.

> *When I first came to Boston, a prominent attorney told me,*
> *upon my entering his office, "You are a Protestant." After a*
> *pause, he said, "You are protesting the environment."*

Some readers may think, "The *Rebbe* is talking to outreach pioneers; it is *they* who need insulation from that other world — but ME? I live in a *frum* community. My family has not been influenced by that outside world." To you I say, "Think again!"

Yes, the outside world is influencing us — even in our Torah bastions. And we must protest this influence when we see how fashion consciousness impacts on the *frum* society.

We are not talking about being in fashion in our style of dress. We refer here to the fads of status symbols that compel us to feel that "I must send my daughter to the most fashionable seminary, to the camp that is in." "My son must get into the yeshivah that is in vogue." Obviously, one seminary or yeshivah cannot accept everybody, nor is the targeted choice necessarily best suited for each child. We ought not feel "It's the end of the world if our child is not accepted." We are not part of the world of class distinctions out there that's aiming for Harvard, and nothing less will do. Our world is one of striving for Torah. In that other world, if you can't make it, you're out. In our world, if we make it in Torah, in our pursuit of the goal of increased Torah observance, Torah knowledge and *Yiddishkeit* in general, then we are in! But to do so, we must know what our goals are, as well as the best way of reaching them — for ourselves, for our children, for our future.

Let us learn from Avraham Avinu. Just as he made sure that he was standing on safe ground, so to speak, when he went out *"Vayeit oholo* — He secured his own tent,"* and he built an altar. Only then did he call out in G–d's Name and reach out to others, always making sure that he was secure first.

Today our position is more secure. We have arrived! And we are reaching effectively into that other world. But we succeed only because we have our protective spacesuit on.

By the same token, as comfortable and secure as it is to be in our own *daled amos*, our own *kollel* or *chassidishe shtiebel*, are we continuing in following Avraham Avinu's scenario? Are we calling out in the Name of G–d, so that others may hear?

You Can Take It With You

Rabbi Ezriel Tauber,
prepared for publication by Yaakov Astor

✢ *Insularity as a Frame of Mind*

There can hardly be a more crucial topic for us today. How do we protect ourselves from outside influences — as we had for generations past — in a Jewish society that no longer is confined to the ghetto or restricted to the shtetl, living with the technology and communications network that can transmit its messages to our doorstep, into our living rooms? How do we stay insular living amidst a society that prides itself on exposure and openness to all forms of ideology and whim — the good and the bad, not to mention the non-Jewish?

✢ *Costs and Benefits*

My credentials for addressing this topic, I assume, are based on the fact that I — as a businessman and a person involved with *baalei teshuvah* — have had to confront this challenge in my own life. I was not trained to do outreach work with assimilated Jews. Neither was I trained to be a businessman. My entire upbringing — all I knew — before I married was the sheltered, protected environment of Yeshivas Nitra, where I warmed myself with the words of my *rebbe*, Rabbi Michoel Ber Weissmandl. Then I married young and suddenly found myself thrust out of this protected environment, literally on the streets, to make a living, though I knew no English and had neither skills nor money.

It was not easy. I had to work amongst the lowest elements of New York City, confronting challenges never directly addressed in yeshivah. I was smack in the middle of a world I had never been aware of.

In retrospect, I can now see that exposure to that situation has afforded me benefits I cannot deny. If nothing else, my confrontation with questions, never directly addressed in yeshivah, helped me come up with answers that have given me a perspective I have used to inspire assimilated Jews, *baalei teshuvah*, and others I deal with. At the same time, my insular upbringing has given me a basis for dealing with this topic. Moreover, had I not made the effort to maintain that insularity in my own home to this day, I would have been in great danger myself.

Thus the problem: We must maintain insularity, yet, paradoxically at times there are benefits to be gained from exposure to the outside, despite the risks. What are we to do?

Fortunately, the question is not new. In fact, the question was wrestled with by our *Avos* and *Imahos* (Patriarchs and Matriarchs) in the Torah. Indeed, the first recorded marital dispute came about over this issue.

✦ The Yishmael Quandary

And Sarah saw the son of Hagar the Egyptian, whom she had borne to Avraham, mocking. And she said to Avraham, "Send out this bondwoman and her son." And the matter was very difficult in Avraham's eyes (Bereishis 21:9-11).

Avraham and Sarah had a *shalom bayis* problem: what to do with Yishmael. Sarah saw the detrimental influence he was already having on her son, Yitzchak. On a simple level, Avraham empathized with Yishmael, since he was his son, and he worried about the devastating effect banishing him from his house would have.

The Chasam Sofer, though, explains this passage, and in particular Avraham's concern, in a unique way: Avraham was raised in an idol worshiper's house. He was directly exposed to all the repulsiveness of the street as it existed in his day — yet, he made himself into a holy man, into Avraham Avinu. And that, the Chasam Sofer explains, is what he had hoped for Yitzchak. He reasoned that it was not ultimately unhealthy for Yitzchak to grow up with Yishmael. He would become a much stronger person for it, in the end, by overcoming the negative influences.

Sarah disagreed. Philosophically, Avraham's argument had merit. Women, however, have a certain intuition, *binah yeseirah*, in these matters and Sarah's told her to banish Yishmael. The matter was finally decided by Hashem when He told Avraham, "Listen to what she tells you." Sarah was right. Yishmael had to be thrown out.

Seemingly, then, we learn from this that children should be raised in a totally insular atmosphere. Do not expose your house to outside, negative influences. However, this is not necessarily so simple because not 60 years later, another dispute took place which apparently suggests a diametrically opposite approach.

✦ *The Reverse Argument*

Yitzchak and Rivkah had the same argument as Avraham and Sarah, except they reversed roles. Yitzchak grew up in a house of *tzaddikim* and had wanted his house to be totally insular as well. He saw that his son Yaakov was a pure soul and Yitzchak wanted him to stay protected in his tents so he could grow to great spiritual heights. Yaakov should never be exposed to the world.

Eisav, on the other hand, was not the studious type — which was acceptable in Yitzchak's mind because he foresaw Eisav as a brother who would support Yaakov in learning for the rest of his life. Therefore, Yitzchak wanted to give the blessings of material well-being to Eisav.

Rivkah, however, saw it differently. She came from a home similar to the home in which Avraham grew up. She was not deceived by Eisav. She knew that if Yaakov had to depend on Eisav's generosity, he would starve to death.

She therefore wanted the material blessings to go to Yaakov.

Again, Hashem resolved this dispute. Yaakov received the blessings for wealth and business success. Rivkah was right in rejecting Eisav as recipient of the blessings, even though she took a stance in opposition to her husband.

How do we reconcile these contradictory positions?

The answer is that there is no contradiction. Different situations require different approaches. *In our homes, in raising our children, there is no room for a Yishmael.* However, once the child has been raised in an insular environment, there are times when it is possible to say that one may run the risk of exposure.

✦ Zevulun and Yissachar

We Jews cannot help but be high profile. A Jewish businessman usually is the best in his field. A Jewish lawyer usually is the best in his field. A Jewish doctor usually is the best in his field. And, unfortunately, a Jewish criminal is also usually the best in his field. Wherever we are, we have one purpose: to create *kiddush Hashem*. Yes, even a Jewish criminal can cause *kiddush Hashem.*

I have the privilege to speak regularly to a "captive" audience of Jewish prisoners in a high security prison in Upstate New York. Some of them have developed beautifully in the past 3 or 4 years. I tell them, "You are not serving time. You are producing time. You are here for the same purpose I am: to make a *kiddush Hashem*, to sanctify the Name of G-d. You made your mistakes. But do you think you were put in here because your judge was an anti-Semite or your lawyer was incompetent? That's not so. There are many people who did what you did, were brought to trial, and nevertheless got away scot free. You are here," I tell them, "because Hashem sent you here. Therefore, you should find Hashem here. You should find yourself." And many of them do.

We Jews are a high profile people: in businesses, in hospitals, in bankruptcy courts, and in prisons. We cannot avoid it. Yes, Hashem wants us out in the world. The point is, though, that He did not in the final analysis put us there to make money, but to make a *kiddush Hashem* wherever we are. Zevulun was blessed to be a tribe of merchants to work in partnership with the tribe of Yissachar, allowing the latter to remain insular, in a learning environment, for their entire lives. The partnership of Zevulun and Yissachar, however, is not one way. It is not simply that Zevulun makes money, gives a share to Yissachar, and thereby earns a share of his Torah. You do not get Torah for money. It does not make sense to say that Zevulun was designated to operate in the work-world because Hashem has no choice but to use him as a pawn in keeping Yissachar insular. In actuality, Zevulun is out there for a positive reason — because Torah has to be disseminated in the business world. Zevulun is there to make a *kidddush Hashem.*

This is the point: Those of us who are perforce exposed to the outside world should know that we are not there to make money. Money comes from Hashem. We are there to represent *Hashem,* to be *mekadesh Shem Shamayim,* to "sanctify the Name of Heaven."

The reverse is also true. Zevulun's success is dependent on Yissachar's diligence. The Chazon Ish once told one of his *talmidim* to close his *Gemara* and take up full-time efforts to save Jewish souls (*hatzalas nefashos*). This *talmid's chavrusa* asked if he too should do as his friend. "No," the Chazon Ish told him. "Your friend will not be successful without the merit of your learning."

Just as a Zevulun supports Torah by giving his money to Yissachar, so, too, does Yissachar support Zevulun, providing him with the Torah that enables Zevulun to remain a *ben Torah* while he is exposed to the outside world. The reason we merit having Agudath Israel professionals represent us in Washington is because we have people learning in Lakewood. The two go hand in hand — like one army. Yissachar is the general, far from enemy lines; yet his efforts have the broadest ramifications concerning events on the front. Zevulun is the fighting soldier, whose survival and success is ultimately dependent upon the Torah, *tefillos,* and *yiras Shamayim* of the leaders behind the lines, who direct and inspire him.

→ *Jewish Commados in New York City*

Because a person is out in the working world, we need not assume that he is exposed to all things evil. Nor can we say that merely because a person is sequestered inside the house, he or she is not exposed to outside influences. Nowadays, insularity or exposure does not depend exclusively on the physical environment.

Shlomo HaMelech said, *"Kol kevudah bas melech p'nimah —* All the glory of the king's daughter is within." The glory of a Jewish woman is that she is a *tzenua,* she is modest, and does not expose herself to the outside. But today's women assume careers to support their *kollel* husbands in learning. In terms of physical location, these women are not *p'nim,* "inside" — they are *chutz,* "outside." Are we then to surmise that Shlomo HaMelech's teaching is not applicable to today's situation?

The answer is, No. We need not concede one inch of *kol kevudah bas melech p'nimah.* We can endeavor to be just as "inside" as our *bubbies* and *zeides* were, providing we develop a proper approach to true insularity.

Years ago insularity was a matter of physical isolation — there was a literal wall, a tangible town boundary. But today a brick wall does not insulate us. One can live in Meah Shearim, Monsey, or Lakewood, and allow the filth of Times Square to seep into the privacy of one's house — and, moreover, nobody will know. At the same time, the reverse can be true. If "Times Square" can penetrate into a Jewish home — into a Jewish *mikdash me'at* (a miniature sanctuary) — then a *mikdash me'at* can penetrate into Times Square.

I came to this realization through my own experience. I was

raised in a very protected environment, which I attempted to maintain as much as possible. For years, however, I commuted to 47th Street in Manhattan. This involved parking my car on 8th Avenue and walking through several blocks distinguished by their moral depravity, just to get to work. At the same time I realized that after a Shabbos in Monsey, and Sunday immersed in learning and *shiurim*, a person need not feel he is in *chutz* — you can still be immersed in *p'nim*.

When the full impact of this thought struck me, I no longer thought of myself as commuting to work with a defensive attitude. It dawned on me that I and all the busloads of Jews who were arriving from the five boroughs and their environs were zeroing in on "enemy territory." *Davening.* Learning. Acting with integrity. Creating *kiddush Hashem.* We were literally an army of commandos penetrating the forty-ninth level of *tumah* — among the most exposed, defiled sections of New York City. Moreover, for decades we soldiers have been establishing a beachhead. We have been making money to set up yeshivos, Bais Yaakovs, *chesed* organizations, and so on. Our children study in *kollelim* all over the world. This is not just a defensive stance. This is where some of the most pitched battles for the soul of *Klal Yisrael* are being fought.

It is important that this approach is neither misunderstood nor left open for distortion. I do not suggest that a Bais Yaakov girl give up her ideals of being a teacher so that she can have the opportunity to "make a *kiddush Hashem* in Manhattan." Nor am I proposing that a Yissachar should leave the four walls of his physically insular environment to become a Zevulun. But I do believe that those who do find themselves in the working world or who are properly advised to enter a business or profession — for such people, your accomplishments, *your spiritual accomplishments,* can be enormous.

But it all starts in our homes. Our homes must be insulated to the utmost. They must never be permitted to be exposed to any external influences. If the home-front is shored up, then when we venture into the outside world — in whatever field it may be — we need not lose our insularity. We can take our *p'nim* state-of-mind with us wherever we go.

Four months ago, I was part of an Arachim Seminar in Los Angeles. Among the participants was an Israeli couple with several children; the husband's hair, in a pony tail, was longer than his wife's. He also wore the earrings in the family. I recently participated in another Arachim Seminar in Los Angeles, where a woman saw me and excitedly called out my name, "Rabbi Tauber!"

"Do I know you?" I asked.

"Don't you remember me from the last seminar? And that's my husband." I didn't recognize her because her hair was covered, the husband's pony tail and earrings were gone, and the children — who had all since been enrolled in yeshivah — looked more like yeshivah kids.

Do we realize the nature of the times we live in? Do we realize what we can accomplish? And how fast things can be turned around? People claim that the drive for instant gratification is a major problem; at the same time there is also a potential for "instant" *kedushah*.

This is not to say that there are shortcuts. However, a person's outlook can indeed be turned around in an instant: A person can actually feel *p'nim* while he or she is physically *chutz*. But it is a status not easy to create or maintain. In actuality, it may require the willpower, cunning, and ingenuity of a commando. But it is possible to learn very quickly how to accomplish great things in our own small ways.

Everything begins and ends, though, by maintaining our insularity, both in our homes and in our minds. We must have ultimate control over these battlefields. And the momentum of the overall "war effort" may depend on you and your next encounter with the enemy. If you remember that "insularity versus exposure boils down to a state of mind," then you have the ammunition not only to survive the battle, but to make a very real and significant impact on the war effort.

Minimizing the Risks
of Exposure

Rabbi Yisroel Reisman

✦ *Reb Yaakov's Message*

I t was the very last time that I had the privilege of hearing Rabbi Yaakov Kamenetsky speak in Mesivta Torah Vodaath. The gathering was sponsored by Torah Umesorah, for young men who were ready to leave the yeshivah and were willing to consider positions taking jobs in *chinuch* or *rabbanus* out of town. When word got out that Reb Yaakov was going to speak, the *beis hamidrash* quickly filled up with a few hundred *bnei Torah* of all ages, most of whom (myself included) were not contemplating leaving the yeshivah.

Reb Yaakov surveyed the crowd, and then spoke. His words (to the best of my recollection) were brief: "I was told that this would be a gathering of *talmidim* who are ready to leave the yeshivah to earn a livelihood. In fact, I see many *talmidim* who plan to remain in yeshivah. I have prepared an address for those ready to go out into the world; my words should not be heard by those who are not at this stage. Instead, let me tell you a *dvar Torah* on this week's *parshah*. Afterwards, those who are indeed considering leaving yeshivah may accompany me upstairs to a classroom, where we can speak privately."

With these words, RebYaakov conveyed an important message. Torah is a guide to all aspects of a person's life; *ki heim chayeinu.* Yet, just as there are many facets to life, so too are there many facets to Torah. Those facets of Torah that guide a person when he is exposed to the secular society around him are not the same as those that guide a *talmid* through his sheltered years in yeshivah. Nor are the guiding principles of our yeshivah years enough to ensure success when the time comes to leave yeshivah.

✈ *The Torah of Shem and Eiver*

This message is spelled out more clearly in Reb Yaakov's commentary on *parshas Vayeitzei,* in his *sefer, Emes L'Yaakov:* Yaaaov Avinu, still a bachelor at the age of 63, is sent by his father to the house of Lavan to find his *shidduch.* On the way to Lavan's house, Yaakov stops to study at the *beis hamidrash* of Shem and Eiver — and remains there for 14 years! After 63 years of study under the guidance of his father Yitzchak, why did Yaakov see it as imperative for him to delay his marriage by stopping to study under Shem and Eiver?

Here, too, Reb Yaakov explains that there are two aspects to Torah: First is the Torah of the house of Yitzchak, which is geared to the student who has the luxury of living in a sheltered environment, protected by the *koslei beis hamidrash.* After 63 years, Yaakov was leaving this yeshivah to be exposed to the dangers of the house of Lavan. To prepare for this, he needed to master a second aspect of Torah, the Torah of Shem and Eiver. Shem and Eiver had lived among corrupt societies — Shem, during the generation of the Flood, Eiver, during the sinful *Dor Haflagah.* Both survived their exposure to surroundings with their personal integrity intact. Thus, the Torah of Shem and Eiver focuses on withstanding outside influences. For 63 years, Yaakov had no need to study Torah in this way. Upon leaving his father's home, Yaakov knew that he could not expose himself to the pernicious influences of Lavan without proper preparation.

In our yeshivah years, we are fortunate to study the Torah of Yitzchak. We spend these years maturing in a controlled environment. The debased society around us seems distant. It is later, when leaving the *beis hamidrash,* that the Torah of Shem and Eiver must be absorbed. When a *talmid* fails to realize this, he will find himself thrust into a society that is far worse than the house of Lavan; and he will face a challenge for which he is ill-prepared.

In my years in yeshivah, I have seen many *talmidim* come and go. In general, our yeshivah is successful in preparing its *talmidim* for life after *beis hamidrash.* Yet, I often see a talmid who had excelled in the yeshivah, but falters badly when he is no longer sheltered. These *talmidim* may have mastered the Torah of Yitzchak, but have failed in the Torah of Shem and Eiver. I am delighted to note that the reverse is also true. Many *talmidim* who did not stand out during their yeshivah years, nevertheless emerge as outstanding *bnei Torah* after leaving the yeshivah. Their dedication to Torah and Torah values, despite the harsh demands of the business and professional world, is extraordinary. They have mastered the Torah of Shem and Eiver.

This discrepancy has bothered me. Why was it that some *talmidim* fall when exposed to the outside influences, while others thrive despite this exposure?

✦ Dr. Asch's Experiment

A psychologist named Asch conducted an experiment on a college campus, and his results shed light on our question.[1] Dr. Asch called seven students into a classroom and told them that they were the subjects of an experiment. Actually, however, six of the students were planted there; only the seventh student was the subject of the experiment.

On the blackboard, two parallel lines were drawn. One was ten inches long; the other, twelve. The lines were close enough, so that their relative size should have been obvious.

The students were told that this was a test of their percep-

---

1. This experiment is cited, in part, by Rabbi Aryeh Kaplan in *Encounters (Moznaim,* 1990) pp. 69-70.

tion. They were asked to carefully examine the board and then decide which line was longer. The six students who had been planted were asked to answer first. One after another, each stated confidently that the ten-inch line was longer than the twelve-inch line. Then, the seventh student was asked the same question. In 60 percent of the cases, the student would respond that the ten-inch line was longer!

In the other 40 percent of the cases, when the subject would answer that the twelve-inch line was longer, the other six students would argue with him and cajole him to correct his obvious "mistake." Under this pressure, an additional 30 percent would concede that the ten-inch line was indeed longer than the twelve-inch line!

This study revealed that under social pressure, 90 percent of people could be influenced to agree that a ten-inch line is longer than a twelve-inch line! This shows the degree to which a person is influenced by those around him, even in cases where a person has no personal attachment to these people.

Most people are sure that they would not have been fooled (if they had been subject to this test). But is this really so? The subjects of these tests were college students and professors, intelligent people, yet their judgment was easily manipulated by the social pressures of the classroom. It is interesting to note that a few years ago this experiment was replicated in Bais Yaakov Academy in Flatbush. The results were virtually identical to those reported by Dr. Asch.

In fact, we are all subjects of this test — in real life. Every young man or woman who steps out into a secular environment to become part of the workforce is put to this test. People around them will insist that wrong is right, that dark is light and that night is day. The corrupt society tears away at the person, day after day. How can a person resist these pressures?

→ *The Experiment: Part II*

Dr. Asch's experiment was followed up by another, similar experiment. Here, seven students were again called into a classroom and shown the same two lines.

This time, only five students were planted, so that the remaining two students were the subject of the experiment. Here again, the first five students would state with certainty that the ten-inch line was longer than the twelve-inch line. The remaining students were then asked their opinion.

The results of this study are revealing. In this experiment, when an individual answered that the twelve-inch line was longer, he had a second person to back him up. In this case, the individual could not be convinced to change his mind. No amount of ridicule would cause him to waiver from the truth.

This is our answer. A young man or woman who leaves yeshivah must remain attached to his spiritual source in a real and active way. This connection will help him withstand the onslaught of secular values (or anti-values) and moral corruption, which abound in today's business and professional world.

✦ Staying Connected

Over the last 15 years in yeshivah, I have maintained a personal connection with many young men after they've left yeshivah. In analyzing the difference between those who feel that they have retained (or improved on) their spiritual level and those who feel that they have not, one common denominator stands out. Those who remained attached to a source of spirituality are best equipped to handle the challenges they face. This "source" maybe in one of many forms. For some, it is an active attachment to a *rosh yeshivah* or a *chavrusa*. For others, it is the *beis hamidrash* where they *daven* and learn. For some, it is the participation in *Daf Yomi* that gives them this sense of attachment.

Incredible though it may sound, too many *talmidim*-turned-professionals have none of these. Their attachment to their yeshivah is through the checkbook only (if that!); their local *shul* is only a place to catch a *minyan,* a place to which they've developed no attachment; and when I inquire regarding *chavrusos,* they tell me of their impending plans to start a *seder* with a friend. All too often these plans remain pending — on a permanent basis.

→ **The Entropy Principle**

The scientific principle of entropy maintains that a system, when left unguided, will have an "irreversible tendency towards increasing disorder and inertness."[2]

Simply put, this principle states that chaos and disorder are the natural result of any action or reaction. When a windowpane breaks, it does not break into smaller, usable squares of glass. Instead, the window shatters in a chaotic way, creating non-useful slivers of glass. Only when there is a guiding hand that controls the breakup of a pane of glass will it break into smaller and useful fragments. (This is one of the problems that scientists concede regarding their theory of evolution. Big explosions do not leave useful creations. When two cars collide head-on, we do not find that they've melted into a limousine. Only a guiding hand causes a "big bang" to yield a constructive and useful product.)

The entropy principle applies to the spiritual world as well. The Torah often compares life to goodness and death to evil, as in the verse, *"See, I have placed before you today life and goodness, death and evil ... choose life"* (*Devarim* 30:15). Rabbi Yitzchak Hutner explains the analogy of life and death to good and evil.[3] A basic requirement for life is a constant source of sustenance and nourishment, without which life could not continue. This is not true of death. The state of death continues without active involvement from any outside source. This is a passive condition, which requires no guiding hand.

The same is true in regard to good and evil. Like life, goodness must be sustained on a constant basis. Even if one attains a level of righteousness, he cannot expect to remain on that level unless he infuses himself with constant sustenance — no matter what one has already achieved.

Evil, on the other hand, does not require this constant infusion. Evil, like death, is a passive state. When there is no spiritual

---

2. Quoted from RD Encyclopedic Dictionary.

3. *Pachad Yitzchak (Rosh Hashanah #8)*. In establishing this principle, Rabbi Hutner alludes to a question posed by another *gadol*. This appears to be a reference to Rabbi Elchanan Wasserman הי"ד in *Kovetz Maamarim*.

sustenance, when a person ignores his spiritual self, his lifeblood of rectitude slowly seeps away. Entropy has taken hold. It is a natural consequence for the soul to fall into a state of chaos and disorder.

This is the challenge of the *ben Torah* who has embarked on a secular career. He must continue nourishing his soul or he risks losing the achievements of his yeshivah years. Like life itself, spirituality cannot continue without constant sustenance.

Entropy sets in when there is no guiding hand. It is the job of a *ben Torah*-turned-professional to ensure that he continues to control his life, that his spiritual self has guidance and direction. This is achieved by the connection he maintains to a source of spirituality, whether via his *rosh yeshivah*, his *chavrusa* or his local *beis hamidrash*. It is this connection and this connection alone that ensures continued growth in the post-yeshivah years.

✦ *The Kuntzenmachers*

The Vilna Goan spent his later days in his personal *beis hamidrash* in Vilna, in the constant study of Torah. He once asked the famed Dubner Maggid to visit him and offer him words of *mussar* (reproof). Although he was reluctant at first (what *mussar* could one prescribe to the *Gra*?!), the Dubner Maggid accepted the invitation.

When he visited the *Gra*, he said, "Is it a big kuntz[4] to be a Vilna Gaon when you stay locked up in your room, unexposed to outside influences? The simple tailors, butchers and tradesmen of Vilna who are exposed to the compromising values of the world, and nevertheless retain their Jewish identity, they are the true *kuntzenmachers* of Vilna!"

The *Gra* was not impressed. His response was simply, "The Torah does not command Jews to be *kuntzenmachers*."

And yet, our *talmidim* are faced with the formidable task of turning the trick, of being *kuntzenmachers* in a world of values far lower than any the Dubner Maggid could have fancied in the

---

4. *Kuntz* is a Yiddish expression for a trick, used here to refer to an unusual accomplishment. A *kuntzenmacher* (lit. trickster) is a person who can pull off unusual feats.

furthest stretch of his imagination. To maintain a level of spirituality despite the crude society around him, an active Torah connection is needed. For anyone to imagine that he is capable of maintaining his spiritual integrity without great effort is to be self-deceiving.

→ *Too Loosely Affiliated*

A *ben Torah* leaves yeshivah to begin a career. He is being exposed to the secular world for the first time. For many years, he has pursued spiritual delights. He has studied Torah, heard *mussar,* and been involved in his own personal soul-searching. He has excelled in the Torah of Yitzchak. But he has not prepared himself for the transition, for the exposure he is about to endure. What happens when he goes out into the world?

The late Rabbi Shlomo Zalman Braun related an anecdote that reflects the experience of an unprepared *ben Torah.*

> *A farmer had two horses, which he used to pull his wagon and help earn his livelihood. One night a thief stole into his barn to steal the horses. The thief first took one horse, then returned for the other. The farmer was alerted to the noise in the barn, and went out to investigate. He arrived at the barn just as the thief was preparing to steal the second horse.*
>
> *The thief sensed that he was cornered. Thinking quickly, he went into the empty stable where the stolen horse had been, and squatted down on all fours. The farmer entered the barn and discovered, to his amazement, that a man was standing in place of his horse!*
>
> *The farmer asked the man who he was. He was astonished when the man replied that he was actually his faithful horse: "I was an evil person in my previous life. Hashem decreed that I return to this world in a gilgul, as your horse. For many years, I labored for you. Tonight, the heavenly courts decreed that my time was up, that I had redeemed myself; tonight I changed back to Yankel, my human self."*

The farmer was amazed. A miracle had occurred in his own farm! Hadn't his horse changed to this man before his very eyes? The farmer expressed his gratitude to his "horse," even giving him a few dollars with which to begin his new life, and sent him on his way.

The next morning the farmer, still marveling at the miraculous events of the previous night, set out for the market, to purchase a second horse.

The farmer arrived at the market and examined the horses that were available for sale. One horse looked strangely familiar. The farmer checked the horse carefully. Yes, there could be no mistake about it, this was his old horse!

The farmer sighed, and patted the horse on its back. "Oy, Reb Yankel. You're out in the world for one day, un shoin vider a ferd (and you're already back to being a horse)!"

→ The Challenge

Our community can be proud of its yeshivah graduates in all areas of life. We have lawyers, accountants, businessmen and doctors who are true *talmidei chachamim*. We can hold our heads up high.

Yet, we must seek to expand on our success. We must ensure that every one of us retains his spiritual integrity even in post-yeshivah days. This can only be done by keeping that spiritual connection intact, that every *ben Torah* retain his lifeline to his yeshivah days.

This is our challenge.

The Time for Tikkun Has Come. Are We Ready?

Aaron Twerski

The crown jewel of our Torah existence — the family — is undergoing serious stress. The tensions need to be identified and steps have to be taken to reduce them to manageable levels. It is time for serious introspection.

✦ Conflict, Crisis and Confusion

O ur charge is to determine how the Jew can serve as a vehicle for *k'vod Shamayim*, i.e., how our daily lives can enhance respect for G–d and His Torah. It is often instructive to understand a concept from its negation. The clearest and most manifest expression of *chillul k'vod Shamayim* arises when Jews worship idols. Of such magnitude is the sin that a Jew is required to sacrifice his life rather than commit idolatry even under coercion. When the Jewish nation first sought to violate this cardinal sin with the creation of the Golden Calf, the Torah relates that they *"gathered unto Aaron and they said to him, 'Come let us make for us gods that will lead us'"* (*Shemos* 32:1). *Rashi* notes that the Talmud was struck by the term *"yeilchu lefaneinu"* (lit. *they will lead us*). The Hebrew word *"yeilchu"* is plural. The request should have been for a singular god that would replace Moshe Rabbeinu. The Talmud explains that the Jews sought not one, but many gods: *"Elohus harbei evu lohem."*

Why a multiplicity of gods? Upon reflection, one can discern a profound lesson about Jews: We either worship one G–d and fulfill His will, or we are pulled in a multiplicity of directions. One source of idolatry will not suffice.

The lesson is clear. When we suffer *pizur hanefesh*, when we are torn in many different directions, it is a sign of deep and serious trouble. A Torah Jew's life must be focused. It must reflect the unity that inheres in the service of One G–d. When we sense that we owe allegiance to a multiplicity of goals, it is time to step back and ask ourselves: Are we still loyal to Hashem and His Torah or do our conflicted lives give evidence of a deep internal division that is inconsistent with the basic tenets of our faith? My own sense is that we are the most stressed-out generation of American Jews in recent memory. Internal stress, conflict and confusion of purpose have become staples of our daily existence. It has begun taking a serious toll on our mental health and that of our children.

I cannot claim to have conducted a scientific inquiry but anecdotal evidence provides more than a little support for my thesis. For example, discussions with those knowledgeable about the sale and dispensing of pharmaceuticals in areas of heavy *frum* population concentration in New York reveal that prescriptions for tranquilizers, anti-depressants and a whole range of soporifics are higher than they should be. Psychologists, mental-health therapists and social workers confirm this observation. It is not that these drugs are being needlessly dispensed; rather the need for them has escalated.

Perhaps even more disturbing are the observations of professional educators. I have heard from several principals and *menhalim*, as well as a random selection of *rebbes* and teachers. They all perceive a decline in performance of entering classes in the past several years. They find more children that are distracted and not able to focus as well as compared to previous years. In some schools, gross academic benchmarks confirm the learned intuition of the professionals. Most of these sources admit to being genuinely puzzled as to why the changes are occurring, but there is little disagreement that something is amiss.

I am neither a sociologist nor a psychologist. My analysis need be taken with a grain of salt. I would be remiss, however, if I did not share with you insights gained from discussions over the past several years with a broad range of people from all spectra of the Torah community.

✦ Those Who Make It, Those Who Don't, and Those Who Make it and Don't

Earning a livelihood has been the topic of considerable discussion and concern to us. It is not merely a societal problem that is tangential to living in a Torah community. The mounting costs of yeshivah education for large families present awesome and often crushing burdens on parents. Concomitantly, inadequate salaries for *mechanchim* and burgeoning class size compromise the ability of teachers to teach with peace of mind and the potential of children to learn in an atmosphere where they are not lost in the crowd.

A sophisticated readership does not need to be told that these are not merely a desideratum which can be wished away. They are matters the *Shulchan Aruch* addresses. They are tied to inexorable halachic imperatives. How does our community cope with these responsibilities? For the sake of simplicity, I will break down our community into three groups. Each is faced with stress that takes its special toll in a Torah-centered community. The wealthy or the "have's," for the most part, meet their financial obligations to family and community with relative ease. Our community, however, has almost no old-line families of wealth.

We are a post-holocaust community. We have no analogues to the Rothschilds, Fords or Kennedys. Our wealth is mostly first- and at best second-generational. It is heavily entrepreneurial. It is thin, fragile and tenuous. There is little margin for comfort.

A second category of well-to-do are professionals who have been highly successful. Once again, these are self-made persons whose income is almost solely dependent on their outstanding individual skills and continuing performance, which is highly demanding both intellectually and emotionally.

Our "have's" are for the most part extremely stressed out. They keep long and grueling hours at work. When they return home, they cannot shuck their worries and responsibilities and park them at the door. The tension level in the home is often extraordinary. Faced with large families and community demands on their time, many of them do not cope well. What passes for communication with children is often polite banter but no real talk. The family is often an unwelcome distraction from what has become an all-consuming involvement with business and profession. Their personal commitments to Torah learning and spiritual growth are sorely tested, and they find themselves torn between unyielding demands on their time and energy. It is little wonder that they swallow tranquilizers and that their children appear more distracted and unfocused than yesteryear.

Even more distressing is the lot of our so called "middle class." I have dubbed this group as "Those That Make It and Don't." This hardworking middle class may be earning anywhere between $50,000-$85,000 per year (either single- or two-income earners). With large families and multiple tuitions, however, these families are choking. They may be in the top 10 percent of American wage earners. Bill Clinton may think they are doing well, but the reality is that the financial pressures are almost unbearable. As the children become older, each family begins facing the day when they will begin marrying off their children. And they often do not have the foggiest notion of how they are going to manage the expenses of a *chasunah, matanos,* let alone the desire and need to help the children in the early years of *kollel* life. They can barely make it through the month — without facing extraordinary expenses. Something has to give, and it does. The tensions of debt, feelings of inadequacy, and social pressures to earn more and work yet harder take their toll.

Recently, a father who fits the above paradigm was chatting with me. He said, "Please, don't take this the wrong way. But, you know, I have days when I'm envious of my Italian neighbor who earns $500 per week. He comes home to his 1.8 children and his wife, and he is a hero. The children attend public school. He lives modestly, and he fulfills all his obligations to society. I earn three times that and I'm a bum. I'm a bum for the tuition committee, an inadequate wage earner for my wife and children, and am slightly above the status of a schnorrer in the community. And now when I think of marrying off my children in the next 10 years — I have nothing but nightmares."

It will not surprise you to learn that this fine *ben Torah* is on anti-depressants and tranquilizers. He has richly earned the right to them. And if the younger children of such folk begin demonstrating diminished performance in school, it is no mystery as to why.

Finally, we have those who do not make it. They are at least spared the agony of unrealizable expectations. Unless they have some special status in the community as that of an outstanding *talmid chacham,* however, they face the ignominy of poverty. The simple truth is that we are wont to place the "have-not's" in the *schlemazel* category. Stratification based on wealth is pernicious and sinful. It is totally foreign to Torah values. But I have heard all too many times about one or another that *ehr iz nisht kein balabatisher yungerman.* Badges of shame are not worn without cost. They too contribute to the never-ending cycle of depression and feelings of worthlessness. Children whose pride as members of a family so tarnished cannot always be expected to easily don the requisite pride so necessary to a healthy ego and to strong scholastic performance.

It is not my intent to proclaim that we live in a state of disaster. The values and beauty of Torah homes provide a multitude of strengths to deal with these problems. We have a deep heritage for survival under adversity and it serves us well. If we seek to ameliorate and correct problems, however, they must be sharply stated. Overstatement is not warranted, but understatement would lull us into inaction. And act we must.

✧ The Social Calendar

If our mental diversion and inattention at home were not sufficient, we have an added dimension that impacts upon our family life. We are all too often physically absent from home. Our social calendars have become so crowded that we have come to dread our social obligations. Several weeks ago, I attended a funeral, ר"ל, one morning. A relative whom I encountered told me that after the funeral he had to attend a *bris,* to be followed on the same day by a *tennayim,* a wedding and a *Sheva Berachos.* Although this is unusual for one day, it is not unusual at all to be booked solid night after night for weddings, bar mitzvas, engagements, parlor meetings, PTA's, *tzedakah* parties, lectures, etc.

A principal of a fine yeshivah recently told me that the two months of the year that are the most tense for students are the very months when parents are absent from home almost every night. January and June are examination months. They are also the prime wedding season. For many of us, however, the phenomenon is not limited to two months of the year. It has become a staple of our lives. We are just way too busy and distracted. There is too much electricity coming over the wires. If we are not careful, we shall give birth to a new generation of latchkey children. Parents should be home for them when they come home. But, if parents must leave night after night to fulfill social obligations, the children will be sorely neglected. The constant tension of having to leave by a certain time, dressing for the event, rushing homework and supper, all exact real costs.

We need more quiet in our lives. We need it for ourselves and we need it for our children. We need to be at home both physically and mentally more, a lot more, than we are at present. Are there practical steps that can be taken to reduce the psychic drain that has become the bane of our existence? To this challenging question I now turn our attention.

→ *Some Modest and Not-So-Modest Proposals for Change*

Before offering any suggestions for reducing the tension, a disclaimer is in order. My proposals will not deal with the issues of *parnasah* in general or the problems of increasing the earning power of members of our community. That is a topic worthy of serious discussion, in and of itself. But the problems outlined above will not be alleviated by marginal increases in wealth. And truly significant increases in earning power are not in the offing. We cannot and should not expect to produce a middle class with an average earning power of $150,000 per year.

What can be done is to find ways to reduce expenditures. We have established that one area that cannot be cut is tuition. We are already operating our yeshivos on shoestring budgets. General modesty in lifestyle is certainly to be encouraged. But, to be fair to our middle class, the general lifestyle is relatively modest. The cost of housing is determined by the market. Unless we are to open up broad new neighborhoods in areas where housing costs are demonstrably less, we face fairly stable fixed costs. One area of our lifestyle must, however, undergo serious reevaluation. The cost of *simchos* of all kinds must undergo sharp and significant downsizing.

The reasons are many. First, it is the one area of our lives where we can realize significant savings without impinging on basic lifestyle. Second, with the increased size of *frum* families, the total financial and psychic burden is crushing both for those who make the *simchos* and for family and friends who participate in them. Third, we can no longer close our eyes to the opulent Jewish *simchos* that constitute such obvious conspicuous consumption that they disgrace us all.

• Bar mitzvas are a good place to start. There is no reason that bar mitzvas should not be limited to close immediate family. For the most part, they can be done at home. Where that is impossible, a small *shul* hall will do just fine. For *Kiddush* in *shul*, a *l'chaim* is quite sufficient. Several *chassidishe* communities have mandated such *takanos* (ordinances). They work beautifully. The entire cost is in the $1,000 range.

• The entire constellation of *simchos* attendant to marrying off a child needs serious restructuring. *Tennayim* should be done at home.

Formal parties, from *l'chaim* to *vort* to actual *tennayim*, constitute a huge financial drain. They are purely an American invention. In pre-war Europe they were unheard of.

• We must find ways to drastically cut the cost of the *chasunah* night itself. Unless tough *takanos* are put in place, we are bound to continue the present system. We invite many friends and relatives because we are obliged to do so. They are obliged to come because they have no alternative. The invitors would be happy to forgo the formal full *suedah* invitation because they are unable to afford the cost. The invitees would be pleased to forgo attending the entire *seudah* because the cost of the present and the babysitter amount easily to $100 for the evening. Both would be happier with an invitation to *simchas chasan v'kallah*. Without formal and binding limitations, however, a sense of obligation mandates that the invitations be made and be accepted.

With burgeoning family size, *b'li ayin hara*, invitations to even immediate family can take on sizable proportions. For some families, married first and second cousins number in the hundreds. Once again without some formal limitations, cutting costs without creating conflicts simply cannot be done.

• The cost of *Sheva Berachos* needs to be sharply diminished. Catered meals on four or five successive nights can run anywhere from $4,000 to $10,000 for the week — excluding Shabbos. It would be quite sufficient to have the *chasan* and *kallah* and parents for dinner and invite a small group of friends for *Bircas HaMazon*.

Takanos with teeth could reduce expenditures enormously. Savings in the magnitude of $20,000 and more per wedding event — i.e. *tennayim, chasunah, Sheva Berachos* — are easily realizable. For families with eight to ten children the total amount saved is staggering. Include the debt service on borrowed money to fund these affairs, and the savings are even more impressive. Finally, consider the psychic toll on parents who are saddled with debt — and the human toll of friends and relatives who look bleary-eyed after a week of mandatory attendance at *Sheva Berachos*. We really must rein ourselves in.

• The need for *takanos* extends to *seudos* of *bris milah, pidyon haben* — indeed, to all *simchos* that are part of the ordinary Jewish life cycle. Putting this entire aspect of our lifestyle in order will, when added together, have a significant impact on the quality of life for all of us. Modesty, true *tzenius*, could become fashionable.

✦ *"But I Really Can Afford It"*

Whenever the issue of *takanos* is raised we hear a hue and cry from some quarters. *Why should we have to restrict ourselves from more lavish simchos if we can afford them? Let the rich make opulent simchos. And let the others scale down in accordance with their abilities.* Many people of substantial means strongly support the institution of *takanos*; however, the argument on the part of the naysayers is stated so frequently and with such vehemence that it needs rebuttal. The primary source of the rebuttal come from *divrei Chazal*. The Talmud (*Moed Katan* 27a-b) relates:

> Formerly, it was the practice to convey food to the house of mourning, the rich in silver and gold baskets and the poor in baskets of willow twigs, and the poor felt shamed; they [*Chazal*] instituted that all should convey food in baskets of willow twigs to uphold the honor of the poor ....
>
> Formerly, it was the practice to bring out the rich for burial on a *dargesh*, i.e., an ornamental bed, and the poor in a plain box, and the poor felt shamed; they [*Chazal*] instituted that all should be brought out in a plain box to uphold the honor of the poor .... Formerly, the expense of taking the dead out to burial fell harder on the next of kin than his death so that the dead man's next of kin abandoned him and fled, until Rabban Gamliel came forward, disregarded his own dignity, and was brought out to his own burial dressed in simple flaxen clothes.

On a similar note, the Mishnah (*Taanis* 26b) relates:

> Rabban Shimon ben Gamliel said: "Israel had no days
> as festive as the fifteenth of Av and Yom Kippur when
> the maidens of Jerusalem would go out dressed in
> white garments that were borrowed so as not to
> embarrass one who had none."

As the Talmud relates, on these days *shidduchim* were made.
And *Rashi* notes that the wealthy maidens were forbidden to
wear their own clothing, lest they embarrass girls from poor
families who had no suitable garments of their own.

Takanos of this sort have a long and honored tradition in
Jewish life. The famed *Vaad LeArba HaAratzos* established standards for *simchos* of all kind. The well-to-do simply had to conform for the greater need of the *klal*. To allow for discretion leads
us to where we are today. The slope is far too slippery. The pressure to conform to the more honored status is too great for mor-
tals to resist. It is interesting that today when we see an elaborate non-Jewish funeral cortege, we react: "That's so goyish!" It
was once very Jewish. No longer. When non-Jews look at our
elaborate weddings they say: "That's so Jewish!" Enough. We
need to embrace the *"hatzne'a leches im Hashem Elokecha,"* and
declare it to be the norm for Jewish life.

✦ Are We Prepared to Listen?

The issue of *takanos* for *simchos* has been on the agenda of the
American Torah community for many years. Most recognize
that they are an absolute necessity. Why have they not been
mandated? Some point the finger of blame at the *gedolei Torah*
for not *sua sponte* issuing a proclamation setting forth the standards. I place the blame on ourselves. Until recently, I believe we
were not ready to listen. And our leaders for good and plenty
reason did not wish to issue decrees that would be honored
mostly in the breach.

But, why have we not been ready to listen? Why have the
gedolim been so reticent to take us on? My own sense is that they

sense in us a cynicism incompatible with the kind of *emunas chachamim* necessary for a true allegiance to Torah. On matters that affect our lifestyle, too many of us are quick to question every perceived inconsistency that may appear to arise, and charge hypocrisy to salve our own sense of guilt.

When I was a youngster, my father constantly cautioned me against falling prey to cynicism. On numerous occasions he told me that when our Matriarch Sarah banished Yishmael from the house of Avraham, her predicate for doing so was that in her view Yishmael was the quintessential cynic. My father interpreted the *pasuk* in *Bereishis* (21:9): "And Sarah saw Yishmael the son of Hagar HaMitzris who was born to Avraham *metzacheik*"—to mean that she saw him scoffing. Sarah concluded that she could not raise her son Yitzchak in an atmosphere where everything sacred was subject to daily cynicism. It was destructive and antithetical to fundamental Torah values.

There is a famous Yiddish saying: *Azoi vee es kristelt zich azoi yiddilt zich.* Loosely translated, it means that Jews pick up quickly on non-Jewish attitudes and traits. The cynicism of the non-Jewish world has spilled over to the Torah world. And our generation has developed cynicism into a fine art. Ours is a generation without heroes. We are far too ready to take cheap shots at Torah leaders and to disregard their edicts. If they are on occasion silent or their words are muted, it is because they realize that we may well treat their pronouncements with disdain. The dictum of *Chazal,* "*K'shem she'mitzvah lomar davar hanishma, kach mitzvah shelo lomar davar she'eino nishma* — Just as there is a mitzvah to speak when one will be listened to, so is there a mitzvah not to speak when one's words will be disregarded," must be taken into account. If we truly want direction from *gedolei Yisrael* on the subject of *takanos,* we will have to communicate to them that we are prepared to put our scoffing aside and abide by their decision.

Purging ourselves of cynicism would do wonders for us all. Let me share a very moving story with you:

> Reb Chaim Tchernovitzer, the author of the Sidduro Shel
> Shabbos and the Be'er Mayim Chaim, was one of the great

chassidic masters. Reb Chaim's kedushah on Shabbos was beyond human comprehension. It was said that from the time he left the mikvah erev Shabbos until the conclusion of Shabbos, he stood a head taller than he was on a regular weekday.

In the city of Mosov lived a famous scoffer — "Hershel Mosover." He was blessed with a fine mind and an acid tongue that he used to heap scorn on all that was holy. He was most entertaining and whenever he would take up residence in the marketplace, he would be quickly surrounded by idle folk who would enjoy his repertoire of fun-making and cynicism. No one and no subject was off limits to him. He was prepared, if the spirit moved him, to poke fun at the greatest of the great and holiest of the holy.

Hershel Mosover was a businessman and his travels once brought him to Tchernovitz. As was his custom, he went to the marketplace and before doing business he was quickly surrounded by people seeking to enjoy themselves at the expense of others. On that day, Reb Chaim set out to collect tzedakah from the businessmen in the marketplace.

From afar Reb Chaim noticed Hershel Mosover and decided to avoid him. Why present Hershel with yet another opportunity to scoff at the Rav of the town? But Reb Chaim came into Hershel Mosover's line of vision. Hershel called out gruffly, "Rebbe, kumt aher!" (Rebbe, come, here!) Reb Chaim disregarded the call, but Hershel would have none of it. "Rebbe kumt aher!"

Seeking to avoid a scene, Reb Chaim walked over to him. "Rebbe, what are you doing here?" Reb Chaim answered softly that he was out collecting money to redeem a family that had been thrown into prison by the poretz (nobleman) of the town for non-payment of rent for a long period of time. The family was starving and freezing in the cold, wet dungeon. Hershel Mosover asked, "Rebbe, how much money do you need?" Reb Chaim responded, "I need 1500 guilden."

Hershel opened his purse and emptied it of its contents — 1500 guilden, a fortune of money. Everyone was waiting for Hershel Mosover to snatch the money back and make a joke out of the whole matter. A minute passed in silence. And then another. Finally, Reb Chaim turned to Hershel and said, "Hershel, how should I bless you? — May you henceforth taste the true flavor of Shabbos!"

Hershel returned home to Mosov penniless. At first he was ashamed to admit to his wife and children that he had squandered his fortune. Ultimately the story came out. The anger of his family knew no bounds, but what were they to do? The deed was done. Hershel returned to his place of honor in the marketplace of Mosov and resorted to his old ways. Things continued normally until Thursday afternoon. Hershel began feeling unwell. He went home and tried to lie down but rest eluded him. Shortly, he was up and about, dancing and clapping, "Shabbos, Shabbos, Shabbos." Friday his ecstasy increased. He had to be peeled off the wall. Shabbos itself was beyond relief. He could find no rest, dancing and singing, "Shabbos, Shabbos, Shabbos." And then Shabbos passed.

Sunday morning, the old Hershel was back to himself. But when Thursday arrived, the scenario of the past week repeated itself. Several weeks followed this sequence. His family then learned from him of Reb Chaim's berachah. They decided that they would have to accompany their father to Tchernovitz and seek the recision of the berachah so that their father could exist as a normal human being.

When they came to Tchernovitz and made their request, Reb Chaim told them that it was not possible to rescind the berachah, but he could make it possible for Hershel to withstand the kedushah of Shabbos kodesh: "Leave him with me for a while and you will see that he will be fine."

Hershel stayed on with Reb Chaim and became his disciple. When he eventually returned to Mosov, he was no longer the same Hershel. So lofty had he grown in avodas Hashem that chassidim who could not make the trip to Tchernovitz would travel to the Rebbe Reb Hershel of Mosov to experience the kedushah of Shabbos that one felt in the presence of Reb Chaim Tchernovitzer.

For one moment in his life, a scoffer put cynicism aside. He was able to act with the compassion of a *Yid*, and became an *ish kadosh*. If we can put aside the cynical attitude that so pervades society and listen with open ears and even more open hearts, we can realize real change in our lives. If we insist on placing our own imprimatur on the *takanos* — if we first ask, *"Ma kasuv bo?"* — we shall never receive the direction we so sorely need.

The time for action and acceptance has come. We must — if we are to survive, both spiritually and physically — reorder our lives. *Takanos* are not a panacea. But they are an important start. And we must begin somewhere.

Where Are We Heading?

Rabbi Aaron Brafman

→ *Our Latest Encounters With Western Culture*

K lal Yisrael's situation in galus America, as the
epitome of current Western culture, is unique in the
annals of Jewish History. All opportunities to do
whatever we desire, and to be whatever we wish to be, are
open to us. Yet, tragically, what Western society stands for
and has to offer us is Nothing. Nothing matters. Nothing
has real value. Nothing has eternal significance.

Never before did we confront a society that stood for
nothing. There were always either idols or ideals; but at least
something mattered. This has devastating implications, as we
will explain.

I. The Demise of Humanism and the Rise of "Nothingness"

The Vilna Gaon writes that the last *avodah zarah* (form of idolatry) will be the worship of man. This was always understood as

a reference to the movement of Humanism, in which man worshiped his intellect, and felt that his reason reigns supreme and could be the arbiter of all decisions of good or evil.

This has deteriorated in the last several decades to the worship of man, not as an intellectual being, but man as animal. Thus entertainment world luminaries as well as sports and other media heroes — the ones who both reflect and define our culture — are progressively more animal-like in their conduct. Immoral or degenerate behavior has become constantly more idealized. Thus the increase in concern for animals, and decrease in concern for humans.

Those of us who attempt to insulate ourselves from popular culture are also subject to the pressure it exudes. Even for such cloistered individuals and families, then, it is important to recognize the nature of the evil that threatens us, as the *Chovos HaLevavos* writes in *Shaar Yichud HaMa'aseh*:

> The chasid told his *talmidim*, "Learn to identify the threat of evil so you can recognize it and distance yourself from it."
>
> [The *Chovos HaLevavos* proceeds to cite proofs to this approach from the *Gemara*. He also writes,] "Only one who is aware of the forces that lay ruin to the good can protect himself from them."

No, we do not want to excessively examine forces of evil or become immersed in them, but we must be aware of what threatens us, to enable ourselves to better defend ourselves and our children from its effects. In addition, those of us who neither go to movies nor have a television or a VCR in our homes are still keenly aware of the trends in the entertainment and information media. Unfortunately, just by driving or walking through our neighborhood streets, or occasionally turning on a radio, thumbing through a newspaper, or even just going to a toy store for a gift, makes one aware of what is going on.

For example, we have gone beyond human heroes to computer-generated animated characters as heroes or heroines.

Some recent movies are of this genre. Thus, we have progressed from heroes who are humans-with-animal qualities to exemplars of Nothingness.

The impact of make-believe in this new world of virtual reality is beyond that of even the old make-believe of Hollywood.

• It is certainly noteworthy that murders are being committed by ever younger perpetrators, and that one continues to hear shocking stores of teenagers killing their babies. Underneath it all is a subculture that has no concern or value for human life. The increase of violence in life and in entertainment is in part due to the meaninglessness that certain trends in society place on everything except immediate self-indulgence and gratification.

Hence the screaming music, which is the defining medium of this subculture, throbs with meanness and resonates with meaninglessness.

• McDonalds had planned to run a special promotion featuring animated characters from a popular movie for children, but had to cancel the promotion because of the violence of the movie.

• The response by public officials to the violence in schools — to spend more money on security devices — would be laughable if it were not so serious an issue.

• There was a time when, generally speaking, ideas carried more weight, philosophers and political scientists had universal impact, and serious intellectual discussion pervaded the upper echelons of society. We, as Torah Jews, had to counter challenging ideas with intellectual responses. Thus our bookshelves are heavy with many philosophical *sefarim* from the Rambam's *Moreh Nevuchim* to the many writings of Rabbi Samson Raphael Hirsch. This is no longer as broadly relevant as it was in the past. What is attracting much of today's youth away from our noble heritage is not so much a fresh idea, or a new guru or philosopher, as the cult of Nothingness — a siren call that says enjoy yourself and do whatever you want. Even vestigial puritan instincts to save money and postpone gratification have become transformed. Nowadays, people invest in eventually realizing enhanced power, or experiencing new frontiers in pleasure, through their expanded wealth.

To counter this pervasive pitfall requires a different defense and strategy. We must seek to be able to point out the ultimate emptiness of this culture and the self-destruction awaiting those who pursue it. We must create an environment in our homes endowed with holiness and meaning. And above all, we must permeate our homes with the *simchah* — the joy — of living a Torah life. Which bring us to a different aspect of contemporary culture.

II. The Family Under Attack

One of the vital institutions in the preservation of *Klal Yisrael,* along with the *batei knessios* and *batei midrashim,* is the family. Just as the *Shechinah* (Divine Presence) rests in the *mikdash me'at* (miniature sanctuary), so too is it present in the ideal home. Thus the family is far more than a grouping for social convenience, which can be altered at will, but rather a unit of great spiritual significance.

> In *parshas Vayishlach,* the Torah describes the pivotal meeting of Yaakov and Eisav, which entails the blueprint (as *Chazal* explain) of our current *galus* experience: When Yaakov encounters Eisav, he finds him accompanied by four hundred heads of battalions. Eisav, as a symbol of Western civilization, is represented by an army. Eisav looks at Yaakov's camp and exclaims, "What are these women and children to you?" (*Bereishis* 33:5).
> He sees Yaakov's family.

Today, our family is our primary defense against the more aggressive forces of Western culture. It is under siege like never before, and on many levels.

On the obvious level, the entire institution of marriage is under attack, with even the New York City government recognizing non-traditional "family" arrangements. But on a more fundamental level, the role of women is being radically changed.

✣ The Changing Status of Women

The feminist movement until now focused on achieving equality between women and men in the workplace. In the process, women developed into self-centered takers, from having been altruistic givers — which in Rabbi E.E. Dessler's treatise on *chesed* (*Michtav MeEliyahu* I) is considered the highest level of human behavior, because one is then acting in the same model as *HaKadosh Baruch Hu*, the ultimate Giver.

A July 10th front-page article in *The New York Times* reported a troubling trend — the progressively lowering birth rate in Europe:

> "There is no longer a single country in Europe where people are having enough children to replace themselves when they die." One after another, the women interviewed gave as their reason for not having children lack of time or interest. "Despite the fact that she lives in Sweden, which provides more support for women who want families than any other country, Ms. ____ doesn't see how she can possibly make room in her life for babies. Ms. ____ would never consider herself a radical, but she has become a cadre in one of the fundamental social revolutions of the century." Even those who take exception to this trend are only concerned in a self-centered way; they fear they will find themselves in lopsided societies with too few young people to sustain the old population.

This shortsighted, self-centered lifestyle will result in an aging, bitter society peopled with desperate, lonely people. But right now this seems to be the dominant wave of the present. Thus the increase in abortion and the unwillingness to have children, if they are "in my way as I climb the professional ladder."

How different this is from the Torah view, where we see (or should see) in addition to the mitzvah imperative, the potential of bringing a *tzaddik* or *tzidkanis* into the world, or an *adam gadol* who will inspire others. (See *Rashi* in *parshas Balak* 24:3: "*HaKadosh Baruch Hu* waits to see which seed will be the one to develop into the *tzaddik*.")

But we have reached a new nadir — not only are women portrayed in current fiction as self-centered and in immoral situations, they are depicted as mean, aggressive and increasingly more violent. The calloused, aggressive feminine executive or lawyer, and the female killer, soldier, or cop is frequently the heroine in current movie and television fare. This is a basic change and fundamental challenge that eats away at the core of society's essential humanity. And we are not impervious to it. Perhaps this is a factor in why the statistics of dropouts among religious teenage girls matches that of the boys. For if we listen to the usual litany of complaints lodged against yeshivos, given as the reason for the yeshivah dropouts, almost none apply to the girls' schools.

While it has become fashionable to make the yeshivos and *rebbe'im* the whipping boys for the increasing rate of dropouts, they are by no means the primary source of the problem. Other sources lie in two area: failure of the family, and the pull of the street society. The dropout problem cuts across all communities and all *frumkeit* levels, and while some of the problems may be due to increased standards of both learning and *frumkeit* in the yeshivos, these play a secondary role at best.

The consensus of professional and lay-activists working with at-risk teenagers and dropouts, has been that the overwhelming majority of their clients come from broken homes, orphaned homes, dysfunctional homes, or unhappy homes. Many of these children carry around much hurt and anger, which they tend to suppress in their younger years, but which explode during the teenage years, to trigger either overtly rebellious behavior or depression. And while this fact no doubt calls for more effort on the part of our yeshivos to deal with this disadvantaged element, we must also strengthen that unit which is most crucial in this area: the family.

→ Save the Family

The billions of dollars that Madison Avenue and the entertainment industry spend to entice and attract the masses to their world of nothingness and emptiness has its inevitable impact — even on those of us who think that we lead insulated lives.

As we mentioned before, theirs is not an intellectual assault, and the strategy for mounting a counterattack is all the more elusive and difficult to launch. It is more important than ever that we practice preventive medicine, and — as mentioned — find ways to strengthen ourselves as individuals and as a community, and focus on the underlying foundations of what we are as a family. We, as parent, must heighten our awareness of the importance of what we are doing and what we are accomplishing as a family. And we will never succeed in infusing *kedushah* and *simchah* into our homes if we ourselves are not inspired and not *b'simchah*.

One of the major problems we all face is our pressured lifestyles, wherein so many different responsibilities pull us in all directions, at all times. The additional drain on our time, due to the increased social commitments to *simchos* and affairs, is certainly robbing our children of much-needed time with us. There is, however, Shabbos. This is, always was, and should be the time we have reserved for ourselves and our families.

The Shabbos table should be marked with an atmosphere of *menuchah v'simchah* (tranquility and joy) — not just in the *zemiros*, but in our demeanor. It is a time to talk and listen to our children. Yet today this, too, is under assault. The typical Shabbos has become a marathon of *Kiddush*-hopping and — worse — weekend *bar mitzvahs*, with the result of the children being shunted aside, left to eat alone or (even sadder) with a housekeeper. In many a home, this corrosion of the Shabbos can result in terrible consequences.

Parents must take stock of what they are gaining and what the potential losses are from indulging in the weekly movable feast.

The same is true of Yom Tov. We can either approach an upcoming Yom Tov with the *simchah* of preparing for a great experience, or try to escape from the responsibilities of the Yom Tov. While there is a point to the song, "Here Come the Pesach Blues," that must not be the impression children receive. The sense and the setting of Yom Tov should resonate with family interaction and celebration as much as possible.

How vital to our stability it is that we maintain the *kedushah* of our homes and create islands of meaning and giving, by filtering out as much of the outside world as possible!

And after all is said and done, we must pray — be *mispallel* — for there is no formula for achieving success with one's children without *siyata d'Shemaya*.

Poison Ivy:
Lessons of the "Yale Five"

Chaim Dovid Zwiebel

O n September 13, 1997, Rachel Wohlgelerenter got married.

But wait, hold the mazal tovs — for her *chasunah* is not scheduled to take place until Chanukah 5758.

Rachel Wohlgelerenter, you see, is a freshman at Yale College in New Haven, Connecticut, one of the five by-now-famous Orthodox Jewish students who sought but were denied an exemption from Yale's requirement that all unmarried freshmen and sophomores under the age of 21 reside in one of the college's co-ed residence halls. She and her *chasan* accordingly went through with a civil marriage ceremony months before the date of their actual *chasunah*, so that she would officially be "married" and thereby eligible to claim exemption from Yale's on-campus residence requirement.

Alas, no such convenient option presented itself to the four other Orthodox students who took religious exception to the immodest environment presented by Yale dormitory life; they have yet to have found their *basherte*. And so, unable to look for a justice of the peace to help resolve their problem, they are looking for a different type of justice — a judicial ruling that Yale's refusal to accommodate their religious beliefs by allowing them to reside off campus or by making available single-sex residential facilities violates a variety of their constitutional and legal rights.

✦ *The Classroom and Beyond*

There is no anti-Orthodox bias at Yale, the college's spokesmen insist. On the contrary: Yale makes kosher food readily available. It accommodates students who are unable to take exams scheduled for religious holidays. It has found a way to enable Sabbath observers to bypass the electronic security system that would otherwise make it impossible for Orthodox Jews to enter their residence facilities on Shabbasos and Yomim Tovim.

But accommodation has its limits. Yale's bulldog-like insistence that students reside on campus in co-ed dormitory facilities is part and parcel of its educational mission, its spokesmen assert, and simply cannot be waived.

As explained by Dean Richard H. Brodhead in a letter to Agudath Israel of America president Rabbi Moshe Sherer, "The students' request in this case … runs counter not just to a well-advertised requirement of Yale College but also to one of our deep institutional values, the education that derives through living together in a collegiate community." Or, in the words of Ivan G. Marcus, professor of Jewish history at Yale, in a letter to the editor of one of the Anglo-Jewish weeklies:

> Yale is not only about classes and a degree. It is also about mixing, meeting, arguing, learning to defend, being different and dealing with different people. It is about people and ideas 24 hours each day, not just in the classes a few hours each week.

For Yale, therefore, there is no room to allow a handful of Orthodox *tzenius* fanatics to opt out of the full Yale experience.

If it means having to defend a lawsuit, so be it, for one does not yield on a matter of principle.

(Or is it a matter of principle? So long as the five students would be willing to pay the college's approximately $7,000 annual room and board fee, the administration would not insist that they actually *reside* on campus. Indeed, in a letter to the students' attorney Nathan Lewin, Yale deputy general counsel William D. Stempel expressly pledged that no disciplinary action would be taken against the students for failing to live on campus, consistent with Yale's general policy of "not monitor[ing] where students sleep." It would appear that students can obtain the benefits of the 24-hour-a-day Yale melting pot simply by paying for it, even without experiencing it. Top that, Harvard!)

✦ *Purposeful Confrontation*

There are several points to be made, I think, about the confrontation between the "Yale Five" and the school's adamant administration.

First, and in certain ways foremost, the entire Orthodox community — including those who would never even consider college, let alone a college like Yale, as an acceptable option for themselves or their children — should take pride in the firm stance taken by these five students. Alone among their many peers, Jews and gentiles alike, these young men and women have dared object to the objectionable. In so doing, they have proclaimed, for all the world to hear, that Judaism demands of its adherents a code of moral conduct totally incompatible with the loose and promiscuous atmosphere that prevails in a modern-day college dormitory. *K'vod Shamayim* has been enhanced — and for that we can all celebrate.

Second, the legal cause being pursued in court is worthy, just, and deserving of the broader Orthodox community's support. One might fairly question whether the students, especially those whose families do not live in the New Haven area, would not have been better off simply avoiding the problem by enrolling in some unenlightened college (Columbia, perhaps?) that has yet to discover the educational benefits of compelling 18-, 19- and 20-year-old students to reside in co-ed dormitories. But the importance of the non-discrimination principle they are seeking to establish is incontrovertible.

If Yale is legally entitled to close its doors to students whose religious beliefs are incompatible with immorality — or, for that matter, to discriminate more generally on the basis of religion — so too are other schools similarly entitled. Orthodox Jews have a stake in a rule of law that precludes such discrimination. We may freely choose not to attend any given college, or any college whatsoever, but the law should guarantee that the choice is ours alone, not forced on us by some insensitive college administrators.

✦ We Are All Yalies

Finally, we would do well to draw a sobering lesson from the "Yale Five": how vigilant one must be when venturing beyond the protective warmth of the "four cubits of *halachah*" and encountering institutions of secular acculturation.

The lesson has broad application. True (and happily so), not too many of us have to deal with the precise challenge facing the students at Yale. But virtually all of us do find it necessary, in one form or another, to confront the outside world — whether working in jobs, studying for professions, reading the newspapers, dealing with neighbors, or even walking the streets. Virtually all of us find it necessary to strike some balance between isolation and interaction, between insularity and exposure. Virtually all of us must therefore learn how to recognize the danger of outside infection and resist it.

As long as we are in this imperfect world, awaiting the redemptive power of *Mashiach*, the Yale dormitory is all around us.

✦ The Beis Din Process

Human Law and Torah Law

Can Modern Legal Disputes Be Settled by *Din Torah*?

Batei Din vs. Secular Courts

A Layman's Guide to a *Din Torah*

The Exalted Status of the *Beis Din* Process

Respect for the Halachic Legal System

The Secular Enforceability of a *Beis Din* Judgment

A Proposal for *P'sharah*: A Jewish
Mediation/Arbitration Service

Human Law and Torah Law

Rabbi Mordechai Gifter

✦ *A Comparison of Purposes*

T he purpose of the Law, as civilized society understands it, is to bring order into the lives and affairs of men, to guarantee — to use a Mishnaic phrase — that "men shall not swallow themselves alive." Where order exists in society humankind can develop to the fullest extent its capacities for progress under freedom and liberty. A society governed by the Law is therefore given a guarantee against anarchy, against chaos and disintegration.

Though this be the purpose of the Law, yet the Law itself can become cold and sometimes even cruel if it is designed only to meet the requisites of an ordered society. Indeed, there is a law even among barbarians. The cruelty and tyranny of the dictator is also framed in the order of law. One is reminded of the words of the Psalmist (94:20) who, in speaking of the tyrant, describes him as being one "who frames violence by statute."

The development of civilized law knows, therefore, also of

the development of equity in the law. Equity has served, we might say, as a guardian over the law, seeking to keep it in line with ethical norms.

It has not been the purpose of the law, however, even when joined with equity, to develop the moral and ethical standards of society and of the individual. This has been the domain of philosophy and of religion. These values nurtured by philosophy, religion, and other kindred branches of ethical and moral teachings became the norms within which the law developed and fructified.

Talmudic jurisprudence is unique in that the very purpose of the law itself is the development of Man's moral and ethical personality. The ambit of Talmudic law is a very wide one indeed, the widest one can imagine, for its scope embraces every facet of human living. It is, by no means, limited to that body of legal matter encompassed by the term "law" as we know it in modern society; namely, that which concerns itself only with those affairs of man *vis-a-vis* his fellow man. Since the purpose of modern law is order in society, it deals with man as part of society, its ambit being the world of human relations. Man, the individual, *per se*, is not the object of the law. Certainly the conscience of the individual is outside the scope of the law. Not so with Talmudic jurisprudence. The very same law which deals with torts, bailments, contracts, and criminal offenses deals also with Man's duties of prayer, of ritual and ceremonial, yea, even with problems of faith in the Divine Creator. Just as the Rabbinic Court was bid to enforce a contract, so was it bid to enforce the observance of the building of the succah on the Feast of Tabernacles. Idolatry in Talmudic law is of the same degree as the criminal offense of murder, subject to the death penalty.

The gamut of the *Beis Din HaGadol*, the High Court, the supreme authority of the law, included such diverse matters as the case of the false prophet, the High Priest who had committed a capital offense, the decision to declare war, extending the boundaries of Jerusalem and of the Temple courts, appointing district courts and decisions involving interpretation of the law. The law embraced all of life, public as well as private, individual as well as social in character.

The ultimate authority for Talmudic law is the Torah, (the Five Books of Moses) containing the commandments of the L–rd revealed at Sinai, and thereafter, through Moses. Since the ultimate authority of the law is the commandment of G–d, there is no room left for man outside the framework of the law. All is open before Him "who tests the hearts of men."

✣ Revelation of the Divine

The law, therefore, in the Talmudic sense, is the revelation of the Divine commandment, of the demands made upon man to raise himself above the level of the beast. It is the law which says to man: *See, I set before thee life and good and death and evil, and thou shalt choose life.* It is the law which posits the freedom of Man to choose the path to nobility and human dignity, the freedom of the individual to determine and direct his destiny, that freedom which is the primary source and the ultimate goal of the sovereignty of the people revolting against the yokes of all forms of tyranny. Maimonides terms this freedom "the pillar of the law and the commandment." But yet the law, in stating this great human principle, bids and commands Man as to the direction of his choice. Within this commandment, *thou shalt choose life,* is contained the entire body of the law, embracing all which is life.

The law is so many times identified, in the language of the Torah, with righteousness — *righteous statutes and judgments* — for its purpose is to make of Man a righteous being, who has chosen freely to be governed by moral and ethical values. The basic premise of the law is the never-ceasing consciousness that one stands always in the presence of his Creator. In order to insure this goal the law sees the necessity for a complete system regulating the conduct of Man, not merely in dealing with his fellowman, but, also, *in dealing with himself.* For he who attempts to achieve moral and ethical perfection and integrity in himself will, of necessity, deal in kind with his fellowman. Society is molded of the individuals who build it. *An ordered and disciplined personality in the individual guarantees a well-balanced and harmonious society.*

How striking are the words of the Torah when commanding the judge to be completely impartial and objective, not to be influenced by the fear of men. Why? *For justice is of G–d.* The court is but the instrument of the will and of the commandment of Him who has created the judge, the plaintiff, and the defendant. How ennobling for all concerned to feel that they stand in the presence of G–d when seeking justice in the court of law!

✧ To Understand the Will of G–d

The student of the Talmud is acquainted with the phrases *Rachmana amar, Rachmana kasav,* "the Merciful One has said, the Merciful One has written." The law is an expression of Divine mercy evidenced in the desire, apparent in the commandment, to raise and elevate Man to the level of that law designed for Man. And ofttimes our opinion would dictate a more stringent liability, but *Rachmana chas alai* — "the Merciful One has eased the penalty." Laws in civil liabilities become lessons in Divine mercy. Is this not a unique approach to law?

That great pillar of Talmudic jurisprudence, Maimonides, created the greatest comprehensive codification of Talmudic law. It seems apparent that he considered his Code as an elaborate commentary upon the 613 commandments of the Torah. He first created his *Sefer HaMitzvos,* the Book of Commandments, containing the cardinal principles in determining the essence of a commandment of the Torah, and thereupon enumerating the 613 commandments based upon these principles. He then proceeded to elaborate upon this work by codifying the entire body of Talmudic law. Every division in his Code, therefore, is introduced with an enumeration of the mitzvos, the commandments, dealt with in the respective division of the Code. This is indicative of the Talmudic approach to the law. The law is the commandment of G–d revealed in the Torah, developed and expostulated down through the ages. *A discussion of the law in the Talmudic academies of learning is an attempt to understand the will of G–d in directing the conduct and affairs of Man.*

Problems in civil law also represent human striving to dignity and nobility, a desire to attune human conduct to the will of G–d. This is the basis of the principle posited by the great Medieval Talmudic jurist, R. Solomon Ibn Aderet (*Rashba, Bava Kamma* 3b), who states that questions involving doubts of interpretation of the basic law in injuries are governed by the principle used in resolving doubts relating to money values.

The effort expended in trying to solve a legal problem is, from the viewpoint of Talmudic law, an attempt to discern the intent of the Divine commandment, so that men may govern themselves in accordance with that Divine Will and Authority.

We find a most interesting and unique feature in Talmudic law. We read in the Talmud (*Bava Metzia* 83a): "Rabbah Bar Bar-Chana had a barrel of wine broken through the negligence of laborers hired to transport the wine. Rabbah thereupon seized the laborers' cloaks as a lien for damages, something permissible by law. The laborers complained to the great master, Rav, who directed Rabbah to return the cloaks. Rabbah asked Rav: Is this then the law? And Rav answered: Yes, for it is written, *That thou shalt walk in the path of the virtuous.* Rabbah returned the cloaks. The laborers then said to Rav: We are poor, we have labored all day and we are hungry, but we have not the means to purchase food. Rav, thereupon, said to Rabbah: Pay them their hire. Rabbah asked: Is this the law? And Rav answered: Yes, for it is written, *And the paths of the righteous shalt thou keep.*"

The ruling of the court in this case was not prompted by the recognition of the equity and justice in the claim of the plaintiffs for, indeed, they had no claim at all. Rather it was prompted by the realization that the ultimate purpose of the law is to develop a disciplined personality, fully imbued with personal morals and ethics. No doubt, the ruling was delivered by Rav because the defendant was Rabbah Bar Bar-Chana, an individual who had proved himself worthy of higher moral demands and standards. The ruling of the court took into consideration the ethical norms of the individuals involved. This is the general principle known as *lifnim mishuras hadin* — going beyond the line of the law, which, in our case, was equated by Rav with *din* — the line of the law itself.

It is quite apparent that this is not a question of an equity which seeks to have the law meet ethical norms, but rather reveals a desire on the part of the law to inject its inner spirit and purpose into the ruling of the court. It is a part of that body of law which describes a lawsuit in terms of *unto the L–rd shall their dispute come.*

→ *Delicate as a Rose*

All which we have attempted to say is so beautifully presented in the poetic language of the *Midrash*. Solomon, in his *Song of Songs* (7:3) speaks of the people of Israel as being like unto a *heap of wheat set about with a hedge of roses.* The Rabbis of the *Midrash* comment thereon: The hedge of roses, these are the words of the Torah, which are as delicate as the rose. Said Rabbi Levi:

> A tempting dish is brought before a person. He prepares to partake of it with great relish. He is told tallow [*cheilev*] has fallen into the food and he refrains even from tasting it. Who has caused this restraint? What serpent has bitten him? What scorpion has stung him to keep him from drawing near to the food to taste of it? Only the words of the Torah, delicate as the rose, for it is written: *Ye shall not eat the fat.*

And yet another illustration:

> A person was walking along a country road. He passed a fruit orchard and the fragrance of the fully ripened first fruits of the season attracted him. He stretched forth his hand to pick a fruit from the tree. He was reminded: These fruits have an owner. He drew back his hand in restraint. What has caused this restraint? What stands between him and the fruit? Only the words of the Torah, delicate as the rose, for it is written: *Thou shalt not rob.*

For the aesthete who has developed an appreciation for the beauty and delicacy of the rose, a hedge of roses is stronger than a wall of iron. He needs but the rose itself to serve as a barrier against trespass. For one reared and nurtured in the law, transgression is trespass.

✣ *Man Is Inherently Good*

Man, created in the image of G–d, is inherently good and noble, striving to fulfill the Divine will which inheres within him. That world of passion, lust and temptation which makes goodness and nobility so difficult to realize, must find its remedy in the law. Man is called upon to develop within himself, through the law, an aesthetic appreciation of moral and ethical values — an everpresent G–d consciousness. The word of the law is the gentle reminder to refrain from trespass in the human soul, handiwork of Almighty G–d.

But certainly a code of law designed to be studied only by lawyers cannot achieve the purpose of which we speak. The law cannot lead men to the lofty heights of moral and ethics, nor can it serve as a guide for the disciplined conduct of the individual, if it remains beyond the reach of the individual. The loftiest principle, therefore, of Talmudic law is the exhortation to study the law, an exhortation directed toward every individual, not only to those who seek their profession in the law.

It is of interest, in this connection, to quote from Josephus in his work, *Against Apion.*

> Moses did not suffer the guilt of ignorance to go on without punishment, but demonstrated the law to be the best and most necessary instruction of all others, permitting the people to leave off their other employments and to assemble together for the hearing of the law and learning it exactly. And this not once or twice, or oftener, but every week, which thing all the other legislators seem to have neglected. And indeed, the greatest part of Mankind are so far from living

according to their own laws, that they hardly know them; but when they have sinned they learn from others that they have transgressed the law. Those also who are in the highest and principal posts of the government confess they are not acquainted with those laws and are obliged to take such persons for their assessors in public administrations as profess to have skill in those laws. But for our people, if anybody do but ask any one of them about our laws, he will more readily tell them all than he will tell his own name. And this in consequence of our having learned them immediately, as soon as ever we became sensible of anything, and of having them as it were engraven on our souls.

So wrote a historian recording Jewish life at about the beginning of the common era.

✦ A Jew Must Know the Law

Maimonides, in his Code, has a division devoted to the laws of Torah study. Therein he postulates: *Every male person in Israel is obligated to study Torah, be he poor or rich, healthy or subject to suffering, young or so old that his strength is ebbing; even if he be burdened with wife and children, he is obligated to set aside a specific time by day and by night to study Torah, for it is written*: Thou shalt study it by day and by night.

This Commandment, this *law* to study the law, is the quintessential of Talmudic jurisprudence. We quote from Talmudic literature:

What were the beginnings of R. Akiva? It is said: When he was 40 years of age he had not yet studied Talmud. Once he stood by the mouth of a well. There he noticed a well-stone. "Who has hollowed out the stone?" he asked. He was told it was the water which fell upon it every day continually. He wondered at this. It was said to him: Akiva, has thou not read: *The waters wear away the stones?* Thereupon R. Akiva drew the implication for himself. If what is soft wears down the hard, all the more shall the words of the Torah, which are as hard as iron, hollow out my heart which is but flesh and blood! With this he dedicated himself to the study of Torah (*Avos d'Rabbi Nosson* VI:2).

The law, through continuous, endless study, can make of Man's heart a receptacle for the living waters of moral and ethical perfection. For, and we quote from Maimonides' Code:

> It is characteristic of every human being that, when his interest is engaged in the ways of wisdom and righteousness, he yearns for those ways and is eager to follow them.

Talmudic law is common law in the sense that its knowledge is common for all men and not the domain of the professional student of the law. The law is therefore truly a Torah — a system of instruction to the people embracing all the problems of life, seeking to make the people worthy of the great heritage of humanity — Man created in the image of G–d.

Can Modern Legal Disputes Be Settled by Din Torah?

Attorney(s) for the Plaintiff
Judah Dick

*J*oe Lyner and Murray Goldman were partners in Gold-
Lyne Gems; Lyner supervised the shop and Goldman
drummed up the business on the outside.

After 12 years of working together, the two decided to
part company. — How much is the business worth? Does
Goldman keep the clients? — Who is entitled to the location?
— What is the Gold-Lyne name worth?

Goldman wants to take their differences to court, but
Lyner refuses. "We're both Orthodox Jews. Anyone who
learned Chumash and Rashi know the opening of Mishpatim:
'And these are the ordinances that you shall place before
them.' Says Rashi — Before them, but not before the Gentile
courts."

Goldman would agree in principle but he doesn't see
anything wrong with going to a modern civil court, which
does not "invoke names of idols," which is Rashi's primary
objection; nor is he certain that a Jewish court has jurisdiction
over a case that is governed by dina d'malchusa — the law
of the land. Besides, he is reluctant to bring such a highly

specialized case to a din Torah — to be adjudicated by a court composed of rabbis.

Would a rabbinical court (beis din) devote the time necessary for such a case?

Are the rabbis of the beis din sufficiently knowledgeable in Choshen Mishpat (the section of Shulchan Aruch that deals with monetary matters) to handle this case?

Do these rabbis have enough expertise in business affairs?

Can the psak din (decision) be enforced?

Might there not be some hidden trap — some unknown aspects of Talmudic law with which they may not be familiar, which they simply didn't take into account?

❖ Whose Jurisdiction?

Although the Goldman-Lyner case is purely fictional, it is typical of a host of disputes that, out of ignorance, people settle in a civil court. Indeed, *Rashi* does quote the Talmud in the warning against bringing a case to a secular court as a "desecration[1] of G–d's name and glorifying the names of idols." This may hardly seem applicable to the neutral atmosphere of modern courts, where a witness even has the option to affirm instead of swearing on a Bible. But the essence of the prohibition is aimed against showing preference for a system of jurisprudence formulated by the human mind over the Divine Law of the Torah,[2] and this applies to all courts — even where the judges and lawyers are Jewish, even when the law of the land happens to coincide with Torah Law. (In fact, the law courts in Israel, which are secular in nature, also fall under this ban; and the Chazon Ish[3] spoke out strongly against submitting business disputes to such courts.)

In addition to violating the restriction against litigating in secular courts, an involuntary transfer of funds that results

---

1. *Gittin* 88.

2. *Nesivos HaMishpat, Choshen Mishpat* XXVI.

3. *Chazon Ish, Choshen Mishpat*, Section XXVI.

therefrom is unauthorized, and is therefore, in effect, *gezeilah* (theft), since Jews are bound to follow Torah law among themselves.

To be sure, *dina d'malchusa* — the law of the land — does on occasion prevail even when Torah Law would generally lead to a contrary result. But the role of *dina d'malchusa* is rather limited, and even according to its broadest interpretation, it applies only to cases where the government has enacted certain legislation for the welfare of the people to meet some pressing need which has arisen; but its supremacy does not apply to a system of general laws or codification of common law, made to establish a legal code for that particular country. If it would have such universal application, its practical effect would be tantamount to the abolition of the *Choshen Mishpat* from an active role in Jewish life.[4]

But even when the principle of *dina d'malchusa* is applicable, its role in a particular situation must be determined by a rabbinical court. An interesting application of this rule can be seen from an article by Rabbi Eliyahu Henkin in *HaPardes* some years ago, holding that since rent-control laws are legislative enactments especially designed to deal with the housing shortage, they are within the scope of *dina d'malchusa* and must be followed by a *beis din*.[5]

There are even views that one must resort to a *din Torah* against a non-Jewish adversary who is willing to submit to one, and for that matter there were many gentiles in Russia who voluntarily did so because of their trust in the integrity of the rabbis.

But when both contestants are Jews — even if one is nonreligious — they most certainly are obligated to submit to a rabbinical court, unless the other refuses to respond to a summons from a *beis din*. In such a case, the *beis din* will grant leave to resort to secular courts to enforce a halachically valid claim.[6]

As for the academic qualification and business orientation of rabbis serving on a *beis din* — a select number of rabbis have emerged who, by virtue of years of experience and specialization,

---

4. *Beis Yosef* on *Tur* 369, in name of *Rashba*.

5. *HaPardes, Nissan* 5714.

6. *Choshen Mishpat* 26.

Talmudic study and practical observation, are indeed highly qualified to act in judgment on highly complex business matters.

But there is still another question haunting Orthodox Jews who would settle their disputes by *din Torah*.

> *M. Samuels & Co. was committed to deliver seventy-five cases of merchandise to J.R. Strickman in time for his spring season, but the Samuels delivery was late. Strickman was forced to pick up other merchandise from a jobber at a much higher price to meet his customers' demand and he did not want to pay the agreed price to Samuels, when the merchandise finally did arrive. They brought their differences to a din Torah, and the psak (decision) allowed Strickman to make a reduced payment over a period of ten months — but Strickman never made any payments.*
>
> *What was Samuel to do? Would he be forced to take Strickman to court and start all over again — or was there a way to harness the legal machinery of the State and enforce the psak (verdict) of the din Torah?*

❖ *The Machinery of Enforcement*

A Jew is enjoined to respond to a summons to *beis din*, at the penalty of being put into *cherem* (ostracized from the community) if he does not respond. Nonetheless, most people usually do not like to depend on their adversary's goodwill, his spirit of compliance, or his fear of *cherem*, and look for more conventional legal buttresses to support an agreement.

There was a time, not too long ago, when the civil courts' calendars were not overcrowded, and the courts were averse to submission of disputes to arbitration — a format for settlement that would include the classic *din Torah* — since this would have meant circumventing their jurisdiction. Nowadays, however, when the dockets are congested, the courts have favored this option, and in almost every state of the Union as well as in Congress, laws have been adopted that recognize the results of arbitration as legally binding, so long as the litigants adhere to the statutory provisions surrounding arbitration — beginning with signing a written agreement to arbitrate. During arbitration both parties must be given a fair hearing, but otherwise no particular procedure or substantive law is prescribed. The awards of the arbitration is then binding on both parties, and the court will then enter a judgment or court order directing the parties to fully comply with the provisions of the award. The only exception to this would be if it could be shown that the arbitrators were guilty of misconduct.

This accommodates the conduct of a *din Torah* in its customary format so completely, that very few modifications would be required to make the results enforceable by law. First would be a written submission to arbitration, signed by all parties. It is disturbing to note that the *New York Court Report* contains a number of cases where it held it could not enforce the decisions of a *din Torah* because of lack of such a signed agreement. It would therefore seem to be of utmost importance to make the signing of such an agreement routine procedure in every *din Torah*. (A model draft of such an agreement appears at the end of this article.)

Should one party refuse to sign such an agreement, it may be considered tantamount to a refusal to appear in a *beis din*, and accordingly would be grounds for authorization to go to a secular court.[7] Partners entering into a contract may provide in advance for submission to a *din Torah* by entering a clause in their contract that would require all disputes to be settled by *din Torah*; a form for this also appears at the article's conclusion.

The model submission form avoids many of the problems which have affected the enforceability of a *din Torah*. The model form authorizes the rabbis to follow the procedures generally followed at a *din Torah*. This is significant, since the procedure followed is somewhat different from that followed by other arbitrators. Also, not all evidence and witnesses normally admissible are acceptable under Jewish Law. For instance, the statute provides that an arbitrator must take an oath to faithfully perform his duties, must swear in witnesses, must give

---

7. *Divrei Gaonim*, Sec. 52 (8) (in the name of several *Teshuvos*).

prescribed notice of hearings, must hear all relevant testimony and evidence presented.

The model form waives these requirements since in conducting a *din Torah,* rabbis do not take an oath nor do they swear in witnesses. It may be desirable to allow departure from the strict *halachah* in the matter of receiving evidence, on occasion permitting the testimony of witnesses who may not be halachically qualified — such as women or relatives. This should be added to the model form of submission if agreed upon.

✦ *The Conditions of Enforcement*

Once the litigants have signed the submission contract, accepting the obligation to settle by *din Torah,* the courts stand behind the document in many ways. First, a court will compel the parties to proceed to litigate the matter before the *din Torah* and will stay any legal action in the courts on the same subject.[8] In certain cases, the court can even appoint an arbitrator — or the third member of an arbitration tribunal — if the parties are unable to agree on one, so that the arbitration agreement will not be frustrated by the one seeking to avoid going to arbitration. In New York and in some other jurisdictions, arbitrators have subpoena powers and can compel third parties to appear before them to testify as witnesses or to produce relevant documentary evidence. When a *din Torah* conforms to the statutory rules for arbitration, the rabbinical court can exercise these powers with state backing. As a practical matter, however, it would be necessary to go to court to enforce such a subpoena; but refusal to comply would subject the reluctant party to costs and/or a civil penalty, and possible liability for damages.

The *din Torah* itself can be conducted in either of two ways, dependent upon the wishes of the contestants: one, where the halachic procedures are followed to the fullest — with the possible exception of circumventing the necessity of an oath. This would entail the reaching of a decision in uncompromising con-

---

8. Berk v. Berk, 8 Misc. 2d 732 (1957).

formity to the *halachah,* with a full verdict of "guilty" (or obligation to pay) or "not-guilty." The other course allows for *p'sharah* — or compromise — which takes into account such factors as the equities of the situation and the concept of *lifnim mishuras hadin,* making greater demands than the law would require from one of the parties using *halachah* as a general guideline only.

In whatever way the *psak* (decision) is arrived at, it can be enforced by the courts, providing the *psak* is put into writing, with the signatures of all rabbis who sat in on the case. A copy of the *psak* should be delivered to each party. It may be written in Yiddish or Hebrew, although it is necessary to have it properly translated if it goes to court. In New York and most other states, the arbitrators' signatures must be acknowledged, which means that they must either sign before a Notary Public or state before the Notary that the signatures are theirs. (A form acknowledgement appears at the end.) While the acknowledgement can always be added later, it would be more desirable to have it done as soon as the *psak* is rendered.

In many states, including New York, one must go to court within one year of the award to have it judicially enforced. Thus, if there is any doubt as to whether any of the parties will abide by the *psak,* it would be wise to have the *psak* entered as a court order or judgment as soon after it is rendered as possible. This is especially true where the *psak* applies to an ongoing relationship which might be violated after the year is up.

> *What happens when by oversight the contestants or the beis din do not prepare a contract of arbitration? Is it still possible that the psak will be enforced by the Courts? Or will the lack of adherence to formal arbitration procedures disqualify the din Torah as a legal proceeding?*

❖ Case of the Missing Form

In a recent case[9] involving substantial sums of money, an award of a *din Torah* was confirmed by the courts, even though

---

9. Kozlowski v. Seville, Inc. 64 Misc. 2d 109 (1970).

the arbitration decision was not duly acknowledged and many of the procedures that are essential to statutory arbitration were simply ignored. The arbitrators were not sworn, nor were the witnesses, and so on. The court held that once the parties agreed to litigate their dispute before a rabbinical court, they had in effect expressed their willingness to waive these customary procedures. Even the acknowledgement before the notary could be done later (eight months had already elapsed since the award was handed down). Nor did it matter that the *psak* was written in Hebrew. The court only refrained from enforcing one aspect of the *psak* — regarding the disassociation of one of the partners from the business — on the grounds that it was expressed in somewhat ambiguous terminology. The important thing was that the parties had signed a written agreement to submit the matter to a *din Torah*.

✦ *Psak of Finality — or Merely Evidence?*

The decision of the rabbinical court is final and is easily converted into an enforceable court order or judgment as long as the statutory procedures outlined above are followed. But this is not always the case. When there is a failure to execute a submission to arbitration or to conduct a *din Torah* in accordance with customary arbitration procedures, the *psak* cannot be entered as a court order. Nonetheless it may still fall into the category of common-law arbitration: The dispute must go through the same routine pleadings and trial procedures as an ordinary action, and the burden of proof rests on the plaintiff to prove that the controversy was indeed submitted to arbitration and that an award was made which was not complied with.[10] In other words, the *psak* is not acted upon as though it were verdict. It only comes into play as plaintiff's evidence for a new verdict. This can be a costly, time consuming process, which can be easily avoided by taking the necessary preventive measures.

---

10. Matter of Hellman v. Wolbron, 31 A.D. 2d 477 (1969); Cooper v. Weissblatt, 154 Misc. 522 (1935); Gruer v. Kramer, N.Y.L.J. Nov. 22, 1971 page 17, col. 8.

✦ When Din Torah Is Not Recognized

There are a few areas where the courts are reluctant to surrender their prerogatives to arbitration, such as where the rights of children are involved. Thus, in one recent case which is presently on appeal, the courts declined to direct a divorced couple to arbitrate before a *din Torah* a dispute involving custody and support of the child of the marriage.[11] The court in that case assumed that judges, with the assistance of professional staffs, are more competent than rabbis are to handle such matters. This is currently being disputed by COLPA (Commission on Law and Public Affairs), which has filed a brief in a Court of Appeals in defense of the process of *din Torah* as applied to custody decisions.

This assumption is certainly open to doubt in view of the competence with which the *batei din* in Israel have handled such matters, showing great concern for the best interest of the child in each individual case, through the flexible application of the guidelines set forth in the *halachah*,[12] as they understood the child's needs. (In case of divorce, the *Shulchan Aruch* suggests awarding all children under 6 to the mother's custody; after 6 years of age, the sons are to be entrusted to the father, and the daughters to the mother. But final decision is left to the rabbinical judges.) It might at least be expected that American courts allow the *din Torah* to proceed — to hear the merits of the case and make a reasoned decision — and then, perhaps, permit a court to set aside such decision when it is convinced that enforcing the *psak* would be detrimental to the best interest of the child.

Other areas which are not entrusted to arbitration are those where the state has a strong public policy, such as the enforcement of securities laws, or where criminal violations are involved. In such cases, the court may decline to enforce an arbitration decision which it believes contrary to public policy.

With these rather limited exceptions, arbitration of disputes

---

11. Agur v. Agur, 32 AD 2d 16, (1970).

12. *Even HaEzer* 82:7.

is now favored by the law as a method of speedy and inexpensive settlement of civil disputes without imposing additional burdens upon the courts and the public treasury.

→ *And the Lawyers?*

Not the least benefit of a *din Torah* is that it allows one to avoid the need for lawyers and substantial legal fees. The sages have traditionally taken a jaundiced view of attorneys, since they often tend to obscure truth rather than aid in its search.[13]

Nonetheless, there are times when lawyers and their services would be salutory to a *din Torah*. There have been *batei din* (rabbinical courts) that permitted their participation in a *din Torah*[14] and it is a common practice today in Israeli *batei din*. This is especially valid when the lawyer is familiar with the applicable *halachah*, as well as with the customs of the trade in question and pertinent *dina d'malchusa*. Ideally the lawyer could then perform as an impartial legal counsel, as a source of necessary information, and to assure that the *psak* be legally binding. He could even function in his customary role as articulator of the interests of his clients, as outlined in the Codes of Professional Responsibility — to assist the court in arriving at the truth and not to mislead it by misrepresenting the facts or law — since there are many people who are either inarticulate or disorganized, and are not able to properly present their case to the *beis din*.

The Torah commands us: "Judges and constables you shall appoint unto thee in all of your gates." Indeed, throughout history Jewish communities jealously guarded their autonomous *batei din* and it was rare that one Jew took his case against a fellow Jew to a secular court — this being grounds for *cherem*. The Jewish community in our country should return to the great tradition[15] which kept alive the *Choshen Mishpat* and made it a living law, rather than just a subject of academic study which has

---

13. *Avos* 1:8.

14. Asaf, Simcha, *Batei HaDin V'Sidreihem* (1922).

15. A comprehensive study and historical review of the subject is found in Asaf's *Batei HaDin V'Sidreihem* ibid.

no present day applicability. The community should encourage the establishment of *batei din,* which would handle claims of all types and varieties for a nominal fee, and assure that no religious Jews be compelled to resort to secular courts to vindicate his legal rights.[16] Then we might earn the realization of Isaiah's prophecy (4:27): "Zion will be redeemed with justice and those returning to it with righteousness."

→ *INDEX OF FORMS*

CLAUSE IN CONTRACT OR AGREEMENT TO SUBMIT ALL DISPUTES TO A BEIS DIN

Any controversy or dispute or claim of any nature whatsoever arising out of or relating to any provision of the agreement or the breach thereof shell be settled by a Din Torah to be held by a Beis Din to be selected as follows: One rabbi by each of the parties and the third rabbi shall be selected by the other two rabbis (by the Beis Din known as............), who shall decide the matter in accordance with Jewish Law (and/or principles of equity generally followed by a Din Torah). The procedure to be followed at the Din Torah shall be consistent with that generally followed by a Beis Din and need not conform to any statutory procedures. It is further agreed that the decision of the Beis Din shall be binding upon the parties and may be entered as a judgment in any court of competent jurisdiction pursuant to Article 75, New York C.P.L.R.

MODEL FORM OF SUBMISSION OF DISPUTE TO BEIS DIN UNDER NEW YORK LAW OF ARBITRATION

MEMORANDUM OF AGREEMENT made this day of ...., between...........who resides at (has its place of business at)............, City of............ State of............ . Whereas a certain dispute(s) and difference(s) have arisen and still exist between the above-mentioned parties, (relative to............) and they have decided to submit such dispute to a Din Torah according to Jewish Law for a binding decision, IT IS HEREBY AGREED by and between them to refer all disputes and matters in difference whatsoever between them (in any way connected or arising out of the above-mentioned controversy) to award, order and final binding determination of a Beis Din consisting of the following 3 rabbis (or to the Beis Din known as............): Rabbi............, Rabbi............, and Rabbi............ The award or decision of the Rabbis or a majority of them shall be enforceable in any court of competent jurisdiction pursuant to the New York Law of Arbitration — CPLR ARTICLE 75. The rabbis shall not be required to take an oath, nor to administer an oath to any witnesses at the hearing, nor to follow any particular rules or procedures except that generally followed at Din Torahs. The decision shall be in accordance with the Halacha (and/or general principles of equity generally followed at a Din Torah). The decision shall be rendered at the conclusion of the hearings or within 30 days

16. For an interesting study of the *beis din* in America, see Kaplan: *Rabbinical Courts; Modern Day Solomons,* Columbia Journal of Law and Social Problems, Jan. 1970, p. 49.

thereafter and a copy of the decision shall be delivered or mailed to each party. The decision shall be signed by the rabbis and upon request of the prevailing party, they shall acknowledge their signature before a notary public so that it may be enforced in court. The rabbis shall be entitled to compensation of $............ per diem to be paid by both parties equally (unless otherwise decided by the Beis Din).

Signed........................

....

Matters in parentheses ( ) are optional and should be stricken if not desired.

– –

FORM OF ACKNOWLEDGMENT OF DECISION OF DIN TORAH

STATE OF NEW YORK, COUNTY OF ....

On the day of ...., before me personally came

Rabbi............, Rabbi............, and Rabbi............ to me known and known to me to be the persons who are described in the foregoing Arbitration Award and Decision of Beth Din and they acknowledged that they executed the same.

Notary Public, State of New York

Batei Din vs. Secular Courts:
Where Do We Pursue Justice?

Chaim Dovid Zwiebel

I.

The *Shulchan Aruch* employs harsh language in enjoining Jews against taking their disputes to non-Jewish courts:

אסור לדון בפני דייני עכו״ם ובערכאות שלהם... וכל הבא לידון בפניהם
הרי זה רשע וכאלו חירף וגידף והרים יד בתורת מרע״ה

Rough Translation: *It is prohibited to litigate before
non-Jewish judges, and in their court .... Whoever does so is
an evil-doer, and it is as if he has blasphemed and raised a
hand against the Torah of Moshe Rabbeinu [Choshen
Mishpat, 26:1].*

One would expect, therefore, that Orthodox Jews would uniformly present their legal claims against one another in *batei din,* that the secular courts in the United States would have to look elsewhere for "business." But reality does not always match expectation. Readers of such legal publications as *The New York Law Journal* and the *Atlantic Reporter* will come across a surprising number of reported court cases involving Orthodox Jew vs. Orthodox Jew. These cases arise in a wide variety of contexts, but most if not all share a striking common characteristic: the preference of at least one of the litigants that the dispute be resolved in secular court rather than *beis din*.

That preference may reflect the halachic advice of a competent *posek* or *beis din* that the general prohibition against resort to a non-Jewish tribunal does not apply in any particular case.[1] It may also reflect some degree of ignorance of the prohibition against resorting to non-Jewish courts, or laxity in its observance. It may reflect a perception among many, warranted or otherwise, that *batei din* in general are not likely to adjudicate the dispute professionally, efficiently or fairly; or that there is no point in going to *beis din* since only the secular courts have the power to enforce their judgments.[2] It may reflect the legal advice of a lawyer that the litigant would be more likely to prevail in the non-Jewish setting.[3] In varying combinations, these

---

1. See, for example, *Choshen Mishpat* 26:2, where the *Shulchan Aruch* permits an individual to seek authorization from a *beis din* to pursue his claim in non-Jewish court if his adversary refuses to respond to a summons to *din Torah*. There may be other circumstances that would also justify resort to the secular courts. Although it goes without saying, let me say it: Nothing in this article is intended as halachic advice (or for that matter as legal advice). Nor is anything in this article intended as criticism of any individual who starts a court case after obtaining halachic authorization to do so.

2. In fact, while it is true that only courts have the authority under American law to enforce judgments, there is a mechanism under law whereby the judgment of an independent arbitration panel — such as a *beis din* — can be invested with the full power of a court judgment. Under New York law, for example, a party to an arbitration proceeding who wishes to convert the arbitration ruling into a formal court order can turn to the court within 12 months of the conclusion of arbitration, and generally obtain judicial confirmation of the arbitration award. Once such confirmation is secured, the arbitration ruling — in our scenario, the *psak din* — is fully enforceable in law just as if the dispute had originally been decided by the court. See Section II, below.

3. An example worth noting is the division of marital assets in a divorce proceeding. Under the broadly recognized secular legal doctrine of "equitable distribution," a spouse may be entitled to claim a substantial portion of his or her partner's assets — a claim that might not be cognizable under *halachah*. Deserving of study, though beyond the scope of this particular article, is the extent to which the much-publicized *agunah* problem is related to or affected by the availability of equitable distribution in the secular courts as an alternative to asset distribution according to *din Torah*.

factors — and perhaps others as well — lead some Orthodox Jews to avoid taking their disputes to *beis din*, and instead to proceed directly to the doorsteps of the local courthouse.

Sometimes, the jurisdiction of the non-Jewish court is invoked even *after* the parties have already gone to *din Torah*. Indeed, if the legal journals and reports are any indication, there appears to be a growing trend in this direction; parties dissatisfied with the way a *beis din* has handled a particular case, or with the *psak din*, are turning increasingly to the secular courts for relief. In so doing, they typically ask the courts to invalidate the *psak* and to prohibit its enforcement by the prevailing party.

This phenomenon would be troubling enough, cause for urgent communal concern irrespective of what actually transpires in the halls of secular justice. If the mere resort to a non-Jewish tribunal constitutes a *chillul Hashem* as *Rashi* states on the first *pasuk* in *Mishpatim*, how much more so is *kvod Shamayim* degraded when the secular court is asked to sit in *post-facto* judgment on an already concluded *din Torah*!

But the *chillul Hashem* extends even further. For it is almost inevitable that when an unhappy party to a *beis din* proceeding seeks redress in the secular courts, he will do his utmost to cast negative aspersions on the members of the *beis din* and their conduct of the *din Torah*. The reported cases are rife with allegations of rabbinic greed, stupidity, partiality and worse. An all too common feature of these cases is the demeaning spectacle of "dueling *dayanim*" — where the party seeking to have the court invalidate the *psak din* presents rabbinic testimony, often from within the very *beis din* that issued the *psak*, attacking the integrity of the *din Torah*.

The fact that we live in an "information age" further compounds the *chillul Hashem*. When an unhappy party turns to secular court for relief from a negative *psak din*, and the court issues a ruling on the matter, it is not just a private matter between the litigants and the judge. Significant court decisions are published in legal periodicals and collected in heavy tomes of case reports. Hundreds if not thousands of judges, lawyers and scholars read these rulings, seeking insights and precedents for their own cases and research. And with the wonders of modern computer technology, these written decisions will entertain and/or dismay legal researchers all across the country, for generations to come.

True, as noted above, there may be extraordinary individual instances where resort to the non-Jewish court system to invalidate a *din Torah* proceeding may be halachically justified. The bottom line in each individual case remains *"a'sei le'cha rav —* obtain competent rabbinic guidance." But whatever the justification in any individual case, taken collectively, the numerous attacks in secular court against *din Torah* proceedings cast an extremely unflattering spotlight on *batei din,* and more generally on the Torah community at large.

II.

The happy news, though, is that most attempts to overturn *piskei din* in secular courts do not succeed. With some notable exceptions, the courts have generally respected the independence and integrity of *batei din,* according them the same status as they would any other non-judicial arbitration panel. So long as the parties have voluntarily submitted their dispute to the *beis din,* and so long as there was no fundamental defect in the *din Torah* process, the *psak* will typically survive *post-facto* secular legal scrutiny.[4]

In May 1992, the New York State Court of Appeals issued an especially important ruling upholding a *beis din* proceeding against an unhappy *baal din's post-facto* secular attack.[5] The ruling was especially important for two reasons: because the Court

---

4. Typically, but not always. In New York, for example, the statute (C.P.L.R. 7511) sets forth a variety of grounds upon which a court may invalidate or modify an arbitration panel's ruling. In addition, there are certain substantive areas of law over which the courts assert exclusive jurisdiction — most notably, child custody and visitation rights, and the distribution of a decedent's estate. In general, though, courts tend to be extremely deferential to arbitration rulings; and while the rate of *piskei din* that are invalidated may be slightly higher than that of general arbitration rulings, it is nonetheless quite low. An effort is currently being undertaken by the National Jewish Commission on Law and Public Affairs, in consultation with several prominent *rabbanim,* to develop standardized guidelines for *batei din* that would further insulate *piskei din* against secular attack.

5. The decision is reported at 79 N.Y. 2d 526.

of Appeals is New York's highest court, whose decisions and interpretations of law are binding upon all courts throughout the State; and because the Court of Appeals' ruling protected countless *piskei din* that otherwise would have been vulnerable to attack in secular court. Indeed, because of the potential far-reaching negative ramifications of this case, the *Moetzes Gedolei HaTorah* (Council of Torah Sages) of Agudath Israel of America authorized the Agudah to make its views known to the Court through an *amicus curiae* (friend of the court) presentation — despite Agudath Israel's longstanding policy of not taking sides in monetary disputes between two parties.[6]

The essential facts of the case were these: Two business partners could not agree amongst themselves how to divide the assets of their partnership. They submitted their dispute to *din Torah*. In so doing, they followed the standard practice of executing a formal arbitration agreement, known as a *"shtar berurin,"* pursuant to which they designated three *rabbanim* who would sit as a *beis din*, *"lodun beineinu k'fi r'os eineihem*, to adjudicate between [the parties] as they see fit," *"bein b'din bein b'pesharah ha'krovah l'din*, whether by strict *din* or by a compromise that approximates *din."* The parties then engaged in a lengthy *din Torah*, which culminated eventually in a *psak* that was largely favorable to one of the parties [Partner No. 1].

The other party [Partner No. 2] then petitioned the New York State Supreme Court for an order invalidating the *psak din*, to which Partner No. 1 countered by asking the court for an order confirming the *psak din*. Partner No. 2 alleged various deficiencies in the *din Torah* proceeding, including bias by two of the *dayanim*, improper private communications, and certain technical defects in the conduct of the *din Torah* and the delivery of the final *psak*. The Supreme Court rejected the bulk of these allegations. Nonetheless, on its own initiative, the court discovered

---

6. In fact, Agudath Israel's presentation to the court did not deviate from its general policy of not taking sides in monetary disputes. Agudath Israel's *amicus curiae* role was limited to the two issues discussed in the text of this article, which had potential far-reaching ramifications for many *beis din* cases. Agudath Israel expressly declined to take any position on several other issues that related exclusively to the specific dispute before the court.

what it deemed to be certain fundamental flaws in the *din Torah* that rendered the entire proceeding null and void, and thus ruled in Partner No. 2's favor.

The first of these flaws was the fact that the *shtar berurin* was written in general terms. According to the court, the failure to spell out the precise issues to be determined by the rabbinical panel invalidated the arbitration agreement between the parties, which in turn invalidated the entire arbitration proceeding itself.

The second fatal flaw unearthed by the Supreme Court related to the compromise nature of the *psak din*. The court ruled that when the parties conferred upon the *beis din* the authority to render a ruling *"bein b'din bein b'pesharah ha'krovah l'din,"* they envisioned that the *dayanim* would either issue a *psak* in accordance with the strict *din*, or attempt to work out some negotiated settlement between the parties. However, continued the court, what the parties did not envision, and what they never authorized the *beis din* to issue, was a compromise judgment that deviated from strict *din*. The court therefore concluded that the *beis din* had improperly exceeded its authority in rendering its own non-negotiated compromise judgment.

Partner No. 1 petitioned the Supreme Court for a rehearing of the case. The court declined, refusing specifically to accept evidence that it had misinterpreted the phrase *"pesharah ha'krovah l'din."* Partner No. 1 then appealed the ruling to a higher court, the Appellate Division. (In New York State, for reasons that surely somebody must understand, the "Supreme Court" is the lowest level court of general jurisdiction.) However, by a vote of 4-0, the Appellate Division summarily affirmed the decision of the court below. In a last ditch effort, Partner No. 1 turned to New York's highest court, the Court of Appeals, asking for a reversal of the decisions in the Supreme Court and the Appellate Division.

As noted above, Agudath Israel of America, with the authorization of the *Moetzes Gedolei HaTorah*, decided to take an active role in the case. The decision to take this unusual step was based on the fact that the *shtar berurin* used by these two partners was essentially identical to *shtarei berurin* used in most other *beis din* proceedings. Were the lower court rulings to stand, countless *piskei din* could have been vulnerable to attack in the secular courts, thereby wreaking havoc upon the entire process of *din Torah*. To protect against that possibility, Agudath Israel submitted an *amicus curiae* brief which — while taking pains to disavow any knowledge of or interest in the specific dispute between the parties — urged that standard form *shtarei berurin* be accorded appropriate recognition under law.

The Court of Appeals ruled, by a vote of 5-0, that the courts below had erred, and that the ruling of the *beis din* should have been confirmed rather than invalidated. In its decision, the Court of Appeals specifically addressed the two issues raised in Agudath Israel's legal brief. It criticized the Supreme Court's refusal to accept testimony that the term *"pesharah ha'krovah l'din"* authorized the *beis din* to issue a compromise ruling. And it upheld the standard *shtar berurin* as an acceptable form of arbitration agreement, despite its failure to specify the issues to be presented to the *beis din*. Said the Court of Appeals:

> Because the decision of the lower courts in this case casts doubt on the validity of broad arbitration agreements in general, and this particular agreement, which apparently is widely used in beth din arbitrations, we consider it appropriate to reaffirm that broad arbitration agreements are permissible. We have never required that arbitration agreements identify with specificity those disputes which are being submitted.

The decision of New York's highest court sends an important message of respect for the venerable institution of *beis din*. Orthodox Jews who hope the secular courts will help them avoid compliance with a *psak din* would be well advised to take the Court of Appeals' message to heart.

III.

Bimeheirah yiboneh haMikdash, our *batei din* and *Sanhedrin* will be re-established in all their glory and judicial power, *piskei din* will be enforced with the full weight of Torah authority, and the pages of the *Law Journal* will no longer be filled with tales of intra-Jewish litigational warfare. For now, though, *batei din* do not have the legal power to enforce their judgments — and if one of the *baalei din* refuses to abide by a *psak,* the case may well end up in court. Such are the facts of *galus* life.

But even before the ultimate fulfillment of our prayer *"Hoshivah shofteinu k'vorishonah,"* there are steps that we as a Torah community can take to enhance the authority of our *batei din.* When an unhappy *baal din* improperly refuses to comply with a *beis din* ruling — or even when an uncooperative party improperly refuses to respond to a *beis din* summons and submit to the jurisdiction of *din Torah* — and the *beis din* sends him the prescribed number of warnings, his ongoing recalcitrance may justify a determination by the *beis din* that the community should treat him as an outcast. The *Rama's Darkei Moshe* on *Tur Choshen Mishpat* 19 quotes the *Nimukei Yoseif* in the name of Rav Paltui Gaon:

אדם שנתחייב לחבירו בב״ד ועבר על גזירת ב״ד כותבין לקהילות ישראל פלוני גזרנו עליו דין וסרב ולא השגיח והחרמנו אותו שלא יתפללו עמו ולא יזמנו עמו ולא ימולו לו ואל יקברו לו מת והוציאו בניו מבית הספר ואשתו מבית הכנסת עד שיקבל עליו בדין.

> Rough Translation: *One who has been found liable to his colleague in beis din, and he transgresses the ruling of the beis din, [the beis din] writes to the communities of Israel that "we have issued a judgment against So-and-so, and he has declined to follow and paid no heed [to our judgment], and we ostracized him that people should not daven with him, and they should not circumcise his son, and they should not bury his dead, and they [should] remove his children from school and his wife from shul, until he accepts upon himself the judgment."*

However strictly the words of the *Darkei Moshe* are to be applied, and whatever the precise circumstances under which they are to be invoked — issues that are beyond the scope of this article and the competence of this author[7] — one thing is clear: the community itself is called upon to play a major role in upholding the honor of *batei din* and enforcing their judgments. And while the restrictions of secular law and secular society may place certain limitations on the community's ability fully to carry out its assigned role, we need not await our redemption from *galus* before taking at least certain important communal steps.

Last winter, the Conference of Rabbanim of Agudath Israel Synagogues — the network of approximately 30 *shuls* in the United States and Canada that are formally affiliated with the Agudas Yisroel movement — adopted internal guidelines designed to isolate any person against whom there is an outstanding *psak siruv l'din* (a *beis din* determination that the individual has been recalcitrant in submitting to the jurisdiction of *din Torah* or abiding by a *psak din*). As a general rule of policy, such an individual forfeits his right to be a member-in-good-standing of any Agudah branch *shul*, to be called to the Torah for an *aliyah*, to be a *shaliach tzibbur*, or to host any *kiddush* or *simchah*. In addition, the individual is to be explicitly advised that he is not welcome in the *shul*.

In developing the guidelines, which are binding on all Agudah branch *shuls* throughout North America, the *rabbanim* spoke about "the importance of strengthening respect within the community for the hallowed institution of *beth din.*" They further noted their concern about "numerous reports of individuals who ignore a *beth din's* summons or defy a *beth din's* ruling, whether with respect to disputes that arise *bein adam l'chaveiro* in the area of *Choshen Mishpat* or disputes that arise *bein ish l'ishto* in the area of *Even HaEzer* (including *beth din* proceedings involving the tragic plight of the modern day *agunah* whose recalcitrant husband inappropriately refuses to give her a *get*)."

Those concerns should be the concerns of all groups, of all *shuls*, of all people. If our communal heart aches, as it should, at the terrible *chillul Hashem* being created by the boom industry of defiance of *batei din* and litigation in non-Jewish courts, our

---

7. Interested readers may wish to study *Yam Shel Shlomo, Bava Kamma* 10:13 (which is cited by the *Shach* [*Sifsei Kohain*] *Choshen Mishpat* 19:5), where the *Maharshal* takes issue with certain aspects of the *Darkei Moshe.*

communal muscle should be flexed to help address the problem and restore *kvod Shamayim*. As the Agudas Yisrael *shul rabbanim* have shown us, it can be done.[8]

IV.

But traffic must flow both ways on this particular street. If *batei din* have the right to expect that the community will discharge its responsibility of pressuring and if necessary ostracizing recalcitrant *baalei din,* the community has the reciprocal right to expect that *batei din* will discharge their responsibility of *"shomo'a bein acheichem u'shefatetem tzedek* — hear [the disputes] between your brothers and judge with righteousness" [*Devarim* 1:17]. Tragically, the perception is widespread that many *batei din* are not living up to their part of the bargain.

Whether the perception accurately reflects reality is almost beside the point. For even if the vast majority of *dinei Torah* are conducted honestly, efficiently and competently — as I believe they are — the fact remains that many Jews have little or no confidence in the system, and would never even consider submitting their disputes to a *beis din.* It is sad but undeniable that, for whatever reason, the venerable institution of *beis din* suffers from an appreciable lack of communal trust — and without trust it is difficult, if not impossible, to demand respect.

Entirely apart from the issue of public trust, the institution of *beis din* suffers terribly from the decline of territorial *kehillos* in the United States. In large cities like New York, with so many different groups and so many different *rabbanim,* and with no clear central *beis din* address whose authority is recognized by all, the very act of convening a *din Torah* — let alone trying to obtain community pressure in enforcing a *psak din* — is often an exhausting nightmarish ordeal.

---

8. To the best of my knowledge, the Agudah branch *shuls* are thus far the only network of *batei kneisios* that have implemented such guidelines on a network-wide basis. A number of other individual *shuls* and *kehillos* have reportedly adopted similar guidelines, including Congregation Yetev Lev D'Satmar in Brooklyn and the Lincoln Square Synagogue in Manhattan.

Many *baalei din*, because of the decline of strong centralized *kehillos*, have difficulty agreeing on the *beis din* to which they will take their dispute. They accordingly select an *ad hoc* panel of *dayanim* through the system of *zabla* (an acronym for *"zeh borer lo echad"* — see *Mishnah Sanhedrin* 3:1), whereby each party chooses one *dayan*, and the two *dayanim* so chosen jointly designate the third member of the panel. This method of appointing a *beis din*, though sanctioned in *halachah*, all too frequently leads to severe problems — as evidenced by the phenomenon of "dueling *dayanim*" noted above, where members of the *beis din* themselves appear to assume the role of adversarial advocates rather than impartial judges.[9]

The questions of how to restore public trust in *batei din*, and how to deal with the realities of our decentralized lifestyle in *galus America*, deserve the urgent attention of our best thinkers and most influential leaders. The challenge is not a simple one, but the stakes could not be higher: enhancing *kvod Shamayim* in the face of massive *chillul Hashem*.

---

9. At a national convention of Agudath Israel of America, Rabbi Yaakov Perlow — Novominsker Rebbe, reported that he had heard from Rav Moshe Feinstein more than 20 years ago that there is a strong preference in our generation to submit disputes to permanent *batei din* rather than to panels chosen through *zabla*. Rabbi Perlow also called upon the leadership of the Torah world, along with Agudath Israel, to establish a national *beis din* that would have broad public recognition, backing, confidence and support.

A Layman's Guide to a Din Torah

Yoseph M. Braunfeld

✧ *Why Not Litigate?*

Mazel Tov! You are finally going to move into your new home built exactly to your specifications. You contract with Boneh-Yofeh Builders, a reputable Jewish firm. When you are about to move in, you notice that the wiring is not as extensive as you specified. The contractor tells you it is and will not incur the extra expense to rewire. No problem, you assume. Like any good American, you will let the courts decide.

Your daughter's wedding last night was an exhausting effort, but — who can deny it? — well worth it. You now take her wedding dress to the local *shomer Shabbos* dry cleaner. He tells you he really doesn't like to do these dresses, but since you are a good customer, he will give it his best. Sure enough, when you pick it up, some ornamentation is ruined. You immediately blame him for ruining your expensive investment which you planned to use for your other five daughters. He says he warned you that it was your risk. No problem, you assume. Like any good American, you will let the courts decide.

Your 10-year-old crashes his bicycle into the non-observant lady who lives at the other end of the block. Before you can placate her that it was only an accident, she berates you for allowing your child to ride on the sidewalk instead of on the street, thereby causing extensive damage to the thousand-dollar fur coat she was carrying. You will be hearing from her lawyer. No problem, you assume. Like any good American, you will let the courts decide.

Then you remember that there is a problem. You've read about it in past issues of *The Jewish Observer*. You've heard it expounded at public addresses. Very likely, you've come across it when learning *Chumash* or *Gemara*. Nonetheless, it is worth repeating: The Torah explicitly prohibits the primary usage of secular courts to adjudicate disputes between Jews.[1]

So what can you do? The Torah prescribes its own court system — *beis din*. Each *beis din* consists of several judges qualified by their Torah expertise. The number of sitting judges in *batei din* vary. We will concern ourselves here with a three judge panel, the number normally required for civil cases.

→ *Allaying Fears of the Unfamiliar*

Lest one think that a *beis din* is just an alternative legal system, a *pasuk* in *Tehillim* informs us that Hashem Himself participates in every *beis din* decision.[2] The problem arises from the fact that the intricate structure of the American legal system combined with ignorance about the *beis din* discourages people from going to a *beis din*. After all, if the legal system with which I am somewhat familiar is too complicated for me, why do I want to start with a totally unfamiliar system? I can just hire a lawyer who will professionally litigate.

---

1. *"And these are the laws that you should put before them* — before the Jewish courts, and not before the gentile courts" (*Gittin* 88b).
2. *Tehillim* 82:1. See *Malbim* and other commentators.

The following lines will hopefully allay the fear of the unknown and familiarize potential litigants with the system. These guidelines pertain to the courts in the United States as well as abroad.

Originating a case or consenting to dispute in a secular court is prohibited. In case of an irreconcilable dispute, the Torah ideally prefers a compromise to a strict ruling. Nevertheless, if a Jew vociferously believes that he (or she — women are equally recognized as plaintiffs or defendants) was wronged, he may recover his loss without undue constraint. The *din Torah* legal process is actually quite simple and is accessible to any knowledgeable person.

• **What constitutes a *beis din*?**

Hashem directed Moshe Rabbeinu to implement a "*semichah*" system beginning with his disciple Yehoshua, whereby those demonstrating their proficiency would be allowed to judge. After this continuous chain was broken subsequent to the destruction of the Second *Beis HaMikdash,* our leaders decreed that anyone properly versed in *halachah* would have limited authority to judge. Throughout our history, cities with a significant Jewish population have organized standing *batei din*. Alternatively, a valid *beis din* may be set up by each of the disputants selecting a judge, and they in turn selecting a third one.

• **Where do I find I find a *beis din*?**

Many large communities and organizations have a standing *beis din* available to their constituency. Anyone wanting to initiate a proceeding should contact his rabbi or a major organization.

• **What kind of dispute can I bring as a *din Torah*?**

Since the exile, our judges are not empowered to judge capital or corporeal crimes. *All* civil altercations between two parties, however, are eligible. Most cases involve financial disputes. *Batei din* may also be called upon to mediate character attacks, and the like. The purpose of the *din Torah* is to evaluate how the Torah sizes up the particular quandary for disputants who want to maintain their lives in its spirit.

• **Must I represent myself, or may I delegate a lawyer?**

The Torah prefers that the parties represent themselves. Nevertheless, when a party may not feel confident that he will present his position properly or when he fears that the case may be significantly complex, some *batei din* allow him to bring along an expert, preferably someone versed in *halachah,* as an advisor (*to'ein*). Some *batei din* actually prefer that a halachically-versed *to'ein* be engaged so as to reduce irrelevant arguments. On the other hand, many *batei din* greatly discourage the use of a *to'ein,* especially one who does so as a professional; they may even totally disallow the use of a *to'ein* if they suspect that he is just trying to twist the case in his client's favor rather than limit himself to presenting relevant arguments.

• **Don't we have a rule of "*Dina d'malchusa dina* — that we are obliged to comply with the law of the land"?**

Dina d'malchusa dina means that we are required to adhere to all governmental laws not antithetical to *halachah.* In a conflict between Torah law and secular law, however, we observe only Torah law. Likewise, it does not mean that personal disagreements may be adjudicated in a civil court. The contrary is true. That is not to say that the *dayanim* will not take accepted business practice into consideration. *Batei din* realize that there are widely-accepted customs which are assumed by all the people of a community. These customs would retain the status of implicit agreements.

• **How can I be sure that the government authorities will recognize the *beis din*'s judgment?**

Beis din has the parties sign a "*shtar berurin* — consent to arbitration." Secular courts will normally treat the *psak* of *beis din* as a legal arbitration as long as certain guidelines are not violated. The *beis din* will ensure that maintaining these guidelines does not in itself violate their independent judicial authority.

• **How is a *din Torah* initiated?**

If the disputants do not come together to the *beis din,* the plaintiff (*tove'ah*) will ask the *beis din* to send a summons (*hazmanah*) to the defendant (*nitvah*). The defendant has the option of requesting a different *beis din.* If, however, he fails to respond, the *beis din* may send two more summonses. If there is still no response, the *beis din* will either issue a *seruv,* which is a public announcement stating that the defendant is not responding to *beis din*'s order to appear, or will allow the plaintiff to pursue his case in a secular court. The secular court would then act as *beis din's shaliach* (agent).

When the *din Torah* does get under way, each party, possibly assisted by a *to'ein*, presents his case to the *beis din*. Women may not generally serve as witnesses, but they may present expertise which the judges will consider. The *beis din* then deliberates privately and issues its judgment.

The *beis din* itself may not be in a position to enforce the *psak*, but may direct the plaintiff to enforce it through the secular courts based on the arbitration agreement. It can then be enforced via the normal enforcement channels.

• **Who pays the ancillary costs?**

The normal practice is to split the *beis din*'s fee. Each party is responsible for his own expenses and lost time. It is therefore advisable to take that into consideration.

• **"I want to swear!"**

The *Gemara* discusses cases where swearing is required or optional. Nowadays, *beis din* will not allow disputants to swear.

• **"Can I bring additional evidence later?"**

The general rule is that a disputant may reconvene the *beis din* to clarify or add to a prior claim. He may not change or contradict a prior statement.

• **Will the judgment be a guilty/innocent type of ruling?**

At the case's outset, the *beis din* will attempt to convince the parties to accept a compromise settlement. If the case turns out to be one not explicitly described in the *Shulchan Aruch*, the judges will then work out a compromise amongst themselves based on the *din,* but allowing for subjective discretion, with extenuating circumstances taken into consideration. Of course, this can only be done if the parties agreed originally to grant the *beis din* this latitude. If the *beis din* is requested to judge on a strict *din* basis, then the choice of rulings would be more limited.

• **Can a judgment be appealed?**

Normally not. The *halachah* recognizes the finality of a *psak beis din*. By submitting a dispute to a *beis din*, the parties accept that particular *beis din*'s ultimate authority. In line with this logic, unlike secular courts, the judges will likely not express their reasoning, although the parties do have the right to request the reasons for the decision.

• **If I receive a summons from a Jewish plaintiff to appear in a civil court, what should I do?**

For practical reasons, respond to the summons. You should, however, have a *beis din* send the plaintiff a *hazmanah* protesting his submitting the case to civil court. If the plaintiff persists, you may defend yourself in the civil court. The plaintiff would be committing the halachic transgression.

• **What if I summon a defendant to *beis din* and he insists on going to civil court?**

The *halachah* would allow you to go. This is tantamount to the case where the defendant ignores the summons. The *halachah* recognizes the civil court as a *shaliach* (agent) of *beis din*.

• **I (or my adversary) initiated a case in civil court, but we want to do *teshuvah*. Or even if our motives are not altruistic, we want to reinitiate the proceeding in *beis din*. Can we?**

If the dispute has not concluded, then there is no question that it may be reinitiated in *beis din*. If the secular court had reached a verdict, however, there is a major discussion amongst the responsa whether it may be reinitiated in *beis din*. As a matter of current practice, most *batei din* will not accept such a case.

• **I know for sure that the judge in the civil court is a Torah-observant Jew. Can I go to his court?**

The Torah places the prohibition on any legal system not under Torah auspices. The background of a particular judge in a secular system is irrelevant. By the same token, even if one knows that a civil verdict will correspond to a *beis din*'s in a particular case, one must go to the *beis din* and not the civil court.

• **What if my adversary is a non-observant Jew or a gentile?**

The rules are the same. If the non-observant Jew forces you to go to a secular court, you may go, just as if you are forced by an otherwise observant Jew. As long as you take an initiative to submit your case to a *beis din*, you do not transgress the prohibition. If you desire, you may also attempt to convince the gentile to attend a *beis din*, but there is no such requirement, and you may settle the dispute in civil court.

• **I have an irreconcilable dispute which both of us want to pursue halachically, but we do not want to go to all the expense and trouble of a *beis din*. Do we have an enforceable alternative?**

The standard civil *beis din* prescribed by the Torah consists of three judges. Nevertheless, altercating parties may agree to present their case to a single *posek*. If they agree to the aforementioned *shtar berurin*, *halachah* will accept the finality of the *posek*'s judgment. Likewise, the secular court system will look upon the decision as a mutually binding arbitration.

When Yisro joined up with the Jewish nation, Moshe described the great deluge of questions and cases being posed to him as the people's search for the teaching of Hashem.[3] That is how we are to approach our conflicts. If we pursue our rights because we feel that we earned our property honestly, according to the laws — and spirit — of the Torah, then we have nothing to fear from a *din Torah*. We should also remember that if we lose the *din Torah*, we should be even more thankful, since we would otherwise have retained property that is not really ours. The Ultimate Judge guarantees that using the *beis din* will elicit the truth. There is no guarantee in regard to a secular court.

---

3. *Shemos* 18:15. See *Rashi*.

The Exalted Status
of the Beis Din Process

Adapted from a shiur by
Rabbi Avrohom Pam

We celebrate Shavuos as "the Time of the Giving of the Torah," commemorating our People's receiving the Torah at Sinai. Besides reliving this pinnacle event in human history, this festival gives us opportunity to reinforce our commitment to live by the Torah's laws — in our daily actions and thoughts between man and his Creator, as in our interactions with others. In cases of doubt or conflict, disputes may be brought to a *beis din*, a rabbinical court, where according to Dovid HaMelech, the proceedings can be appreciated in terms of "G–d standing in the Divine assembly, in the midst of judges shall He judge" (*Tehillim* 82:1). Moreover, the maintenance of equity and justice is a prerequisite for the continued existence of the world (*Rosh Hashanah* 31a, *Maharsha*, loc. cit.).

While *The Jewish Observer* has published articles featuring explanations of the process of submitting disputes to a *din Torah,* as well as criticisms of some aspects of the system, it is important to stress that not only is a Jew forbidden to resort to secular courts, he will ultimately find the experience more frustrating than any *din Torah.*

With this essay, we would like to underscore the obligatory nature of using the *beis din,* when necessary, and its exalted nature in the Torah scheme of things. The following thoughts on the topic are adapted from a shiur by Rabbi Avrohom Pam, *Rosh Yeshivah* of Mesivta Torah Vodaath and member of the *Moetzes Gedolei HaTorah* (Council of Torah Sages of Agudath Israel of America).

✦ *The Central Role of Torah Law*

When the queen travels, she is customarily preceded by her attendants, and then followed by an entourage of guards. They serve her and protect her. Similarly, says the *Midrash, Klal Yisrael's* encounter with the Divine Royal Presence at Sinai, as recounted in *Parshas Yisro,* is preceded in the *Chumash* by Yisro's discussion with Moshe Rabbeinu regarding *dinim,* counseling him to establish an effective judiciary system, and is followed by *"Ve'eileh hamishpatim* — And these are the laws that you should place before them." Just as the royal guards protect the queen from all sides, so too do obligations regarding *dinim* protect the basic fundamentals of the Torah.

> The *Gemara (Bava Metzia* 68) relates that Rav Pappa served as the judge in a dispute between two partners. One of the partners had withdrawn his half of the capital in a joint investment without the knowledge and consent of the other, who brought the case to the *beis din.* Rav Pappa ruled that since exactly half of the assets were taken by the partner, he was within his rights in accordance with *halacha.* A year later the same two people again entered a partnership in purchasing

several barrels of wine together. This time the other partner liquidated half of the barrels without his partner's consent. So the other decided to take his partner to Rav Pappa for a *din Torah*. This time Rav Pappa ruled against the partner who had liquidated the partnership without the consent of the other.

Rav Pappa realized that he should elaborate on his ruling, lest the litigant who had lost both times feel that the *Rav* had some personal animosity against him. He explained that in the first case, where the partnership consisted of capital, one could take back half of the money without any question of impropriety. In the second case, however, where wine was involved, how could one partner take some of the barrels and sell them? Certainly the quality of the wine varied from barrel to barrel. One person could not independently sell part of the assets without the risk of being unfair.

The lesson learned from this *Gemara* is that had Rav Pappa not explained his ruling, the second partner would have certainly felt a grudge against *batei dinim*.

✦ When Objectivity is Invariably Lacking

Rabbi Yisrael Salanter once commented that when one poses a question of *issur* and *heter*, and the *Rav* says that an item is *treif*, even if it involves great financial loss or, as a result, one has no meat for Shabbos, the person does not begrudge the *Rav*. If he loses a *din Torah* in monetary matters, however, the loser invariably has complaints against the *Rav*. He answers that in a case of *issur* and *heter*, there is no contest between a winner and a loser. But in a *din Torah*, one party wins, giving the other litigant cause to be upset. Another reason, he adds, is that in matters of *issur* and *heter*, one realizes that he is not proficient in the laws of *basar v'chalov* (mixtures of meat and milk) or *taruvos* (other mixtures of the forbidden and permitted). In the area of *Choshen Mishpat* (business law), however, everyone thinks that he is as proficient in the *halachah* as the *Rav*. Yet even *talmidei chachamim* who have mastered the relevant *halachos* can lose sight of the fact that they can lack objectivity. The Nesivos HaMishpat (Rabbi Yaakov Lorberbaum) writes to his children in his *tzava'ah* (ethical will) that even if they become great *talmidei chachamim*, in a case of a monetary question, one *must* ask another *Rav* because "No man [is capable of] seeing his own faults"; one must be even more careful than in cases of *issur v'heter*.

The Ksav Sofer (Rabbi Shmuel Binyomin Sofer) writes three *teshuvos* (halachic responsa) about whether a son can summon a father, or a *talmid* can summon a *rebbe* to a *din Torah*.

The one who posed the question had felt that it was a *bizayon* (disrespectful) for a son to take his father to *din*. The Ksav Sofer unequivocally answers that resorting to abjudicate a *din Torah* is not a *bizayon* and should not be treated as such. He does caution, however, that one must exercise caution in how he expresses himself at the *din Torah*, because engaging in an adverserial exchange could detract from one's *kibbud av* or *kibbud rav*. He then relates an incident he had heard from his father, the Chasam Sofer:

> The S'MA had had a monetary dispute with someone, and later had occasion to raise the question during a gathering of the gedolei hador. He presented the case to them, and pointed out why he felt his position was right. One of the gedolim opened up a Choshen Mishpat and showed him how his reasoning was wrong, pointing out that the S'MA rules against him. He then arose and said, "Now I understand the comment of Chazal that declares 'No man [is capable of] seeing his own faults.' Even a gadol b'Yisrael cannot rely on his own reasoning when he is a party to a monetary dispute and must ask a she'eilas chacham."

✣ Striving for Shalom

Rabbi Yisrael Salanter once gave a letter of introduction to an indigent person to help him collect funds. His students, upon learning of this, were outraged because the individual was known to be a fraud, so they plotted all sorts of ways to get the letter back from the individual. When Reb Yisrael heard of this, he summoned his students and admonished them that they were acting in total oblivion of questions of *gezel* (thievery); he had legitimately given the letter to the individual, and they have no right to take possession of it without the man's consent.

> The Chofetz Chaim points out that after Yisro had presented Moshe Rabbeinu with his proposal for a structured judicial system, he added, "And the entire nation will go to its place *b'shalom*"— with peace (*Shemos* 18:23), an expression that seems inappropriate. According to the *Gemara* at the end of *Berachos*, when one addresses living people, one should say, "Go *l'shalom*" — *to* a higher level of *shalom*. Only in reference to a dead person ל״ר does one say *"b'shalom"* — as if to say go *with* the peace that you have acquired. Why, then, does Yisro use the term *"b'shalom"* in regard to living people?
>
> The Chofetz Chaim explains that if one is ל״ר guilty of theft, then after 120 years, when his *neshamah* ascends to heaven, it may be sentenced to return to earth in the form of a *gilgul* — a transient soul — so as to return the stolen goods to the family of the party that had suffered the loss. This is what Yisro was referring to when he specified *b'shalom*: After 120 years on this world, when one's *neshamah* is called to heaven for its ultimate accounting, may it be *b'shalom* — to eternal peace.

People seek excuses to avoid a *din Torah*. And even after a person goes to a *din Torah*, he may misrepresent the facts. This is similar to a patient who has a pain in his foot and consults a doctor; when asked where it hurts, he shows the doctor his other foot because he fears the doctor might cause him pain when he examines the sore foot. Shouldn't he realize that the only way the doctor can heal him is if he knows all the symptoms? So, too, how can a *beis din* rule correctly if it is not given all the relevant facts? One must know that going to a *beis din* is at least as important as going to a doctor, for one's spiritual well-being is at risk.

→ *Justice: An Eternal Need*

When *Mashiach* comes and the world is filled with *daas Torah*, as the *Navi* describes it, one might assume that *batei din* will cease to exist. Quite the contrary. As people search in earnest for *emes* and *daas Torah*, *batei din* will certainly increase. This ultimately will lead to *kiddush Hashem*.

> *The Midrash relates how Alexander the Great, in his travels, visited a royal court just as two litigants came before the king. The dispute was as follows: One person had sold a parcel of land to another. Upon digging up the property, the buyer discovered a great treasure. He claimed that the treasure did not belong to him, as he had purchased only a piece of real estate. The seller argued that he had sold the property and all of its contents to the buyer, and the treasure rightfully belongs to the buyer.*
>
> *Alexander the Great had never heard such an unusual case, and was very curious as to how the king would rule. The king called over one of the parties and asked him about his family — if he had any children of marriageable age. He affirmed that he, indeed, had a daughter to marry off. He then enquired of the other party regarding his family, and if he might have a son of marriageable age. He also answered in the affirmative. The King ruled: could one imagine a better shidduch than one uniting two such honest families! The daughter of the one should marry the son of the other, and the treasure be given to the young couple as a wedding gift. This search for truth on the part of the litigants and its ultimate resolution made a profound impression on Alexander the Great.*

The time to reflect on these ideas, and to commit oneself to seeking the opinion of a *beis din* and abiding by it, is before a person becomes involved in litigation, before he has vested interests in a specific outcome. Properly conducted *mishpat* has the potential of creating a great *kiddush Hashem*, and will be instrumental in bringing *Mashiach* speedily in our days.

Respect for the Halachic Legal System
Concern Over Its Misuse

Based on an address by the Novominsker Rebbe,
Rabbi Yaakov Perlow

I deem it extremely important to raise an issue that requires our serious attention and that bears directly on the challenge before us at all times, *"t'hei Shem Shamayim misaheiv al yadecha."* In recent years, it has become the practice of some Orthodox Jews and some Orthodox lawyers to defame and vilify the sacred institution of *batei din b'Yisrael*, of Jewish ecclesiastic courts. Not only do people refuse to respond to a summons from such courts, but they resort to secular courts, before and after a *din Torah*, in the process destroying the credibility and prestige of the Jewish legal system.

The following quotation from a brief submitted by an Orthodox lawyer on behalf of his client, seeking to upset a *psak din* of a duly-constituted *beis din* of *talmidei chachamim*, says more than my descriptive phrases: "I am now no longer under the thumb of a biased, corrupt, unfair and fraudulent *beth din*." It is well-known that secular judges are shocked at the extent to which Orthodox Jews will go to undermine the decision of a *beis din*, up to and including poison pen letters against *rabbanim*. This is a tremendous *chillul Hashem*.

In a somewhat different situation, a husband suing for a civil divorce refused to give his wife a *get*. This man's lawyer, an Orthodox Jew, testified upon examination by the court that "not all Orthodox rabbis require a *get* to be given before a woman remarries, and there have been Orthodox rabbis who perform such marriages, even intermarriages ...."

This from an Orthodox lawyer, mind you. He even submitted a statement by a Reform rabbi, with three academic degrees after his name, asserting that "... in accordance with the Talmudic principle of *dina d'malchusa dina*, the civil divorce is recognized not only civilly but also religiously, and each party is free to remarry civilly and religiously ..."*Rachmanah l'tzelan.*

The corruption of unscrupulous people, unfortunately *shomrei mitzvah*, has resulted in the desecration of the Almighty, the desecration of the honor of the Torah, and desecration of the honor of the Jewish People before the legal profession, before the secular world.

Admittedly, the subject of *batei din* today is a double-edged sword. People have complaints about different *rabbanim, dayanim, borerim* and *to'anim* (functionaries in the *beis din*). This is not the place to explore this sensitive issue. But I would like to recall for public consumption how more than 20 years ago, Rabbi Moshe Feinstein, remarked in my presence that in these times it is preferable to go to a standing *beis din* of three, in contrast to resorting to *borerus* (where each party to the dispute selects one judge, and the two judges appoint a third) – a *beis din* of *zabla'a*. Such courts, while well-grounded in *halachah*, are subject to many pressures and pitfalls, whereas a totally neutral *beis din*, where none of the individual members of the court is chosen by either of the disputants, is more likely to function smoothly, and to arrive at judgments in line with Torah principle.

Years ago, I had the merit to sit on a *beis din* with Rav Breuer and Rav Schwab in K'hal Adath Jeshurun. The *aimas hadin*, respect for the Law, the *mora Shamayim*, the fear of Heaven, the trembling before the realization of *hamishpat l'Elokim hu* (*Devarim* 1:17) that judgment is ultimately the exclusive realm of the Almighty, which prevailed in that *beis din*, was simply overpowering. One could truly sense the presence of G–d as Jews came for a *din Torah* in that court. Understandably, that *beis din* commanded the respect and obedience of the litigants.

I would suggest that the time has come for the leadership of the Torah world, along with Agudath Israel, to establish a high-level *beis din tzeddek*. Made of individuals with the highest credentials, *talmidei chachamim*, both young and old, these *dayanim* will alternate and serve the community with the honor and respect that *din Torah* requires. Such a respected *beis din* will promote fulfillment of the verse, "*Tzedek, tzedek tirdof* — Pursue only justice" (*Devarim* 14:20), as our Sages have explained it: "*Haloch achar beis din yafah* — Search after a worthy court." It would be fearless, just and dignified; it would win the allegiance of the entire Torah community. Moreover, it would help reinstate *kavod Torah, emes, din* and *shalom* in our midst. And it would certainly help us all fulfill "that the Name of Heaven be made beloved through you."

The Secular Enforceability of a Beis Din Judgment

Shlomo Chaim Resnicoff

O thers have cogently articulated the contours of the halachic imperative to submit disputes to *batei din* rather than resort to secular courts. Alas, today's rabbinic courts often lack, as a practical matter, the independent power to effectively enforce their rulings. Although we pray that this temporary situation is soon remedied, this article emphasizes that in many instances, it is possible — and halachically permissible — to utilize the secular judicial system to enforce a *beis din's* decision. With proper planning, we can even have a secular court affirmatively order a person to fulfill his promise to have a dispute resolved by a *beis din*.

Why would American courts support the *beis din* process? Secular law realizes that the litigation system is terribly flawed and, as a result, federal and state statutes encourage the employment of alternative systems of dispute resolution, including the use of arbitration. When a written arbitration agreement is governed by such statutes, courts will specifically order parties to proceed to arbitration and will implement any arbitral awards. Indeed, secular support for arbitration is so strong that a *New York Law Journal* article likened the chances of overturning a properly obtained arbitration award to a snowball's chances of surviving *Gehinnom*.[1] American law regards an agreement to have disputes resolved by a rabbinic court as a rabbinic arbitration agreement and the *dayanim* as arbitrators.

Wouldn't enforcement of a rabbinic arbitration agreement violate some constitutional principle regarding the supposed separation of church from state? In most instances, the answer is "No." Religious Jews have the same right as anyone else to contractually agree to submit their decisions to arbitration and to have such contracts secularly enforced. A refusal to enforce a rabbinic arbitration agreement might be an unconstitutional deprivation of a religious Jew's right to contract.[2]

Each matter, however, involves many factual nuances and legal intricacies. For example, even though a case arises between parties located in New York, this does not necessarily mean that the New York arbitration statute, as opposed to the Federal Arbitration Act, applies. Before proceeding in any particular case, the parties and the *dayanim* should consult a licensed attorney who is familiar with arbitration law.[3] The purpose of this brief article is simply to highlight a few fundamental — and avoidable — problems that may arise because of ignorance of the law, often despite everyone's good intentions.

✧ *Drafting and Executing an Appropriate Arbitration Agreement*

To be statutorily enforceable, an arbitration agreement must be in writing and should be signed by all relevant parties. The agreement should clearly state whether a person is signing on his own behalf, as an agent for another person or on behalf of an

---

1. David E. Robbins, "Vacating Arbitration Awards," 9/22/94 N.Y.L.J. 1 (col. 1).

2. See, e.g., Elmora Hebrew Center, Inc. v. Fishman, 125 N.J. 404, 413-414 (1991).

3. The 12-page outline I distributed at the Conference, which contained numerous citations to specific cases, and the audio tape of my presentation, although hopefully useful, do not serve as an adequate substitute for speaking to a lawyer. An attorney may help a *beis din* establish a standard set of rules and procedures that would comply with all federal and state requirements.

entity, such as a general partnership, limited partnership, limited liability company or corporation. Anyone purporting to sign for another should warrant that he has the legal authority to do so and should produce satisfactory evidence of such authority. One of the many reasons why competent secular attorneys should be consulted is that they can provide critical advice in a particular case as to which parties are necessary and as to whether persons claiming to represent such parties have the legal authority to do so.[4] An arbitration award will not be enforced if it purports to affect the rights of persons who have not participated in or agreed to be bound by the arbitration.

In one case, a single member of a yeshivah's board of trustees signed a contract to sell a piece of land owned by the yeshivah. The other members of the board of trustees took the signer to a *din Torah*, and the *beis din* ruled that the signer had no authority to bind the yeshivah. Nevertheless, because the party who entered into the contract as purchaser of the property was not part of the arbitration, that party was not bound by the *beis din's* ruling.[5]

An arbitration agreement should specifically identify the *beis din* or the *dayanim* to whom any dispute should be submitted. Statutes may contain a "default mechanism" whereby the court will designate arbitrators if they are not named in the arbitration agreement. Nevertheless, whether rightfully or not, secular courts may balk at appointing arbitrators where a matter is to be considered in light of Jewish law.

As a practical matter, an arbitration agreement should ideally be drafted and executed *before* a dispute arises, because that is when the parties are most likely to sign it. There may be greater trust between the parties at this point than after the trouble begins. In addition, some *batei din* are known to take particular

---

4. Attorneys could also assist in suggesting, or drafting, additional provisions that the parties or the *beis din* may consider desirable, such as clauses concerning the confidentiality of any information produced in connection with the arbitration, the time periods within which any arbitration award is to be issued, etc.

5. Levovitz v. Yeshiva Beth Henoch, Inc., 120 A.D.2d 289 (2nd Dept. 1986). Other New York state or federal courts where the capacity in which someone signed — or whether all necessary parties signed — an arbitration agreement became an important issue include Mikel v. Scharf, 105 Misc.2d 548 (Kings Co. 1980); Glauber v. Coren, 204 A.D.2d 389 (2nd Dept. 1994); Waldman v. Bausk, N.Y.L.J. 2/7/94 (p. 34, col.2); Sound Around, Inc. v. CE Electronics Sales Corp., 1998 WL 199871 (E.D.N.Y.).

positions with respect to certain controversial halachic issues, such as the extent to which secular law is halachically significant. Because the parties may be unable to predict the precise problems that may arise, there is less reason to quarrel over the selection of a *beis din* at the outset than after the halachic issues are clear.

The agreement should be written in English, because this is the language secular courts will understand best. If a party does not comprehend English, the agreement should also be written in a language he does understand. The agreement should expressly authorize the arbitrators to base their award on Jewish law, on compromise close to Jewish law, or on what the arbitrators consider to be just. Such a clause should prevent an arbitration award from being overturned because the *dayanim* demonstrated "a manifest disregard of the [secular] law."[6] Because the arbitrators are unlikely to base their award on strict Jewish law (*din*), the agreement, for halachic purposes, should specifically provide that any decision made by a majority of the arbitrators shall be binding.[7]

Any reason why a *dayan* may be perceived as partial should be explicitly revealed, and the arbitration agreement should contain an explicit waiver by each of the parties of any such bias. A case involving a Monsey, New York, *beis din* underscores the need for complete disclosure. In that case, there was a reason why one member of the *beis din* may have been biased against a particular party. For purposes of its ruling, the court assumed both that this *dayan* had openly offered to explain the possible bias to the adversely affected party and that the party expressly waived such disclosure. Nevertheless, the court ruled that while a possible financial bias can be waived once it is disclosed, a party cannot effectively waive the disclosure itself.[8]

In order to be enforced, an arbitration award must be considered "final." One quite questionable Florida decision revealed how expansively this requirement could be (mis)construed.[9] In that case, the arbitration agreement stated that "[t]he decisions of

6. This ground is not mentioned in New York State's arbitration statute.

7. See, e.g., R' Yitzchak Weiss, *Minchas Yitzchok* VI:158.

8. Fein v. Fein, 160 Misc. 2d 750 (Nassau Co. 1994).

9. Ainsworth v. Schoen, 606 So.2d 1275 (Ct.App. 3 Dist. 1992).

this Arbitration will be legally binding upon us with no recourse to any other authority whatsoever." Notwithstanding this language, two of the three *dayanim* acknowledged — one in deposition and the other in an affidavit — that the *beis din* award might be "incomplete," either because, in theory, a higher *beis din* might accept a case that was already ruled upon by a "lower" *beis din* or because the parties, under the terms of the agreement, would "have an opportunity to appeal the decision to a higher Jewish court." Consequently, the court refused to confirm the arbitration award. To minimize the possibility of such a result, the arbitration agreement should explicitly state that any award is to be "final," that the parties waive any right to appeal, and that no other court — including any other rabbinic court — would have any right to review the award. Halachic authorities should be consulted as to whether any particular steps are necessary to ensure that such a provision is halachically effective.

✦ Conducting the Arbitration Proceeding

Virtually all state and federal arbitration statutes incorporate — in one guise or another [10]— the requirement that the arbitration be conducted in accordance with secular notions of fundamental procedural fairness. An attorney should be specifically consulted as to which procedural rules may be waived, and it may be desirable for the parties in the arbitration agreement to clearly waive any objection based on noncompliance with these rules.

Some rules may not be waived. The New York statute, for instance, states that a party has a non-waivable right to be represented by an attorney.[11] This does not mean that every party to a *din Torah* must bring an attorney. Instead, it means that at any point in the *beis din* proceeding, a party may choose to have an attorney. Any prior agreement by the party supposedly sur-

---

10. These requirements are sometimes designated as a *priori* procedural rules and sometimes as bases for overturning an arbitration award. They may appear explicitly in the statues or they may arise in case law either interpreting or supplementing the statutes.
11. See C.P.L.R. 7506 (d), (f).

rendering the right to an attorney is void, and the *beis din* may in no way penalize the party for using a lawyer. The right to counsel includes the right to have the attorney produce and examine evidence, as well as the right to have the attorney present and cross-examine witnesses.

Another common problem is that prior to, or during, the arbitration proceeding, one or more of the *dayanim* may speak privately with one, but not all, of the parties. Such *ex parte* conversations can be fatal to the secular enforceability of an arbitration award — and may raise serious halachic questions as well. The secular problems may be minimized by including an explicit waiver in the arbitration agreement.

Secular — and perhaps halachic — problems also arise when a *dayan* independently investigates a dispute, without the presence or permission of the parties, by contacting witnesses (even "expert" witnesses who have no specific knowledge about the dispute but who supposedly have general knowledge about industry practices), visiting the scene of an accident or viewing purportedly damaged property. Although the *dayanim* may correctly or incorrectly[12] believe that such independent investigations will more effectively yield the "truth," such practices may prevent the arbitration award from being enforced. Once again, however, it is possible that the parties may be able to effectively waive any applicable objection by a waiver in the arbitration agreement.

✦ When Secular Enforcement May Be Unavailable

For assorted "public policy" reasons, courts in different jurisdictions may not enforce certain arbitration agreements or awards. Thus, in many jurisdictions, courts will make their own independent determinations as to child custody or child

---

12. *Ex parte* conversations with a witness may actually give rise to miscommunications that might have been avoided had the parties been present. Similarly, a *dayan's ex parte* investigation of a location or of property may cause him to reach erroneous conclusions. The current status of the location or of the property may not accurately reflect its respective condition before, at, or immediately after the event giving rise to the dispute.

support matters to ensure that the results are "in the best interests of the child."[13] Nevertheless, whether or not a particular *beis din* award is secularly enforceable does not affect the halachic obligation to submit the dispute to *beis din*.

There is considerable controversy concerning the enforceability of a prenuptial agreement to submit to a *beis din* the question as to whether, in a family dissolution context, a *get* must be given or received. While the highest court in New York ruled, by the slimmest of margins, that such agreements are enforceable, not all courts in other jurisdictions agree.[14] If they are to be enforceable, these agreements should be precise.[15] Ideally, they should specify the composition of the *beis din* to whom any dispute would be submitted.

✦ Conclusion

Rabbi J. David Bleich explains that a person who wrongfully goes to secular courts rather than to *beis din* engages in a grave *chillul Hashem*. Such a person implicitly praises Gentiles and their beliefs, and it is as if he blasphemed, cursed and committed violence against the Torah.[16] The contrary should also be true. One who eschews secular courts and submits himself and his disputes to *beis din* glorifies Hashem's Name and exalts and honors the Torah. With such mitzvos, come *berachos*. At present, if the *dinei Torah* are handled properly, we may in most cases use the secular courts as tools to help carry out the verdicts of *batei din*. We pray that we are soon *zocheh* to another *berachah*, the *berachah* that *batei din* regain the ability to enforce their own judgments.

---

13. See, e.g., Glauber v. Glauber, 192 A.D.2d 94 (2d Dept. 1993).

14. Contrast Avitzur v. Avitzur, 58 N.Y.2d 108, cert. denied, 464 U.S. 817 (1983), to Aflalo v. Aflalo, 295 N.J.Super. 527 (1996).

15. Courts have cited lack of specificity as one of the reasons for refusing to grant specific performance based on the oral declaration at a Jewish wedding that the marriage is entered into according to the laws of Moses and Israel or on a *kesubah*, a written agreement, often in Hebrew and/or Aramaic, referring to the couple's financial responsibilities. See, e.g., In re Marriage of Victor, 177 Ariz. 231 (Ct.App. 1993). But see In re Marriage of Goldman, 196 Ill.App.3rd 785 (1990) (requiring specific performance based on a *kesubah*).

16. *Shulchan Aruch, Choshen Mishpat* 26:1.

A Proposal for P'sharah: A Jewish Mediation/ Arbitration Service

Yitzchak Kasdan

*H*immelfarb and Goldberg had been friends and sole shareholders in a large, successful real estate development company for 10 years. As the regional economy where the company was based changed, the company began experiencing a downturn in business. With the decrease in profits came a deterioration in the relationship between the friends. Each accused the other of taking self-serving actions which allegedly were detrimental to the business as a whole. Before long, Himmelfarb claimed that Goldberg had misappropriated company funds. In turn, Goldberg accused Himmelfarb of breaching certain of his fiduciary duties. One thing led to another until the parties became embroiled in a lawsuit — Himmelfarb having sued Goldberg for $500,000 and Goldberg having counterclaimed for $750,000.

Both Himmelfarb and Goldberg entered into the litigation convinced of the justice of their respective positions and certain of complete vindication in court. However, after countless depositions, subpoenas, document requests and *interrogatories — all legitimate discovery tools — hundreds of thousands of dollars in legal fees, and seemingly interminable time dedicated to the case, the antagonists learned the painful and expensive lesson that there are two sides to a dispute. Like (an estimated) 95% of other parties in litigation, the erstwhile friends decided to settle without going to trial. They agreed to dissolve the business, split the remaining assets and drop the claims against each other without admitting culpability. They still remain angry with one another.*

Himmelfarb and Goldberg were vaguely aware that according to Jewish law, halachah, Jewish disputants are not supposed to resolve their differences in secular court, but rather in a Jewish court, a beis din. However, they mistakenly believed that the prohibition of arkaos — litigation in secular court — did not apply to today's judicial system. In any event, they had rejected suggestions that a beis din adjudicate the dispute.

Had Himmelfarb and Goldberg heeded the advice of their lawyers who had forewarned them of the expensive and time-consuming nature of courtroom litigation, they might have decided not to sue each other. They might have opted for private, less costly and more expedient alternative dispute resolution proceedings such as mediation or arbitration — forms of p'sharah discussed in Jewish law — either of which could have been conducted in an halachically-acceptable manner. By choosing to litigate in a public forum, these disputants ended in a "no-win" situation which cost them dearly, both financially and emotionally.

The mistakes of our fictitious antagonists need not be repeated ....

Halachah generally prohibits a Jew from initiating legal action against a fellow Jew in a court other than a *beis din*.[1] Despite this Torah-based prohibition,[2] religious Jews, like others in today's

---

1. *Shulchan Aruch, Choshen Mishpat* 26.
2. *Shemos* 21:1, based upon *Gittin* 88b. See also Responsa *Minchas Yitzchak* Vol. 4 No. 51, and the sources cited therein.

litigious society, unfortunately turn to the courts of this land to resolve disputes in which they become embroiled.

The conceivable reasons behind the derogation of this *halachah* are manifold.

First, it appears that the restriction against proceeding in *arkaos shel nochrim*, the reference to non-Jewish courts,[3] is not well-known. Relatively few responsa over the past few decades[4] have delved exhaustively into issues surrounding secular litigation. Only recently have articles on this topic begun to appear in popular halachic journals.[5]

Second, many Orthodox Jews who even have a general knowledge of the problem, miscomprehend the parameters of the issue of *arkaos*. Two misconceptions abound: (1) that our judicial system cannot be considered *arkaos* and, therefore, is not covered by the prohibition, and (2) that the law of the land, *"dina d'malchusa dina,"* automatically sanctions secular court lawsuits.

The initial misconception stems from the mistaken notion that *arkaos shel nochrim* encompasses only idolatrous or corrupt courts. In fact, the *halachah* prohibits a Jew from litigating in any non-Jewish court.[6] By not proceeding in *beis din*, the individual raises the potential *chillul Hashem* inference that Jewish law is incapable of resolving the case at hand.[7] Additionally, should a civil court order monetary relief in a case where the

---

3. See *Rashi, Shemos* 21:1 *"Lifneihem."*

4. These include the following: *Mishneh Halachos* Vol. 7 No. 255; *Noam* Vol. 9 *"Binyan Arkaos"*; *Tzitz Eliezer* Vol. 11 No. 93; *Tzitz Eliezer* Vol. 12 No. 82; *Y'chaveh Daas* Vol. 4 No. 65; *She'eilos Ut'shuvos T'shuvos V'Hanhagos* Nos. 793-796.

5. See, e.g., *Journal of Halacha and Contemporary Society*. Vol. II, Rabbi Simcha Krauss. "Litigation in Secular Courts" (hereinafter "Litigation"); id., Vol. IX, Rabbi Dr. Dov Bressler. "Arbitration and the Courts in Jewish Law" (hereinafter "Arbitration"), *CROSSROADS: Halacha and the Modern World*. Vol. 11, Rav Yaacov Ariel, "Secular Courts in the State of Israel," id., Prof. Yaacov Bazak. "The Status of the Israeli Court System."

6. See, e.g., "Litigation" at 37 note 6.

7. *Shulchan Aruch, Choshen Mishpat* 26:1. One, unfortunately, of many examples of *chillul Hashem* resulting from civil litigation in secular court is found in a recent *Washington Post* editorial which publicized how two factions within a synagogue sued each other under the Racketeer Influenced and Corrupt Organizations Act (RICO). Cases of this nature are regularly published in State and federal law reporters. See, e.g., Grunwald vs. Bornfreund, 696 F. Supp. 838 (E.D.N.Y. 1988).

halachah would not, a plaintiff could come to transgress the prohibition of *g'zelah*.[8]

Moreover, *dina d'malchusa dina* in no way condones the bypassing of *beis din*. The law of the land is more narrowly applied in *halachah* than, perhaps, is commonly recognized.[9] In any event, it is a substantive rule of law and does not specifically speak to the question of choice of a Jewish or non-Jewish forum to resolve a dispute.

A third reason why many may disregard the primacy of *beis din* jurisdiction in favor of secular courts, concerns the inability of *beis din* to enforce its own decrees. Of course, this problem may be solved by the advance agreement of parties to be bound by the *beis din's* holding and permit state or federal court enforcement of the judgment. Nonetheless, instances arise where a *beis din's* decision is not upheld due to procedural and/or substantive challenges to the *beis din* proceeding.[10]

Another possible explanation for the lack of enthusiasm for *beis din* is the concern putative litigants have regarding what substantive law applies. Jewish law certainly does not always coincide with the statutory or common law that, in people's minds, formed the basis for the transaction or circumstance now in dispute. Parties refuse to subject themselves to the jurisdiction of a *beis din* which might, it is perceived, unfairly elevate halachic dictates and responsibilities over commonly accepted, albeit secular, laws and customs.

Regardless of whether the various rationales to avoid *beis din* are valid or are misplaced, the fact remains that the halachic restriction against *arkaos* proceedings cannot be supplanted. Without obtaining the permission of a *beis din*, the plaintiff's attorney halachically is required to abstain from aiding in the instigation or continuance of a lawsuit outside the confines of *beis din*.[11]

---

8. *Chidushei R' Akiva Eiger, Shulchan Aruch, Choshen Mishpat* 26:1, *"Uv'arkaos shelahem."*

9. See generally *Journal of Halacha and Contemporary Society*, Vol.1, Rabbi Hershel Schachter, *"'Dina D'Malchusa Dina':* Secular Law as a Religious Obligation."

10. See. e.g.. Kozlowski vs. Seville, Inc., 64 Misc.2d 109 (Sup. Ct. 1970); Katz vs. Uvegi, 187 N.Y.S.2d 511 (Sup. Ct. 1959). See also *New York Law Journal*. July 19, 1989 p.1 "Court Vacates Rabbis' Award In Arbitration," discussing Meisels vs. Uhr (Supreme Court, Kings County July 13, 1989).

11. See *Rama Choshen Mishpat* 26:1:
"Likewise we ban one who strengthens the hand of the one who goes before a heathen

For the client who, for whatever reasons, refuses to turn to a *beis din* and for the lawyer who does not wish to lose litigation business, two alternatives exist which are halachically viable and practicable: mediation and arbitration. These two methods of alternative dispute resolution are well-founded in *halachah* in the form of *p'sharah* or *bitzua* and can be tailor-made to serve the needs of Jewish litigants.

✦ *Arbitration*

Arbitration is the voluntary reference by disputants of their disagreement to one or more (typically, three) impartial individuals who, after a hearing at which evidence and argument are presented, render a binding decision called an award. Although the arbitration proceeding is private and less formal than litigation in a court of law — e.g., discovery is circumscribed and strict evidentiary rules are not applied — it is governed by rules and procedures to which the parties have agreed in advance. At times, these rules and procedures are standardized, such as when the parties agree to arbitrate in accordance with the rules of an arbitral organization like the American Arbitration Association. In other instances, the procedures governing the arbitration are formulated, negotiated and agreed upon separately by the parties and their attorneys.

In addition, state and federal statutes provide guidance on the conduct of arbitrations to ensure fairness in the process.[12] Arbitration awards may be appealable under various statutes, but the grounds for court review are narrow. Generally, a court will not vacate an arbitrator's decision unless presented with evidence that the arbitration proceeding was tainted by fraud or

---

court." See also *Y'chaveh Daas* Vol. 4 No. 65 note **; *She'eilos Ut'shuvos T'shuvos V'Hanhagos* No. 795. An exception from the need to obtain advance permission of *beis din* may apply in a case involving non-religious Jews who undoubtedly will not obey a subpoena ("*hazmanah*") issued by a *beis din*. See *She'eilos Ut'shuvos T'shuvos V'Hanhagos* No. 795.

12. See, e.g., the Federal Arbitration Act, 9 U.S.C. § 1-15, and the Uniform Arbitration Act ("UAA"), which has been adopted in whole or in part by 32 states and the District of Columbia.

bias, or that the arbitrators exceeded their powers[13] in a manner which results in a manifest disregard of the law.

→ Mediation

Mediation is a dispute resolution method by which an outsider helps persuade parties to settle their differences voluntarily. Unlike arbitration, no decision is rendered in mediation. Any suggestions the mediator makes for resolving the dispute are not binding upon the parties.

The *modus operandi* of the mediator is not prescribed. He may preside over face-to-face meetings between parties, caucus with each side separately, or (and most likely) use both of these approaches freely and interchangeably. The mediator listens to the parties' real or imagined grievances and seeks to gain understanding of their respective positions. He attempts to define the issues and areas of dispute, and determine what common ground, if any, the parties may share.

The mediator is available to the parties as an objective "sounding board" to offer an impartial evaluation of the merits of their case. In this regard, the parties can choose to share confidences with the mediator, who, without prior consent, will not divulge such information to others. Conversely, the mediator can serve as a conduit through which the two sides can exchange information or settlement proposals. In the end, the mediator resorts to his skills to find creative compromise solutions which are palatable to the antagonists. If acceptable, the mediator's proposals are finalized in a written, enforceable agreement which the parties execute.

→ P'sharah and Bitzua

The terms *p'sharah* and *bitzua* are used interchangeably by the Talmud in the first chapter of *Massechet Sanhedrin* and, as explained below, apparently refer both to arbitration and mediation processes.

---

13. See. e.g.. 9. U.S.C. §§ 10; UAA §§ 12.

The Talmud reports a dispute between Rabbi Meir and the *Chachamim* as to the number of individuals needed to preside over *p'sharah* and *bitzua*.[14]

ביצוע בשלשה דברי רבי מאיר: וחכמים אומרים פשרה ביחיד

"*Bitzua* is with three [individuals] according to R. Meir; and the *Chachamim* say that *p'sharah* is with one [individual]."

The Soncino translation defines the terms *p'sharah* and *bitzua* to mean "arbitration": "Arbitration is by three, so says R. Meir. The Sages say that one is sufficient."

The continuation of the *Gemara* focuses upon the respective rationales of R. Meir and the *Chachamim* and concludes that their argument is based on whether *p'sharah/bitzua* can be compared to "*din*," formal court proceedings:[15]

דכולי עלמא דין בשלשה, והכא בהא קמיפלגי: דמר סבר מקשינן פרשה לדין. ומר סבר לא מקשינן פרשה לדין. — "All [both R. Meir and the Sages] agree that legal decision is by three, and the point in which they differ is this: One [R. Meir] holds that the force of arbitration should be regarded as equal to that of legal decision, while the other disputes it."

The view of the *Chachamim* is codified by R. Yosef Karo in the *Shulchan Aruch* which holds that *p'sharah* may be conducted by a single individual,[16] unlike strict legal proceedings which require three judges.[17]

Because *p'sharah* is not comparable to *din*, the *Shulchan Aruch*,[18] in accordance with the continuation of the *Gemara* in *Sanhedrin*,[19] requires parties submitting to *p'sharah* to pledge themselves, through *kinyan*, to adhere to the award rendered. *Rashi* in *Sanhedrin* opines,[20] and the *Shulchan Aruch* concurs,[21] that a *kinyan* is necessary for enforcement of the award even where the *p'sharah* is conducted by three individuals, i.e., the number necessary for *din*.

---

14. *Sanhedrin* 6a.

15. Id.

16. *Shulchan Aruch, Choshen Mishpat* 12:7.

17. Id. 3:1.

18. Id. 12:7.

19. *Sanhedrin* 6a.

20. *Rashi, Sanhedrin* 6a: "*V'hil'ch'sah p'sharah tz'richah kinyan.*"

21. *Shulchan Aruch, Choshen Mishpat* 12:7.

Although, as noted above, the Soncino translation of both *p'sharah* and *bitzua* is "arbitration," whether those Talmudic terms refer to the present-day concepts of arbitration or mediation turns, in part, on the timing of the *kinyan* necessary for enforcement of the *p'sharah/bitzua*. If a *kinyan* is made in advance, thereby binding the parties to a decision, then *p'sharah/bitzua* is in this sense akin to arbitration. If a *kinyan* is required as an after-event, then the *p'sharah/bitzua* is like non-binding mediation in which settlement of the dispute is made enforceable only by the subsequent agreement of the parties.

Tosafos in *Sanhedrin*[22] actually contemplates both circumstances: (i) A *kinyan* may be made by the parties at the outset to become bound by the judgment to be rendered at the conclusion of the *p'sharah* proceeding or (ii) a *kinyan* may be made by the parties after pronouncement of the *p'sharah* decision to fulfill otherwise non-binding terms.

That *p'sharah* and *bitzua* encompass not only an arbitration but also a mediation format is also clear from the explanation of the *Shiltei Giborim*[23] to another statement in *Sanhedrin*:[24]

נגמר הדין אי אתה רשאי לבצוע — "After a case has been decided by legal judgment, one must not attempt a settlement."

The *Shiltei Giborim* qualifies this proscription: While judges may not, after rendition of the strict law, impose a settlement, they may encourage voluntary conciliation, i.e., mediation, in the form of *p'sharah*. Indeed, according to the *Shiltei Giborim*, not only is it "worthy" for the judges to do so through assuagement and persuasion, it is a "great mitzvah," because voluntary conciliation brings "*shalom*" — harmony — between opposing litigants.[25]

→ P'sharah/Bitzua Today

According to all opinions, *p'sharah/bitzua* is certainly acceptable, if not preferable, at least before disputants approach a *beis*

---

22. *Tosafos, Sanhedrin* 6a: "*Vhil'ch'sah p'sharah tz'richah kinyan.*"

23. *Shiltei Giborim, Rif* on *Sanhedrin*, 1b note 1.

24. *Sanhedrin* 6b.

25. *Shiltei Giborim.*, note 23 supra.

din for a strict *din* proceeding.[26] Indeed, the *Shulchan Aruch* rules that even a *beis din* must ask litigants whether they wish to proceed in *p'sharah* or in *din* before commencement of the latter process.[27] The *Aruch HaShulchan* further rules that it is a mitzvah for the judges to encourage the parties to proceed on the basis of *p'sharah* rather than *din*.[28]

Today, those litigants who choose to go to *beis din* generally agree to accept a decision of the judges termed *"p'sharah karov l'din"*[29] or *"din k'ein p'sharah,"* i.e., a compromise judgment for which the judges need not adhere absolutely or strictly to the law.[30] To the extent, however, that disputants do not bring their cases to *beis din,* they obviously are not afforded — and probably are not even aware of — the options of *p'sharah* or *p'sharah karov l'din* under *beis din* auspices. Unfortunately, even when apprised of these alternative proceedings before a *beis din,* some otherwise Torah-abiding Jews simply refuse, for whatever reasons, to become involved with a rabbinic, judicial or quasi-judicial panel. For these individuals who otherwise will turn to secular courts, the question arises whether arbitration or mediation proceedings outside the jurisdiction of a formal *beis din,* e.g., before Jewish or non-Jewish attorneys and other professionals acting as arbitrators/mediators, is permissible.

While non-Jewish arbitration or mediation panels may be halachically acceptable,[31] it would be preferable, where possible, to have parties voluntarily appear before fellow, *frum* Jews. First, keeping squabbles "within the family" would help reduce

---

26. Even the opinion of R. Eliezer, who prohibits *bitzua* (see *Sanhedrin* 6b) is limited to the time after the litigants arrive at the doors of *beis din*. See *Rashi, Sanhedrin* 6b: *"Asur livtzoah."* See also *Peirush HaRif* on *Ein Yaacov, Sanhedrin* 6b: *"R. Eliezer omer asur livtzoah."*

27. *Shulchan Aruch Choshen Mishpat* 12:2.

28. *Aruch HaShulchan* 12:2. See also *Nesivos HaMishpat, Choshen Mishpat* 12 note 3; *Igros Moshe, Choshen Mishpat* Vol. 1 No. 17.

29. See, e.g., *Igros Moshe Choshen Mishpat* Vol. 2 No. 8: *She'eilos Ut'shuvos T'shuvos V'Hanhagos* No. 793.

30. The concept of *p'sharah karov l'din* is intended not only to encourage a spirit of compromise, but also is designed to help protect the judges themselves from the consequences of (even inadvertently) not rendering an indisputably correct and foolproof decision. See "Arbitration" at 107.

31. See generally "Arbitration," supra. See *Aruch HaShulchan* 22:8 citing *Shach, Choshen Mishpat* 26 note 15.

the potential for *chillul Hashem*. Second, a mediation or arbitration over which a halachically-knowledgeable lawyer or other professional presides can consider not only common law and statutory customs and principles, but also principles of *Choshen Mishpat* and the spirit of *"yashrus."*[32] So long as the litigants voluntarily agree to have their case mediated or arbitrated on these bases, there should be no halachic objection to these forms of *p'sharah* or *bitzua*.[33] In this regard, Rav Eliezer Yehudah Waldenberg has ruled it permissible for neighbors in a shared housing or condominium-type facility to have disputes decided without any reference to Torah law.[34] Rav Waldenberg relied, in part, on sources cited by R. Akivah Eiger[35] that permit businessmen to have their arguments resolved on the basis of their industry-accepted practices and customs — again without reliance upon the laws of the Torah.[36]

There is strong precedent for the conduct of *p'sharah* outside the jurisdiction of *beis din*. The first and foremost arbitrator/mediator was Aharon HaKohen. The *Gemara* in *Sanhedrin* extols Aharon as one who "loved peace and pursued peace and made peace between man and man ...."[37] *Tosafos* in *Sanhedrin*[38] notes specifically that Aharon fulfilled *p'sharah* in his individual capacity, in contrast to his brother Moshe Rabbeinu,

---

32. See *Rashi, Devarim* 6:18: *HaYashar v'hatov: "Zu p'sharan, lifnim mishuras hadin."*

33. Whereas the agreement of disputants to litigate in secular courts (including the State of Israel's court system) is prohibited even in instances where the secular court would apply Torah law (see *Shulchan Aruch, Choshen Mishpat* 26:2; "Litigation" at 49-53), agreement to arbitrate before a Jewish arbitration panel which would not necessarily apply strict Torah law should nonetheless be permissible. See notes 34, 35 and 36, *infra*. The distinction may lie in the permanence of the secular court system, its usually compulsory nature and its rigid adherence to precedent, versus the temporal status of the arbitral panel, its non-compulsory nature and its ability to exert flexibility and discretion in the decision-making process. These latter characteristics would not render arbitration an affront to, or rejection of, *beis din* or halachic authority, or create the spectre of *chillul Hashem* on those occasions when it [arbitration] is used. Cf. "Litigation" at 51-52.

34. *Tzitz Eliezer* Vol. 11 No. 93.

35. *Chidushei R. Akiva Eiger, Shulchan Aruch Choshen Mishpat* 3:1: *"V'hem danim."*

36. *Tzitz Eliezer* Vol. 11 No. 93. בלשון הציץ אליעזר: "שהי' מנהג אותו מקום שלא לדון בעסקי משא ומתן כפי דין התורה מפני שאם היו דנין כן על פי התורה לא היו קיום והעמדה להם. לכן היו דנים על פי מנהג הסוחרים כפי נמוסיהם וכפי תקנותיהם. וכמו כן היו דנין כל זה אפילו בדייני ישראל על פי המנהג...."

37. *Sanhedrin* 6b.

38. *Tosafos, Sanhedrin* 6b: *"Aval Aharon."*

who applied strict *din* in his capacity as a *dayan* (judge). Similarly, R. Yoel Sirkus, the *Bach*,[39] speaks of *p'sharah* conducted by *"baalei batim"* — lay individuals who are not part of a formal *beis din*. According to the *Bach*, the decisions or suggestions of the *baalei batim* become binding through a *kinyan*, as discussed above. Finally, R. Shlomo Ganzfried in his *Kitzur Shulchan Aruch*[40] upholds the validity of a *p'sharah* proceeding separate from *beis din*:

לפעמים הבעלי דינים בוררים להם אנשים שיעשו להם פשרה ביניהם, אם בצירוף הבית דין או שלא בבית דין. דבר זה הגון הוא, שכל אחד מצדד בזכותו של זה אשר בחר ויצא הפרשה כראוי. — "Occasionally, litigants choose arbitrators to sit either jointly [in conjunction] with the *beis din* or without [apart from] the *beis din*. This is a proper procedure, because each arbitrator advances the cause of the one who has chosen him, and thus a just settlement will be reached."

✣ A Proposal for P'sharah

A Jewish mediation/arbitration service staffed by Torah-abiding attorneys, with access to competent rabbinic authorities for consultation where necessary, can act as a modern-day Aharon in the pursuit of *shalom*. Such a service could afford Jewish disputants who, for whatever reasons, are unwilling to appear before a *beis din*, the opportunity to have their cases settled or decided in a more private, speedy and cost-effective manner than courtroom litigation. More importantly, such a service would enable both lawyers and their clients to avoid the potential of transgressing the prohibition against litigation in *arkaos*, and attendant problems of *chillul Hashem* and, possibly, *g'zelah*.

Cases brought to the service, by advance agreement, would be settled in mediation or decided in arbitration by reference to Torah law, secular customs and practices based upon common and statutory law, and by taking into account general notions of fairness and equity and *yashrus*. Also by advance agreement, the

39. *Bach, Tur, Choshen Mishpat* 12 note 7: "*Af al pi.*"
40. *Kitzur Shulchan Aruch* 181:8.

fees and costs could be allocated by the mediator(s)/arbitrator(s), or shared equally by the parties.[41] The parties could represent themselves or, if they preferred, be accompanied and represented by their own attorneys. Finally, the parties would also agree not to appeal the results of the mediation or arbitration to court, and to have the arbitrator(s)/mediator(s) retain jurisdiction to ensure compliance.

This writer was recently involved in mediations involving religious Jews. In each case, with the aid of the mediator, the parties came to appreciate some of the strengths and, more importantly, the weaknesses in their respective positions. They thus were able to gauge their probability of success (or lack thereof) in subsequent court action or arbitration. They also came to recognize the potentially enormous outlay in time and expense that further proceedings of any kind would engender. As a result, in each case, the parties negotiated an amicable settlement through the mediator who conducted "shuttle diplomacy" between them. Although mediation will not resolve every conceivable dispute, in these cases the disputants left the process wiser (and wealthier) for having made the good faith efforts they did to avoid litigation.

In this time of overuse and misuse — halachically and otherwise — of the courts, it is time for a Jewish mediation/arbitration service.

---

41. *Aruch HaShulchan, Choshen Mishpat* 9:6.

✦ Legislative Concerns

The Rising Cost of Life

Using Secular Government
to Promote Religious Interests

The "Halachic Health Care Proxy"

The Rising Cost of Life

Yisroel Mayer Kirzner

✦ A Torah View on the Economics of Choosing Life

I t was a distinctly chilling experience to read of current suggestions being put forward asking that new criteria be used in the legal determination of the cessation of human life. A panel of legal, medical and other experts — including, inevitably, a "theologian" — grappled with the problem of the definition of life and of death, in the light of contemporary medical developments. It seems that the conventional criteria employed to determine the instant of death impose, in certain instances, heavy costs upon the family, or upon society in general, in order to preserve patients in a state of irreversible coma, a state which, beyond a certain point, it is now urged that society consider as a state of death. The costs that are involved here arise out of modern developments in medical technology that make possible the artificial prolongation of certain physical processes normal to life, as well as the more recent possibilities opened up of transplanting vital human organs, possibilities that may be precluded if conventional criteria for the definition of death are adhered to. In the light of the high costs involved, the experts now urge a redefinition of life and of death that shall permit physicians to halt efforts to prolong — what has hitherto been considered — life artificially, and to remove vital organs from patients from whom such removal would have hitherto been considered murder.

Now, this writer refrains, on the grounds of lack of competence, from passing judgment on the relationship between the alternative criteria that are at issue here, and those prescribed by our codes in the halachic determination of the instant of death. Needless to say the clarification of this relationship must be of crucial concern to Orthodox Jews. Nor, despite the obviously ominous possibilities for extensions of their approach, is one entirely shocked that the experts, theologian and all, seem to consider the criteria for the definition of life and death to be simply a matter for arbitrary determination, a matter of agreed convention. What this writer found chilling in the reports of the deliberations of this panel was the emphasis laid, in explaining the need for revisions in the accepted legal criteria for the definition of death, upon the element of *cost*. The difficult problems raised by organ transplant possibilities, in situations where the "cost" of the donor's life is the life of another human being, may be, for present purposes, left on one side. But, apart from these difficult problems, these reports are, in effect, telling us that because of the high monetary costs of keeping some patients alive, it has become a matter of acute importance to search about for some way of defining death that shall, without doing offense to popular ethical norms, make it possible to avoid these costs. The following notes on the nature of costs and of the cost of preserving life, arose out of reflection on the attitudes suggested by these chilling reports, and on the gulf that separates these attitudes from the Torah-outlook.

Why does mention of costs in the same breath as the preservation of life have this chilling effect? We are accustomed to taking it for granted that no material sacrifice is too great for the preservation of life. Conversely the renunciation of life is invariably referred to as the "supreme sacrifice," and is, barring pathological cases, thought of only in the context of causes possessing transcendent significance. It is probably because we are accustomed to this cast of thought that we are jarred by the cool calculation of the relative costs of alternative definitions of the cessation of life. While it is true that threats to life that are avoidable at either high cost in material resources (air-pollution?) or high cost in renounced pleasure (smoking?) are often ("irrationally") *not* avoided, *we are not normally used to deliberating upon the worthwhileness of keeping oneself alive at high cost.* Indeed the panel of experts pondering the appropriate definition for death did not, of course, dream of suggesting that where the preservation of life carries with it a sufficiently high cost, murder, or even the deliberate refusal to prolong life, is to be countenanced. Instead the awareness of the high cost of preserving — what has been hitherto considered — life has called attention to the possibility that on an ethically and medically acceptable redefinition of death, this cost is entirely uncalled for. Nonetheless it cannot be denied that hard-boiled calculations in the context of the preservation of life run sharply counter to patterns of thought based on a deep-seated reverence for the inviolateness and the sanctity of human life.

The truth is that in one important sense cost calculations seem to be inherently inappropriate with respect to the preservation of life. In the literature of economics the notion of cost is interpreted in broad terms of *sacrifice.* Where an individual is faced with a choice between two courses of action, the outcome of each is viewed as the "opportunity cost" of the other. Whichever course of action is adopted, is adopted by *renouncing* the results offered by the alternative course of action. What any one pleasurable experience costs, is the alternative experience that is being sacrificed in order to enjoy the first. But it follows from this insight into the nature of cost, that where an individual chooses a pleasurable experience, the alternative to which is a state in which he would no longer *exist,* then this pleasurable experience is costing him nothing at all. He is renouncing *nothing,* in order to enjoy this experience. There *is* no alternative (enjoyable or otherwise) that is being sacrificed, in this situation, for the sake of the pleasurable experience being embraced. To the extent, therefore, that death connotes the absence of experience and of sensation, its rejection constitutes no sacrifice whatsoever. Of course it is only in the narrowest of senses that death may be described as connoting the absence of experience and of sensation. But to the extent that death does connote the absence of sensation and of existence, the preference for life over death involves no sacrifice. Nothing at all is being renounced. Despite the material resources which may be required for the preservation of life, the true cost is zero. In renouncing such resources in order to preserve life, one is renouncing nothing; the alternative to life, in such situations, is not the alternative enjoyment of these resources, but simply non-existence.

Something of this is no doubt responsible for our haibits of thought in which life is viewed as beyond the yardstick of cost calculations. In considering the preservation of life we are accustomed to view all possible relevant sacrifices as of the palest significance. In considering life we are well aware that there simply is no alternative, so that nothing at all is being sacrificed, no cost at all is being incurred, when life is preserved, no matter how heavy the material expenditure that may be involved. It is true that in strict logic the costlessness of life as discussed here pertains only to one pondering the expenditure of resources to save his *own* life. But the *attitude* towards life which is consistent with the recognition of its costlessness, applies no less to the life of one's fellow man. Whether, then, it is one's own life that is to be saved with the expenditure of one's resources, or whether one expends one's resources to save the life of another, we are accustomed to a cast of thought in which life is inherently costless.

These observations are of particular interest in the light of the frequent comparisons between Torah and life itself. Torah is *Toras chaim*, a Torah of life: we are told in the Torah itself to identify the good with life, and we are admonished "choose life." At the giving of the Torah at Sinai, we were shown that our very lives and existence — and indeed the very existence of all Creation — depended upon our acceptance of the Torah. Again and again the

Torah, its study and the observance of its mitzvos, are likened to life, to the tree of life, to life-giving water, and so on.

For the Jew, therefore, identifying as he does the fulfilment of Torah with the preservation of life, it follows that no sacrifice is too great when the fulfilment of Torah is concerned. *More correctly, when the fulfilment of Torah is concerned, no notion of sacrifice can possibly be involved at all.* A life without Torah, is, for us, a contradiction in terms. There *is* simply no alternative, for the Jew, to a Torah life, as there is no alternative to life itself. Just as cost calculations with respect to the preservation of life involve an almost blasphemous disregard for the bottomless gulf that separates life from its absence, so does use of the notion of sacrifice and the yardstick of cost calculation in the context of Torah observance almost blasphemously imply the possibility, at least in principle, of an existence free of the Torah yoke. Theoretical recognition — at least — of the utter identity of life with Torah, is surely part of the mental equipment of every observant Jew, with numerous degrees of graduation possible with respect to the depth of his everyday *practical* consciousness of this identity. The readiness to assume greater and greater material burdens, to renounce more and more imperiously beckoning pleasures, for the sake of Torah and mitzvos, reflects, then, not only greater and greater awareness of their transcendent value, but even more fundamentally perhaps, the awareness of their *inevitability,* the consciousness that existence without them constitutes a state of paralysis. Our *baalei mussar* tell us that although it is of the essence of man that he is a *baal b'chirah,* one with the freedom to choose, nonetheless the consistent pursuit of the Torah life should point to a spiritual plane where *the very possibility of choosing evil fades away into nothingness.* One measure of one's progress towards this plane surely consists in the degree to which one's awareness of the utter *impossibility* of an existence without Torah has permeated one's being and dominated one's practical actions.

There are Jews who maintain a kosher home, but who, with greater or lesser sense of guilt, suspend their *kashrus* observance when away from home. Each of us is aware of circumstances in which one feels sorely tempted to relax observance of some Torah precept — more weighty or less — that one normally holds inviolate. The economist is accustomed to interpret this in terms of cost; whereas at home or under normal circumstances the sacrifice called for in order to observe the Torah precept is small enough to render observance preferable to transgression, the sacrifice at other times or under other circumstances becomes sufficiently great to make observance seem the less desirable of the two possible courses of action. From the Torah perspective what is to be condemned in such instances is not merely the perverted sense of values that renders observance less desirable than its worldly alternatives; to be deplored is the very notion that the cost calculus is at all appropriate to the question of Torah observance.

Of course the Torah itself makes provision for situations in which the proper choice may be the *non*observance of (what in other circumstances would be) a Torah-precept. There are systematic priority rankings governing cases where one precept comes into conflict with another, where a precept calls for the expenditure of large fractions of one's wealth, and, of course, where a precept comes into conflict with the preservation of human life. But where a precept yields ground, this is never to be interpreted as an act of deliberate calculative choice made from some vantage point located *outside* the Torah life. This is never to be interpreted, it should hardly require to be pointed out, as an instance where the cost of Torah observance is too high for observance to be worthwhile. Even the case of *pikuach nefesh* (when a mitzvah yields as a result of its conflict with the preservation of life) does not, of course, mean that the Jew himself independently ranks the preservation of his life higher than the observance of the Divine Will. It means that *in the Torah ranking of priorities,* the preservation of life takes precedence, in general, over other precepts. And in those cases where the preservation of life does not take precedence over relevant Torah precepts, this means that continued existence in violation of these precepts is, in the Torah view, unthinkable under *any* circumstances.

For the Torah-Jew the observance of Torah is inseparable from life itself. His very identity is merged with that of Torah observance. Just as all living things struggle passionately to preserve their lives, so does the Torah-Jew as an individual, and so does *Klal Yisrael* as a whole, struggle passionately to preserve its life and existence, through unswerving commitment to the Torah. As we have seen, cost calculations have little place in the context of the preservation of life. And it is because of this that men cling to life passionately, recklessly, even irrationally. Even so does *Klal Yisrael* cast all calculations to the winds in its yearning and striving for life, the life of Torah, the life of a people that cleaves to its Soul and Creator — the G-d of Life.

And if for no other reason than the awareness of all this, it is entirely healthy that we feel chilled, jarred and shocked whenever we encounter attitudes in which the preservation of human life is treated as something less than sacred, as something for which the material cost calculus is, in principle, a matter of relevance.

Using Secular Government to Promote Religious Interests:

What Are the Boundaries?

Chaim Dovid Zwiebel

→ *Auto Parts, Designer Jeans and "Tashmishei Kedushah"*

I n early 1986, at the request of Agudath Israel of California, Assemblyman William Filante introduced a bill in the California legislature requiring sellers of religious articles such as *tefillin* and *mezuzos* to disclose to consumers the identity of the manufacturer of the article and any supervising authority.

The genesis of Assemblyman Filante's bill, according to Rabbi Chaim Schnur, director of Agudath Israel of California, was a series of complaints brought to his office concerning blatantly unkosher *tefillin* and *mezuzos* that were flooding the California market. Asked to crack down on the perpetrators of this consumer fraud, the California Attorney General's office issued its legal opinion that "it would be extremely difficult" to address the problem under existing anti-fraud law. Hence the need for new legislation, to ensure (in Rabbi Schnur's words) that "purchasers of religious articles receive no less consumer protection than those who purchase mislabled designer jeans or defective auto parts."

Where Agudath Israel and the Attorney General's office saw enhanced consumer protection, however, others saw dangers lurking in the shadows. The local Reform Rabbinate, especially, took strong exception to Assemblyman Filante's bill. Typical was the protest voiced by Rabbi Sanford Ragins of the Leo Baeck Temple in Los Angeles: "For any relatively small group within the Jewish community to seek to impose its will upon the rest of the community and, moreover, to impose its will with the use of the state's power, is outrageous" ("Bill on Misrepresented Mezuzos Stirs Controversy Among Jews," *Los Angeles Times*, April 19, 1986).

Another Reform spokesman, Rabbi Leonard Thal, Pacific Southwest regional director of the Union of American Hebrew Congregations, echoed the same theme:

> By and large, Reform Jews will not care very much whether it [i.e., a *mezuzah*] is done by hand by a scribe ... or whether it is mass-produced....
>
> If this were the only bill of religious consequence promoted by Agudath Israel, that would be one thing. However, these are the same individuals who promoted the unfortunate ... *get* (Jewish divorce) legislation, the *kashrus* legislation and who now have initiated a time-of-death bill which would establish separate criteria for Jews.
>
> [I object] to the continuing efforts of a small segment of the Jewish community to turn to well-intentioned legislators in an effort to use the legislative process to impose their own Jewish practices and observances on others who, in our open society, have chosen to embrace a different set of Jewish practices and observances (Ibid., *letter of April 24, 1986 to Assemblyman Filante*).

Apparently these protestations proved persuasive. Assemblyman Filante's bill failed to pass.

→ Woeful Ignorance or Willful Distortion

The charge that Orthodox Jews in general, and Agudath Israel in particular, seek to utilize the secular governmental process to impose their own view of Jewish law upon those who do not share that view, is hardly a new one — although, as Rabbis Ragins and Thal so eloquently demonstrated, it is often a frivolous one.

Consumer fraud statutes, including labeling requirements and full disclosure provisions, have been enacted throughout the United States. To press for similar legislation to protect consumers of *tefillin*, *mezuzos* and the like, is a perfectly appropriate exercise of political advocacy. On the other hand, to resist such legislation on the patently false ground that it represents an effort by the Orthodox to use government to impose *halachah* on the non-Orthodox, is to seek to deny Orthodox Jews the same legal rights enjoyed by other consumers. Who, then, was really guilty of manipulating California's "well-intentioned legislators"?

There are numerous other recent contexts in which our critics betrayed either woeful ignorance or willful distortion of Agudath Israel's legislative objectives. Some examples:
• the contention of some prominent New York-based Reform rabbis that a bill mandating hospitals to advise parents of newborn baby boys that hospital circumcision may not satisfy religious requirements was designed to force *bris milah k'halachah* upon willing parents, when in fact it was designed to protect parents who want their son to have a proper *bris milah* but in their ignorance assume that hospital circumcision satisfies *halachah*;
• the charge that New York's *"get* law" was developed by Agudath Israel to "impos[e]...Orthodox Jewish religious requirements upon virtually all New Yorkers" (September 1984 letter to *The New York Times* from the Director of the New York Federation of Reform Synagogues), when in fact the law would encourage the giving of a *get* only where the couple had

initially been married by a rabbi who would insist on a *get* as the means of terminating the marriage;

• the argument that our endeavors to obtain tuition tax relief and other forms of public aid for parents whose children attend religious schools are aimed at obtaining special status for religious education, when in fact we are fighting only for the right of taxpaying parents to recover a fraction of their educational tax dollars to help defray the costs of exercising their constitutionally guaranteed right to educate their children in non-public schools;

• the claim that Agudath Israel's efforts to secure a legislative exemption to the commonly accepted "brain death" standard "would establish separate criteria for Jews" (Rabbi Thal, *supra*), when in fact our efforts in this regard are designed solely to safeguard the civil liberties of individual patients whose religious beliefs regarding the definition of life and death do not coincide with government's.

✦ Testing Our Critics' Underlying Premise

Often, then, our critics' charge that we seek to use the machinery of secular government to compel an unwilling public to observe *halachah* is transparently false. But there are contexts in which the charge is not so easily dismissed.

In recent years, Agudath Israel has spoken out on a host of contemporary social and moral legislative issues. We have opposed "gay rights" bills and the Equal Rights Amendment. We have supported proposed laws to restrict the availability of pornography and abortion on demand. Having taken such positions, are we not guilty as charged of utilizing government to impose on others our own parochial religious views?

Before entering a plea of innocent or guilty, let us pause for a moment to consider a more fundamental question: So what if we are guilty?

Our critics' charge of impropriety is based on the premise that there is something sinister about enlisting the secular law to help promote halachic values. Some in our community would contest the validity of the premise. They would argue that it is perfectly proper for organized Orthodoxy to employ whatever means available, including political advocacy and legislative enactment, to encourage respect for and observance of the eternal truths embodied in Torah. They would further argue that government inevitably teaches when it legislates, and that we in turn have the right to seek to influence the substance of that teaching on the basis of our religious beliefs.

Others in our community would agree with our critics' basic premise that enlisting secular government as an active partner in promoting Torah values and observance is a mistake. Orthodox Jews in the United States are, after all, a minority within a minority. Thus, the argument goes, American Jewry has a great stake in preserving the so-called wall separating church and state; were it to crumble, it is indeed the church — not the synagogue — that would dominate the state. According to this view, in the long run our community is better off keeping Jewish religious values out of the legislative process, else majoritarian religionists could utilize the same process to impose anti-Jewish values on us.

✦ The Implications of our Limitations

Without taking sides in this debate, I believe that certain basic facts dictate the posture the American Torah community should adopt vis-à-vis government. (The reader is cautioned to take note of the two disclaimers implicit in the previous sentence: that what follows is my own personal view; and that I offer my opinion only in the context of the American system of government.)

Orthodox Jews in the United States are a community of limited means and limited political clout. Common sense dictates that we must husband the resources we do have and establish a hierarchy of legislative priorities. With all due respect to those in our camp who would press government to make Rosh Hashanah and Yom Kippur national holidays, and to those who would expend their energies on having certain street blocks renamed in honor of leading Orthodox figures, we should be concentrating on issues that are more fundamentally crucial to our ability to survive and thrive as a Torah community.

Establishing a hierarchy of legislative priorities requires us to identify those issues in which our stake is substantial and direct, and those in which it is only peripheral and indirect. Where our primary motivation in seeking legislation is not to preserve our own rights, but to compel society at large to act in conformance with *halachah,* we should think twice before committing ourselves to such an initiative. Granted, we have a responsibility to promote Torah values and observance among the ignorant or forgetful. (More on that subject in the final section of this article.) Enlisting the secular law to help us discharge that responsibility, however, is no easy task, could prove counterproductive, and is a questionable use of limited resources.

It is thus in our community's ultimate interest, I believe, to recognize the secular character of American government and the limited resources that we have for influencing government, and to formulate our legislative priorities accordingly. In that limited sense, critics like Reform Rabbis Ragins and Thal may have a point. American Orthodox Jews should not focus their energies on persuading government to make *halachah* the law of the land, thereby converting the police power of the state into an enforcement arm of the *Shulchan Aruch.* Rather, our domestic legislative agenda should be designed primarily to preserve and advance our right to lead full lives as Torah-observant Jews in the United States.

✧ *Osmosis and Beyond*

To return now to the question posed above, have we not strayed from our basic purpose in speaking out on the broad range of social and moral issues that come before legislative bodies in contemporary U.S.A.? Is it not a misuse of our limited resources to seek laws that promote general social morality? Are we not in fact guilty of asking secular government to impose our religious views upon society at large?

I think not. Our stand on these types of issues is designed primarily to protect ourselves and our families. The Torah community's way of life is threatened when government encourages or permits conduct that leads to social and moral decay. I refer not merely to the indirect threat posed by the osmosis of contemporary secular mores into our own homes and values — *azoi vee es kristelt zich, azoi yiddilt zich* — but to a direct and substantial threat to our ability to lead our lives in accordance with *halachah.*

Thus, we oppose "gay rights" not so much because of the negative moral impact such legislation is likely to have on society at large, but because parents whose religious and moral convictions demand that they shield their children from conduct they believe to be deviant should not be required by law to violate those convictions. We oppose E.R.A. not so much because we want government to deliver the message that woman's role in life is different than man's, but because E.R.A. could lead to a "gender neutral" military draft and the withdrawal of tax exempt status from single-sex religious institutions. We support curbs on pornographic materials not so much because proliferating pornography debases society at large, but because it makes it impossible for our families to walk the streets without being assaulted by offensive images. Stated otherwise, in each of these contexts we seek first and foremost to protect our own civil rights.

✦ Our Stake in the Abortion Debate

Agudath Israel's support of legislative efforts to ban or curtail abortion on demand is perhaps the most difficult of all to justify within the framework of Orthodox Jewish civil rights. After all, no woman is compelled by government to terminate her pregnancy. Nothing in the law permitting abortions impacts directly upon our community's ability to lead full lives as Torah-observant Jews. How, then, can we justify our appeal to government to deny women the right to choose whether or not to carry their pregnancies full-term? Isn't that appeal an attempt to use the secular law to impose our own religious viewpoint on others?

The question is a good one. Perhaps it is precisely because our community's stake in the debate over legalized abortion is not so direct or substantial that Agudath Israel's *Moetzes Gedolei HaTorah* has instructed us not to make this issue the high-level legislative priority it has become for certain other religious groups (*l'havdil*). In fact, when we have spoken out on the subject, we have expended as much energy in insisting that anti-abortion legislation not preclude abortions in cases where *halachah* would permit or require them — a classic example of advocating Orthodox Jewish civil rights — as we have in expressing our basic support for laws prohibiting abortion on demand.

Nonetheless, we have expressed our support for such laws, and in no uncertain terms. In my view, there is substantial justification for doing so, despite the absence of any readily discernible impact on the Torah community.

A woman's decision to abort her child is fundamentally different from virtually any other decision one can make. For the innocent fetus whose life (or, at a minimum, potential life) is being snuffed out, the woman's decision to abort is tragically irrevocable. To speak out against legalized fetacide upon demand is to speak out for the rights of the weak and helpless, not for religious coercion; it is less an imposition of our views on others than a protest against permitting women blanket license to impose their views and conveniences upon the unborn.

The propriety of pressing government to protect fetal life becomes even more evident when one considers the magnitude of the abortion tragedy. An estimated 1.5 million legal abortions annually have been performed in the United States since the Supreme Court's decision years ago that abortion is a constitutionally protected right. More than one of every four pregnancies now end in abortion, at the rate of approximately 4,000 each day. Indeed, as a recent cover story in a national magazine makes clear, the legalization of abortion may be only the first step down a slippery slope leading to unfathomable depths:

> "I don't think abortion is ever wrong," argues
> psychiatrist and anthropologist Virginia Abernathy of
> Vanderbilt University's School of Medicine. "As long as

an individual is completely dependent upon the mother, it's not a person." In this view, which is shared by other pro-choice theorists, an individual becomes a person only when he or she becomes a responsible moral agent — around age three or four, in Abernathy's judgment. Until then, she thinks, infants — like fetuses — are nonpersons: defective children, such as those with Down's Syndrome, may never become persons. The claim they have on persons, she says, is compassion, not a moral right to life: "Compassion is always very important, but [it] loses when weighed against the rights of a person" (*Newsweek, "America's Abortion Dilemma," January* 14, 1985).

Dare we remain silent in the face of attempts to legitimize the unthinkable?

I stated before that our community's stake in the debate over legalized abortion is neither direct nor substantial. In a very real sense, that is incorrect. Jews, especially, should require no reminder that a society that permits euthanasia and other forms of killing the innocent is a society that desanctifies and devalues human life — and, ultimately, permits or encourages the destruction of Jewish life.

✦ Delivering the Message Without Government's Help

Government, I have argued, is not an ideal partner to help Torah Jewry deliver the message of Torah to the ignorant masses. That does not mean the message should not be delivered.

We can and should make better use of modern media to articulate and disseminate the Torah viewpoint on issues of contemporary relevance. *Klal Yisrael* has a responsibility, collectively and individually, to serve as *ohr la'goyim,* a light unto the nations; and to fulfill *"hochei'ach tochi'ach es amisecha* — rebuke your fellow Jew" when he strays from the path of righteousness.

Discharging that responsibility requires us not only to lead by example, but to raise our voices and make our position known.

We can and should tell the world that there is a Supreme Being who created the entire universe and who commanded Noach and his descendants a series of laws that are universally binding upon all mankind; that human beings were created *b'tzelem Elokim,* in the Divine Image, and are accordingly entitled to life, dignity, respect and sustenance; that men and women have different roles to play in G-d's master plan for the human race; and that activities and policies that undermine the traditional family structure strike a body blow at the very foundation of civilized society.

By the same token, we can and should tell our brothers and sisters who are ignorant or forgetful of Torah that the Jewish nation is the *am hanivchar,* chosen by Hashem for a special mission on this world and a special portion in the World to Come; that Torah is both the legacy and responsibility of every Jew; that the rabbinic leadership of those expressions of Judaism that are premised on the denial of the simple fact that Torah as it was given at Sinai is both eternal and constant are falsifiers of our heritage whose teachings have led countless Jews astray.

And, yes, we can and should let our fellow Jews know that *teflllin* and *mezuzos* are acceptable only if they conform precisely to the requirements of *halachah.*

The "Halachic Health Care Proxy":

An Insurance Policy With Unique Benefits

Chaim Dovid Zwiebel

S hortly before the summer, the highest policy making body within Agudath Israel of America, the *Moetzes Gedolei HaTorah* (Council of Torah Sages), arrived at a historic decision: Agudath Israel should develop and then initiate a major national campaign to encourage people to sign a "halachic health care proxy" — a standardized form designed to help ensure that all medical and post-death decisions made by others on an observant Jew's behalf would be made pursuant to *halachah*.

In this article, we will address three basic questions:

I. Why the need for a "halachic health care proxy"?

II. What are the legal considerations that underlie such a document?

III. What are the specific components of the standardized form developed by Agudath Israel, and how can individual Jews avail themselves of its protections?

I. The Need for a
"Halachic Health Care Proxy"

✦ Nancy Cruzan and the
Legacy of Modern Medical Technology

The Orwellian-sounding phrase "right to die" became firm-ly entrenched in the American lexicon in 1990 when the U.S. Supreme Court issued its ruling in the celebrated case of Nancy Beth Cruzan.

The facts of the case were undeniably tragic. Ms. Cruzan was in an automobile accident some seven-and-a half years ago. Since that time, she has been lying in a Missouri hospital in a "persistent vegetative state," having lost her upper brain func-tion, legally alive but permanently unconscious. However, Ms. Cruzan is not terminally ill; she could continue to live for many years in her vegetative state so long as she receives adequate nutrition and hydration. Ms. Cruzan's parents asserted that their daughter would never wish to be maintained in such a state, and they asked the court to compel the hospital to "pull the plug" on Ms. Cruzan's feeding tubes. By a vote of 5-4, how-ever, the Supreme Court denied the parents' request, and upheld the State of Missouri's right to continue providing life-sustaining nutrition and hydration to Ms. Cruzan.[1]

Cruzan may have been the first case of its kind to reach the U.S. Supreme Court, but it is illustrative of the types of agoniz-ing issues that arise so frequently in this era of rapid advances in medical technology. Those advances have enabled doctors to preserve and prolong many lives. At the same time, they have

---

1. In so ruling, the Supreme Court reached the result urged by Agudath Israel of America in its *amicus curiae* (friend of the court) brief — the only such brief submitted by a Jewish organization to the high court. The Court's reasoning was essentially this: Even assum-ing that an individual would have a personal constitutional right to refuse lifesaving measures, states are free to insist that there be "clear and convincing evidence" that a comatose patient would in fact have refused life support before any outside party could make that decision on the patient's behalf. Since there was no such "clear and convinc-ing evidence" of Ms. Cruzan's own wishes, her parents could not compel the State of Missouri to "pull the plug" and end her life.

created a painful question that confronts countless individuals and their families: Are there any limits to the resources and efforts that should be devoted to the maintenance of a person whose quality of life is severely diminished, whose chances of recovery are slim or virtually nil, whose continued maintenance is exacting a severe economic and emotional cost? Where, if anywhere, is the line to be drawn?

The question is one that is faced not only by growing numbers of individuals and families, but also by society as a whole as it struggles to develop public policy in an area of extreme moral complexity.

Some in the "pro-life" community advocate an uncompromising public commitment to the preservation of human life under virtually all circumstances, no matter what the costs, no matter what the medical prognosis, no matter what the wishes of the family or even the individual patient. A growing number of others, in contrast, advocate the "right to die with dignity" — a policy that would allow patients and their families to decide, at least at some point, that the patient's quality of life was so severely diminished as to justify the withholding or termination of medical life-support.

Although most proponents of the "right to die" position would hasten to disavow any support of suicide or of "euthanasia" (mercy killing), those concepts are inevitable outgrowths of the "right to die" philosophy and are already beginning to emerge from the shadows of the "death with dignity" movement. Laws have been proposed in a number of jurisdictions that would authorize physicians to assist patients who wish to commit suicide. One senses that stories like the one recently reported about Dr. Jack Kevorkian, a pro-euthanasia physician who had supplied a woman suffering from Alzheimer's Disease with a "do-it-yourself" suicide kit, which she promptly used to take her life, will soon fail even to raise eyebrows among most people.

For yet others, dying is more than merely a matter of right; it rises to the level of an obligation. In 1984, for example, Colorado Governor Richard Lamm told a group of attorneys that terminally ill seniors have "a *duty* to die and get out of the

way with all of our machines and artificial hearts and everything else like that and let the other society, our kids, build a reasonable life." This attitude is reflected in health care rationing
plans like the one recently developed in Oregon, which would
deny Medicaid patients the right to receive certain types of medical services that are not deemed "cost-effective." Thus, in determining whether any given life-sustaining measure makes medical sense, the key consideration is rapidly turning into one of
dollars and cents.

With these developments taking place all around us, what is
to be the attitude of the Torah community?

✧ The Primacy of Halachah

Halachah, the law of Torah, encompasses every facet of
human life. It also encompasses every facet of human death.
There are *halachos* that teach us how a person's remains are to be
buried; under what circumstances, if any, a decedent's body
may be autopsied or dissected; whether it is permissible, or perhaps even a mitzvah, to donate body organs for purposes of
transplantation into needy others.

So too does *halachah* govern the many issues that may arise
in near-death situations: the types of medical circumstances, if
any, that may justify the withholding or termination of various
forms of medical care; the permissibility, or non-permissibility,
of undergoing experimental treatment that could shorten life if
it does not cure the disease; the extent, if any, to which an individual's personal preferences with respect to medical care are
relevant halachic considerations in determining the course of his
treatment; the special laws that apply when a person reaches the
stage of *gesisah* (in the throes of death), as well as the means by
which *gesisah* is determined; the criteria by which to determine
a person's death.

Obviously, to state the self-evident axiom that *halachah* provides answers to all of these questions is by no means to state
that there is always definitive halachic consensus as to what
those answers are. Indeed, with respect to certain especially

complex matters, the rabbinic responsa and other halachic literature reveal a considerable disparity among a number of contemporary *poskim* (halachic decisors). Moreover, the enormous technological and physiological complexity involved in many of these *she'eilos* (questions of Jewish law), as well as the high stakes, may result in a reluctance on the part of certain *rabbanim* to render halachic rulings in specific cases.

For the believing Jew, though, the bottom line is that the resolution of such issues must come through the halachic system, not through personal predilection as molded by contemporary culture. There are inevitably bound to be disparities between *halachah* and the mores of the time; the underlying philosophies are in fundamental conflict. As Rabbi J. David Bleich has written:

> Man does not possess absolute title to his life or his body.
> He is charged with preserving, dignifying and
> hallowing that life. He is obliged to seek food and
> sustenance in order to safeguard the life he has been
> granted; when falling victim to illness or disease he is
> obliged to seek a cure in order to sustain life. The
> category of *pikuach nefesh* (preservation of life) extends to
> human life of every description and classification
> including the feeble-minded, the mentally deranged and
> yes, even a person in a so-called vegetative state. Shabbos
> laws and the like are suspended on behalf of such
> persons even though there maybe no chance for them
> ever to serve either G–d or fellow man. The mitzvah of
> saving a life is neither enhanced nor diminished by virtue
> of the quality of the life preserved."[2]

2. Bleich *The Quinlan Case: A Jewish Perspective,* reprinted in Rosner & Bleich, *Jewish Bioethics*, p. 270 (Heb. Publ. Co. 1979).

Sadly, certain others who allegedly represent the Jewish viewpoint propound a different philosophy. The October 17, 1989 edition of the *Congressional Record* contains the statement of Rabbi Dayle A. Friedman (Reform) in support of the "Patient Self-Determination Act of 1989," a bill pending at that time that would encourage patients to prepare living wills or health care proxies. In the context of his remarks, which were presented by the bill's sponsors as part of a series of "statements from authorities on the ethical teachings of the three main-line religions' traditions." Rabbi Friedman explains the Reform movement's endorsement of a person's ultimate right to choose to die:

Thus, "death with dignity," the rallying cry of the modern day euthanasia movement, clearly does not find its roots in the law or values of Torah. Elderly persons who speak of their desire to die rather than become a financial or emotional "burden on the children" may have the most noble of intentions, but nobility of intention is not the yardstick by which Jews measure conformity with Hashem's will. Those who champion only the *quality* of human life as the overriding value in health care decisions disregard the longstanding Jewish emphasis on the *sanctity* of human life, even in its most diminished qualitative form.

In sum, the complexity of the halachic issues, the diversity of views among rabbinic authorities with respect to certain *she'eilos*, the relative difficulty of finding *rabbanim* prepared to offer halachic guidance — none of these considerations detracts from the fundamental fact that for the Jew, the framework of analysis and decision on these issues must be the *halachah*.

✦ Who Will Ask the Questions? Who Will Make the Decisions?

In ordinary circumstances, when a person has a *she'eilah*, he will pose it to the halachic authority whose guidance he personally accepts as binding — the *Rav* of his *shul*, his *rebbe*, his *rosh*

"In contrast to our heteronomous tradition, Reform Jews have held that individuals have a direct, personal relationship with G-d in addition to their relationship via the Jewish people's covenant with G-d....We Reform Jews champion the right of individuals to make choices regarding their own conduct, including the "right of conscientious dissent" from the dictates of tradition when mandated by individual conscience, or by individual understanding of contemporary circumstances (Borowitz, *Choices in Modern Jewish Thought*, p. 269). We reject imposition of specific choices from external authorities, either contemporary or historical.... What is being proposed here is that the value of autonomy must be a guiding principle in a Reform Jewish discussion of choices in medical ethics. In the instant case, based on the principle of autonomy, we would have to hold that the patient, a competent, mature adult, has made a decision which must be respected. We would hope that the decision which such a person had made would emerge from a confrontation with the values expressed in Jewish tradition, both *halachah* and *aggadah*. Ultimately, however, the principle of autonomy requires us...to respect even choices which might seem to conflict with our understandings of the values of the tradition.

yeshivah, someone recognized as a halachic decisor for all of *Klal Yisrael* — whomever. Yet that is obviously impossible with respect to the many medical and post-mortem issues that may arise when the person about whom the *she'eilah* is being asked is incapable of posing the question himself.

One would hope that the *she'eilah* under those circumstances would be posed by those who will be making decisions on the individual's behalf — in most cases, the members of his family — and that it would be posed to the very same halachic authority to whom the individual himself would have turned were he capable of doing so.

But not always can it be so. Some people do not have family members with whom they retain contact or upon whom they can rely to contact their *morei hora'ah* (halachic decisors) in times of emergency. And, even for those who do, not always will the *she'eilos* arise under circumstances where those family members will be available to contact the individual's halachic authority. When, for example, a person is involved in an accident far from home, emergency decisions will be made for him by doctors and nurses who may not even know that he is Jewish, let alone who his relatives are or who his rabbi is. The likelihood is all too great in such situations that medical procedures will be performed, or withheld, in ways that constitute a violation of *halachah.*

The problem arises even more frequently in the context of post-mortem procedures. Many horror stories have come to light involving autopsies, post-mortem procedures and non-halachic burials of Jewish decedents who have passed away under circumstances where nobody was available to ensure that *halachah* would be followed after the person's death.

Hence the need for some form of protection — a mechanism whereby one can obtain at least a measure of assurance that when he becomes incapable of making his own health care decisions, when he dies and is unable to direct the course of his own burial, when he becomes incapable of asking the *she'eilos* himself, that others will take the steps necessary to ensure that *halachah* will be followed. As detailed below, the "halachic health care proxy" is designed to respond to that need.

II. Legal Underpinnings

✤ The Doctrine of Personal Autonomy

The renowned American jurist Benjamin N. Cardozo established in 1914 the principle that continues to guide medical jurisprudence to this day: "Every human being of adult years and sound mind has a right to determine what shall be done with his own body; and a surgeon who performs an operation without his patient's consent commits an assault, for which he is liable in damages."

This principle, which has come to be known as the "doctrine of personal autonomy," has been applied in numerous contexts to allow a patient the right to dictate the course of his own medical care, including the right to choose among various treatment alternatives and even the right to decline life-sustaining measures. In the famous Karen Anne Quinlan case, the New Jersey Supreme Court held that an individual's right to choose whether or not to receive treatment was of constitutional dimension, encompassed within the constitutional "right of privacy." The U.S. Supreme Court came close to endorsing this view in *Cruzan*, stating that "a competent person has a constitutionally protected liberty interest in refusing unwanted medical treatment."

That is not to say that the doctrine of personal autonomy is absolute. Some legal limitations do exist. Prohibitions against suicide or assisting others in committing suicide, for example, run contrary to the notion of unlimited personal autonomy; yet such prohibitions are recognized as legally valid. Indeed, the Supreme Court in *Cruzan* intimated that under certain circumstances, at least, a state may have the authority to override a patient's constitutionally protected "liberty interest" and insist that the patient receive life-support even against his own wishes.[3]

---

3. For the record, it should be noted that Agudath Israel, in its *amicus curiae* brief to the Supreme Court and innumerous other contexts, has expressed its strong opposition to the notion of unlimited personal autonomy. For example, in testimony submitted to the New York State legislature earlier this year, Professor Aaron Twerskl (chairman of Agudath Israel's Commission on Legislation and Civic Action) and I observed that the

Limitations notwithstanding, it is fair to say that the clear trend in American law is to accord virtually unfettered deference to the wishes of the individual patient in matters of medical care. But what if the patient is not physically able or competent to express those wishes?

✢ Ascertaining the Patient's Wishes

A patient's inability to express his wishes with respect to health care decisions does not necessarily negate the doctrine of personal autonomy. The law typically imposes an obligation on those who will be dictating the course of an incompetent patient's health care to do so in a manner that complies with what the patient would have wanted, were he able to express his own wishes. Stated simply, it ordinarily will be incumbent for third party medical decisionmakers to ask the question: "What would the patient have wanted us to do?"[4]

---

doctrine of personal autonomy under New York law would generally permit a person to refuse medical treatment even where the prognosis is that such treatment would lead to full recovery. We stated as follows: "Agudath Israel is troubled by the message this notion of unlimited personal autonomy delivers. It embodies a value judgment that society's interest in the preservation of human life must bow before an individual's decision that his life is no longer worth living. The implications of this message run directly counter to prohibitions against suicide and euthanasia that have long been accepted among civilized societies, and portend ominous changes in these social norms."

4. In addition to the general doctrine of personal autonomy that requires surrogate decisionmakers to attempt to ascertain what the patient would have wanted, a number of governmental bodies around the country have enacted statutes or regulations designed specifically to protect the religious rights of patients and decedents. In New York, for example, the state with the most comprehensive series of religious accommodation provisions (thanks to the efforts of organizations like Agudath Israel and COLPA, and of individual public officials like Assemblyman Sheldon Silver and Health Commissioner David Axelrod), the following protections have been explicitly written into the law:

General: Section 2803-c of the New York Public Health Care Law provides, in part, as follows: "*Every patient's civil and religious liberties...shall not be infringed.*"

"Do Not Resuscitate' (DNR) Orders: Section 2965 of the Public Health Law, which relates to decisions by a surrogate with respect to the cardiopulmonary resuscitation of a patient who has suffered cardiac or respiratory arrest, provides that such decisions shall be made "on the basis of the adult patient's wishes *including a consideration of the patient's religious and moral beliefs.*"

Very often, though, it may not be possible to ascertain with any degree of certainty what the patient would have wanted. It is under those circumstances that there is a broad disparity of legal guidelines throughout the United States. Some states insist that all forms of life support must be provided to incompetent patients unless there is "clear and convincing evidence" that the patient would not have wanted such support. Others accept less definitive evidence as sufficient indication of the patient's wishes. Yet others allow the withholding or withdrawal of life-sustaining measures from an incompetent patient even if there is absolutely no evidence of the patient's wishes, so long as it is determined that the patient's "best interests" would be served by allowing him to die.

These legal considerations have given rise to organized efforts to encourage competent persons to provide clear evidence of what their wishes would be with respect to medical decisions when they become incompetent. Two basic means of

---

Health Care Proxies: Similarly, section 2982 of the health care proxy bill (discussed in the text accompanying footnote 5 below) authorizes an agent to make health care decisions on behalf of his principal "in accordance with the principal's wishes, *including the principal's religious or moral beliefs.*"

Determination of Death: Under section 400.16 of the New York State Department of Health regulations, hospitals are required to develop "a procedure for the reasonable accommodation of the (patient's) *religious or moral objection to a determination of death based upon the irreversible cessation of all brain function*" (the neurological condition known as "brain death," which is nearly universally recognized by the secular law as constituting legal death, yet is held by many *poskim* not to constitute halachic death).

Autopsies and Dissections: Section 4209-a of the Public Health Law generally prohibits the performance of an autopsy or dissection on the body of any person who carries a card stating his personal opposition to such procedures. Similarly, section 4210-c prohibits, in the absence of a compelling public necessity, the performance of an autopsy or dissection *"over the objection of a surviving relative or friend of the deceased that such procedure is contrary to the religious belief of the decedent, or, if there is otherwise reason to believe that a dissection or autopsy is contrary to the decedent's religious beliefs."*

Anatomical Gifts: Under section 4222 of the Public Health Law, a coroner or medical examiner may seek the removal of a decedent's corneal tissue or pituitary gland tissue only if *"such removal does not conflict with [the] decedent's religious or other views."* More generally, section 4301 authorizes relatives of a decedent to donate the decedent's organs for transplantation and other medical purposes, but only "in the absence of actual notice of contrary indications by the decedent, or actual notice of opposition by [a relative], *or other reasons to believe that an anatomical gift is contrary to the decedent's religious or moral beliefs."* If there is reason to believe the decedent would have religious or moral objection to an anatomical gift, the hospital administrator is enjoined from requesting such a donation (section 4351), and a potential recipient is enjoined from accepting such a donation (section 4301).

achieving this purpose have been developed: the "living will" and the "health care proxy."

→ The "Living Will"

A "living will" is a document prepared by a competent adult that provides specific instructions with respect to a number of medical procedures that may arise if that person becomes incompetent. For example, the "Society for the Right to Die," an organization in the forefront of the "death with dignity" movement, encourages people to sign a form (which was reproduced in *The New York Times* two days after the Supreme Court issued its *Cruzan* decision) that includes the following:

"I direct my attending physician to withhold or withdraw treatment that serves only to prolong the process of my dying, if I should be in an incurable or irreversible mental or physical condition with no reasonable expectation of recovery.

"While I understand that I am not legally required to be specific about future treatments, if I am in the condition(s) described above, I feel especially strongly about the following forms of treatment:

"I do not want cardiac resuscitation.

"I do not want mechanical respiration.

"I do not want tube feeding.

"I do not want antibiotics.

"I do not want maximum pain relief."

By the same token, obviously, a "living will" could specify the individual's desire that those various medical procedures *should* be maintained in the event of the individual's incompetence. The point of the document is simply to enable an individual to make his specific wishes known.

→ The "Health Care Proxy"

The "health care proxy" takes a different approach to the issue. Rather than specify the types of medical procedures to be undertaken, or to be withheld, the proxy simply appoints someone to serve as the health care agent of the person signing the proxy form, empowered to make health care decisions on the person's behalf if the person ever becomes incapable of making such decisions on his own. The health care proxy thus operates essentially as a power of attorney (and is indeed known in many jurisdictions as a "durable power of attorney").

A number of states have enacted health care proxy laws, providing specific guidelines as to the formal requirements of the proxy, as well as the scope of the agent's authority and other pertinent substantive issues. New York, in the final days of its 1990 legislative session, shortly after the Supreme Court's *Cruzan* ruling, passed the "Health Care Agents and Proxies Act," scheduled to go into effect in early 1991.[5]

The two approaches outlined above — the "living will" and the "health care proxy" — are by no means mutually exclusive. One may, in the same document, accomplish both purposes: appoint an agent to make health care decisions when the individual cannot make such decisions on his own; and provide the agent with specific guidance as to the types of procedures that should or should not be undertaken.

As will now be seen, that dual approach is embodied in the "halachic health care proxy."

III. The "Halachic Health Care Proxy": Its Components and Mechanics

With the assistance of its Commission on Legislation and Civic Action, as well as a number of knowledgeable *rabbanim*, doctors and lawyers, Agudath Israel has developed a "halachic health care

---

5. Agudath Israel opposed the New York health care proxy bill, objecting to the broad authority it accorded to agents to decide that patients should die. "Even though the bill is couched in terms of the agent making decisions in accordance with the principal's wishes or best interests, Agudath Israel believes that the potential for abuse of that awesome decisionmaking authority is self-evident. If the social good of permitting people to designate trusted relatives or friends to make health care decisions on their behalf can be achieved only by granting such third parties an essentially unlimited right to decide that their principals should die, we think the price to pay is too high."

proxy" that is now available for broad distribution and use.[6]

Actually, the "halachic health care proxy" consists of two separate standardized forms: (1) a legally binding, formal document, entitled "Proxy and Directive With Respect to Health Care Decisions and Post-Mortem Decisions," which has been designed to conform to all the technical requirements of the recently enacted New York State health care proxy law; and (2) a short, credit card-sized form, entitled "Emergency Instructions," which summarizes the key provisions of the first form and is designed to be carried in a person's wallet or handbag. Both forms should be used in conjunction, as each serves a distinct purpose.

✣ *The "Proxy and Directive"*

As its title implies, the "Proxy and Directive" form accomplishes two essential functions.

First, it is a *proxy*: the appointment by a competent adult (the "principal") of another person to serve as an agent to make health care decisions on the principal's behalf if the principal becomes incapable of making such decisions on his own. Subject to certain statutory exceptions, the agent can be virtually any competent adult — a family member, a friend, anybody the principal trusts to carry out his wishes. The principal can also appoint a second person to serve as an alternate agent if the original agent is not available or willing to make decisions. The agent's authority commences only upon a medical determination of the principal's lack of capacity to make health care decisions for himself.

Second, the form is a *directive*: an instruction by the principal to the agent to make all health care decisions, as well as post-mortem decisions, in accordance with *halachah*. In order to ensure that the agent will direct *she'eilos* to the rabbinic authority the principal himself would consult were he able to do so, the

6. Copies may be obtained by contacting Agudath Israel of America, 84 William Street, New York, N.Y. 10038, (212) 797-9000.

form includes a section allowing the principal to designate a specific rabbi to be consulted by the agent whenever a *she'eilah* arises. Or, if such rabbi is unavailable or unwilling to rule on a particular halachic issue, the form further allows the principal to designate an Orthodox Jewish organization or institution to be contacted for purposes of referring a competent rabbinical authority.

The "Proxy and Directive" form should be completed and signed by the principal. However, if the principal is physically incapable of signing the form, he may ask another adult to sign his (the principal's) name on his behalf. In either event, the signing should be done in the presence of two witnesses, who in turn should sign their names to the document as well.

→ The Wallet-Size "Emergency Instructions" Form

Copies of the "Proxy and Directive" should be kept among the principal's important documents, and with a number of key people: the agent and alternate agent, members of the principal's family, his doctor, his lawyer, his rabbi and whomever else may be called upon in cases of emergency. At the same time, however, an unforeseen emergency may arise far away from family and home, where the "Proxy and Directive" will be of no avail unless the principal happens to be carrying a copy with him — hardly a likely happenstance in view of the sheer bulk of the document.

Hence the second "halachic health care proxy" form developed by Agudath Israel: a small, credit card-size form designed to fit in a person's wallet or handbag. The text of the card makes reference to the fact that its bearer has executed a formal "Proxy and Directive." It then proceeds to outline, in abridged form, the key provisions of the larger formal document; and provides the names, addresses and telephone numbers of the agent and rabbinical consultant designated by the principal.

It is questionable whether the wallet-size form, on its own, would be regarded as a legally binding document. Nonetheless, carrying it (on days when carrying is permitted!) is an effective means of ensuring that one's wishes with respect to medical and post-mortem decisions will be known under virtually any eventuality that may arise. And, when used in conjunction with the more formal "Proxy and Directive" outlined above, it will provide considerable legal protection against the possibility of such decisions being made in violation of *halachah*.

✦ *Inherent Limitations*

There are some things the "halachic health care proxy" does *not* do. For one, it does not attempt to spell out precisely what types of procedures, under what types of circumstances, should or should not be undertaken as a matter of Jewish law. This omission reflects a conscious policy decision by the *Moetzes Gedolei HaTorah*. They concluded that the range of halachic issues was too great, the changes in medical technology too rapid, the *she'eilos* too dependent upon individual circumstances, to presume to identify in advance the precise course of action to be taken under all future hypothetical situations. Rather than engage in such a speculative and possibly misleading exercise, the *Moetzes Gedolei HaTorah* felt that the form should simply provide a mechanism that would ensure that *she'eilos* would be posed in whatever circumstances may eventually arise.

Yet another thing the forms do not purport to do is tell individuals which rabbis or organizations they should choose to serve as halachic consultants/decisors with respect to medical and post-mortem procedures. This, too, was a conscious decision of the *Moetzes Gedolei HaTorah*. As noted above, there is a diversity of viewpoints among contemporary *poskim* with respect to a number of the issues an agent may have to decide. The *Moetzes* decided that it was not the role of an umbrella organization like Agudath Israel to identify specific *rabbanim*, to the implicit exclusion of others, as "competent" authorities in the area of medical *halachah* — especially in developing a form designed to be used by all communities and segments of *Klal*

Yisrael. Rather, each individual should designate as a halachic consultant the particular *moreh hora'ah* whose guidance he himself would seek — recognizing, of course, the specialized and highly complex nature of some of the *she'eilos* that may arise.

It should also be recognized that the "halachic health care proxy" is by no means the answer to every problem that may arise. Among its most obvious limitations is the fact that by law, only competent adults can sign such forms. Children, and adults who are not mentally competent, will not be able to avail themselves of its protections. Agudath Israel is currently pursuing with the New York State Department of Health the possibility of developing a variation of the basic form that would enable adults to protect their children and guardians to protect their incompetent wards against medical or post-mortem violations of *halachah.*

Another question that requires careful consideration, and consultation with competent halachic authority in individual cases, is whether encouraging gravely ill patients to sign such forms could itself constitute a violation of *halachah* by creating the possibility of *tiruf hada'as* — emotional shock that could further jeopardize the individual's fragile health. (See generally *Shulchan Aruch, Yoreh Deah* 337.) Obviously, the optimum time to encourage people to fill out and sign a "halachic health care proxy" is when they are in sound health and in full possession of their faculties, not after they have already entered a hospital or nursing home.

One final caveat: As noted above, the forms developed by Agudath Israel have been designed to conform with the specific formal requirements and other provisions of the New York State health care proxy law. Although the concept underlying the "halachic health care proxy" would likely be recognized as binding throughout the United States (and presumably in most other countries as well), other states may have certain particular requirements that might require minor modifications in the basic form. For example, whereas New York law provides that a proxy will remain in effect indefinitely unless specifically revoked by the principal, California law limits the effectiveness of its proxy (known in California as a "durable power of attorney") to a seven-year period.

Agudath Israel is in the process of developing alternate "halachic health care proxy" forms for use in jurisdictions where the New York model may be inappropriate. Individuals who reside outside of New York may wish to consult with a local attorney to determine whether the New York model would be recognized in their jurisdiction; or they may wish to contact Agudath Israel for additional assistance.

✦ Conclusion

Life is a precious gift from Hashem. Generally speaking, man is not permitted to squander the gift no matter how difficult or even unbearable the circumstances of human existence may become. As believing Jews, we must cling firmly to these basic values even when the secular world all around us is abandoning them. A society that subscribes to the principle that each person is entitled to choose death — the "right to die with dignity" — is a society that fails to appreciate fully the sanctity of human life. Stated simply, the doctrine of unlimited personal autonomy in medical decision making is totally repugnant to the foundations of our faith.

Yet, in one of the ironic twists that is so common to our millennia-long experience in *galus* (exile), the very same doctrine of personal autonomy provides each individual Jew an opportunity to obtain protection that will allow him to serve Hashem even when he is totally devoid of consciousness, even when he is at the brink of death, even after he has returned his soul to his Maker. The "halachic health care proxy" is an insurance policy that costs no money to obtain, is available to all, and provides the types of benefits that no insurance company can ever offer.

✈ Public Posture and Policies

The Jew in Galus:
How High a Profile?

Based on an address by
Rabbi Shimon Schwab

✦ The Foundation for Halachic Guidelines

To address the theme of "The Jew in *Galus*" — our relationship with the nations of the world in our *galus* situation — we must first take measure of the greatness of *Klal Yisrael* in the context of the other nations. An incident recorded in the Talmud can help us gain insight into this relationship.

Rabbi Elazar's *talmidim* (disciples) asked him, what are the demands of the mitzvah of *kibbud av v'eim*, honoring one's parents? Rabbi Elazar told them to learn from the conduct of a non-Jew in Ashkelon, Damma ben Nesina by name. His was the greatest expression of *kibbud av v'eim* imaginable: The sages once came to Damma to purchase a diamond for the *choshen* (the breastplate) of the Kohen Gadol, and they were willing to pay any price. But the key to the jewelry box lay under the pillow on which his father was sleeping (others say it was under his father's feet). He refused to awaken his father, forfeiting the gain of millions of dollars because of his respect for his father!

Now, the question of the *talmidim* was in regard to "*Kabeid es avicha v'es imecha*," one of the *Aseres HaDibros* (Ten Commandments). These were given only to Israel, not to the nations of the world. The answer to their query should have been based on *halachah*, or at least on the conduct of people who live by *halachah*. Why go for guidelines to Ashkelon — to an idolater, no less — and endow him with such importance as to refer to him by name? To be sure, it is fascinating that a heathen somewhere once did honor his father to such an extent, but that does not seem to answer their question.

In truth, there are two levels of *kibbud av v'eim*. One is universal, and applies to all mankind; the other is a mitzvah, addressed exclusively to *Klal Yisrael*. The world existed for twenty-six generations from Creation, until Israel stood at the foot of Mount Sinai, on the basis of *derech eretz* — civility and ethical conduct. Not only was mankind charged with *sheva mitzvos bnei Noach* — the seven Noahide commands — it was instructed in the principles of *derech eretz*, proper *middos*. Within this context, the basic responsibilities of *kibbud av v'eim* belong to the entire world.

This is evident in an incident in *Chumash*: When Eliezer proposed marriage to Rivkah on behalf of Yitzchak, the Torah records that, "Lavan and Besuel replied" (*Bereishis* 24:50). *Rashi* notes that from this passage, it is evident that Lavan was a *rasha* (wicked) because he spoke up before his father, Besuel, could reply. Now, Lavan was not a Jew; furthermore, honoring one's father is not among the *sheva mitzvos bnei Noach*. Nonetheless, *Chazal* (sages of the Talmud) declare him a *rasha*, for *kibbud av v'eim* is an aspect of *derech eretz*, which a non-Jew is also expected to fulfill. It is a matter of *hakaras hatov* — gratitude for all that parents do for their children especially when the parents are respectable people.

Apparently Nesina was a respectable man, and Damma ben Nesina carried the concept of gratitude to his father to its highest form. Thus, when the *talmidim* had inquired about the *halachah* of *kibbud av v'eim*, Rabbi Elazar replied by first laying the groundwork by showing how far a non-Jew carries this concept, without the guidelines of *halachah*. This response to the question tells us the extent of *kibbud av v'eim* as an expression of the human being as a *tzelem Elokim* — formed in G–d's image. That is where it peaks with the non-Jew ... and that is where the *mitzvah* of *kibbud av v'eim* begins in the Jewish scheme of things. The special nature of the Jewish mission is summarized in Moshe Rabbeinu's final words to *Klal Yisrael* before his passing: "How fortunate you are, O Israel ... you will tread on the high place [of the nations]" (*Devarim* 33:29). Where the non-Jew reaches his highest level of achievement, there, at that point, must the Jew begin to grow. Such are the demands being made of *Klal Yisrael*.

❖ An Approach to the Non-Jew

In one respect, the Jew must strive for prominence — the highest profile imaginable. This is based on *Klal Yisrael's* elevation from amongst the nations: "And you shall be for Me an *am segulah* — a nation treasured more than all the nations" (*Shemos* 19:5). The *Sforno* points out that "although the entire human race is more precious to Me than all other, inferior creatures, for man alone represents My purpose [as our Sages say, 'Precious is a man who was created in the Image' (*Avos* 3:14)] still you shall be to Me a treasure beyond all of them." If one simply looks with disdain at other nations, what is the gain of being treasured — the best of an ignoble heap? To bless G–d daily for being a member of the Jewish nation is more than simply expressing gratitude for not having been born into a family of Nazis or PLO-members. The *berachah*, to be of value, must refer to being treasured as one of a group of noble creatures.

If all the nations of the world — and it's a tendency today to think this way — are depraved, foolish and wicked, it is no distinction to be better than those who are depraved, foolish and wicked. That is no basis for praise to the *Ribbono Shel Olam*. By the same token, gratitude for being given the Torah cannot be meaningful if all non-Torah science is nonsense, if all secular knowledge is without value. What glory is ascribed to Torah knowledge if its distinction is simply that it is superior to nonsense? To the contrary, *Chazal* have told us that there is indeed *chachmah* (wisdom) amongst the nations. As a matter of fact, upon seeing a wise non-Jew, one pronounces a blessing, praising G–d "for having given of His knowledge to [a creature of] flesh-and-blood." But all their knowledge — all their sciences and all their wisdom — shrinks into absolute nothingness before the majesty of one *kutzo shel yud* (small stroke in the sacred Torah).

Yet an attitude of disdain for the other nations is to be expected, as a natural outgrowth of having suffered the recent decimating *churban* in Europe — and I am a witness to it. After such barbaric behavior by one of the world's most civilized nations, and silent indifference on the part of so much of the rest of the world, many of us have lost basic respect for the opinions of mankind. Because of our anger and our deep pain, we have developed an attitude of, "Who cares what other nations say?" We have seen their civilization and culture collapse in a major catastrophe. We have been deafened by the silence of the so-called moral majority of decent people. We no longer care. *Let them say what they want!*

Permit me to share a personal experience: I cannot forget a trip I made, returning to Germany some 25 years ago; my father had requested that I visit the burial places of my grandparents and great-grandparents. I arrived at the airport of my home-town, Frankfurt, where I had lived until 30 years earlier, and I saw these clean-shaven, immaculately dressed Germans, with their high-gloss shoeshines — so clean smelling, so vainglorious. *Guten Morgen, mein Herr...* I heard the old language, expressing the same haughtiness as before. I saw before me men of my age — among them must have been former SS men who had tortured little children. *They killed a third of my people!* In the clean smell that wafted about them, I choked on the stench of the gas chambers .... A taxi took me to the *beis ha'olam* (cemetery), and from there to my former home on my former street where I saw nothing but *churban* — desolation. Of the *shul*, just a piece of stone was left. Where the *beis midrash* and the yeshivah had been, an office building and a garage stood. I looked up at every window, where I had known everyone who had once lived in those apartments, and I saw Germans looking down at me. And I felt sick.

At the time, I recalled *Rashi's* comment on the first *pasuk* in the Torah, and I wondered. *Rashi* asks why the Torah starts with "*Bereishis*" and not with "*Hachodesh hazeh lachem* — this is your first month" — the very first mitzvah given to *Klal Yisrael*. He replies that the *goyim* will say, "*Yisrael listim atem* — Israel, you are thieves! You are not entitled to the Land of Israel!" G–d's account of Creation demonstrates His right to award the Land to the People of His choice. At that moment in Frankfurt, I thought: *Who cares? Let them say it! Is it necessary to structure the Torah to appease these sadists, these cruel people? Let them say what they want!*

The Torah promises us that the Jews will be *chachamim u'nevonim b'einei ha'amim* — wise and understanding in the eyes of the nations. Who cares what they say?

As these thoughts were flowing through my mind, I suddenly caught sight of a fleet of military trucks passing by, loaded with American servicemen. I was so excited that had I not been embarrassed, I would have waved to them. At this moment, I realized that there are two kinds of nations — the *malchuyos horishah* (wicked nations) and the *malchuyos shel chesed* (kingdoms of kindness). The prophecy that "The nations will be destroyed," only refers to *certain* nations, the *malchiyus horishah*, the likes of Nazi Germany, Austria, Russia and Libya .... A *malchus shel chesed* is, by contrast, a place where we are permitted to develop ourselves as we wish, and create yeshivos, form *kehillos* and establish our own houses of worship, without interference ... a country such as America, where *Yiddishkeit* has developed and can develop, and is making such admirable strides forward. In regard to such nations, we are keenly interested in the type of impression we make. In regard to them, we are concerned that our "wisdom and understanding" be appreciated, so they may comment favorably in regard to Jewry: "This is a singularly wise and understanding people." And when we express our hope: "Let all nations praise G–d, all peoples extol Him" (*Tehillim* 117:1) we refer to such *malchuyos shel chesed*.

In all our dealings with others, we must distinguish between these two types of nations.

→ Dealing With a Nation of Evil

A word of caution is in order here. Religious Jews are often accused of having a "*galus* mentality." We, for our part, must have the courage of our convictions even if they are unpopular, because we stand on firm ground. The *Ramban* in *parshas Vayishlach* cites a *midrash* that relates that whenever Rabbi Yannai went to Rome to deal with the government on behalf of the Jews, he would take along a *Chumash* and review *parshas Vayishlach* which describes the encounter between Yaakov Avinu and Eisav: Seven times Yaakov prostrates himself before his brother and calls him "*adoni* — my master," and refers to himself as "*avdecha* — your slave." The *Ramban* explains that *Chazal* recognized this as the *parshah* of *galus*, telling us for all times how to deal with every *malchus horisha*, based on Yaakov's conduct in his confrontation with Eisav.

I recall from my days as a *talmid* in the Yeshiva of Telshe, how the Telshe Rav, Rabbi Yosef Leib Bloch, described the entire episode as a comedy. I understood this interpretation later when I saw in the *Zohar Chadash* that the Torah never really says that Yaakov bowed down to Eisav. Yaakov Avinu saw G–d's presence before him. He knew that Eisav was nothing but a pawn in the hands of G–d, Who had placed him temporarily in a position of power, for reasons of His own. When Yaakov bows down seven times, he bows to the *Ribbono Shel Olam*. When he says "*avdecha*," he refers to his status before the *Ribbono Shel Olam*: "I, Yaakov Avinu, am Your servant." And "*adoni*" is not addressed to his brother who is one minute older than he is; "*adoni*" means the *Ribbono Shel Olam*. Eisav, the vainglorious fool, believes that it is directed toward him.

Chazal instruct us to proceed this way whenever we deal with a *malchus horishah*. Even today, when we live in the free society of this *malchus shel chesed*, America, we must not abandon this guideline when dealing with hostile nations. Others, who do not know how to learn *Chumash* — and some who do know how, but seem to have forgotten the lessons — ridicule us for our "*galus* mentality." It takes a great measure of courage to have an opinion other than that of the majority, but we can draw strength from our knowledge that we have a solid precedent: We carry our *Chumash* in hand, so to speak, when we seek the counsel of *gedolei Yisrael* before we embark on a project for the *hatzalah* of *Klal Yisrael*. (This approach may not apply to problems in *Eretz Yisrael*, which is surrounded by a raging ocean of enmity. *Baruch Hashem*, G–d has placed our most eminent *gedolei Yisrael* in *Eretz Yisrael*, and they are the ones to be consulted regarding their problems.)

Yaakov Avinu did make one error, *Chazal* say: He should not have sent emissaries to give regards to Eisav and pay his respects to him. They quote a *pasuk* in *Mishlei*, "Somebody who grabs hold of the ears of a dog will get into an unnecessary fight." Eventually he will get bitten. He should not have told Eisav a thing. When dealing with sworn enemies of Jewry, there is only one approach: do not provoke them; do not anger them; do not embarrass them. Eisav never forgets, and only harm can come from antagonizing him. If anti-Semites in Austria want to elect one of their ilk, a former Nazi criminal, as their president, let them. Do not meddle. It is not our concern .... If a foreign leader chooses to embrace Arafat or Waldheim, let him do so. He has demonstrated his inner leanings. We cannot afford to forget that whatever statements we make, whatever actions we take, can antagonize the *resha'im*, and may bring harm to *acheinu Bnei Yisrael* .... In Russia, more than two and a half million Jews are virtual hostages. There is a sizable Jewish population in South Africa and in Arab countries. Our primary concern in our *hatzalah* efforts on behalf of our Jewish brethren must be in terms of actually helping them, not simply to show that we Jews can also raise our voices or make the newspapers in the manner that the others do. We are meant to be different from all the others, and so is our image.

People who choose to travel to Washington to demonstrate for Soviet Jewry should "take along the *Chumash*" and consult *parshas Vayishlach*. If the tone of such gatherings is set by non-Torah leaders, who do not recognize *Toras Elokim* and do not accept the authority of the *Chumash*, then we certainly are endangering ourselves as well as the welfare of our brethren, who might be helped in other ways. Quiet diplomacy entails a great *mesiras nefesh* of its own — avoiding the reassurance of headlines. The purpose of discreet activity is *not* to show that we also have a voice. To be sure, "We are not doormats anymore!" "Never again!" and whatever other slogans are currently popular may sound beautiful to the ear, and saying them, or hearing them shouted, can make one's chest swell with pride. But the basic question is: How do we truly help *Acheinu Bnei Yisrael*?

→ The Kingdoms of Kindness

The rules of dealing with a *malchus shel chesed* are totally different from those for negotiating with hostile powers. The first point is never to forget that we are in *galus*, even when under the most benign circumstances. We should recognize that if at this juncture in history, we are blessed with the good will of the authorities in this country, that is the *Ribbono Shel Olam's* doings. He has His own Master Plan, and under this warm relationship with our host country, Torah is a thriving reality in the growing number of yeshivos, *kollelim*, Bais Yaakov schools, *kehillos*, and generally in communal life. But in this *galus* status of ours we dare not forget the letter that Yirmiyahu HaNavi sent to *Galus Yehoyachin* in Babylon. (The Jews were treated very decently there.) He says, "Further the welfare of the city into which I have exiled you. And pray to G–d for the welfare of the city [the country of Babylon]. For in its well-being, will you find well-being" (*Yirmiyahu* 29:7). *Kavod hamalchus* — respect for the government — has been the hallmark of Jewish dealings with the host country wherever Jews have lived. Respect for the rule "*dina d'malchusa dina* — the law of the land prevails," as long as it does not conflict with Torah law, has been the guideline for Jewish conduct of affairs for generations. It should be no less in the case in our current stage of *galus*.

The second rule is always to endeavor to make a *kiddush Hashem* — to bring glory to G–d's Name through our actions. The Prophets instruct us to emulate Avrahom Avinu, and invoke the respect of the nations as he did, earning the greeting: "You are a prince of G–d in our midst" (*Bereishis* 23:6). This fulfills G–d's vow to Avraham: "All the families of the earth will be blessed with you" (*Bereishis* 12:3). And indeed, they did feel that they were blessed because of his presence. In our time, too, we must present to the world a symbol of dignity. The *berachah* we recite every morning, "*Oter Yisrael besifarah* — You crown Israel with glory," carries a message of avoiding boisterous behavior, and by contrast fulfilling the rabbinic dictum of "greeting every person first — even a heathen in the marketplace."

Also, we must beware of causing *chillul Hashem* — desecration of G–d's glory through our conduct. Let us be in the forefront of those who are meticulously honest. Those who make the headlines through deceit and swindle and smuggling and forging and defrauding the government and the public — no matter how devout they are in their outward appearance — have the blood of *Klal Yisrael* on their hands. Stealing from a non-Jew is more severe than stealing from a Jew, for whoever is guilty of the former has no atonement, should he die without doing *teshuvah* (repenting), because of the *chillul Hashem* involved. *Chazal* have gone on record including those who lie or steal from the Gentiles among those who are *mechalel Hashem*, for they provoke non-Jews to say, "There is no Torah within Israel." Liars, swindlers, thieves who appear to be *frum* Jews are actually considered as if they proclaim, "There is no Torah unto Israel," for the Torah instructs the Jewish people not to commit dishonest acts, and they put the lie to this command. Should they actually adhere to this directive, then the greatest *kiddush Hashem*, in this respect, would result.

Several years ago, newspapers and magazines published stories about a great Jewish family renowned for both its remarkable business successes and its philanthropy. The stories stressed that everybody trusts them because they are honest; that their word is gold, because they are Orthodox Jews.

Another rule. Let us beware of *lamah tisra'u* — do not be conspicuous in your wealth even if it is honestly earned, as Yaakov Avinu warned his children: Why display yourselves before others as if you have sufficient food, when everyone else is going hungry? His sons did have enough, but others did not. Thus his admonition: *Don't flaunt your wealth!* How, then, does one deal with the public display of wedding extravaganzas, public celebrations covered by the media, detailing how many thousands of dollars the *kallah's* dress cost, and how many thousands were spent on the ring? Another example of imprudent excesses is the twenty-six page display advertisement in *The New York Times* to "sell" an institution of Jewish learning. Or for that matter any display of excessive luxury, lavish dress and opulent appearance. These all send the wrong signals to the world at large. It creates greed, jealousy and hatred. Listen to the old *zaken*, the father of the twelve tribes, Yaakov Avinu: *"Lamah tisra'u."*

Another point that is somewhat similar centers on the widely-touted gala exposition of kosher gluttony. The purpose of *kashrus*, says the *Chumash*, is to promote "Men of holiness you shall be unto Me" (*Shemos* 22:30). An exposition dedicated to *kashrus* should spotlight the *kedushah* of keeping kosher, rather than project the image of being a *"zoleil ve'sovai* — glutton and drunkard" of the highest magnitude .... How high a profile? Unfortunately, when we identify the kosher Jew with a Viennese table, it is a very low profile, indeed.

→ *High Profile Advocacy*

Even in a *malchus shel chesed* we can face grave dangers to our existence, in the spiritual sense. When we face the prospects of a Gay Rights Bill, or the Equal Rights Amendment, it is a matter of *pikuach nefesh* — spiritual survival. Such issues call for vigorous action to protect our very existence. As time goes on, new areas of contention can arise, wherein the law of the land can interfere with leading a Torah existence.

In such cases, the first rule is to be unafraid, and not be ashamed because people may mock us. Yes, we are in *galus*, but the Torah is not in *galus*. This, of course, requires the guidance of *gedolei haTorah*: no step may be taken without the counsel of the most prominent *talmidei chachamim* of our time. In this respect, we must pay homage to Agudath Israel of America, which consults Torah authorities in formulating its policy and in carrying it out so effectively. When the profile delineates loyalty to values and methods consistent with Torah, then the profile must be high, proud and uncompromising.

The Sweet Galus

Rabbi Chaim Dov Keller

Can we live a miracle as if it were natural?

✦ History Lessons for Future Conduct

U nfortunately — or perhaps fortunately — we must stress
that which should be obvious; that the Jew is in *galus*. For
what may be obvious to the Jew who went through the *churban*
in Europe may not be obvious to the American-born Jew, not
even the American-born *ben Torah*. He was born here, he feels
comfortable here. Indeed, G–d has been good to us here. Jews on
the whole are getting ahead, and Orthodox Jews in particular
are succeeding spiritually as well as materially. So the Jew is a
member of an ethnic minority. America is made up of many
minorities. We have rights like the rest of them. If we are indeed
in *galus*, it's a sweet *galus*.

There is an oft-quoted saying that he who does not learn
from history will have to relive history. When we speak of the
Jewish people, we must paraphrase that statement: The Jew *will*
relive history and therefore he *must* learn from history. The
Ramban in his commentary to *parshas Lech Lecha* teaches us,

"Maasei avos siman l'banim." That which happened to our Patriarchs — Avraham, Yitzchak and Yaakov — is a portent of what will happen to their children, the Jewish People.

The *Avos HaKedoshim* in their personal lives laid the foundations and set the pattern for all subsequent Jewish history. This is what we mean when we say the Jew will relive history. The corollary to this rule is that we must learn from how the *Avos* dealt with those history-making situations in which they found themselves. The *Ramban* (see commentary to *Bereishis* 32:4 and 33:15) teaches us that Yaakov's preparation for and his meeting with Eisav is the *parshas hagalus,* indicating what would happen to us in future encounters with Eisav's descendants. It also provides us with a formula for coping with our present-day *galus* among Eisav's children. If we fail to learn from it, we will have to relive that *parshas hagalus* at very great risk.

Even in actions where our Sages were critical of the *Avos'* conduct, they nonetheless followed their example: The *Midrash* tells us that because Yaakov Avinu referred to Eisav eight times as *"Adoni* — my master," eight kings arose from the children of Eisav before Yaakov's children had even one king.[1]

Yet when Rebbe Yehudah *HaNasi* saw that his scribe, Rabbi Efes, had addressed a letter: "From Yehudah *the Prince,* to my master, the Emperor Antoninus," he told him to rip up the letter and to write instead: "From Yehudah *your servant,* to my master, the Emperor Antoninus." When Rabbi Efes asked him why he lowered himself and his prestige as *Nasi,* Rebbe answered, "Am I better than my father Yaakov who, when he addressed Eisav, referred to himself as *avdecha Yaakov* — your servant Yaakov?"

Rabbi Yosef Leib Bloch, the Telshe Rav and *Rosh Yeshivah,* explained that Yaakov was found wanting for not having attained a level of spirituality that would have made it unnecessary to humble himself before Eisav; yet the actual state in which he found himself left him no choice but to refer to Eisav as "my master" — and this became the model for future generations.

---

1. "And these are the kings that ruled in the land of Edom before a king ruled over the children of Israel" (*Bereishis* 36:31).

⤳ *Patriarchal Survival Tactics*

The Jewish People throughout the millennia here survived because whenever they were persecuted and driven from one country, they found refuge in another country. This pattern was directly established by the *maasei avos* of Yaakov Avinu, who, in preparation for his confrontation with Eisav, divided his people into two camps: "*Im yavo Eisav el hamachaneh ha'achas vehikahu vehayah hamachaneh hanishar lifleitah.* And he said, if Eisav will come upon one camp and smite it, then the remaining camp will survive" (*Bereishis* 32:9).

Says the *Ramban*, this is also an indication of what will happen: In future generations, the children of Eisav could never completely destroy us. They may persecute us, even torture us, in some of their countries. A ruler in one land will make decrees against our possessions or against our persons, while another government in a different part of the world will have mercy on the refugees, and protect them.

It does not take too much imagination to realize that our generation is living witness to this recurring pattern of Jewish history: "If Eisav will come upon one camp and smite it" — if Hitler brought about an almost total annihilation of European Jewry — "then the remaining camp will survive" — we here in America were that remainder. If today Jews in other parts of the world are suffering privation and persecution, then we here in America and in *Eretz Yisrael* are the *machaneh hanishar* — the other camp.

But we do have one thing in common with "the other camp" — and we make a grave error in not realizing it — that we here are just as much in *galus* as are our brethren in Russia, in Iran and in Arab lands. Except that they suffer from the first half of the *pasuk* — "if Eisav will come upon one camp and smite it" — and we are the beneficiaries of the second half — "then the remaining camps will survive." And we have no guarantee that the roles cannot ח"ו be reversed.

We must be keenly aware of this *galus* status, even when we are blessed to be among the survivors, as the Vilna Gaon points out in his commentary to the Pesach Haggadah:

In "*Vehi She'amdah*," where we recount how G–d is keeping His oath guaranteeing the survival of Avraham and his offspring, we say, "For it was not only one who rose against us, but in every generation they arise (present tense!) against us to destroy us, and the Holy One Blessed Be He saves us (present tense!) from their hands." But what if we don't realize this? What if we live under a *malchus shel chesed* — a benevolent government — and we don't see those who are out to destroy us? That, says the Vilna Gaon, is the connection with the next paragraph: "Go out and learn — what did Lavan want to do to our father Yaakov? Pharaoh leveled his decree only against the males, whereas Lavan sought to destroy everyone." That is, even though we do not consciously sense them, G–d is constantly performing great miracles for us. If it is not obvious to us and we are overly secure, it is time to leave our comfortable illusions and learn from Lavan HaArami.

At first glance we can't see what Lavan intended to do to Yaakov, yet the Torah tells us that *Arami oveid avi* — he sought to uproot the entire Jewish People:

Yaakov is living with his uncle, Lavan, married to his two daughters. (Some say that even Bilhah and Zilpah were also Lavan's daughters, by concubine — see *Targum Yonasan ben Uziel*.) Yaakov's children are Lavan's grandchildren. He is making vast sums of money for Lavan, and along the way, becoming independently wealthy and building his own family. Yaakov does not have the slightest inkling that there is a problem. And then he begins to hear rumblings: "And he heard the words of the sons of Lavan saying, 'Yaakov has taken all that belongs to our father, and from our father's possessions he has acquired all this honor.' And Yaakov saw the face of Lavan that it was not with him as it had been yesterday and the day before" (*Bereishis* 31:1-2). Yaakov steals away, not yet realizing the full import of that change in Lavan's face. Lavan pursues him. And then, in the final moment of truth, Lavan reveals his true intentions: "It is within my power to do evil with you; and the G–d of your father appeared to me last night and told me, 'Do not speak with Yaakov good or bad'" (*Bereishis* 31:29). Lavan, the loving uncle, father-in-law, grandfather, and business partner, has revealed himself. Don't delude yourself. *Lavan b'keish la'akor es hakol* — Lavan sought to destroy everything!

→ *Existence by Miracle*

Over 200 years ago, Rabbi Yaakov Emden wrote: "The existence of the Jewish people among the nations of the world is a greater miracle than that of the Exodus from Egypt."

This same observation was made by the *Chovos HaLevavos*[2] hundreds of years before. "If a person wants to see miracles in his times similar to those performed by the *Ribbono Shel Olam* at *Yetzias Mitzrayim* and *Maamad Har Sinai,* let him look with a truthful eye at how the Jewish people survive among the nations of the world since they have gone into *galus,* and how their needs are being met. We flourish even though we differ essentially from our host nations. Our inner values and outer behavior are different from theirs, and they know it." These are factors that normally arouse hatred between groups, and yet we still live among them. Moreover, they know that the Jew is "making it," sometimes even doing better than them. "Their middle- and lower-classes often work harder than ours do. And yet we exist among them — as the *Ribbono Shel Olam* had promised us: 'Even when they are in the lands of their enemies I have not despised them and I have not rejected them to destroy them, to nullify my covenant with them, I am Hashem their G–d' (*Vayikra* 26:4)."

Do you think we are not in *galus*? *Mir zennen shoin ein moll in galus*! We are in *galus* — but the *Ribbono Shel Olam* is with us.

If we are fortunate enough to live in a *malchus shel chesed*, it is because we are beneficiaries of that second half of the *pasuk,*

---

2. In *Shaar HaBechirah,* Chapter 5.

"And the remaining camp will be a refuge." The danger is that we look at this awesome miracle of our existence, and we consider it to be natural. We think that we exist in *galus* because we get along so well with non-Jews, because we're so clever, so resourceful, so industrious, so ambitious ... because the Jew, no matter how you throw him up in the air, is going to land on his feet. But it just is not so.

✣ *On the Back of the Fish*

Among those wonderful *Aggados* in *Perek HaSefinah,* Rabbah Bar Bar-Chana relates: *"We were traveling on a ship and we saw a huge fish. Sand had collected on its back and a meadow of grass had grown there. We had thought that it was dry land, so we landed on it. We lit a fire, baked and cooked our food there. And when its back got hot, the fish turned over...Had our boat not been nearby, we surely would have drowned"* (*Bava Basra* 73b).

This, like all the other *Aggados* there, is obviously an allegory. Rabbah Bar Bar-Chana is teaching us that there are times in our *galus* when we mistake the back of a fish for a beautiful, grassy island of refuge. It appears to us as dry land, and we forget that we are in the middle of a stormy sea of *galus.* We decide to enjoy ourselves. We light our fires, we bake, we cook, we drink *"l'chaim,"* and we live it up as if we were here to stay, and as if nothing is going to bother that fish. We make the mistake of thinking that this state of existence in *galus* is natural and permanent. The wonderful illusion lasts until we make those fires a bit too hot and the fish turns over! And if the ship of Torah — our only real guarantee of survival — is not nearby, we run the risk of sinking to the depths of that sea of *galus.*

People talk about the unprecedented situation of Jews in America. Nonsense! Nothing is unprecedented in the history of the Jewish people. We are always reliving history:

The so-called "Golden Age" of the Jews of Spain lasted for over a century. The Jewish people in Spain were under the impression that Spain was their island of tranquility — they had produced philosophers, doctors, merchants, poets and ministers.

But then things began to change. In 1492, even though Don Yitzchak Abarbanel was the Finance Minister and one of the closest advisors to Ferdinand and Isabella, the Jews were thrown into a turmoil — not by the discovery of America, but by *Gerush Sefarad*, the expulsion of the entire Jewish community from Spain.

The Jews of Germany, beginning from the Emancipation in the early 19th century, labored under the same kind of illusion. In the First World War, they fought loyally by the side of their non-Jewish compatriots for the glory of the Kaiser. In the Weimar Republic, which followed, they enjoyed civil rights and rose to positions of influence and power, producing some of Germany's greatest scholars and scientists, poets and musicians. There were those who said, *"Berlin ist Jerusalem"* — until an insignificant corporal, with the same master plan as Lavan's for a final solution, appeared on the scene. *And the fish turned over!*

High Profile ...

Let us not be misunderstood. The message here is not: "It can happen here unless we watch out for the neo-Nazis and the Aryan Nation." In effect we are saying the opposite: that Jews in *galus* are living a miracle and one dare not confuse that miracle with *teva* — nature. We cannot apply political or sociological laws to a miracle. Schools of higher learning and advanced think-tanks cannot teach us anything that can realistically apply to the categories of Jewish history.

In order to understand Jewish history, you must understand Torah: As Rabbi Shimon Schwab has said, "The Jew in *galus* has to take along the *Chumash*." Consulting the *Chumash*, we find that there are no simple guidelines to *galus* conduct. On one level, we are bidden to maintain an extremely high profile, and on the other, we are commanded to keep out of sight — possibly both at the same time.

We are the children of Avraham, Yitzchak and Yaakov. The hallmark of the *Avos* was *"Vayikra b'Shem Hashem"* — they proclaimed the Name of Hashem for the world — publicly declaring the Divine significance of that Name (*Bereishis* 12:8 — see

Ramban). Before Avraham came upon the scene, Hashem was known as G–d of Heaven. After Avraham proclaimed His Name, He was known as the G–d of *Heaven and Earth* (*Bereishis* 24:7 — see *Rashi*). Yitzchak continued this mission (*Bereishis* 26:28). And Yaakov proclaimed the Divine Name by dwelling in the tents of Torah and learning with all who sought G–d's teachings (see *Sforno* to *Bereishis* 36:51). The *Ramban* explains that Yaakov's form of proclaiming G–d's Name was by bringing into the world a family whose very existence bore testimony to the true *emunah* among the nations of the world.

This is our *tachlis* — our mission as a People. We have no other *tachlis*. As the *pasuk* says: "I have created this People to declare My praises" (*Yishayahu* 43:21). In fact, the whole purpose of the creation is, as *Chazal* tell us, for *k'vod Hashem*.

If this is our purpose, can we shirk our responsibilities? Must we not proclaim the *Shem Hashem*? Should we not teach Torah to our fellow Jews, and teach the world by our example how a human being was meant to live? Our mission is to show the world by our service to G–d that there is a Creator, and demonstrate by our conduct how His creatures should live. If in this we maintain a high profile, then we are fulfilling the purpose of our *galus* among the nations of the world. (See *Smag, Mitzvas Asei* 84.)

❖ ... Hidden From Sight

On the other hand, we are also bidden to hide ourselves as much as possible. The Torah records: "We [the Jews] circled Mt. Seir for many days and G–d said, 'You have gone around this mountain enough — turn to the north'" (*Devarim* 31:3). On the simple level, this was a message to proceed toward their goal, *Eretz Yisrael*. The *Kli Yakar*, however, draws from a *midrash* and says that this passage "plumbs to the depths." It explores the depths of the *tehom*, which is a reference to *galus Edom*.[3] This *pasuk* is an allusion to the Jewish condition at that time, and for all generations.

---

3. *"Tehom"* is the fourth *galus* — that of Eisav, which is alluded to the beginning of *Sefer Bereishis*.

We are traveling around Mt. Seir, the territory of Eisav, not yet having attained our final goal. Nor will we attain that goal until *Mashiach* comes. But, says the Torah, while you are going around among the descendants of Eisav — that is, during Eisav's period of ascendancy in this world — hide yourselves. (Implicit in the word *tzafon* — literally, north — is *hatzpinu atzmechem*, hide yourselves.) The *Kli Yakar* explains: "If a Jew finds some sort of success in this world, he should conceal it. Don't show it to Eisav because no one hates the Jews as do the children of Eisav. In their eyes, everything we possess was stolen from them when Yaakov took the *berachos* from Eisav. Therefore, '*hatzpinu atzmechem* — hide yourselves.'"

Says the *Kli Yakar*, "This is the exact opposite of what Jews are doing today. If the Jew achieves a little success, he has to flaunt it. Somebody who has a hundred gold coins clothes himself and his family and lives in a house in the manner of a person who has thousands, and this arouses the hatred of the gentiles. In this, they are transgressing the *pasuk's* command: '*Hatzpinu atzmechem!*'" (The *Kli Yakar* wrote these words during the late 16 century!)

Those who ignore this *pasuk* (and unfortunately this has become inordinately common) do so at great risk .... It is no secret that this has been one of the main sources of the anti-Semitism from which the Jewish People has suffered throughout the years of *galus*.

✦ A Confused Agenda

This, then, is our agenda: When it comes to proclaiming the Name of Hashem, we should be seen *and* heard. Our pronouncements and actions should be instrumental in making Him "the G–d of the Heaven and the Earth." In this, we must maintain a high profile. But when it comes to our material success, we should try to keep out of sight. We should proclaim for the world, *"Hashem hu haElokim,"* not show them how much we own. We seem to have *fardrayt di yoitzrois* — reversed the agenda. When it comes to proclaiming the Name of Heaven in the world, not only are Jews as a whole not manning the ramparts, but unfortunately there are all too many in the forefront of what is perceived as a battle to secularize America. However, when it comes to conspicuous consumption — letting the non-Jews know to what extent we've made it and how we can spend it — we can't be beat.

When typically Jewish-sounding names are broadcast throughout the land in connection with insider stock trading, using controlled substances and child abuse, there is obviously too high a Jewish profile. When pornography and images of violence are propagated by an elite of East and West Coast Jewish authors, publishers, movie and media moguls, whose first amendment rights are defended by a highly visible corps of Jewish ACLU types, then we are too obvious.

There is little you and I can do about this. But if by our apathy and inaction we allow the American Jewish establishment to speak in the name of the entire Jewish People, ultimately we will have to give an accounting. For the situation has so evolved that should we want to know what position to take on almost any given issue of public policy dealing with religion, morality and related affairs, we can almost unerringly say that, whatever position is taken by the secular-Reform Jewish establishment and the ACLU, we should take the opposite. To give just a few examples, on the ERA, abortion, "gay rights," government aid to private schools, or any issue dealing with the so-called separation of church and state, the Catholic Church and the fundamentalist Christians have taken stands that are closer to the Torah position than the so-called "Jewish position" is. I believe that it is our sacred duty to proclaim the Name of G–d not only for its own sake, but also to remove the *chillul Hashem* resulting from the perception that the Catholic Church and the Moral Majority have become the guardians of America's morality, against the Jews.

✦ Dispelling the Grotesque Caricature

We must also do whatever possible to dispel the grotesque caricature of the Jew that is projected by so-called Jewish weddings and bar mitzvahs. It's not enough to have a wedding attended by thousands of people. One must engage a public relations outfit to handle the press and call in the T.V., who then make it into a media event, which someone obviously feels is a *kiddush Hashem*. But that is not the end. The paper has to dutifully conduct interviews with the caterer who reveals how many thousands of chickens and how many tons of chopped liver and gallons of dressing he'll be using.

When this happens, or when *The New York Times* runs a prominently featured story on the *Queen Elizabeth II* being chartered for a bar mitzvah celebration, we are heating up the fire on the back of the fish. *Gedolei Torah* have for the past several years been raising their voices against the excesses in this area — it would seem to little avail. But the time has come for intelligent and dedicated Jews to realize not only the adverse effects that extravagance has on the individual and on the family, but of the real and present danger that it presents to *Klal Yisrael* in *galus*. And we must realize that it's not only weddings and *simchos,* but our entire lifestyle that stings the eyes of our neighbors. One has only to pick up a Jewish publication and look at the ads to realize to what appalling extremes the ostentatious display of our material success has reached.

This tendency has been aggravated by the insidious assimilation of an objectionable character trait of our host society. Unfortunately, even the most committed Jew, who would never dream of outright assimilation, cannot help but absorb certain attitudes from the very air of the society in which he lives. On the whole, Americans are the world's nice guys. But they do have certain *middos ra'os* (pernicious traits), no different from all other nations of the world. One of them, perhaps the main one, is a lack of *tzenius.* By this we mean not only improper in dress, we mean an inordinate preoccupation with hype and P.R., and an appalling lack of personal modesty and humility. Publicity in all forms and varieties becomes an end unto itself. And we absorb all this by social osmosis.

Even our actions on behalf of Torah are affected. *Chazal* tell us that the first *Luchos* (Tablets of Law), which were given in a public, awe-inspiring fashion, did not last. The second *Luchos* were given quietly, and they did last. The message should be obvious. Yet even some of our most dedicated Jews — and even our most sacred institutions — have been making the mistake of acting as though the medium were the message. Getting your name or your institution's name in *The New York Times* — or any other paper, for that matter — is an accomplishment in itself.

There are those who think that if they put up a menorah on public property in the city square, they've accomplished great things for *Yiddishkeit* even if they have to defend their position by declaring that the menorah "is not a religious symbol." We thus witness the ultimate absurdity of arousing the hatred and derision of the gentile world and, at the same time, removing the *Shem Hashem* from the very Jewish symbol that we are trying to publicize. I personally believe that there should not be a nativity scene in the public square, but that we should not fight against it I also believe that there should not be *l'havdil* a Chanukah menorah on public property and we certainly should not go to court to fight for it.

✦ *Choosing the Issues —*
No Foolproof Formula

There can be no specific formula for choosing issues on which to take a stand. There must be a case-by-case evaluation. The general guidelines, though, suggest that we agitate for issues of significance for the interests of *Klal Yisrael,* on which we have sound legal and moral rights, and which will not unduly arouse the enmity of our neighbors. I use the term "unduly" advisedly. For almost anything we do or say in defense of our rights is bound to arouse some negative reaction in some quarters. But we should not become so drunk with the successes that we have had in this area, that we go to the legislatures or the courts on every trivial issue. In any case, quiet *hishtadlus* should be pursued before strident public positions are broadcast over the media and in print.

This does not mean to say that when we see a non-Jew walking down the street, we must step off the sidewalk for him. Nor does it mean that we should go to the City Council or the State Legislature or Washington, hat in hand, bowing obsequiously, humbly petitioning for the favor of "Your Honor, the Mayor," "Your Excellency, the Governor," and "Your Majesty, the President," as the subjects of the Czar were once forced to do. We must pick our issues carefully, work for them discreetly, and if necessary, defend them with vigor and dignity.

On the positive side, I believe that Agudath Israel has led a dignified, low-key revolution in championing the rights of the Orthodox Jewish community, without being shrill or compromising Jewish values in the process.

✦ *Dignity, not Pride*

Finally, let us realize that there is a difference between Jewish dignity within humility and the pride of Eisav. When Eisav offered to accompany Yaakov on his journey, Yaakov said, *"Let my master go before his servant and I will conduct myself slowly and quietly, at my pace, in keeping with the work which is before me and in keeping with the pace of my children, until I come to my master, to Seir"* (*Bereishis* 33:14).

Yaakov Avinu, even while he ostensibly humbled himself before Eisav, revealed the inner secret of the Jew's formula not only for survival, but for ultimate ascendancy. *I cannot go with you,* said Yaakov to Eisav. *I have to go my own way at my own pace, modestly and quietly, without noise and fanfare, in keeping with the tasks that I have to accomplish in this world, and in a manner which befits the chinuch of my children, until that day will come — and surely it will come — "when we come to Seir."*

As *Rashi* explains, Yaakov had no intention at that time of going to Eisav's country. But Yaakov did not lie. When will he come to Seir? With the advent of *Mashiach,* as the Prophet Ovadiah said, "The savior will ascend the Mountain of Zion to judge the Mountain of Eisav. And on that day we shall see the Kingdom of G–d" (*Ovadiah* 1:12).

A Matter of Life and Death: Organ Transplants and the New RCA "Health Care Proxy"

Chaim Dovid Zwiebel

"A landmark decision," trumpeted the Jewish Telegraphic Agency. "A victory for *halachah*," cheered the *Washington Jewish Week*. "A bold and creative effort ... to provide proper religious guidance to the community ... not only correct according to *halachah*, [but also] deeply sensitive to the real needs of society today," exulted Rabbi Marc D. Angel, president of the Rabbinical Council of America (RCA).

The cause for celebration? Ari L. Goldman's June 15, 1991 "Religion Notes" column in *The New York Times* tells the story:

> In its continuing effort to apply traditional Jewish teaching to modern life, the largest group of Orthodox rabbis in the world has formally endorsed the donation of organs from brain-dead patients.
>
> The action was taken at the 55th anniversary convention of the group, the Rabbinical Council of America, which concluded Thursday in Spring Glen, N.Y. The position puts the 1,000-member group at odds

with some other Orthodox authorities, who are opposed to organ transplants because they do not accept the end of brain functioning as death.

The council's approval came in a key paragraph of a "health-care proxy" prepared by the Orthodox rabbis in response to new Federal guidelines, which take effect next December, that require every health-care provider to make available a health-care proxy to patients. The new proxy, prepared under the direction of Rabbi Moses Tendler of Yeshiva University, declares that organ transplant procedures are in full compliance with *halachah,* traditional Jewish law."

A landmark decision, indeed. Yet not everyone greeted it with quite the same enthusiasm its promoters displayed. In fact, as of the date of this writing — little more than two weeks after the *Times* broke the story, and only days after *The Jewish Press* splashed the news ("Organ Donations Now Permitted") across its front page — the RCA's new foray into the field of medical *halachah* has already generated a firestorm of controversy.

✧ The Brain Death/Organ Donation Equation

The controversy over organ donation centers around the critical question of whether *halachah* recognizes "brain death." A person is brain-dead when his entire brain, including the brain stem, has irreversibly ceased functioning. Medical science has concluded that the brain stem controls respiratory activity; and that accordingly, if a person's brain stem has irreversibly ceased functioning, he is no longer capable of breathing independently. With the assistance of a respirator, however, his heart can continue beating, if only for a relatively short period of time.

Secular law, at least in the United States, now accepts that a person who has suffered brain death is legally dead. Therefore, upon his prior consent, or the consent of his relatives, doctors may "harvest" his vital organs for purposes of transplantation. Under current law, doctors would not be permitted to harvest such organs before brain death, even with the donor's prior consent, because removal of the organs would cause the donor's legal death. On the other hand, to wait beyond the donor's brain death until his heart has also stopped beating would be impossible; once cardiac activity has ceased, the vital organs will have deteriorated to the point where they are no longer suitable for transplantation. Vital organs are thus candidates for harvest only during that period when brain stem function has irreversibly ceased yet the heart continues to beat. Hence the linkage between brain death and organ donation.

(Parenthetically, it should be noted that organs such as kidneys and corneas may be suitable for transplantation even after the cessation of cardiac activity. The publicity generated by the new RCA health care proxy form relates specifically to the transplantation of vital organs such as the heart and liver, which can be done only so long as the heart still beats. Kidney and cornea transplants present different sets of medical, legal and halachic issues.)

✣ *The Halachic Debate*

What is the halachic status of a person who has no brain activity and no independent respiratory activity, but whose heart still beats? If he is alive, then one may not disconnect his life-support machinery or remove his vital organs; to do so would be an act of murder. If, on the other hand, he is dead, then he should be buried as soon as possible, and his organs may be removed — with the consent of his relatives to save the life of another sick person.

It is this modern-day life and death *she'eilah* (halachic question) that the Rabbinical Council of America has now purported to *pasken* (render judgment). In publishing its own version of a "health care proxy" as an alternative to the proxy/living will form developed by Agudath Israel of America, the RCA encourages people to make an "anatomical gift" of their "life saving organs," to take effect after their death; and offers the following "Torah Perspective" on organ donation:

> The saving of a life takes precedence over all but three halachic imperatives — murder, idolatry and adultery.

Therefore, no halachic barriers exist to donation of the organs of the deceased if they are harvested in accord with the highest standards of dignity and propriety. Vital organs such as heart and liver may be donated after the patient has been declared dead by a competent neurologist based upon the clinical and/or radiological evidence. *In accord with the ruling of the Rav, Reb Joseph Dov Soloveitchik and HaGaon HaRav Moshe Feinstein, and of the Chief Rabbis of Israel, death as determined by neurological criteria [i.e., brain death] fully meets the highest standards of halachah.* [Emphasis added.]

One wouldn't know it by reading the RCA proxy form, but there is another "Torah Perspective" on this issue as well. Thus, four years ago when the *Rabbanut* issued the pro-brain death/pro-organ transplant ruling referred to and relied upon by the RCA — a *psak* we will soon revisit in greater detail — a number of distinguished *rabbanim* in *Eretz Yisrael* denounced the ruling in no uncertain terms. These authorities included the late Dayan Yitzchok Yaakov Weiss (head of the *Eidah HaChareidis,* Jerusalem), and Rabbi Elazar Menachem Schach *(Rosh Yeshivah,* Ponevezh), Rabbi Shmuel Wosner, Rabbi Nissim Karelitz, Rabbi Nosson Gestetner (all three, widely respected *rabbanim,* of Bnei Brak) and Rabbi Eliezer Waldenberg (a noted authority on medical *halachah,* Jerusalem), each of whom wrote publicly that removal of a heart from a person who had suffered "brain death" but whose heart was still beating would be an act of murder. Reliable rabbinic sources report that Rabbi Yosef Sholom Elyashiv, (one of the foremost *poskim* of our time), has also expressed his opposition to brain death. Here in the United States, rabbinic opponents of brain death include such a diverse group as Rabbi Menashe Klein, Rabbi Aharon Soloveitchik, Rabbi David Cohen and Rabbi Yehuda Dovid Bleich[1]

---

1. The reader is cautioned not to conclude that any list of names in this article is comprehensive. It is based on my own records and files, which may be quite incomplete. I would be glad to share my *"marei mekomos"* for any of the assertions in this article, or copies of pertinent documents from my file, with interested parties, who may contact me through *The Jewish Observer.*

→ The Sources Relied Upon by the RCA

As we have seen, the RCA cites the rulings of Rabbi Moshe Feinstein and Rabbi Yosef Dov Soloveitchik and also that of the Israeli Chief Rabbinate, in support of its position on organ donation. Here too, however, the RCA's statement is extremely controversial.

The question of whether Rabbi Moshe Feinstein did or did not support brain death has generated a great deal of scholarly attention and debate. Some scholars maintain that Rabbi Feinstein's writings — in particular, the *teshuvah* Rabbi Feinstein wrote in 5736 to his son-in-law, Rabbi Dr. Moshe Dovid Tendler *(Igros Moshe,* III *Yoreh Deah* 132) — does support brain death, as the RCA statement recites. Others, however, contend that Rabbi Feinstein in fact did not support brain death or vital organ transplants. They point in particular to Rabbi Feinstein's 5728 *teshuvah* to Rabbi Yitzchok Yaakov Weiss *(Igros Moshe,* II *Yoreh Deah* 174) — which he subsequently reaffirmed in a 5738 letter to Rabbi Kalman Kahane *(Igros Moshe,* II *Choshen Mishpat* 72) — wherein Rabbi Feinstein employs extraordinarily strong language to condemn heart transplants as *"retzichas sh'tei nefashos mamash,"* the murder of both the recipient and the donor.

Reliable sources have testified that in his later years, Rabbi Feinstein permitted people to *receive* heart transplants. Presumably, the improved success rate for heart transplants gave Rabbi Feinstein basis to reconsider his earlier written ruling that the transplant procedure was an act of murder upon the recipient. Still, there is no indication that Rabbi Feinstein also reconsidered that portion of his *psak* that spoke of removal of the donor's heart as an act of murder upon the donor; allowing a sick person to receive a heart that has already been removed from a donor does not necessarily imply that removal of the heart was permissible.

Rabbi Feinstein's unequivocal written rulings that removal of a donor's heart is murder imply either that he rejected the entire concept of brain death, or that he did not consider the tests used to ascertain brain death halachically sufficient, or that the transplant doctors could not be relied upon to wait for brain death before removing the donor's heart. Under any of these explanations, the RCA's reliance upon Rabbi Feinstein would seem to be misplaced. Moreover, as his son Rabbi Dovid Feinstein pointed out to me, there is certainly nothing in any of Rabbi Feinstein's rulings that encourages people to do what the RCA document encourages them to do: fill out a standardized form to make a general "anatomical gift" of their "life saving organs" after death.

The debate over Rabbi Feinstein's views revolves around the written legacy of the *teshuvos* he left behind. In contrast, Rabbi Yosef Dov Soloveitchik, does not appear ever to have written on this subject. In attributing a pro-brain death/pro-organ transplant view to Rabbi Soloveitchik, the RCA apparently relied on the testimony of someone who claimed to be familiar with his views. However, informed sources report that prominent members of Rabbi Soloveitchik's own family have written a formal letter to the RCA firmly denying that Rabbi Soloveitchik ever issued a ruling supporting brain death.

Tragically, Rabbi Feinstein is no longer with us; and Rabbi Soloveitchik [may he have a *refuah sheleimah*] is in no position to speak for himself today. There is thus no way definitively to resolve the debates over their respective halachic positions. In attributing such unequivocal views to these authorities directly in the body of its new health care proxy document, the RCA has apparently decided to resolve those debates without even acknowledging their existence.

The RCA's citation to the Israeli Chief Rabbinate's ruling as further support for its position is also problematic, though for a different reason.

The Chief Rabbis did indeed express their view that heartbeat alone, without independent respiratory activity, is not a halachic sign of life; and that therefore irreversible cessation of brain function is an acceptable means of establishing death. However, in issuing the *psak* authorizing transplant surgeons at Hadassah Hospital in Jerusalem to remove hearts from brain-dead persons, the Chief Rabbis insisted upon a number of stringent conditions, including (among others) the performance of an additional medical test to confirm the prospective donor's brain death, and participation by a representative of the *Rabbanut* in making the medical determination. No such safeguards appear in the RCA document.

The debate over brain death has been going on for many years, and there is a great deal more that can be said on the subject. For now, however, what is written here should suffice to demonstrate how controversial an issue it is, despite the unequivocal nature of the RCA's statement.

→ *Other Noteworthy Aspects of the RCA Form*

In light of the highly controversial nature of the RCA's ruling with repect to brain death and organ donations, it is quite understandable that a great deal of public attention has been drawn specifically to that aspect of the RCA's new "health care proxy." However, by no means is the brain death/organ donation provision the only component of the new RCA form that is halachically controversial.

Most notable in this regard is the broad authority the RCA health care proxy confers upon an individual or his health care agent to decline life-sustaining treatment. Thus, the RCA form allows a person to check a box indicating his advance desire to decline virtually all forms of life-sustaining procedures if he ever develops, for example, "brain damage or some brain disease that in the opinion of my physician and several consultants cannot be reversed and that makes me unable to recognize people or to communicate in any fashion, but I have no terminal illness, and I can live in this condition for a long time" [i.e., an advanced stage of Alzheimer's Disease]. Moreover, the document declares, "a quality of life that is burdensome to the patient may justify passive euthanasia ... Only *the patient and his/her proxy can declare a quality of life unacceptable.*" [Emphasis added.]

The implications of these provisions are staggering. They suggest that *halachah* embraces the notion of personal autonomy in medical decision making — permitting an individual to decide in advance that his life will not be worth living, and hence not worth preserving, when its quality is severely diminished. Moreover, they suggest that a designated relative or friend, no less than the individual himself, can make that same decision when the individual is no longer capable of deciding for himself. I am no halachic expert, but these implications are contrary to virtually everything I have studied or heard on the subject.

Another puzzling aspect of the new RCA form is the fact that it fails to state explicitly that all health care decisions are to be made in accordance with *halachah*. In fact, the document labels as "optional" the instruction that the health care agent should consult with Orthodox halachic authority prior to making his decision. If one chooses not to exercise that "option," in what substantive way does this form differ from similar forms developed by totally secular groups?

✤ A Matter of Integrity and Courage

Rumor has it that there is considerable dissatisfaction within the RCA itself over the substance of the new proxy document, and also over the means by which it was adopted as the organization's official form. The document was apparently published without prior consideration by the RCA's own *halachah* committee, at least several of whose members, if not the majority, are reportedly not prepared to go along with certain of the controversial halachic statements and implications contained therein.

In addition, the current Chief Rabbi of England, Lord Immanuel Jakobovits — himself a noted scholar in the field of medical *halachah,* and a member of the RCA — has taken sharp issue with the RCA's adoption of its new health-care proxy. And, as noted above, eminent members of Rabbi Yosef Dov Soloveitchik's family have formally objected to the RCA's reliance upon Rabbi Soloveitchik in support of its stance on brain death/organ donations.

Perhaps the *post-facto* ferment within the RCA will result in an internal reconsideration of the propriety of publishing a form, designed to be used by masses of people, that embodies such controversial halachic positions and even appears to depart in several ways from accepted halachic consensus. Such reconsideration would be a welcome development indeed — an act of integrity and courage in an era so sorely lacking in both.

❖ ❖ ❖

The Summer 1991 issue of The Jewish Observer featured an article, "A Matter of Life and Death," by Chaim Dovid Zwiebel, general counsel and director of government affairs for Agudath Isreal of America, wherein he took issue with many aspects of the widely publicized Health Care Proxy Form issued by the Rabbinical Council of America.

The article generated a large response, of which two representative letters were selected for publication, from Rabbi Moshe D. Tendler, who authored the RCA proxy form, and Dr. Yoel Jakobovits, who is a member of the faculty of Johns Hopkins University.

This is followed by a rejoinder by the article's author, Chaim Dovid Zwiebel.

This exchange is prefaced by a statement by Agudath Israel of America, which includes publication of a recently issued relevant *psak* from the world-renowned *poskim*, Rabbi Shlomo Zalman Auerbach and Rabbi Yosef Sholom Elyashiv.

⤳ *A Statement From Agudath Israel of America*

18 Elul, 5751
August 28, 1991

Rapid advances in medical science and technology, as well as recent legal developments, have resulted in numerous complex medical questions and scenarios facing Torah-observant Jews. As Jews we must recognize that these medical matters, like all other circumstances of human existence, must be approached through the perspective of Torah, and under the specific direction of *halachah.* Toward that end, it is incumbent upon each individual to consult with his or her own competent rabbinical authority to obtain guidance with respect to specific issues pertinent to his or her medical circumstances.

One of the most serious and complex issues that has arisen in this field relates to the criteria for determining death. This issue also impacts upon the related halachic question concerning the removal of organs for transplantation purposes. Various questions and opinions concerning these issues have been expressed in halachic circles.

The rabbinic leadership of Agudath Israel of America has traditionally refrained from halachic decision-making as a group. Therefore, an inquiry concerning the aforementioned critical issues, presented by a distinguished delegation on behalf of the *Moetzes Gedolei HaTorah* of America, was made to two of the foremost contemporary halachic authorities — HaRav Shlomo Zalman Auerbach and HaRav Yosef Sholom Elyashiv of *Eretz Yisrael.* The following is their written expression of their views:

בס"ד

יום ח"י מנ"א תנש"א

נתבקשנו לגלות לגלות דעתינו, דעת תורה, בענין השתלת הלב או שאר איברים לצורך חולה מסוכן בזמן שלב התורם פועם ומוחו כולל גזע המוח אינו מתפקד כלל הנקרא "מיתת המוח" - דעתינו שאין שום היתר להוציא אף אחד מן איבריו ויש בזה משום שפיכת דמים.

‏[הרב] שלמה זלמן אויערבאך

‏[הרב] יוסף שלום אלישיב

[translation]
18 Menachem Av, 5751

We have been requested to declare our view, da'as Torah, with respect to the transplantation of a heart or other organs, for the benefit of a sick person whose life is in danger, at a time when the heart of the donor is beating and his entire brain including the brain stem is not functioning at all, which is known as "brain death": It is our view that it is absolutely not permissible to remove any of his organs; and to do so would involve the taking of a life.

(HaRav) Shlomo Zalman Auerbach
(HaRav) Yosef Sholom Elyashiv

✦ Confusion: Brain Stem Death, Pikuach Nefesh, and Halachic Integrity

To the Editor:

In his article, "A Matter of Life and Death: Organ Transplants and the New RCA 'Health Care Proxy'" (JO June, '91), Chaim Dovid Zwiebel, Esq. questions various aspects of the health care proxy form developed by the Medical Bio-Ethics Commission of the Rabbinical Council of America. As the chairman of that commission, and as the author of the RCA proxy form, I wish to respond to the article, and especially to dispel the confusion that has arisen in certain circles regarding the views of Reb Moshe Feinstein upon which the RCA health care proxy form is based. I pray that this summary of the views of my sainted father-in-law, and analysis of the medical and halachic realities, now in the glare of the public eye of the Torah-committed readership of The *Jewish Observer,* will better serve the goal of לידע איך לברר הלכה על בוריה and resolve the confusion in this area of life-and-death decisions for those in need of vital organ transplants.

"Reb Moshe" made *psak* look easy! A telephone response to questions involving life and death, *issur v'heter,* monetary matters between partners, neighbors, or family members took only minutes. But how he toiled, labored, searched, to determine the *din emes l'amito!* The same was true with respect to the issue at hand. It goes without saying that Reb Moshe spoke to cardiologists and radiologists, and discussed the medical realities with them. And then, after an exhaustive study of *Shas* and *poskim*, he concluded that brain stem death is tantamount to *"hutaz rosho b'koach"*[1] or decapitation. It is therefore in concurrence with the classic definition of death found in the Mishnah,[2] repeated in the *Gemara*[3] and codified in the *Shulchan Aruch*.[4] No waffling, no ambiguity! Those who cast doubt, even only the "doubt" of the *"machmirim"* as to what my father-in-law said or meant to say, undermine the integrity of the entire halachic process that enables our Torah to be a *"Toras Chaim."*

There was no doubt about Reb Moshe's *psak*. Indeed, he went so far as to communicate his views clearly to secular government officials considering legislation in this vital area. Thus, on May 24, 1976, Reb Moshe wrote a letter in English to the Hon. Herbert J. Miller, Chairman of the N.Y. State Assembly Committee on Health, in which he explicitly supports brain death legislation, *if* total absence of respiration is confirmed.* That Reb Moshe subsequently supported a legislative religious exemption from the brain death standard (8 Shvat 5737), despite his own approval of brain stem death, was in keeping with his lifelong behavior pattern never to demand *"kablu da'ati* — Do as I say!"

Clarification of Terms and Concepts

Now to resolve the confusion in the minds of those whose background does not include training in Torah law and/or biomedical sciences:

(1) Brain stem death does not mean that the brain died and the body lives. It is not analogous to cardiac failure or liver failure, which is the failure of an *organ*. The Mishnah (*Oholos* 1:7) instructs

---

1. *Igros Moshe*, Y.D. III, 132

2. Oholos 1:7

3. Chullin 21a.

4. Yoreh Deah 370.

* Editor's Note:
Rabbi Tendler enclosed copies of several documents referred to in his letter, including Rabbi Moshe Feinstein's May 1976 letter to Assemblyman Miller and a handwritten note from Rabbi Dovid Feinstein.

us that anatomical decapitation results in halachic death of the entire body even though the heart still beats and the limbs twitch. The Talmud (*Chullin* 21a) in its statement "זקנה שאני" concludes that anatomical decapitation is not an absolute requirement. Even if no external wounding occurs, if the connection between brain and body is interrupted, the entire body is dead, i.e. organismal death. Therefore, a Kohen must not enter the room; it is forbidden to transgress the Sabbath for such a "cadaver"; and there is a duty to bury the body. The clinical picture is described by *Rashi* in *Yoma* 85a referring to a man buried under rubble on Shabbos: "If he appears clinically dead, does not move his limbs, how much do you dig to determine the truth?" The Talmud concludes "until you expose his nose" so as to determine if he makes any respiratory efforts because "the source of life is in the breath."

Brain stem death, which is determined after careful neurological examination, affirms that there is: completely unreactive pupils, no spontaneous or elicited eye movements, no motor response to stimulation; no grimacing, blink response, gag response; and no respiratory movement, cough, sigh or hiccup, confirmed by an apnea test in which patient is hyperoxygenated prior to disconnecting the ventilator.[5]

One should not confuse a polio patient (or one who ate tainted food — botulism) who can talk, write, procreate, but requires a ventilator, with the "respiratory dead" patient we are discussing. All testing whether death occurred is done only on patients who "appear" clinically dead ... not those choking on a piece of steak who need a Heimlich "hug," not a coffin!

Brain stem death occurs when, due to trauma, the brain swells, and the pressure in the skull rises to exceed systemic blood pressure. The brain is therefore without blood or oxygen for a period of time. Since brain cells are extremely sensitive to enoxia, the cells die and begin to liquefy (lyse). The best way to determine brain stem death is by nuclide scanning. A harmless radioactive substance is injected though the I.V. tubing already in place, and a subsequent picture taken with a portable camera shows that blood

---

5. Bleck, T.P. and Smith, M.C. "Diagnosing Death and Persistent Vegetative States," *Journal of Critical Illness* 1989 4(11): 60-65.

circulation ceases below the base of the brain. If repeated 24 hours later, it is the single most incontrovertible proof that death had occurred. There has *never* been an error made in determining death by means of the neurological criteria outlined above!

(2) Reb Moshe wrote *five* responsa concerning determining time of death. In *three* responsa[6] he clearly refers to the type of patient now known in medical literature as Karen Quinlan or Cruzan cases. He clearly defines his patient as *yachol linshom* — can breathe independently. This is *NOT* a brain stem dead patient but one referred to as cerebral dead, or P.V.S., or locked-in syndrome. Such a patient is entitled to full medical care as I expressed in my *amicus curiae* brief to Supreme Court in the Cruzan case. In his fourth and fifth responsa on brain stem death, Reb Moshe identifies the patient as: "The doctors put him on a ventilator, so that he breathes even though he is dead — such breathing does not qualify to consider him alive." *(Igros Moshe Y.D.* III 132). This *psak* is reiterated *(C.M.II* − 73) in his lengthy responsum on critical care (viz., p. 304).

While the *Jewish Observer* article refers to opinions of Rabbi Dovid Feinstein (son of Reb Moshe), it is noteworthy that Reb Dovid has never questioned his father's acceptance of brain stem death as halachically valid. This was clearly, definitively stated in the investigative report on Reb Moshe's opinion regarding brain stem death in ASSIA (December 1989); and, indeed, Reb Dovid has written a note that affirms this fact. [See ed. note on p. 383.]

(3) The RCA health care proxy was designed to meet the needs of the Torah community in light of the Federal law known as the "Patient Self-Determination Act" to go into effect December, 1991. It is in full accord with the halachic norms promulgated by my father-in-law. The key points are:

> (a) It is a great mitzvah to donate organs to save lives
> *(Igros Moshe, Y.D.* II 174).
>
> (b) Brain stem death is a halachically proper way to
> determine that the patient had died.

---

6. Y.D. II — 146, 174, and C.M. II — 72

Mr. Zwiebel perpetuates the confusion by failing to note what is clearly stated in Reb Moshe's responsa:

— a patient who can breathe is considered alive;

— a patient who appears clinically dead and cannot breathe is dead.

The "unequivocal ruling" he alludes to (the removal of a donor's heart is murder) was in reference to a patient who can breathe independently. It is indeed murder by all standards — halachic as well as secular law.

The RCA and the Proxy

The proxy is not "a new foray" by the RCA into the field of medical *halachah.* In 1988, when Dr. Bailey was using anencephalic newborns as heart donors, the RCA Executive Board (before the Halachic Commission was appointed) issued a policy statement condemning this practice as murder, because although the upper brain did not develop, the neonate could breath independently. In that statement there was also the recognition that if the anencephalic is placed on a ventilator, and brain stem death is subsequently ascermined, then organs may be removed.

This policy statement was based on the *psak din* of Reb Moshe and of the Chief Rabbis of Israel.

Mr. Zwiebel misreads the instructions in the RCA health care proxy. The instructions clearly state: "It is important that the health care proxy you appoint be personally knowledgeable in both medical and halachic considerations." He accuses: "The document labels as optional...to consult with halachic authority." Indeed it is an "optional" choice — only if the one appointed as proxy is *not* a halachic authority.

The "more stringent" requirements of the Israeli Chief Rabbinate who fully accept the *psak* of Reb Moshe and permit vital organ donations and therefore cardiac transplants from brain stem death patients, are more than adequately duplicated by the standards of the American medical profession. Indeed, I asked Rabbi Moshe Sherer (president of Agudath Israel of America), almost three years ago, to allow me to present the correct Torah view on brain stem death to the *Moetzes Gedolei HaTorah,* and then to join me in my effort to have nuclide scanning included in the New

York State Brain Death Bill. This is the most stringent requirement — one I insist on, in every case in which I am consulted.

The General Directive in the RCA proxy form to appoint a halachically knowledgeable proxy will be used by most. The Detailed Directive — a first draft issued so far only to *rabbanim* for their edification — directs attention to the real world. These are the questions that are asked of family members by physicians. As seen in the sample copy that was prepared — NO is also an answer. The intent is indeed to direct the medical staff to offer care even though modern medical thought advises benign neglect. It is not intended to offer the patient the choice of refusing life-saving therapy, unless it is in accord with halachic guidelines.

Rabbi Soloveitchik's View

Although a *talmid* of HaGaon HaRav Yosef Dov Soloveitchik for almost half a century, I cannot recall a clear *psak* from him on this issue. I can recall numerous conversations in which his only expressed reservation was to the accuracy and reproducibility of the testing protocol. Rabbi Walfish — executive vice president of the RCA, and also a *talmid* — asserts that the "*Rav*" did unequivocally accept brain stem death as halachically valid. Rabbi Walfish is a man of great integrity whose respect for *halachah* and love of the "*Rav*" is second to none.

I would also record that the "*Rav*" established as RCA policy to support all halachic decisions of the Chief Rabbinate of Israel that are of international, not local import.

The issue we are discussing now in the public arena must be resolved. Reb Moshe, when alive, was the most beloved and respected *posek* of our generation because of his unimpeachable integrity and his *Ahavas Yisrael.* I am convinced that all who respect truth and hallow Torah law will continue to follow his instructions, and thus merit the blessings of Hashem: ברוך תהי' מכל העמים.

RABBI MOSHE DOVID TENDLER,
תתנא דבי נשיאה
ראש ישיבה, ישיבת רבינו יצחק אלחנן
Professor: Biology and Medical Ethics, Yeshiva University
Rav: Community Synagogue of Monsey, New York

→ A Letter from Dr. Yoel Jakobovits

To the Editor:

The debate regarding brain death and health care proxies (i.e. living wills) continues unabated. The issues surrounding brain death (readers may consult my article discussing the technical aspects of brain death in *Tradition*, 24[4], Summer 1989) and those springing from the living will are really quite distinct, related only in their temporal juxtaposition with the end of life. Regarding both those vexing topics, it is a wonder and concern that communal organizations have, to some extent, usurped the traditional quintessential role of individual *rabbanim*. Although communal organizations can provide indispensable help in designing guidelines for legally mandated documents, the specific issues, and particularly those with direct impact on life and death decisions, ought to evolve through traditional avenues of halachic discourse and are outside the purview of organizational policy statements and press releases.

But let me turn rather to the specific topic of living wills, a subject of much more usual application than brain death. As a practicing physician "in the trenches," I can attest to the real need for some form of advance directive mechanism. These needs exist independently of, and antedate, governmental regulations. Our society's much vaunted pluralism frequently leads to a surfeit of fundamentally conflicting opinions which surface during the extraordinarily trying days and hours which characterize our patients' modern, technologically-mired death. Conflicts occur among physicians and care-givers, lawyers and administrators, and — most tragically — among family members. Precise pre-knowledge of the patient's own wishes would greatly reduce the tensions during the dying period as well as the guilt which often follows.

On the other hand, the whole concept of "advance directives" with respect to forgoing terminal treatment is basically quite foreign to the Jewish way of thinking. Frankly, I would be abrogating my responsibility as a Jewishly conscientious physician by throwing these decisions onto the patients' shoulders. No airline pilot, for example, would be expected to consult with his passengers regarding how to negotiate a cloud bank, even though his professional judgment also has direct impact upon the very lives of his clients. Furthermore, it seems to me that the patient, being the most *noge'a b'davar*, should in fact have the *least* to say regarding these capital decisions. Neither can I find any halachic rationale to give the family a decisive vote in the patient's care.

The truth is, of course, that the whole *parshah* of Living Wills and Durable Powers of Attorney arises directly from the contemporary secular notions of personal autonomy, individual rights, and self-determination as assumed to exist under Constitutional protection. These concepts, in turn, flourished in the fertile ground of the "do-your-own-thing" generation of the 1960's. These philosophies are entirely alien within a Torah framework. Even the widely-adopted term "living wills" assumes the implementation of what used to be a document of instructions for after death in the pre-death period, as if this were already the post-mortem period. The linguistic sleight of hand may not be deliberate, but its subtlety can be morally even more pernicious. Granted, we have little choice but to face the current norms as they exist, but as Jewishly committed physicians — and rabbis and lawyers — we should be doing everything we can to discourage these trends, not to encourage them.

Undermining the Role of Rabbis and Physicians

To my mind, the promotion of detailed living wills serves to undermine both the role of the rabbi and that of the physician in caring for patients. It erodes the authority and function of the local rabbi by making a blanket halachic statement well before the circumstances of the *she'eilah* have occurred, let alone been asked. This approach also erodes the role of the physician in reaching a decision tailored to the particulars of the case at hand, rather than using an "off-the-shelf" approach. I am not suggesting that doctors be allowed to make these decisions alone. Clearly doctors need halachic guidance in these matters which are not really medical decisions at all. Therefore I welcome the recent introduction in most hospitals in this country of Ethics Committees whose very existence emphasizes the extra-medical dimensions of health care, even though they are not often bound to Torah ethics.

I might add, parenthetically, that it is quite remarkable that the very sophistication of advancing medical technology has resulted in the currently widespread recognition — even beyond our camp — of the indispensability of applied ethics in medical practice. Many might have expected the opposite: that the "scientification" of medicine would ultimately subvert its "sanctification."

Mindful of these considerations I prefer the simplest possible living will model, similar to the one described in *The Jewish Observer* of Tishrei 5751/September 1990. Such a document should confine itself to directing the physicians and family to consult with a qualified rabbi in the event of terminal care decision making — without any more detail than that. By relying on the proven traditional methods of *sho'el u'meishiv*, this technique would augment the rabbi's role, and hence that of *halachah*, while also relieving the family of inordinate pressures and ensuing post-mortem guilt. At the same time, it would limit physician's (non-halachic) bias and yet preserve the need to make specific clinical evaluations and recommendations.

YOEL JAKOBOVITS, M.D.
Baltimore, Maryland

♦ *Chaim Dovid Zwiebel Replies:*

My article for the Tammuz 5751/Summer 1991 *Jewish Observer* generated a large and varied volume of reaction. It is encouraging that people take such sensitive and complex issues seriously. In offering this reply to certain points raised by Rabbi Moshe Dovid Tendler's letter, I fully share in Rabbi Tendler's prayer that the discussions in these pages will help dispel some of the confusion that has surrounded these critical issues of life and death.

This reply is divided into two parts. Part I revisits the main points of my earlier article in light of Rabbi Tendler's critical comments. Part II reports on a significant development that occurred after my article had already gone to press, and reflects upon the fundamental difference between the approaches embodied in the Rabbinical Council of America's "Health Care Proxy" form and the "Halachic Living Will" form developed last year by Agudath Israel of America.

I.

My article focused on three different aspects of the RCA's new health care proxy form: (1) the broad authority the form confers upon an individual to decline, in advance, various forms of life-sustaining treatment under a variety of medical scenarios that may arise; (2) the failure of the form to state clearly that all health decisions are to be made in accordance with *halachah* and under the guidance of a halachic authority; and (3) the form's inclusion of an anatomical gift/organ donation clause, based upon its explicit and unequivocal halachic endorsement of "brain death" (i.e., irreversible cessation of the entire brain function, including the brain stem, notwithstanding the presence of spontaneous heartbeat through the assistance of a ventilator or respirator).

With respect to the first of these points, my article contended, the RCA health care proxy form appears to embody an *anti*-halachic position; with respect to the second, a *non*-halachic position; and with respect to the third, a *highly controversial* halachic position. Rabbi Tendler's defense of the RCA document — which is surely definitive, coming as it does from the author of the document — casts a new light on these issues, and requires careful reconsideration of my earlier contentions.

(1) Personal Autonomy in Medical Decision Making

The back of the RCA document offers the following "Torah Perspective": "A quality of life that is burdensome to the patient may justify passive euthanasia such as withholding resuscitation, blood pressure raising medication, or antibiotics. Only the patient and his/her proxy can declare a quality of life unacceptable." The proposition that *halachah* confers upon a patient or his proxy the authority to "declare a quality of life unacceptable" based upon its being "burdensome" would itself be quite noteworthy. It becomes all the more noteworthy when one examines an earlier portion of the document, which allows a *perfectly healthy person*, one who is *neither a patient nor a proxy*, to make a prospective declaration refusing to accept various forms of treatment should it ever come to pass that at some point in the future he will become afflicted with, for example, a non-terminal advanced stage of Alzheimer's Disease.

To be sure, there may be instances when *halachah* would permit a patient, or a family member or other outside person acting on an incapacitated patient's behalf, to choose to forgo certain forms of life-sustaining treatment. At a bare minimum, though, it appears clear that the halachic imperative to preserve human life, even in diminished capacity, will often overcome the determination of an individual or his proxy that his "quality of life" is, or may at some subsequent time become, "burdensome" or "unacceptable." While the halachic scholarship on the subject is complex, the bottom line appears to be that these life and death decisions are highly fact-sensitive; and that *poskim* called upon to rule on such matters will make a careful case-by-case evaluation of a multiplicity of factors — e.g., the degree of pain suffered by the patient, the nature of the treatment, the medical prognosis — before offering specific guidance. (A number of these issues are treated in *Igros Moshe*, II *Choshen Mishpat* 73-75.) A far cry, most certainly, from the type of unequivocal "I do want — I do not want" advance declaration checklist offered in the RCA proxy form.[1]

Rabbi Tendler does not dispute that it would be contrary to

---

1. There is growing recognition even in secular circles that an advance medical directive of the "I do want — I do not want" variety is seriously flawed. In its recent cover story on "Choosing Death," *Newsweek* (August 26, 1991) offered the following observation:

"Even patients, or families, who think they know often do not ...That's why the MICU [the Medical Intensive Care Unit at Boston's Beth Israel Hospital, where the *Newsweek* established halachic norms for a person to choose in advance to refuse various types of life-sustaining treatment under some of the scenarios envisioned by the RCA document. He writes that the "the RCA Proxy form makes clear that NO is also an answer" [I assume Rabbi Tendler means "I do want" when he says "NO"]; and that the intent of this portion of the form is simply to enable an individual to "direct a medical staff to offer care even though modern medical thought advises benign neglect. It is not intended to offer the patient the choice of refusing life-saving therapy, unless it is in accord with halachic guidelines." But if so, why offer the masses an opportunity to choose a variety of "I do not want" options that are *not* in accord with halachic guidelines? If indeed the advance directive part of the RCA proxy form is merely "a first draft issued so far only to *rabbanim* for edification," and if the RCA intends ever to issue a revised second draft for public use, I would respectfully suggest that at a minimum those "I do not want" options which contravene *halachah* be deleted.

I would also respectfully suggest that Rabbi Tendler and the central RCA executive office need to do a better job of coordinating their approach to this issue. When the RCA published its new health care proxy form, it issued a public news release announcing that "copies of the Health Care Proxy are available" to interested parties. An acquaintance of mine took the RCA up on its offer and received in the mail a handsomely printed document containing both the "General Directive" referred to by Rabbi Tendler and the "Detailed Directive" which Rabbi Tendler believes is being distributed only to *rabbanim* in draft form. To the best of my knowledge, the RCA never informed members of the public who requested the form that the "I do want — I do not want" section was only a first draft for the edification of *rabbanim*, not yet intended for public use.

reporters did their field research] staff regards 'living wills' as less than perfect: these documents stipulate what a patient will and will not want, but they cannot anticipate the grim complexities of disease ... It may be better to designate a health proxy, someone who understands the patient's attitudes toward dying.The proxy is charged with making medical decisions when the patient cannot, and can weigh the specific circumstances of the illness and the choices available."

(2) "Optional" Halachic Guidance

To my article's observation that the RCA health care proxy form fails to state explicitly that all health care decisions are to be made in accordance with *halachah,* and indeed that the RCA document labels as "optional" the instruction that the proxy should consult with Orthodox halachic authority prior to making his decision, Rabbi Tendler responds that I have misread the RCA form. In fact, he writes, the form contains an explicit instruction which makes clear the need to obtain halachic guidance: "It is important that the health care proxy you appoint be personally knowledgeable in both medical and halachic considerations."

But that is only *part* of what the instruction on the RCA form says. The full instruction, as I have it, reads as follows:

> It is important that the health care proxy you appoint *either* be personally knowledgeable in both the medical and halachic considerations in making critical health care decisions *or that you specify the persons your health care proxy is to consult or if you prefer, you may state at the discretion of my health care proxy."*[Italics denote words omitted in Rabbi Tendler's letter.]

The instruction thus advises the person filling out the form that he has three options. The latter two — directing the proxy to consult designated persons, and leaving the matter entirely to the proxy's discretion — say nothing about halachic guidance. Rabbi Tendler's explanation that the "option" to consult with halachic authority is meant to be exercised if the proxy himself is not a halachic authority is a welcome clarification, but it is entirely absent from the RCA form.

(3) Brain Death/Organ Donations

In my article, I raised two separate points concerning the RCA form's endorsement of organ donations based on its unequivocal statement that *halachah* accepts the concept of brain death.

My first point was that the issue was far from settled in halachic circles, with many contemporary *poskim* specifically rejecting brain death criteria and removal of organs from brain-dead individuals. In the months since I wrote my article, the controversial nature of the RCA's brain death/organ donation *psak* has become even more pronounced.

In addition to the various halachic authorities from many varied circles whose names I cited in my article as opponents of the brain death standard, two of the foremost contemporary *poskei hador* — Rabbi Shlomo Zalman Auerbach and Rabbi Yosef Sholom Elyashiv — have now signed a clear written *psak* prohibiting the removal of organs from a person whose heart is still beating, even if the entire brain, including the brain stem, has irreversibly ceased functioning. (Reports from *Eretz Yisrael* indicate that shortly after Rabbi Auerbach and Rabbi Elyashiv issued their *psak*, they received a medical/halachic presentation offering a contrary perspective on the issues of brain death and organ donations, and urging them to reconsider their ruling; but Rabbi Auerbach and Rabbi Elyashiv rejected the presentation and instead reiterated their *psak*.) In addition, several members of the RCA's own *Va'ad Halachah* have reportedly gone on written record questioning the halachic validity of brain death criteria, and requesting that the RCA retract this aspect of its health care proxy form.[2]

---

2. Indeed, there appears to be less than perfect unanimity even in secular medical circles as to the concept of brain death. For example, in a September 1982 editorial in the *Journal of the American Medical Association*, Dr. Daniel Wickler and Dr. Mark Siegler take note of several clinical studies of pregnant women who suffered brain death yet were maintained on life support for several weeks, nurturing their child in utero and ultimately delivering healthy babies. They offer the following observation:

> Now we are told that a brain-dead patient can nurture a child in the womb, which permits live birth several weeks "postmortem." Perhaps this is the straw that breaks the conceptual camel's back ... The death of the brain seems not to serve as a boundary; it is a tragic, ultimately fatal loss, but not death itself. Probably death occurs later, when integrated functioning ceases.

Drs. Joseph C. Evers and Paul A. Byrne offer yet another medical perspective on the issue in the Fall 1990 edition of *Pharos Medical Journal*:

> We believe that there can be destruction of the entire brain, but there has not been found any criteria that has been established to reliably determine this. A cessation of brain function is not the same as destruction. At the present state of the art of medicine, a patient with destruction of the entire brain is, at the most, only mortally wounded, but not yet dead. Death ought not be declared unless and until there is destruction of the respiratory and circulatory systems and the entire brain.

I do not mean to suggest that these views represent a commonly held consensus within the medical community. Nonetheless, the fact remains that there is controversy even within secular medical circles over the concept of brain death, and that at least some medical researchers would take strong issue with the equation of brain death and "physiological decapitation."

My second point was that the RCA document's stated reliance upon Rav Moshe Feinstein, Rabbi Yosef Dov Soloveitchik and the Israeli Chief Rabbinate was itself controversial — in the case of Rabbi Feinstein, because a number of *rabbanim* have offered varying interpretations of his *teshuvos* in the field; in the case of Rabbi Soloveitchik, because members of his family firmly deny that he ever issued a ruling on the subject; and in the case of the Israeli Chief Rabbinate, because its *psak* authorizing transplant surgeons at Hadassah Hospital in Jerusalem to remove hearts from brain-dead persons was accompanied by a number of stringent conditions that do not appear in the RCA document.

The Reservations of Rabbi Soloveitchik and the Rabbanut: Rabbi Tendler recalls numerous conversations with Rabbi Yosef Dov Soloveitchik "in which his only expressed reservation was to the accuracy and reproducibility of the testing protocol." Given Rabbi Tendler's recollection of that reservation, it is all the more difficult to comprehend how the RCA could claim reliance on Rabbi Soloveitchik in promoting an organ donation policy for masses of American Jews. For even if the RCA form is correct that Rabbi Soloveitchik does accept the concept of brain death — a contention vigorously disputed by close members of Rabbi Soloveitchik's family and by certain of his *talmidim* — its endorsement of organ donations must inevitably rely upon something Rabbi Tendler heard Rabbi Soloveitchik question: the accuracy and reproducibility of the brain death testing protocol.

In a similar vein, one of the express conditions upon which the Israeli Chief Rabbinate permitted heart transplants at Hadassah Hospital was that a representative of the *Rabbanut* must participate "as a full member" of the medical team that establishes the donor's brain death. Absent such a representative, ruled the Chief Rabbinate, "there is still no permission to perform heart transplants in Israel." The RCA document, in contrast, states that "an Orthodox halachic authority must be consulted as to proper protocol to follow," but does not insist that the halachic authority be involved in the medical determination of brain death. Moreover, the *Rabbanut* expressly limited its conditional endorsement of heart transplants to cases where the donor is an accident victim. No such limitation appears in the RCA form. I question whether the *Rabbanut* itself would endorse the RCA form.

In fact, I am unable to understand Rabbi Tendler's own endorsement of the RCA form. He writes that he always insists on a particular test to determine brain death — nuclide scanning — which is "the most stringent requirement." Yet doctors I have consulted tell me that nuclide scanning is not typically performed in determining brain death. If the test that is typically performed fails to demonstrate brain death with the degree of certainty Rabbi Tendler always insists upon, why is he not concerned that the RCA document will result in vital organs being removed from individuals before they have in fact died?

Rabbi Moshe Feinstein's Views: In my article, I wrote: "The question of whether Rabbi Moshe Feinstein did or did not support brain death has generated a great deal of scholarly attention and debate." Rabbi Tendler's letter presents one side of the debate. The fact remains, however, that there is another side. As Rabbi Tendler himself has acknowledged, in an article he co-authored with Dr. Fred Rosner for the *Journal of Halachah and Contemporary Society* (Pesach 5749/Spring 1989), the view that "Rabbi Feinstein's written responsa ... indicate that Jewish law clearly recognizes that death occurs before all organs cease functioning ... is our interpretation, not necessarily accepted by others."

Among the "others" who interpret Rabbi Feinstein's writings as providing no support for the concept of brain death are Rabbi Aaron Soloveitchik and Rabbi Yehudah Dovid Bleich.[3] Both of these *rabbanim* make the observation I related in my earlier article: If it is true that in his 5736 *teshuvah* to Rabbi Tendler (*Igros Moshe*, III *Yoreh Deah* 132), Rabbi Feinstein specifically endorsed the use of a test to establish brain death, why would

---

3. An English-language presentation by Rabbi Soloveitchik appears in the Pesach 5749/Spring 1989 edition of the *Journal of Halachah and Contemporary Society*. One of Rabbi Bleich's many written presentations on the subject appears in the Spring 1989 edition of *Tradition*, the RCA's own English-language journal of *halachah*.

he continue in 5738 to label heart transplants murder of the donor (*Igros Moshe*, II *Choshen Mishpat* 72)? As I wrote in my article, the 5738 *psak* would seem to imply either that Rabbi Feinstein rejected the concept of brain death entirely, or that he did not consider the tests used to ascertain brain death halachically sufficient, or that he felt the transplant doctors could not be relied upon to wait for brain death before removing the donor's heart.

I do not understand Rabbi Tendler's response to this point. He writes that Rabbi Feinstein's unequivocal 5738 ruling "was in reference to a patient who can breathe independently. It is indeed murder by all standards — halachic as well as secular law." On this latter point Rabbi Tendler is most assuredly correct: Removal of a heart from a patient who is still capable of independent respiration is an act of murder even under secular law. Apparently, then, Rabbi Tendler is attributing to Rabbi Feinstein the view in 5738 that transplant surgeons were committing murder under secular law by removing hearts from still-breathing donors — despite the fact that at that time (at least since 5736) the criteria for measuring brain death already existed. If Rabbi Feinstein's assumption in 5738, *halachah l'maaseh*, was that transplant surgeons were committing murder, and that therefore heart donations could not be permitted, what has changed in the years since that would cause the RCA to discard that assumption?

It is true that in his 5728 *teshuvah* to the late Dayan Yitzchok Yaakov Weiss (*Igros Moshe*, II *Yoreh Deah* 174), Rabbi Feinstein explicitly encouraged relatives of a dead person to consent to the removal of the decedent's organs for the purpose of saving another life. But nothing in that *psak* deals with the criteria by which death is to be determined; in fact, that *psak* is part of the same *teshuvah* in which Rabbi Feinstein first labeled heart transplants an act of murder upon the donor. Moreover, as I reported in my article, Rabbi Dovid Feinstein has told me that his father's rulings do not necessarily imply that he would have encouraged people to fill out an RCA-type standardized form to make a general anatomical gift of their own organs after death.

Rabbi Tendler cites Rabbi Feinstein's May 24, 1976 letter to Assemblyman Herbert J. Miller "in which," Rabbi Tendler writes, "he explicitly supports brain death legislation, if total absence of respiration is confirmed." I have reviewed the letter, as well as other materials in Agudath Israel of America's archives that provide its context, and I see no such explicit support. What is explicit is the letter's rejection of proposed brain death legislation. The proposed law read in critical part as follows:

> If artificial means of support preclude a determination that [a person's spontaneous respiratory and circulatory functions] have [irreversibly] ceased, a person shall be pronounced dead if in the announced opinion of a physician based on ordinary standards of medical practice such person has experienced a total and irreversible cessation of brain function.

Rabbi Feinstein's unequivocal advice to Assemblyman Miller: "This bill as written is and has always been unacceptable." The letter then goes on to spell out the requirements for any bill defining death. In so doing, Rabbi Feinstein does state clearly that "[the] sole criterion of death is the total cessation of spontaneous respiration." Nowhere, however, does the letter state that the brain death test should be used as a means of ascertaining total cessation of spontaneous respiration.

Rabbi Feinstein's 5736 *teshuvah* merits closer examination. In it, he considers (among other things) the case of an individual who has suffered an accident that causes him to stop breathing. Cessation of respiration in that case, observes Rabbi Feinstein, may only be temporary; and the traditional means of ascertaining absence of respiration — i.e., by placing a feather near the person's nostrils — may not be conclusive evidence that the person has irreversibly ceased breathing. Accordingly, he writes to Rabbi Tendler:

> *Since you tell me* that there is now a test whereby big doctors are able, through the injection of a certain liquid through the veins, to ascertain that the connection between the brain and the rest of the body has been severed, i.e. that if this liquid does not reach the brain it

is clear that the brain no longer has any connection to the body and also that the brain has become destroyed [*nirkav*] entirely so that it is as if the head has been chopped off by force, *therefore we should be stringent* [*yesh lanu l'hachmir*] with such an individual [an accident victim]. Even though he feels nothing, even through a needle prick, and even though he is not breathing at all without a respirator, [the doctors] should not conclude that he is dead until they perform this test; and if they see that there is a connection between the brain and the body, despite the fact that he is not breathing, they should place the respirator in his mouth even for a long time, and only when they see through this test that there is no connection between the brain and the body can they conclude by virtue of the fact that he is not breathing that he is dead." [Literal translation; emphasis added.]

The language of this *teshuvah* would appear to suggest that Rabbi Feinstein endorsed performance of the brain death test only as a *chumrah* (stringency) in specialized cases where the standard test for measuring irreversible absence of respiration may not be conclusive. To proceed from that *chumrah* to a generalized endorsement of brain death testing — even, for example, where the person is on a respirator — requires a leap of logic that appears nowhere in Rabbi Feinstein's published writings.[4]

The Agudath Israel of America archives contains an internal diary memorandum written by Agudath Israel's president Rabbi Moshe Sherer during the months of April and May 1976, when the New York State legislature was considering the proposed brain death legislation cited above. This was also the time

---

4. The language of the *teshuvah* would also appear to suggest that Rabbi Feinstein relied for his information about the brain death test, including his statement that the test demonstrated total destruction of the brain, upon the representations of Rabbi Tendler. Close members of Rabbi Feinstein's family have in fact informed me that statements in Rabbi Feinstein's *teshuvos* describing medical *metzius* may not necessarily reflect his own personal knowledge.

that Rabbi Feinstein issued his 5736 *teshuvah*. Rabbi Sherer's diary reports on several conversations he had with Rabbi Feinstein which make quite clear that Rabbi Feinstein opposed using the brain death test in cases where the patient is breathing through a respirator. Following are two excerpts from Rabbi Sherer's diary:

> May 11 [,1976], 11:15 A.M. — Phoned Rabbi Feinstein to ask for his meaning of the *psak* re: "blood flow" test of Rabbi Tendler. He said:
>
> ס׳איז בליוז א חומרא, און בליוז און פאלן פון עקסידענט
>
> ["It is only a stringency, and only in cases of an accident."] I then asked: What is the *din* if an ordinary sick person on a respirator is breathing and has a heartbeat, but we don't know whether he would continue breathing if the respirator is removed — can we then trust the "blood flow" test to determine death?

Rabbi Feinstein's reply:

> בפירוש ניט, איך האב געשריבען קלאר אז א נאראמאלער קראנקער טאר מען ניט אויפהערן די מאשין אויב ער אטעמט - און דער ׳טעסט׳ מיינט גארניט גארניט. ס׳איז בליוז א חומרא וועגן עקסידעסנט.
>
> ["Explicitly not. I wrote clearly that with an ordinary sick person one is not permitted to stop the machine if he is breathing — and the test means nothing. It is only a stringency concerning accidents."]

> May 12, 9:30 A.M. — Rabbi Feinstein phoned ... Rabbi Feinstein repeated explicitly what I had said yesterday, that the "blood flow test" is only a *"chumrah"* in accidents. To my question as to whether a "blood flow" test has any significance when a patient is breathing only through a respirator, Rabbi Feinstein replied:
>
> אוודאי ניט, ווי איך האב קלאר געשריבן אין אנפאנג פון פסק און דער טעסט טאר מען בכלל ניט מאכן וויל ער איז דאך א גוסס.
>
> ["Certainly not, as I clearly wrote in the beginning of the *psak* — and the test should not be performed

altogether since the person is after all a *goseis* (in the throes of death).]

Let me state clearly that it is not my purpose in offering this very brief and incomplete overview of Rabbi Feinstein's written statements to express my personal disagreement with Rabbi Tendler's exposition of his father-in-law's position. I fully concede that I am only a layman, expert in neither *psak halachah* nor medical science, and I have no standing to agree or disagree with one interpretation or the other of Rabbi Feinstein's writings. I certainly have no personal knowledge of any unpublished statements by Rabbi Feinstein, written or oral, that might shed further light on his views. My point in this section is simply to observe and report, as others greater than I have already done, that Rabbi Feinstein's published writings are susceptible of an interpretation contrary to the one upon which the RCA's health care proxy form is based.

II.

The RCA has now taken at least one small step to soften the unequivocal nature of its health care proxy form. In a cover letter circulating the form to RCA *rabbanim* around the country early this summer, after my earlier article had gone to press and other criticisms had emerged, Rabbi Marc D. Angel, president of the RCA, acknowledged that not everybody would agree with the halachic viewpoints embodied in the form:

> We recognize that the issues of brain death and organ transplantation are controversial. Certainly, there are great rabbinic authorities — including members of the current [RCA] Va'ad Halachah Commission — who do not accept brain death and who do not allow organ transplants ... We urge our colleagues to study the issues involved very carefully, since they are virtually matters of life and death. No health care proxy should be used until you have thoroughly studied the issue and until you have consulted experts in the field.

This statement is most welcome. Still, to the best of my knowledge, the health care proxy document itself remains intact; the RCA as an organization still stands behind its form; and there has been no public acknowledgment of the controversial nature of the *piskei halachah* embodied in the form, despite the broad publicity the form received upon its initial introduction.

It is that absence of public acknowledgement that prompted me to write my initial article. A health care proxy form, after all, is a document designed to be used by masses of people — some of them knowledgeable in *halachah*, many of them ignorant. Members of the public who choose to sign such a form rather than a standard secular living will/health care proxy form do so because they are looking for something special: a degree of protection and assurance that medical decisions made on their behalf when they are incapable of making them on their own will fully conform with *halachah*.

But sometimes there is no clear consensus as to what the *halachah* requires or permits in any given circumstances. Sometimes — such as with respect to the issues of brain death and organ donations — there are even serious conflicts among halachic authorities.

Given those realities, there are two basic approaches one might adopt in developing a health care proxy/living will document for broad public use. The first is to adopt a very specific halachic viewpoint, and then promulgate it among the masses under the philosophy of *"kablu da'ati"* — accept my particular halachic viewpoint in signing this form, despite the fact that other respected halachic figures may disagree. That, essentially, is the approach embodied in the RCA form, at least with respect to the issues of brain death and organ donations.

The other possible approach is to develop a form that does not embody any specific halachic viewpoint, but instead merely enables each individual to declare that all health care decisions made on his behalf in the event that he becomes incapacitated should be made in accordance with *halachah*, and then gives the individual an opportunity to designate the specific halachic authority whose guidance he wishes his agent to follow whenever questions of Jewish law arise.

This latter approach, endorsed by Dr. Jakobovits' letter, is precisely the approach embodied in the "Halachic Living Will" form developed more than a year ago by Agudath Israel of America, under the direction of its *Moetzes Gedolei HaTorah*.

Unlike the RCA form, the Agudath Israel Halachic Living Will makes no effort to anticipate various medical scenarios that may arise. It does not afford people an opportunity to insert their own personal predilections, which may not conform to *halachah*. It issues no *piskei halachah* on substantive issues that divide contemporary *poskim*. It can easily be used by persons on either side of the brain death/organ donation debate. In short, the Agudath Israel form follows in the path which Rabbi Tendler so correctly points out was established by the long-standing chairman of the *Moetzes Gedolei HaTorah*, Rabbi Moshe Feinstein, of not seeking to impose a viewpoint of *"kablu da'ati."*

To the RCA's credit, its president Rabbi Angel has now offered to make the Agudath Israel document available to all RCA members (though in his offer Rabbi Angel misstates that the Agudath Israel form "does not accept brain death or organ transplantation"). One can only hope that RCA *rabbanim* will look beyond organizational labels and objectively consider the pros and cons of the varying approaches reflected in the two respective organizational forms.

Discordant Notes: An Essay on Galus and Egalitarianism

Dr. Aaron Twerski

C armelite nuns erect a convent within the gates of Auschwitz. The act offends the sensibilities of Jews for reasons that need no elaboration. The response of Cardinal Glemp and the confrontation with some militant American Jewish activists is now history. The issue has been on and off the front pages of world newspapers for the last two years. The rhetoric has been extreme and the clash engendered more than verbal jousting. Question: Was the Jewish reaction wise?

Crown Heights explodes as a result of an unfortunate automobile accident in which a black child was killed. The driver of the car that caused the accident was a Lubavitcher *chassid.* Almost immediately following the incident, Yankel Rosenbaum, a young Orthodox Jewish scholar visiting Brooklyn from Australia, is deliberately murdered by a gang of marauding blacks. Crown Heights is bathed in violence. None of it emanates from the chassidic community. Irresponsible rabble rousers bring in gangs to wreak havoc on the neighborhood. The Mayor vacillates for almost three days before he takes decisive action. In the meantime Crown Heights takes on the appearance of a *shtetl* following a Cossack attack. What should the Jewish response be to these events?

The President of the United States, George Bush, decides to delay ten billion dollars in loan guarantees to Israel to help the resettlement of Russian emigres. His purpose in doing so is to exert pressure on Israel to halt settlements in the West Bank so as to facilitate the peace talks. When questioned about the subject at a news conference, the President expresses annoyance at "thousands of lobbyists" who fan out over Washington seeking to assert their influence. How should a Jew respond to this public rebuff?

In general, are there a set of Torah-inspired guidelines to help inform our reactions to hostile events and to remarks that can be interpreted as less than friendly in nature?

Anti-Semitism is not a new phenomenon. It has an ancient pedigree. Manifestations of anti-Semitism and reactions thereto are set forth in *Sefer Bereishis* and are spilled over the pages of the Talmud. Torah leaders throughout the ages have left us a legacy rich in content as to how they responded to a wide variety of anti-Semitic attacks. Not merely individual responses relevant to a particular time and a particular circumstance, these reactions over the centuries suggest some broad patterns, which indicate a clear halachic approach. After all, with the stroke of a pen or with an improvident word one can let loose forces that are as deadly as a loaded gun. It would indeed be strange that the question of whether to remove a critically ill patient from a respirator is a halachic problem, and whether to undertake a demonstration that could trigger violence and loss of life would be subject to whim and personal opinion. The societal factors that must be considered are *pikuach nefesh* — matters pertaining to life and death — and clearly within the realm of *halachah*.

✦ Proceeding From First Premises

Before engaging in discussion as to what are appropriate responses to anti-Semitism, it is necessary to first ask, what does one seek to accomplish? The most obvious answer is pragmatic in nature.

One hopes to alter either the conduct or views of the anti-Semite, or that of the people who are likely to be influenced by him, by appealing to their logic and sense of decency. There may be yet another goal. By raising the issue to public light there is a belief that people who are unaware and insensitive to anti-Semitism will be subject to "consciousness raising" and thus become more alert to the scourge of anti-Semitism.

By definition, one who seeks to accomplish pragmatic goals is bound to undertake some form of risk-benefit balancing to decide whether the proposed action is warranted. And as we shall later see, the Torah is not neutral as to how to weigh the factors in balance. But first let us examine the views of those who believe that the battle against anti-Semitism is grounded in the need of the Jewish people to accomplish "equality" and "first class citizenship" in their own eyes and in the eyes of the nations of the world.

→ The Egalitarians

Those who predicate their response to anti-Semitism on egalitarian grounds will either refuse entirely to undertake risk-benefit balancing, or even if they purport to do so, will almost always opt for a strident response. The goal of attaining — or, more often, *portraying* — true equality when placed in the balance will simply outweigh competing considerations.

The most recent salvo challenging American Jewry for not demanding their full equality is the best-seller by Professor Alan Dershowitz of the Harvard Law School. In his recent book entitled *Chutzpah*, Dershowitz castigates American Jews for viewing themselves "as second class citizens, as guests in another people's land," and urges that "we must demand the first class status we have earned in America." His concluding line in the book tells it all: "One conclusion is certain: unless we regard ourselves as first-class Americans and as first-class Jews, no one else will so regard us."

Dershowitz's prescription is thus predictable. We must be prepared to take up the cudgel to respond to virulent or subtle anti-Semitism. In one poignant passage, Dershowitz describes why he decided to represent Rabbi Avi Weiss in a defamation action against Cardinal Glemp. After Rabbi Weiss and his group had a confrontation with the nuns at the site of the convent, Glemp addressed an audience and essentially said that had Weiss and his group not been apprehended, the nuns might have been killed and the convent destroyed. These allegations were patently false. In 1989, Glemp was invited to the United States by Polish-American groups. Dershowitz wrote to Glemp informing him that when he came to the United States, either he or his attorney would be served with legal process for a tort action alleging malicious defamation. Immediately thereafter, Glemp canceled his trip to the United States. Dershowitz was exultant. He had won a great victory.

> It *was* a great victory for decency. It was also a victory for Jewish power. It sent a clear message to Cardinal Glemp and his ilk: Jews no longer take this kind of bigotry without fighting back. We don't just hide in our homes and pray that there will be no pogrom. We don't come hat in hand begging for justice. We invoke our rights as equals. We fight back as equals. And we get results.

Combativeness, assertiveness and tough one-upmanship is the order of the day. Only heavy doses of *Chutzpah* will save us from devastation. Dershowitz's thesis is not new. Since time immemorial, the battle cry for political equality as an inherent good has been sounded by dissidents within the Jewish nation. And the subtext has been, "Let us be like all the nations, Israel!" It began with those who sought the establishment of a monarchy in the days of the Prophet Samuel, so that we could be "like all the nations that surround us." And it came to full flowering in its *golah* expression with the *maskilim* and others who sought political salvation in the egalitarian principles of socialism. Their message has been the same: Step up and demand your rights. You will attain political equality only if you fight for it.

→ Listening to Voices of the Sages

Is Jewish first-class citizenship attainable? Is it unequivocally desirable? The answer to both questions is clearly in the negative. Fortunately, it is not necessary for me to seek out the original sources or divine their meaning. Several universally respected *gedolei Yisrael* faced with the Dershowitzes[1] of their day have gathered the sources and fashioned the *teshuvah*. The reality of *galus* is such that equality is unattainable and is by definition undesirable.

Listen to the words of the **Meshech Chochmah,** the world renowned Reb Meir Simcha of Dvinsk:

"And he [Yaakov] sojourned there" — to teach us that Yaakov Avinu did not descend to Egypt to settle there, but only to sojourn there (Sifri).

That is, Yaakov was instructing us how to conduct ourselves in every galus, throughout the generations; that one must realize that Jews are not meant to settle in every particular place, only to sojourn...until the End of Days, not thinking of themselves as citizens...

For that reason, the passage (Shemos 1:12) describes the Jews in Egypt as "Vayakutzu ... and the Egyptians became disgusted with the Jews," implying that they thought of the Jews as kotzim — thorns (Sotah 11a). This means that just as a thorn does not interbreed with other trees or plants, neither do the Jews: they did not think of themselves as similar to the Egyptians. They were distinct from them in nature and in attitude, to the point that the Egyptians thought of them as thorns. The great leaders of the JewishPeople — Ezra HaSofer and Anshei Knesses HaGedolah (the Men of the Great Assembly) in the forefront — learned from this the need to draft the Eighteen Ordinances of Separation i.e., not to drink the wines or eat the cooking of non-Jews, etc. (see Shabbos 13a) to ascertain that the Jews will preserve their uniqueness in all their activities; that Jews recognize that essentially they are strangers, guests in an alien land

---

1. This is not meant to dismiss Alan Dershowitz's admirable accomplishments in defending Jewish interests nor to disavow his altruistic motives. We take issue here with his basic ideological premise as expounded in *Chutzpah*.

... like the olive twig that cannot be grafted onto any other type of tree.

The Gemara says that even Eliyahu HaNavi will not be able to abrogate any of these Eighteen Ordinances (*Avodah Zarah* 36a). This means that until Mashiach arrives and abolishes the Jews' subjugation to other nations — even if Eliyahu has already come to herald the imminent advent of Mashiach — these ordinances will still be in effect for they sustain the Jewish nation in the golah, and serve to remind them that they are Jews, dwelling in a land that is not theirs...

Ignoring this can have devastating consequences. Those who have renounced Jerusalem for Berlin will someday suffer from destructive fires that will erupt from Berlin.

Similarly, the **Noam Elimelech** comments on the passage in *Bereishis* (32:5), where Yaakov instructs his messengers in how to address his brother, "So shall you say to my master, Eisav ...":

The Torah teaches us how to conduct ourselves in this bitter galus, where we are under the dominion of other nations, and we are obliged to accept this galus with love until that time when G-d will have mercy on us and redeem us swiftly. For as long as we are in this bitter galus, we must be subjugated to them and call them "Our master" as did Yaakov to Eisav.

The **Netziv** (Rabbi Naftali Zvi Yehudah Berlin) — head of the famed Volozhin Yeshivah from 1852 through 1892 — who was one of the leading figures of Russian Jewry during some of the most oppressive years under the Czars' tyrannical rule, approached the issue from a somewhat different perspective.

He wrote Sefer Sh'er Yisrael, on anti-Semitism, urging his fellow Jews to avoid its underlying causes. First and foremost, he wrote, the Jews are destined to be a nation apart; separate from all the others. If they do so out of their choosing, then they will be secure, in keeping with the passage: "Vayishkan Yisrael betach badad ... ayn Yaakov — Israel shall dwell securely alone... the eye of Yaakov" (Devarim 33:28) — meaning that this state of isolation represents Yaakov Avinu's deepest aspiration, the vision in his eyes.

The **Degel Machaneh Ephraim** strikes a similar theme in explaining Bilam's pronouncement that *"Am levadad yishkon, bagoyim lo yis'chashev."* He explains that Bilam recognized that if *Klal Yisrael* remained *levadad* — "separate and alone" — it would dwell in tranquility; but that if it sought to find status among the nations then the Jews would lose their importance — their *chashivus.*

And finally, the saintly **Reb Elchonon Wasserman** in his *Ikvasa D'Meshicha* relates the following:

Aside from the precepts and prohibitions, the Torah contains wise counsel. As the Chofetz Chaim used to say: With perceptive vision, one can find in the Torah all the advice one can possibly need — for individuals and surely for the Jewish people as a whole, including guidelines for conduct in galus. Ignoring the Torah's counsel in such areas can have extremely harmful repercussions. Until recently, Jewish leaders always consulted the Torah in regard to galus-policy. In fact, the Tannaim (rabbis of the Mishnaic era) studied the Torah's account of Yaakov's confrontation with Eisav whenever they made one of their frequent trips to Rome to negotiate an annulment of harsh decrees (see Ramban, Vayishlach).

Today, people have departed from this practice; they only consult Torah wisdom to know if and when to say "Kaddish." National concerns are referred to professional politicians and journalists.

The source of their theories and insights? "Let us be like all nations, O'Israel!" The Torah is rejected! But secular criteria are as unsuitable for the conduct of Jewish affairs as a yardstick is for measuring milk, or quart bottles for figuring out acreage. Our policies must come from eternal sources fashioned for the eternal People — the Torah itself.

And what does the Torah say? "G-d made Israel swear three oaths: 'Do not rebel against the nations ...'" (Kesubos 111a) ... To which the Rabbis commented, "If you keep these oaths, it will be well for you; but if not, your blood will run." Also: "If you see an evildoer upon whom fortune temporarily smiles, do not provoke him." Said Rabbi Chiya, "If Eisav threatens you, do not battle with him, but hide from him, until his time passes." Where shall we flee? G-d answered: "If you see that he stirs up conflict, flee to the Torah, as it says, 'Turn and go to Tzafon (northward)' and Tzafon is none other than Torah, as it says, 'Through Tzafon shall He give the upright salvation'" (Midrash, Devarim).

The sources are unimpeachable. *Galus,* by its very terms, precludes full achievement of the kind of unconditional equality that the egalitarians seek. The long tragic history of *Klal Yisrael* demonstrates it is foolhardy to expect that, even if temporarily attained, it will have any lasting power. One need only remember that in the Weimar Republic the Jews of Germany sensed that the millennium had arrived. They were equal in every sense to their non-Jewish neighbors. Within 10 years, the equality gave way to the worst brutality that Jews have experienced in their 3,000 year history.

It is important that we understand the limitations placed upon us by *chachmei Yisrael*. We begin our inquiry into the parameters of sensible Jewish reaction at a very different point than does Dershowitz. He and other Jewish secularists begin with equality as good in and of itself. We reject it because *Chazal* teach us that it runs *contra* to the basic concept of *galus*.

Once it is clear that we are not doing battle to establish an immutable egalitarian principle, we can discuss the nature of our response to anti-Semitism. Having left the world of principle, we must confront the world of pragmatics. The issue before us is the terms of Jewish survival. Does the Torah counsel total passivity? If not, how do *Chazal* weigh the pragmatic factors necessary to make the hard choices as to how to respond?

→ *The Rules of Risk-Benefit Balancing*

"And [when] this nation will go astray...My wrath will burn ... and many evils and troubles will befall it" (Devarim 31:16-17). [This refers to] evils that will prove troubling to each other, like the bee and the scorpion. Cold water relieves the pain of a bee bite, and hot water cures a scorpion sting, while the reverse treatment is actually life threatening. Thus, a person stung by both a bee and a scorpion does not know what to do, for what relieves one aggravates the other. This is how it will be when the nations persecute the Jews in galus. The Jews fear to protest, for then the nations will despise them more. Yet if they do not cry out, the nations will feel that they can continue to persecute them with impunity.

Daas Zekeinim Mi'Baalei Tosafos

We now face the dilemma of how to respond to the simultaneous bee and scorpion bites. Passivity and active response both present their own sets of dangers. We can ill afford knee-jerk reactions. At times the balance will weigh in favor of a strong and even militant response. On other occasions a more muted response — or even silence — may be called for. That histrionics is not called for on all occasions is quite clear. Once again the words of Reb Elchonon are enlightening.

All the above quotations point to one thing: that in galus the Jews must not stand in combat against their adversaries. A wise man said: It is worthwhile to fight an enemy if I am stronger than he, and he more virtuous than I; but if he is stronger than I, and I more virtuous than he, I had better not fight him. The various groups that rise up against us are superior in strength and inferior in virtue to us; therefore no good can come out of active opposition...

"Do not show yourselves before your brothers, the sons of Eisav and Yishmael!" (Bereishis 42:1, Rashi). This is a clear warning not to be conspicuous and give the nations cause to speak about us. The less they discuss us, the better off we are. Except when they make decrees against the Torah; then we must be as hard as a rock and not yield a hairsbreadth.

When Nevuchadnetzar decreed that the Jews must bow down to his image, Chananyah, Mishael and Azariah refused to submit to this decree and said to him: "You are the king, and you are Nevuchadnetzar." That is, if you decree taxes and tributes, fine; for this you are king. But to tear us from the faith of our Torah, you are not the king, but merely Nevuchadnetzar — you and the dog are equal.

This, in brief is the Torah's approach in regard to our attitude toward the nations, and the Jews acted in accordance to these guidelines in all times, until the latter generations, until "leaders" arose who refused to recognize the Torah and its counsels, and direct Jewish policies in exactly the opposite way. Their gospel? The Jews must fight and make demands. Whom must we fight? The strongest powers in the world. We must boycott them, and assemble at conventions to assault them with newspaper articles, and thereby bring fear and trembling into their hearts.

Where does all this lead us? Does the counsel of *Chazal* provide clear and unambiguous direction to the resolution of each of the questions I posed at the outset of the article? I think that the answer is that it does not. But, does it give us substantial guidance as to how to go about formulating a response? Without doubt, the guidance is there for all who care to seek it out. First, careful and sensitive evaluation has to be undertaken as to the effects of any intervention. I believe that Rabbi Weiss' confrontation with Cardinal Glemp and the subsequent Dershowitz lawsuit fails every sensible test based on risk-benefit balancing. Powerful forces in Poland and the Vatican were baited for little real benefit. Yes, Glemp is an anti-Semite and there are more like him in the Catholic church around the world. Many of them are in positions of power in countries with dominant Catholic populations and Jewish minorities whose existence was and remains precarious. Whether their lives and fortunes should have been placed in jeopardy for the sole purpose of branding Glemp as an anti-Semite seems to me highly questionable. My hunch is that *Gedolei Yisrael* resolving this *she'eilah* would have prohibited the intervention.

✦ A Word About Crown Heights

The immediate focus of the media attention in Crown Heights was the alleged tension between blacks and Lubavitcher chassidim who reside side by side in that integrated neighborhood. In my discussion with thoughtful Jewish community leaders in Crown Heights, I learned that they believe that the source of the difficulty was not the internal community. First, they note that the black community in Crown Heights has been hit particularly hard by the economic downturn. The streets were virtually packed with large numbers of unemployed who were bitter and angry. There is no question but that blacks and disadvantaged minorities are especially vulnerable to fluctuations in the economy. In short, Crown Heights was a tinderbox ready to explode. At the first provocation it erupted. The most likely available white targets were local Jews. Second, and even more important, the tragic auto accident came after three weeks of virulent attacks on Professor Leonard Jeffries.

It will be recalled that the chairman of the Black Studies Department in the City University of New York, Leonard Jeffries, had delivered a speech accusing Jews and Italians in Hollywood of conspiring to portray blacks in a negative fashion. Moreover, he accused the Jews of Western Europe of having masterminded the slave trade of the 18th and 19th centuries. The Jewish reaction to this speech was extraordinary. The leading Jewish secular organizations came out swinging. The story captured the headlines in the New York tabloids on a daily basis. It was clear that organized Jewry had found a target worthy of their ire.

My Crown Heights friend believes that the background of the Jeffries affair was a strong contributing factor to the horrendous reaction following the auto accident. He relates that caller after caller on the black radio station talk shows delivered the same message. ("They brought down our Martin [Martin Luther King]; they brought down our Malcolm [Malcolm X], and now they want to bring down our Lenny.") It is not necessary to explain that the first two "theys," which refer to Whitey, and the last "they," which refers to Jews, are very different entities. For the embattled black the enemies appear the same.

The justifications of the black community are not on the agenda at this writing. This discussion deals only with the risk-benefit calculus, which must guide Jewish response to anti-Semitism. The question is: Was it necessary, was it wise to escalate the Jeffries speech into a *cause celebre*? Jeffries is obviously an anti-Semite. His statements since his infamous conspiracy speech leave little doubt on that score. But what did we accomplish by responding with such vituperance? We projected a virtual nobody (who had ever heard of Jeffries?) into an important spokesperson for black Americans. Rather than his words falling as a dud on deaf ears, he was treated as someone whose words should be reckoned with. Now when he appears in Crown Heights he comes in as a hero.

In the process of engendering an elaborate defense mechanism on the part of the black community, we, the New York Jewish community, set ourselves up as targets. For what purpose, for what benefit? If all that can be said is that it feels good to hear the sound of our voices affirming that anti-Semitism is bad, then it seems rather clear to me that we do not pass the risk-benefit test articulated earlier.

Paradoxically, when the riots were in progress and Jewish lives were in danger and their property was being demolished, the secular Jewish community was slow to recognize that the riots were anti-Semitic. Now that a response was in order to save the lives of *chassidim*, it took several days for Jewish leadership to come together and to denounce the riots as anti-Semitic. Instead of reacting immediately with delegations to the appropriate public officials, they sat back on their haunches — contemplating as to whether what was going on in Crown Heights was truly anti-Semitic in nature. Only after the rhetoric of the self-appointed rabble rousers turned ugly — long after Yankel Rosenbaum was killed — did they finally get the gumption to demand that the city put an end to the anti-Semitic rioting.[2]

✦ Responsible Intervention

Finally, as to the questioning of whether President Bush's "thousands of lobbyists" remark should have called forth a response, I have no doubt that a vigorous response was very much in order. President Bush is not Leonard Jeffries, nor is he a cardinal in a country in which the Jewish population has dwindled down to a small group of several hundred aged survivors. He is the President of the United States and it had to be made clear that his language was totally unacceptable. But in making the response there was no warrant in branding him an anti-Semite. Common sense and fairness demanded that the criticism be delivered without invective.

---

2. In seeking to respond to anti-Semitism, it seems to me that Orthodox Jews must understand that the dangerous flash point of black communities which results from chronic unemployment is a matter of true concern to us. In a recent *Coalition* article, Chaim Dovid Zwiebel, general counsel of Agudath Israel of America, argued with considerable justification that we must become advocates supporting the social economic strengthening of inner-city communities. Not only should these positions be taken because they are just — they must be taken because we are in great danger when we live side by side with communities whose alienation from society is profound.

Because we denounce grandstanding for its own sake in favor of *seichel* and restraint does not mean that we preach passivity under all circumstances. To the contrary. We at Agudath Israel, for example, have been strong advocates to help better the conditions of Jews and to seek fair treatment from all sectors of government. It is for this reason that the Agudah devotes so much attention to its Commission on Legislation and Civic Action. We are active participants in the legislative process at the state and federal level, and are involved in litigating issues that bear heavily on the quality of life for Jews. When we lobby or use our contacts in government, we present our case as equals before the law. This is how it should be to be effective in a democracy. But it should not be essential for our self-image as Jews that Americans fully accept us as equals. In our *galus* situation, that will never be the case, and we are not impoverished for lack of their genuine acceptance. Yet, wherever possible, we create coalitions with groups that have similar interests, for many Jewish concerns coincide with those of non-Jewish groups. It is not only politically wise to broaden our base, it accomplishes a secondary goal of reducing the primary focus of the specific activity as Jewish in nature.

Intervention (*shtadlonus*) has a long and honored tradition within Jewish history. It was most often pursued with vigor and considerable intensity. The power of right and justice should not be negated. It can be forcefully presented and highly persuasive. But there is a line between vigorous diplomacy and offensive advocacy. Anyone who has been part of this process knows the difference. That the line is a fine one does not mean that it does not exist.

Some will point to some political successes which they will attribute to highly militant and confrontational posturing. My response is what it must be. We measure our successes and failures using non-conventional measuring devices. We recount our victories utilizing a measure whose time-line is eternity and whose judge is an omniscient G-d. Torah through the voice of *Chazal* mandates that we act wisely in response to assaults on Jewish interests. But unlike other minorities, we cannot be strident without weighing the countervailing considerations.

For some, the position taken by *Chazal* will be hard to swallow. We were, after all, raised to believe that we are part and parcel of the American dream. But our past teaches us that we are also part of a very long *galus* nightmare. Some will argue that we must protest anti-Semitism to reaffirm our own sense of self worth. I prefer to define myself not by responding to the dregs of the earth, but by focusing on the nobility of man as seen through the prism of Torah. The legacy of Sinai is a uniquely Jewish experience. It is the key to our self-definition. It is the final and only response to the Jew-haters throughout the centuries.

The Orthodox Jew in the Workplace — a Legal Perspective

Abba Cohen

✣ Discrimination — in the News

As members of a free society in the world's oldest democracy, American Jews should be reasonably secure in their quest for equality in the workplace. This expectation is protected by the law, and when a Jew — or a member of any minority group, for that matter — believes that he is a victim of discrimination, he can turn to the government for help. Indeed, the federal government receives thousands of religious discrimination complaints each year of which hundreds involve an employer's failure to accommodate an employee's religious practices. Hundreds of religious discrimination cases are brought specifically by Jews each year and the number grows steadily.

Many religious discrimination cases have made the news recently, such as the one involving Wal-Mart, the nation's largest retailer, which forced an employee in Missouri to quit because he would not work on his Sabbath. Or the hotel in Virginia — part of a national chain — that refused to hire a woman because she wore a head-scarf for religious reasons .... The company in Maryland that won't hire men with beards .... And the case in New York regarding transit workers and their right to observe their Sabbath.

And then, of course, there is Texaco, which has recently been in the news because its directors were caught on tape griping about how they were being asked to accommodate the religious observances of its employees, including Jewish employees who celebrate Chanukah. To us, of course, this is not news. It was Texaco that, a few years ago, sued a franchisee for not keeping his gas station open after sundown on Friday — this, despite the fact that he was Texaco's all-time top gasoline pumper, who earned in excess of $470,000 a year. In that case, the judge ordered the franchisee to open his station on his Sabbath.

Sabbath, holidays, beards, scarves — how familiar this sounds!

At Agudath Israel, over the past year, we have been approached by a legal secretary who told us the anger and resentment she faces at work because of her leaving early on Friday; by a guidance counselor in a junior high school who lost her job, despite her record of distinction, because of complaints relating to her Orthodoxy; by a postal worker in Texas who was being threatened with dismissal. We have received calls from Orthodox Jews from all across the country, from every profession, from every level on the employment ladder, who are being forced to choose between their livelihood and their religion.

→ *A Familiar Refrain*

In truth, we are familiar with the problem of religious discrimination in the workplace. So many of our parents and children, our husbands and wives, our friends — we ourselves — have confronted the ugly face of discrimination in the workplace; and we know the questions — the persistent, biting questions:

• Why do you just sit there while the rest of us are enjoying our dinner? Why don't you order something, too? Is water really all you can have?

• Why do you have to wear a dress with such long sleeves? Why can't you be a little less prim and a little more stylish? Why do you have to stick out?

• Why do you have to be so obstinate about leaving early on Fridays, and about never coming in on Saturdays? Can't you come in for even a half hour? You know, you are the only one who doesn't.

• Don't you care about our business? Don't you want us to be successful? Don't you want to be part of the team? Do you want to offend our clients?

• Why are you always asking for special treatment? What do you mean you won't be coming to the firm's parties or holiday celebrations? If you want that promotion, shouldn't you be a bit more reasonable, a little more flexible?

We know the threats, the looks, the snide remarks — and it hurts.

This may seem strange. After all, isn't this America? Aren't religious freedom and tolerance the pillars upon which this nation was founded? Doesn't the Constitution protect us from the government intruding on our rights? Don't Federal Civil Rights Laws protect us from religious discrimination in housing, in education — and in the workplace?

✧ The Bitter History of Discrimination

To understand the problem, we must, indeed, look at the law — its history, its language and how it has been interpreted by the courts.

The history is sadly a bitter one. In the early part of the century, before the civil rights era, there was little to protect Jews from discrimination. We know all too well about "no Jews need apply," about the "quotas" our parents and grandparents faced. That bitter experience, among other things, compels Agudath Israel today to support legislation in Washington that makes quotas and similar hiring practices illegal.

We also know about the "if you don't come in on Saturday, don't bother coming in on Monday" rule, and the tremendous pressures — economic and otherwise — that Jewish refugees and immigrants faced. How many millions of Jews, how many generations have been lost to *Yiddishkeit* because of the decision to take that first, fateful and tragic step of *chillul Shabbos*? How many times do we hear nowadays about fellow Jews who are marginally committed and who would entertain the possibility of being *Shomer Shabbos* if they were not so afraid of losing their livelihoods?

Indeed, the issue of discrimination in the workplace was, and is, not only a concern in the material realm, but one of profound importance to the *neshamah*, as well. It touches both *gashmius* and *ruchnius*.

→ The Landmark Civil Rights Act

An important step forward was taken in the 1960's, when the landmark Civil Rights Act was passed. It soon became apparent, however, that it did not adequately address the problem. Yes, it was now illegal to discriminate against Jews in the workplace, but the law only related to firing Jews just for being Jews, and not because of difficulties that come as a result of their religious observances or practices. An employer would say, *I hire many Jews, and I'm happy to hire Jews, but the employee wanted me to let him take time off for the holidays — and I want my workers, all my workers, to be available to work. After all, I have a business to run.* And, indeed, the Supreme Court, in 1971, let stand a lower court's ruling that, though blanket discrimination against members of a religious group was illegal, employers did not have to accommodate an employee's "religious practices and observance."

As *frum* Jews, we understand that being "ethnically Jewish" and being practicing Jews are inseparable, and that it is our religious observance that defines us as Jews. Thus, in 1972, Agudath Israel joined other groups in successfully seeking a change in law. Under this new law, an employer would have to "reasonably accommodate" the religious practices of an employee, unless such an accommodation would result in "undue hardship" on the employer's business. And so, in 1972, it seemed as if Orthodox Jews had a powerful weapon in fighting for their rights in the workplace.

→ *Cracks in the Protective Wall*

Again cracks began to appear. The statute did not define what a "reasonable accommodation" was. It did not pinpoint who was responsible for working out the appropriate accommodation. Nor did it tell us what constitutes "undue hardship" on the employer. And, it did not assign the burden of proving discrimination. On those and other questions, the law was silent, leaving these questions to the courts. And, unfortunately, because of the decisions handed down by the courts, the 1972 religious accommodation law has never lived up to its original promise.

While we cannot go into too much detail in regard to the pertinent Supreme Court cases, we could summarize three particular decisions that have had a profound effect on the legal protections afforded Orthodox Jews in the workplace.

• The *Hardison* Case, in 1977, involved a non-Jewish Sabbatarian who was fired because he refused to work on Saturdays. The Supreme Court ruled that the dismissal was legal because "anything more than the most minimal amount of hardship on the employer will relieve an employer of the obligation to accommodate his or her religious employee." This "anything more than the most minimal" standard is an easy burden for any employer to meet and has proven to be a very difficult obstacle for religious Jews in the workplace.

It is no wonder that Justice Thurgood Marshall in his dissent observed that the Court's ruling deals a "fatal blow to all efforts under Title VII to accommodate work requirement to religious practices." In a similar ruling, one Federal Court of Appeals put it as follows: "A standard less difficult to satisfy than the diminimus standard for demonstrating undue hardship is difficult to imagine."

• In 1986, in the *Philbrook* Case, the Court further eroded the rights of religious employees. In that case, the Court ruled an

employer has only to offer an employee an accommodation —
any accommodation — no matter how onerous it might be for
the employee in other ways.

For example, an employer might say, "Of course, I will
accommodate you — instead of coming in on Saturdays, make
up the time for me every morning between 8-9." The employee
responds: "I appreciate your sensitivity, but it just so happens
that during those particular hours I must tend to family responsibilities — but I would be happy to make up the time by working late each night between 5-6." The Supreme Court says that
once an employer has given you a way out of working on
Shabbos, he is off the hook. If you can't accept his accommodation — even if your suggested alternative is not in any way a
hardship on him — you can be fired. In other words, take it or
leave it.

• In the famous 1985 *Caldor* Case, the Supreme Court ruled
that even if a state passes a law, as Connecticut had done, that
gives religious employees the *absolute* right not to work on the
Sabbath, that law has no force or effect because it violates the
constitutional doctrine of separation between religion and state.
In other words, that kind of law goes too far in protecting religious rights in the workplace.

✈ *The Real-Life Application*

In sum, the original religious accommodation law has not
provided the protection the Jewish community hoped for — and
which we believe Congress intended — in 1972. The laws that
are currently on the books have been significantly watered
down by the courts, to the point where they have offered little
protection against dismissal or other forms of discrimination.
The deck is simply too heavily stacked against them. The
inevitable result is that often *frum* employees do not even bother exercising their legal rights, and hostile employers do not
even bother trying to accommodate the religious needs of their
employees.

The state of affairs is such that at least one major company has even been comfortable enough to actually advise others on how to avoid hiring workers who take time off for their religious holidays — and get away with it under the law.

> Several years ago, it was reported that New York Telephone sent to nearly 200,000 small businesses an article that had appeared in Inc. Magazine, a popular business magazine, entitled: "Questions You'd Love to Ask a Job Prospect — But Can't." The article pointed out that certain questions, asked in certain ways, could violate the law. It therefore suggested other ways to pose these questions. For example, instead of asking a prospective employee, "Will you be taking time off from work to observe Passover?," the magazine suggested something a little bit more general: "Will the time of your religious observance conflict with the regular work periods of this company?"
>
> Incidentally, the magazine was informed that even this more "parve" form of questioning was illegal. For this type of misleading information and for other reasons, including bad public relations and political pressure, New York Telephone apologized to the public, and Inc. Magazine retracted the article.

✦ Today's Recourse

Can we do anything today, in 1997, about the law? Are there alternatives for us to pursue to strengthen the religious accommodation law?

First, we can attempt to return to the Supreme Court, and ask it to reconsider its earlier decisions. In fact, we have. In a case last year involving a Seventh Day Adventist who resigned from the police force because it would not accommodate his Sabbath observance, Agudath Israel (amongst other groups) submitted a legal brief asking the Supreme Court to hear the case and to reconsider its previous interpretations. Agudah's director of Government Affairs and General Counsel, Chaim Dovid Zwiebel, pointed out in the brief how devastating the court's rulings have been for Orthodox Jews, how greater protection was needed, how in fact other workers — handicapped workers — are afforded by federal law a higher level of protection, and how — by not giving religious workers that same level of protection — constitutional questions must be raised.

It would be gratifying to report that the Supreme Court was persuaded by these arguments and agreed to hear the case. Unfortunately, that was not the case. The Court apparently has little interest, at this time, in strengthening workplace protections for religious employees. In the meantime, we will wait for another case, another opportunity to urge the Court the strengthen the law.

There is, of course, another way to strengthen the law, the legislative route — to go back to Congress and ask it to amend the current law. And, indeed, in the recently convened 105th Congress, legislation will be introduced by Congressman Jerrold Nadler (D. Brooklyn) which is intended to give new meaning — and new teeth — to the religious accommodation law. The Agudah has worked closely with the congressman and with other groups in developing and fashioning legislation that will, among other things:

• Replace the current low standard with a higher degree of protection that will let employers off the hook only when they confront *significant* — not minimal — hardship when accommodating their religious employees.

• It will require the employer to implement the accommodation that is least onerous on the employee. An employer will no longer be able to say "take it or leave it."

• It will require an employer to make a bona fide, serious attempt to accommodate — to actually take affirmative steps to try to work the problem out. No longer will an employer be able to just say no.

• It will allow certain voluntary arrangements between employees that will allow a *frum* employee to take time off for Yom Tov — arrangements that, under current law, employers do not have to allow.

It is an important bill and, if enacted, would represent an important step forward for the religious employee.

The prognosis, however, is uncertain. This legislation will face formidable opposition, foremost by the business community, which is fearful of any legislation that imposes new requirements and higher standards on employers. We might even find resistance from the labor community, which — despite its commitment to the goal of protecting workers — is also concerned about any legislation that gives individual workers greater power, sometimes at the expense of the union's power. Indeed, the challenge before us on Capitol Hill will be great.

✣ *Other Factors at Work*

This is a look at the law — past, present and, hopefully, the changes we would like to see in the future. There is, of course, more to the story. Several realities that have developed over time help complete the picture, and must be included in any meaningful look at the law. Let us briefly review some of them.

First, we must acknowledge that, despite its flaws, the law has helped us. It has helped observant Jews enter the market place, and if the cases of discrimination have gone up, part of the reason is because there are more *frum* people being employed in positions that were previously closed to them.

It is also true that the law has been a deterrent. Employers who have no desire to go through the expense and hardship of litigation — even if the law is in fact more sympathetic to them — will more often follow the path of accommodation over confrontation. Indeed, the law has been effective in keeping cases out of court.

A second point is the fact that religious needs themselves are changing, and that the reality is reflected in the different types of challenges religious employees are facing. We are accustomed to thinking of religious accommodation in terms of *shemiras Shabbos.* But the law is certainly not limited to that one scenario. There are now issues related to religious garb, and even modes of dress and grooming. We have even heard from Orthodox

Jews who are facing transfer to far-flung cities and worry about *kashrus, mikveh, chinuch,* a supportive *kehillah* and other religious needs. As our community grows and changes, its needs change, and we have to consider the effect this will have on issues we confront in the workplace.

Third, it is important to keep in mind that our discussion has been limited to federal law. States and localities, of course, have passed their own legislation in regard to various forms of discrimination in the workplace — legislation which in several instances offers greater protection than federal law in safeguarding the rights of religious employees. Orthodox Jews residing in states where religious accommodation laws are strong will be well advised, and on firmer legal ground, to base their "religious accommodation" claims on those statutes. Those where state laws are weak might want to organize and initiate an effort in the state legislature to enact stronger legal protections.

There is yet another issue we must consider — one which involves not only the rights of religious employees, but also the rights of religious employers: specifically, when the religious rights of an employee of one faith conflict with the religious rights of an employer of a different faith. No one can deny that individual employers have their religious rights, including the right to free religious expressions. No one can insist on a totally religion-free workplace. But there are times that an employer might use the leverage he has in the employment relationship to missionize or proselytize — when religious expression may indeed rise to the level of religious harassment.

That is why Agudath Israel refused to follow the lead of the organizations on the so-called "religious right," who last year opposed new federal guidelines on religious harassment in the workplace. They were concerned about chilling the free religious expressions of religious employers. That concerns us too, but no less than we care abut *Acheinu Beis Yisrael* who do listen to an employer's missionizing and proselytizing because they are afraid of antagonizing the employer and possibly losing their jobs. Remember, once again, discrimination issues are matters of both material *and* spiritual dimensions.

This leads to a final point — that while the law is important, and while we seek to improve it, there is a much more profound dynamic here. We refer to an observation made by Professor Aaron Twerski at an Agudath Israel Convention several years ago.

When a young man or woman leaves the sheltered environment of the *beis midrash* or Beis Yaakov and enters the secular workplace environment, he (or she) encounters enormous pressures to conform to the surroundings corporate or business culture. A *frum* employee may feel that unless he conforms, he is making himself an easy target for bias or ridicule. He will want to blend into the surrounding culture to avoid standing out. These temptations relate to mode of dress, to diet, to social relationships, to informal banter, and to countless other aspects of the workplace.

When the day is done, we must ultimately realize that even if laws against religious discrimination and harassment in the workplace were strong and effective, that even if overt discrimination and harassment disappeared from the workplace, we and our children will continue to face formidable pressures in the workplace — challenges in both *ruchnius* and *gashmius*.

In conclusion — as always — we must remember that we speak about government and laws and courts and Congress, but we only speak in these terms because that is the language that is commonly understood. We must bear in mind that whether we are successful or not in facing the pitfalls and potential of the workplace ultimately depends on *siyata d'shemaya* (Divine assistance) and on He who is *Mamlich melachim v'Lo HaMeluchah* (appoints the temporal rulers, while He is the true Ruler).

✈ Introspection/ Self Improvement

Why Do They Say Those Things About Us?

Rabbi Nosson Scherman

An examination of the causes of overt and subtle expressions of "Orthodox-bashing," and some responses

✦ Victims of a Double Standard

The evidence is in. David Landau quotes Tom Dine speaking about "Smelly Orthodox Jews and badly groomed diamond dealers." That's the way polite people talk behind closed doors. *The New York Times* and other publications say, for example, that if David Dinkins gets 97 percent of the black vote, that's legitimate pride, but if 90 percent of the *Charedi* population of Yerushalayim votes against Teddy Kollek, then this can be described only in language unfit for polite company.... It is quite obvious: There is a double standard.

Much of it is born of prejudice against people who are visibly at odds with progressive notions of what Jews should be and do. We see it. We've seen it in the last couple of years in the response to Crown Heights. To my way of thinking, the most shocking thing about Crown Heights was not the violence. The pogrom was not all that surprising — frightening, yes; surprising, no. The lack of response on the part of the mayor? The city has not responded to many things over the years. But where was the Jewish Establishment? Where were the mainstream Jewish organizations? It was a while before any strong statements were forthcoming from their quarters. A.M. Rosenthal put it well in his column in *The New York Times*. In commenting on the Girgenti Report on the Crown Heights riot, he spoke directly to the Establishment Jews who did not respond because they were embarrassed by the black hats, the beards, and the rumpled appearance of the "Hassidics," which call attention to the unpleasant fact that Jews are different. Rosenthal had one magnificent line: "Sweetheart, by you, you're Park Avenue. By your wife, you're Park Avenue. But to the anti-Semite, you're a Hassid."

So it is true that we are victims of prejudice, and to a great degree I think we should be proud of that. We should be proud of being different, and of being identifiably loyal to Torah and mitzvos.

Conversely, however, some of us translate our "victim" status into a license for being obnoxious, and it shows up in embarrassing ways. When someone double-parks on 13th Avenue in Borough Park in the middle of a busy shopping day, inspiring a metermaid to write out a ticket, and the double parker shouts, "Gestapo!" — which happens — I suggest that something is wrong in our own perception of our role and responsibilities. A catering hall opened up in Brooklyn several years ago, and bought a house behind the hall, for use as the entrance and lobby to the hall. The "entrance" was on a residential block which was not zoned for public function, nor did the owners bother getting a building permit. The neighbors complained — nobody wants to live next to a wedding hall where traffic and honking punctuate the midnight hours. When the city closed down the annex, the owner complained that he was a concentration camp survivor and how could they use such tactics against him?

Sometimes we overdo it.

✦ Taking a Market Research Approach

There is a third point of view to this problem. Any sensible person who is the subject of criticism should wonder whether or not that criticism is true. Large corporations do market research to find out what the public thinks of their products: If the public is not happy with my product, then either I modify it or I discontinue it. Let us think in terms of market research. Why *are* they saying those things about us? Are they right to any degree? And if they are, what can we do to change their attitudes?

At the outset, we should recognize that prejudice against *Klal Yisrael* always exists. *Halachah b'yadua Eisav sonei l'Yaakov* — it is a law of human conduct that Esau hates Jacob. That law will remain with us for as long as we are Yaakov. And if we stop being Yaakov and become so indistinguishable from Eisav that he begins loving us, then we are truly in trouble. Our responsibility as Jews is to guarantee that we are resented because the Eisavs — or even the Jews who have rejected the Torah — cannot countenance a *shomer Torah u'mitzvos.* Let the prejudice, the hatred, be based on that. But let it never be based upon something that should trouble us, as well.

Let us also be clear about something else. We have serious problems in our camp. We suffer unduly because of a limited number of bad apples who very publicly and very blatantly damage the image of us all. And that is not the problem of society or the media; that is *our* problem. If *l'havdil*, Jesse Jackson and Al Sharpton are touring high schools in the United Sates, urging black teenagers to stay away from guns, to stay away from drugs, and turn in drug dealers, because they are killing more black people in one year than have been lynched in the United States in the entire history of the republic — then maybe it's time for us to start thinking in those terms as well. Maybe it's time for us to start working within our own community, exerting pressure that is within halachic bounds, within the bounds of decency, and doing the things that *can* be done.

But let us not delude ourselves into saying of our fellow Orthodox Jews and our institutions, "They're *all* that way ...." A recent magazine article spoke about Rabbi Moshe Sherer, praising his public stance concerning morality in the general society, in the schools, on the subways and everywhere else, and describing him as a leader of unquestionable integrity and moral authority — someone who should be a role model for all American society. That same article described Agudath Israel of America's general counsel, Chaim Dovid Zwiebel, as one of the most brilliant young lawyers in public life, in particular praising a brief that he wrote recently to the Transit Authority, setting forth the legal and constitutional grounds for having the right to reject obscene and pornographic advertising on subways and buses. The author of that article was Cardinal O'Connor.

That is the sort of public image every one of us should project. And it is something we can strive for, realistically. Now, both Rabbi Sherer and Mr. Zwiebel are roundly attacked by the liberal elements of the Jewish community, as is the author of that article. Such attacks we can live with. Such attacks should be our *ambition*. We should long to be the target of people who say that we are trying to interfere with the First Amendment because we are in favor of morality, and because we feel society should exert itself to curb the forces that are causing the moral climate of this country to deteriorate.

But there are other kinds of attack that should disturb us mightily — attacks against our honesty and integrity, attacks against our lack of sensitivity. If they are true, then we should respond not by lashing out against our attackers, but by examining ourselves.

✦ *The Ripple Effect From Society at Large*

What is happening in general society is having a deleterious effect on us. During the Vietnam War, Senator George Aiken of Vermont, one of the more civilized opponents of the war, responded to hose who said that national honor compels us to continue the fight, "Let's declare victory and leave." If you repeat something often enough, it becomes true.

More recently, Senator Moynihan came up with a marvelous phrase: "Defining Deviancy Down." To wit: Those of us who live in New York, or other such major metropolitan areas, have probably had a car or at least a battery stolen, suffered a burglary, or something of that sort. You go to the police station, and they fill out the report required to make an insurance claim. But no one has a thought of investigating the crime, because automobile theft and simple burglary have become so routine, that they are considered mere annoyances. Such ordinary crimes do not matter any more. Marijuana does not matter any more. Most narcotics crimes do not matter any more. These things use to be "deviancy" and were classified as criminal behavior. They used to be intolerable. But what do you do if they are so common that the police department cannot cope with them, courts are overloaded to the breaking point, and society is numbed almost to the point of acceptance? The same thing you do if most of your high school students cannot read 12th-grade level: You can take what *used* to be the 10th-grade level and label it 12th grade. And then a few years later, you do what is done in every large school district in this country: you take the 8th-grade level and call *that* twelfth-grade level.

"Defining Deviancy Down" means that behavior that was unacceptable is now defined as the norm. It becomes acceptable, not deviant. It is not criminal, it is normal.

When you live in a society that defines deviancy down, and you listen to that society's news, and you read its magazines and newspapers, and you do business with it, and you walk its streets, then you end up defining deviancy down. And you say, "The money is *hefker*, it is there for the taking!"

In my yeshivah principal days, I would often give *mussar* to students about their sometimes rambunctious behavior in the afternoon. They would respond, "But the teachers say that they love to come here after public school, because here they don't have to worry about somebody pulling a gun or a knife."

I answered, "Do you realize what you're saying? You're telling me that our code of conduct is not based on what the

Torah says, or the *Shulchan Aruch* says. Our code of conduct is based on what goes on in the worst public schools of the worst neighborhoods of this city. And if on a scale of one to ten they are at three, and we are at four and a half, then we are doing very well, because we are 50 percent better. But we are *not* doing very well. Our standard should be *ten*, not 4.5."

✦ Of Availability and Entitlement

The prevalent attitude among many people is that because the government wastes money, "throws it away," it is free for the taking. And why not? "Whatever I get is much, much less than that of other people who are far less deserving." In the 60's, Senator Everett Dirksen quipped, "In Washington you have a couple of million here and a couple of million there, and before you know it, you're talking about real money." That real money seems to be there for the taking, and many people are ready to take it. The availability of such funds can warp the judgment of normally honest people. Doesn't the Torah warn us of what even a small bribe can do to the judges of the highest caliber?

Rabbi Yaakov Kamenetsky once told me, "The possibility of bringing in extra income through government programs has caused a great deal of damage in our community. When you were in the *kollel*," he said, "you were poor, and your *chaveirim* were poor. All of you struggled, but there was no feeling of jealousy that 'Someone else has something that I don't have, and why can't I get it? Why shouldn't I have it?' But today, with the availability of funding for qualified families, there is a temptation to become eligible, and there is jealousy of those who find a way to do it. That causes a great deal of harm."

Many years ago, the Telshe *Rosh Yeshivah*, Rabbi Elya Meir Bloch, spoke at an alumni gathering, and instead of the usual 45 minute *shiur da'as* (a philosophical discourse) he pounded on the *shtender* and said, "*Men tor nit ganvenen!* It is forbidden to steal!" and he sat down.

Another time, he came back from a fund-raising trip and he said in a *shiur da'as* that he had run out of funds and asked his host to cash his personal check. This gentlemen said, "It's hard for me, I already gave to the yeshivah." Reb Elya Meir wept as he said, "If the plumber or electrician had asked him to cash a check, would he have hesitated? But because it was a *Rosh Yeshivah*, he thought the check would not go through. He was afraid that I would not honor my check. Can there be a greater *chillul Hashem*?"

These occurrences took place many years ago, but have attitudes changed? If not, let us not ask why *they* are saying those things about us. We know why. The *Smak*, one of the *Baalei Tosafos* and a great orator, used to travel and give *mussar* to Jewish communities. He writes, "I used to preach in Jewish communities that those who lie to gentiles and who cheat are in the category of *mechallelei Hashem*, because their behavior causes gentiles to say that Jews have no religion, that Jews have no Torah." The *Smak* was not speaking only to his own generation.

Why are we saying those things about *ourselves*?

I would like to pose another question: We are worried about "Why are they saying those things about us?" I would ask, "Why are we saying those things about *ourselves*?" When we hear about a fire in one of our businesses or institutions, are we *dan l'kaf zechus* (judge circumstances favorably), or do we smirk? What is our reaction to *din Torah* in general? To the institution of *beis din* versus the court system?

A most serious illustration of our own rush to negative judgment is an item that has been in the news as of late: the so-called Pell Grant scandal, regarding certain schools and other institutions that were getting government money to fund supposedly ineligible students. How many of *us* felt, instinctively, that the overwhelming majority of our institutions are aboveboard, and any wrongdoing is surely limited to a very small, *fringe* minority? And how many of us chuckled in sweeping condemnation?

A reporter searches for tidbits that will make headlines; we all know that an editor will not run a story that says that the yeshivos are doing marvelous work. So the papers ran stories suggesting widespread fraud and chicanery.

As a case in point, a recent newspaper series, purporting to be investigative reporting, blasted the Congress, the Department of Education, and colleges and trade schools for looseness and worse in their handling of Pell Grants and student loans. Prominent targets of criticism were Jewish institutions, including some that had always been considered models of probity. These articles are further proof that the First Amendment is abused at least as much as Pell Grants.

A revealing statement not publicized in the media was in the official staff report of Senator Nunn's committee on investigations. It said that the "rabbinical seminaries" — i.e. the traditional mainstream *yeshivos gedolos* — are *not* targets of the Senate investigation. Nearly all of our *mosdos* are members of the Association of Advanced Rabbinical and Talmudic Schools (AARTS), an accreditation organization that is recognized by the U.S. Department of Education, and these yeshivos have not been accused of any wrongdoing whatsoever, Yet, the newspapers kept talking about the "yeshivahs" as if all *mosdos haTorah* were one large undifferentiated conglomerate.

The newspapers reported that nearly two dozens "yeshivahs" — again, a misapplication of the term — were deemed ineligible for federal funding. But here too, there is less than meets the eye. The problem with these schools, says the U.S. Department of Education, is that they are not "vocational," meaning that they do not confer a degree, nor do they train people for particular jobs or professions. These courses were instead characterized by the Department as "avocational." Whether or nor the institutions in question fit the definition of eligibility is a technical question of statutory interpretation that will likely be determined in a legal process. But these programs have been in existence for years. In previous years, when the schools in question filed their curricula, the Department of Education routinely approved the programs for funding with *full knowledge* of what was being taught. The "vocational-avocational" distinction never became an issue until this year.

Even if such "avocational" programs are ruled ineligible, it is surely unfair to bludgeon the schools for doing what the government sanctioned for more than a decade.

Employing a common reportorial technique, many stories brought together a hodgepodge of abuses found nationwide in many institutions, religious and secular, implying that the institutions named in the story were guilty of them all, which was not the contention of the Senate Committee of the Department of Education. In a glaring example, one institution was named in the papers as allegedly guilty of a particular charge; later, that very school was upheld by the Department's law judge, and that particular charge was withdrawn. This news never made it into the press.

I am in no position to judge the institutions under question. But one thing is certain: Media engage in their excesses. An editor at one of America's leading newspapers once told me, "A reporter for a daily will be able to ask two or three questions of a participant in a story, and that makes him more knowledgeable than his readers. But he really doesn't have the time or ability to become a real expert on a breaking story." Whatever may appear on the TV screen and emanate from the lips of sensation seekers, judgment is still premature, and therefore wrong.

This leaves us a troubling question: Why do *we* believe every accusation we read? What happened to us and our own attitudes towards ourselves? What has happened to our religious obligation to judge people favorably and give them the benefit of the doubt? True, there may well be rogues among us, but there are honest people, too.

A prominent politician in the 1980's spent two years and over $2,000,000 defending himself against a variety of very serious charges. When a jury found him not guilty and he was mobbed by reporters asking him for comment, he said one thing: "Now where do I go to get my reputation back?"

✦ Focusing on Number One

I have no illusions about the outcome of these discussions. The Sanzer Rav, used to say that he would change the world. Then he thought he would change Galicia. Then he thought that at least he would change Sanz. Then he though he would perhaps change his chassidim: then he thought he would change his family. He concluded, "Now I'm trying to change myself." My *Rebbe*, Reb Gedalia Schorr, once said that a person should never neglect "*der yochid vos ruft zich 'ich'* — the individual called 'myself.'"

Indeed, let us think about our personal self-improvement. We have been brought up with the attitude that in the aftermath of the Holocaust we must build and strengthen our own community, our *mosdos haTorah* — that we must circle the wagons around our community and ignore the rest of the world. There is much legitimacy in that. But there is another side of every coin. Part of that other side is the feeling that — as we tell our children — we are not like the outside world and we should not accept its standards. True. We do not carry knives, and we do not carry guns, and we do not steal cars... we're not like that, *Baruch Hashem*. But that comforting notion can be carried too far.

Ask hospital nurses what they think of Orthodox Jews. They will tell you about Tomchei Cholim, about the Satmar ladies who come with Thermos bottles of hot chicken soup for patients and their families; no questions asked — *frum*, not *frum*, Reform, Orthodox, Conservative — it doesn't matter. But the nurses will also tell you that even though there is a limit of two visitors to a patient, Orthodox Jews will crowd up the room like Madison Square Garden at a basketball playoff. And when visiting hours are over, you can't get them out. Nurses will complain, "They don't let us do our work."

Mention such complaints to our people, and they say, "So the lady said not more than two visitors! *Bikur cholim* is a mitzvah, the patient feels better. And *I* can't wait in the lobby until somebody comes out!"

"Someone decreed a speed limit of 55 miles an hour. What does he know?" For such contempt for the rules of the road we pay a heavy price every summer when our 17- and 18-year-old drivers think that red lights and stop signs and double lines and 55-mile-an-hour speed limits are stupid — because what do *they* know? Fire drills? So they said you need a fire drill. What do *they* know?

We must reorient our ideas of what is important and what is not, and where our pride should come into play. We *should* come into play. We *should* be proud when people like Cardinal O'Connor say that our leaders are men of impeccable integrity and intelligence. And when gentiles and non-observant Jews are uncomfortable with us because we are dedicated to *Torah u'mitzvos*, uncompromisingly so, let us stand tall.

Indeed, let us take seriously the question of "Why are they saying those things about us?" Why are they saying *which* things about us? Our goal is not to be loved. If we act as we should, they will not love us, because we will be living repudiations of everything that today's First Amendment society stands for. But let us never give people cause to call us hypocrites, to say that apparently we have not read the Ten Commandments lately. Let us be not popular, but respected. We *can* be that. And we have people among us who *are* that. And one by one, family by family, institution by institution, we all have to work to become that.

In closing, let me respond to those many among us who are angered by the frankly self-critical tone of these discussions. When I was a child, Orthodoxy was considered the dinosaur of American Jewry. The senior Orthodox rabbi in most cities would be invited to recite the *Motzi* at the local federation's *tereifah* dinner, and then be patted on the head and ignored. The establishment did not criticize the Orthodox in those day because we were moribund and sliding towards extinction, and one never attacks the terminally ill.

Times have changed. Today, the Torah world is thriving, fast-growing, vibrant, influential. Thanks to the dedication and self-sacrifice of the *gedolim* who built *kehillos* and institutions after the War, and the lay leadership that responds to their directives, we and our children are proud of our achievements and confident of our future. And our opponents train their heavy artillery against us and capitalize on every real or perceived shortcoming.

That we devote time and space to introspection and self-criticism is a sign of health and strength. We want to better ourselves as the nation that lives to create *kiddush Hashem* in the world.

Let us be cognizant of these successes — in order to solidify and increase them, let us not be afraid to search for areas for improvement.

Accepting Reproof With Grace: A Formula for Growth

Rabbi Noach Orlowek

Humility, which lies at the root of the ability to accept reproof, is a sign of intrinsic greatness, for there is no fear that my accepting your reproof will in some way diminish my stature.

A Jew is obligated to give constructive criticism, as expressed in the mitzvah to rebuke a fellow Jew who is committing a sin (*Vayikra* 19:17). There may be times, however, when we need to be on the receiving end of that rebuke. If the mitzvah of giving rebuke is a difficult one to master, perhaps the ability to accept rebuke is even more difficult. This subject can be addressed in two parts: One, why it is so important to learn to accept rebuke gracefully; and, once motivated, to learn some of the ideas and attitudes that will help us profit from the critical insights of others into our actions or character.

So let us begin by enumerating some of the benefits that accrue to someone who learns to accept criticism.

→ The Rewards of Receiving Reproof

1. Happiness and Meaningful Relationships

My life has a better chance of being a happy one if I'm open to correction, for then people are going to be more willing to point out my mistakes and shortcomings, offering me a better chance to rectify them.[1]

The ability to accept criticism is one of the cornerstones of a meaningful relationship, for if my friends, children or wife are afraid to give me criticism, then they can never feel that the relationship is open and secure, and the entire relationship is likely to suffer. Indeed, *Rabbeinu Yonah*[2] tells us that one of the functions of a friend is to offer reproof. To the degree that I understand you, I can love you. It therefore follows that if I cannot let you know me, then the love will be stifled.[3]

---

1. See *Yoma* 9a, where the *Gemara* relates that the generation that experienced the First Destruction (of the Temple in Jerusalem, circa 420 B.C.E.) knew the reasons for the Destruction, and hence were able to merit to rectify them and return to Jerusalem. They were a generation that could still, to a degree, accept the criticisms of the prophets. (This was changing and hence the gift of prophecy was to get lost, as any gift which is unused or misused gets lost.) They had prophets and these prophets were quite clear as to the reasons for the impending Destruction. As I was privileged to hear from Rabbi Yitzchok Hutner (explaining the Vilna Gaon's statement that the end of prophecy was linked to Greek culture and the existence of prophecy during the First Temple era was due to the fact that the salient sin during that era was idolatry) that the prime sin of the First Temple period, idolatry, was, in effect (to use his words), a קבלת עול שקר, the accepting upon oneself the yoke of something false. As long as one still possessed the capacity to accept a yoke upon oneself, there was still someone to talk to about accepting the Yoke of Heaven; hence prophecy persisted throughout the First Temple era. At the time of the Second Destruction (circa 70 C.E.), however, people were into Greek philosophy which was (again to use Rabbi Hutner's words) an act of פורק עול אמת, where people were casting off the yoke of truth. People were negative to the whole idea of having a yoke upon themselves; they wished to be the final arbiters of right and wrong. There was no one to talk to about accepting Heaven's Yoke, and therefore prophecy ended. There were no longer prophets to tell us where we had erred and therefore we stood far less of a chance at rectifying the underlying cause.

2. *Rabbeinu Yona* of Gerona (1200-1263), author of the famed *Shaarei Teshuvah*. Here he is quoted from his Commentary to *Avos*.

3. *Rashi, Bereishis*, tells us that "to know" is a term of endearment, for the word *daas* in Hebrew always refers to some sort of connectedness (see *Alei Shur*, vol. 1 page 138), in this case the connectedness between Hashem and Avraham. You can only love someone to the degree that you know him or her, for otherwise, you do not even know what you are "loving." This seems to be why the study of Torah is directly related to Love of Hashem — and is representative of Hashem's love for us — for when a person studies Torah, he is in effect engaged in finding out what is important to Hashem, knowing

The *Mesillas Yesharim (Path of the Just)*,[4] which is known for its concise style, is quite emphatic about how vital it is to be able to accept advice, even if it implies criticism. He writes:

> Above all, one should constantly reflect upon the weakness of human intelligence and the many errors and deceits to which it is subject, for it is always closer to error than to true understanding. He should *constantly* be in fear, then, of this danger and seek to learn from all men; he should give ear to advice lest he go astray. As our Sages of blessed memory said (*Avos* 4:1), "Who is wise? One who learns from all men." (emphasis mine)

Such a reiteration of emphasis on the part of the *Mesillas Yesharim*, considering his generally terse style,[5] is nothing short of a shout.

2. Becoming a Candidate for Divine Mercy and Bounty

Divine Mercy is that trait of Hashem that looks into the future and gives the person time to rectify his deeds and perfect his character. *A person who can accept reproof has a future, which makes him a candidate for Divine Mercy.* The more a person is willing *and eager* to learn of his/her shortcomings, the more likely it is that someone will indeed be willing to offer that criticism.

The *Sfas Emes*[6] tells us that Moshe blessed the Jewish People after giving them reproof, because it is the ability to accept reproof that makes one a candidate for bounty. I suggest that these two points are interrelated. Just as an ability to accept

---

Him. When we study for its own sake, we are saying, in effect: "Hashem, what's important to You is important to me. I am therefore making an effort to find out what's important to You, how You look at the world."

4. Written by Rabbi Moshe Chaim Luzzatto (1707-1746), it is considered one of the greatest works on character and ethics ever written.

5. The Vilna Gaon (1720-1797), who was never given to exaggeration, is reputed to have said that there is not an extra word in the opening chapters of the book.

6. Written by the Gerrer Rebbe, Rabbi Yehuda Aryeh Leib Alter (1847-1905), the *Sfas Emes* is an awe-inspiring work of immense scope and depth. We quote here from the *Sfas Emes, Devarim*, p. 10 (*Devarim* 1:11).

reproof improves my future potential, making me a candidate for Divine Mercy, in the same vein the ability to accept reproof makes it easier for me to receive bounty, for there is less danger that that bounty will make me arrogant. This is because the ability to accept reproof is generally an outgrowth of humility, which causes a person to become more humble, the more bounty or good fortune is bestowed upon him.[7] This is related to our next point:

3. Becoming a Candidate for Leadership

The Vilna Gaon, in his commentary on the *pasuk*, "And the one who hears will always speak," tells us:

> One who hears and accepts upon himself reproof, will, as reward, merit to lead everyone.[8]

One might explain that this is so because a true leader is someone who does not depend on honors from those whom he leads, and is willing to do what is correct without thinking of any consequential loss of honor.[9] A leader is someone who is giving leadership and direction, without thought for his own honor.[10] He can therefore eagerly accept criticism, for what matters is only what is right and good, with no thought as to his own image. People sense this and eventually he will emerge as a true leader. The Telsher Rav, Rabbi Yosef Leib Bloch (1850-

---

7. The *Gemara* (*Chullin* 89a) maintains that this trait — whereby bounty and success cause increased humility, rather than an ever-larger ego — is the special aspect of the Jewish People that evokes Hashem's special love for His People.

8. *Mishlei* 21:8.

9. This seems to be analagous to the famous explanation of Rabbi Yisroel Salantar (mentioned in *Shiurei Daas*, Rabbi Yosef Leib Bloch, *Meluchah*), regarding the prediction that in the time preceding the advent of Mashiach, "the face of the generation [i.e., the leadership] will be as the face of a dog" (*Sotah*). Said Reb Yisroel, a dog runs ahead of his master, giving the appearance of leadership, but upon reaching a fork in the road it waits for its master to catch up and give direction. Then the dog once again "takes the lead." So too do today's "leaders" look anxiously towards the good will of the people, notwithstanding the fact that the masses may be totally uninformed and mistaken as to the correct path.

10. This may be why a king cannot forgive a slight to his honor (*Kesubos* 17a), for he has no personal honor; his honor is the honor of the people whom he leads, and one cannot forgive a slight to someone else's honor.

1929), gives us a graphic illustration of what typifies a genuine leader.

> During a meeting, when someone enters the room, who will arise from his chair to give it to the newly-arrived guest? The most distinguished, sensitive soul, who feels that the new guest is in a quandary when entering and finds no chairs available .... But the simpler man will not get up, for he fears that his honor will be lessened if he surrenders his place to the newly-arrived person.[11]

3. True Humility, True Greatness

The Maharal[12] tells that this is what our Sages meant when they said,[13] "Wherever you will find the Greatness of Hashem (mentioned in the Scriptures), you will find (mentioned in the same place) His Humility," because His Humility is His pre-eminent Greatness.[14]

Humility, which lies at the root of the ability to accept reproof, is a sign of intrinsic greatness, for there is no fear that my accepting your reproof will in some way diminish my stature. Humility, in its truest sense, is the awareness of my strengths — and the subsequent realization that these gifts are from Hashem and make me feel responsible to use them, rather than arrogant. As Rabbi Leib Chasman[15] tells us:

> It is obvious that a humble person is not someone who is not aware of his essence and abilities. Such a person is a fool and not humble. Who is humble? One who has a total recognition that all that he has is not his, but a result of the mercy of Hashem on His creatures — Who

---

11. *Shiurei Da'as, Meluchah,* ד"ה גם בחיינו.

12. 1512-1609, the famed Maharal of Prague.

13. *Megillah* 31a.

14. Beginning of Chapter One, *Nesiv HaAnavah.* The *Maharal* is commenting on why the Sages were stressing that in every place that you will find mention of Hashem's Greatness will you find mention of His Humility, why it is necessary to note this point in every place.

15. The *Mashgiach* of the yeshivos in Telshe and Chevron (1869-1935).

wished to bestow upon him kindliness, and gave him what He gave him! The more a person realizes this, the more humble he is.[16]

All greatness is intrinsic for nothing is truly mine if it is merely relative, for then it is only a reflection of your weakness or inferiority, not of my strength or ability.[17] It is therefore not a threat to me to be shown that I may be in error. If I have intrinsic worth, then my worth is not diminished by having been wrong about any particular matter. Two dramatic incidents in Jewish history portray the ability of great men to accept the fact that they have been wrong about something, even if it is a cherished, long-held belief.

• Firstly, when Yitzchak Avinu learned, suddenly and poignantly, that he had erred about his children: Yaakov was meant to be the father of the Chosen Nation, not Eisav, as Yitzchak had thought. Yitzchak's turnabout, as painful as it was, was instantaneous, without any attempt to rationalize. Yitzchak declared, firmly and dramatically, "And (indeed) he (Yaakov) shall be blessed!" [18]

• The second occurred many centuries later, when the *Tanna* Shimon, or (according to some) Nechemia HaAmsuni, who had taught that wherever the word "את" appears in Scriptures, it signifies that some matter beyond the simple message of the *pasuk* is to be included in the *pasuk's* teachings. At one point the students posed the question as to what can be included in the honor of Hashem, for it is written את ה' אלוקיך תירא. When Shimon (or Nechemia) demurred, the students asked, "What will be with all the times that you taught את as an inclusive word?" (If in even one place the rule would not hold true, then the entire principle's veracity was threatened.) The immortal reply was, "Just as I received reward for

---

16. *Ohr Yaheil*, vol. 2, *parshas Shemini.*

17. This is why the Maharal says that the *Mishnah* (*Avos* 4:1) stresses that wealth, strength and wisdom are of an intrinsic nature and not measured in term of financial assets, muscle power or information gleaned, for these are relative, depending on where one lives to determine whether this is really a huge sum of money, or truly physical strength, or indeed in possession of a wealth of information.

18. Our Sages tell us that when Eisav entered and Yitzchak discovered his mistake, he saw *Gehinnom* open up before him. See *Rashi, Bereishis* 27:33.

teaching, so too will I receive reward for desisting from teaching" (even though all of his lessons will now face possible rejection).[19]

Rabbi Zelig Pliskin tells of one of his most memorable moments during the years that he had studied in Telshe Yeshivah in Wickliffe, Ohio. One of the deans of the yeshivah was delivering the weekly *shiur* to the senior student body. In the middle of the shiur, a student asked a question. The dean said, as if to himself, "If so, then such-and-such will follow, which would mean such and such will be true. If so, I have been refuted." He then proceeded to step down, without making any attempt to defend his position, which without a doubt he could have done.

The great leaders of the Jewish people merited their leadership because they were eager to accept reproof, and this was indicative of their wisdom, as it says, "Reprove the wise man and he will love you."[20]

4. Clarity of Life Direction

Perhaps the major benefit to be gleaned from an ability to accept criticism is that you are more likely to have a clearer idea of the correct path to take in life. The Vilna Gaon says so explicitly:

> Because of his listening to criticism, he will know what (life) path to take.[21]

→ *Some Pragmatic Approaches*

There are several attitudes which a person can assume to help him learn to desire criticism.

1. Focusing on the End Result

One of the functions of the intellect is to enable a person to look into the future and to act on his insight as if it were the

---

19. *Pesachim* 22a.

20. *Mishlei* 9:8.

21. *Mishlei* 15:33.

present. This is what our Sages meant when they said[22] that a wise man sees the future. For it is the sense of sight that acts upon the emotion, and it is emotion that causes us to act.[23] King Solomon said it, as well: "The wise man (has) his eyes in his head."[24] In Jewish tradition, a wise man acts on what he knows; he is not content merely to know it.

This means that a person can develop the ability to undergo certain discomfort now, because he or she is already able to feel that the benefits of a certain future act will outweigh the present discomfort.

In yeshivah, I give the students the following exercise:

> When on a bus, a person can occasionally seek out the faces of old people, and identify those who lived a secular, materialistic life and those who lived a life guided by spiritual values. The contrast is stark. People who lived a life centered around physicality are more likely to show signs of unhappiness, of a sense of being in a world no longer theirs. The faces of those who lead a spiritual-centered life, however, are more likely (in the absence of painful disease) to reflect a sense of continued purpose and usefulness.

It is the use of the sense of sight in the present that helps us act today to affect our future. This may be because a wise person, when "seeing" the future, is in reality "pulling" that picture into his present and thereby arousing his emotions so as to act on it.

But not only can a look to the future help us bear the difficulties of hearing criticism, it can actually make it a rewarding experience.

The Vilna Gaon, in his Commentary to *Mishlei* (9:8), gives a striking parable for this idea — the mirror that a woman uses so as to ferret out any traces of grime that could ruin her complexion:

---

22. *Tamid* 32a.

23. The Vilna Gaon says that emotion is related more to sight than to hearing, and it was for this reason that Moshe was more affected when he saw the Golden Calf, even though Hashem Himself had already informed him of the Calf's existence.

24. *Koheles* 2:15.

For it is the way of the righteous that reproof for them is like the mirrors of those women who congregated at the entrance to the *Mishkan* ... A mirror that enlarges any trace of dirt is to be preferred, for she wants to remove it... and then she will be cleaner and purer. So too do the righteous desire and love someone who will *exaggerate* (emphasis mine) the sin that they may have done, even if in truth it is small, for they will thereby become pure and clean.

It is with a sense of triumph and joy that each imperfection is discovered, for it is that discovery which will enable my future to be better and purer. This leads us to a second attitude that will enable us to endure the pain of correct criticism.

2. The Result, not the Intention

One of the differences between intellect and emotion is that while emotion is basically experiential, and rooted in the present, the intellect is capable, as stated, of reaching into the future and concretizing it to the degree that it becomes part of one's present.[25]

Often, people criticize us for the wrong reasons. Instead of being a way of expressing love or friendship, it is a vehicle by which they vent their frustrations upon us. Either they feel the need to put us down, to ease their own feelings of low self-worth, or they enjoy poking fun at someone or something. Sometimes their motivations are more sinister, for they wish to deter us from accomplishing something worthwhile and wish to belittle us or our project.

We often understandably balk at accepting such criticism, feeling instead the sting of the reproof.

It is at this point that we must bear in mind the words of Rabbi Chaim Shmuelevitz:[26]

---

25. This is related to maturity, for the more mature a person becomes, the more he is able to concretize the abstract; one application of this is being able to make some type of sacrifice or compromise today, which is more concrete, for a better tomorrow, which is more abstract. The ability to make a real or perceived sacrifice in This World for the sake of meriting the World to Come is therefore an expression of maturity of the highest order. It would therefore follow that developing maturity in other areas will help a person in this most mature of endeavors, earning eternal life in the World to Come.

26. The beloved and revered *Rosh Yeshivah* of Mirrer Yeshivah, Yerushalayim (1901-1978).

The *Midrash* tells[27] the following story:

> A man, having been bitten by a scorpion, rushed to the river, where the water would help him save himself. Arriving there, he saw a young child drowning, and saved him. When the child thanked him for having saved his life, the man replied, "Don't thank me, thank the scorpion."

Reb Chaim applied this concept to married life. Quoting the *Gemarah*[28] that notes that even though a person may feel that his wife is not treating him properly, he should appreciate her for raising his children, and for helping him ward off the temptations of the *yeitzer hora*. True, her actions are not necessarily done for his sake, for, after all, they are her children as well; nonetheless, he should feel gratitude for the results, for the fact that his children are receiving a proper upbringing.[29]

When faced with criticism, we must learn to look at the benefit to be accrued, with the improved quality of life that we will have when we learn to rectify the fault, and separate it from the motivations of our critic.

3. Self-Worth Is Intrinsic

Perhaps the most important thing to bear in mind is that my self-worth, as a Jew and creation of Hashem, is inalienable. I am intrinsically pure and beloved by Hashem even if I am imperfect in my actions. When I know this, I can bear the thought of having made a mistake or of being imperfect in my character make-up, knowing that as I strive to become better, Hashem's love for me is ever-present. Then I will be better able to hear from others where I have erred, as painful as it may be, and thank them for helping me better myself and draw closer to the Master of Perfection.

May we, as the *Sfas Emes* notes, become eligible for Hashem's blessing as a result of our ability to accept criticism.

---

27. Shemos Rabbah 1:32.

28. *Yevamos* 63a.

29. *Sichos Mussar 5732, Hakaras HaTov.*

Whisper Above the Roar: Making the Case for Subtlety

Rabbi Matis Roberts

✦ The Temptation to Preach

It is not exactly news that the Torah Jew is a cultural alien in modern American society. Moral relativity dominates the landscape, reducing all of the values we hold dear to a murky bog of hazy confusion. No value is sacred and no evil unacceptable. And there is no escape to the *shtetl* of our grandparents. Thus, in the midst of a world that produces constant violence, accepts wanton promiscuity, and debates the morality of abortion for convenience, we have to raise our children — as well as ourselves — to pursue a life of Divine service.

This situation creates a problem that has no easy solution. If we meet the world head on, we expose ourselves to a vast range of evils that inevitably affect our attitudes and actions — often to a much greater degree that can ever be tolerable. But insulating ourselves in religious enclaves also has its dangers. For one thing, it fosters a mentality of *Us vs. Them*, which can cause us to rationalize various moral compromises. In addition, there is no way to isolate ourselves completely, and many who grow up protected fall with a heavy thud when they are suddenly exposed. So we all juggle with various blends of protection and exposure, trying to imbue our children with the depth of faith and strength of character to carry them through life.

Because the evils we face are so pronounced, and the values so contrary to all we hold sacred, we clearly need to make full use of every resource at our disposal.

For this reason, there is a prevalent trend to feed our children a steady diet of strong moral messages, employing a great deal of preaching and sermonizing. Everything is spelled out in capital letters and exclamation points — and often broken down to simplistic levels of black and white.

Thus, many educators who use meaningful stories to convey the Torah's morals fortify their tales with lengthy sermons that dwell on those morals. The same applies to the realm of creativity. In school and at home there are many opportunities for children to express their spiritual values creatively. They do so in picture and in verse, in drama and in song, in prose and in poetry. Here, too, there is a common tendency to hammer away at the points being made — to express them so clearly and repeatedly that no one can possibly miss them.

But the clamor of relentless preaching often drowns out the message being conveyed. When we spell things out so clearly that there is no challenge in receiving them, we fail to engage a child's mind — or anything more than his superficial interest. And when we repeat ourselves over and over again until our point is coming out of their ears, they begin to associate the values we teach with the suffocation they experience in learning them.

✦ The Penetrating Power of Subtlety

The Torah, however, prescribes a different approach to cultivating values, one that is exemplified by the way we celebrate the Passover festival. At that time, we devote an entire night to reliving the Exodus from Egypt, and a full seven days to its commemoration. Why then, asks Rabbi Yosef Leib Bloch, do we fill

our *Seder* with mere symbols and vague allusions? Why not really bring those events to life — with plays and reenactment of all
that occurred? Wouldn't that drive home the lessons of the *seder*
much more effectively? Rabbi Bloch answers with an insight
that is absolutely vital in our age of ultra-decibels:

> True spiritual achievement comes through those
> things that leave only subtle impressions but do not
> arouse emotional intensity. These, and these alone,
> can reach the delicate strands of the human soul and
> inspire them. That which is more concrete and
> conspicuous can bring a person to great passion, and
> may seem — for the moment — to make a deep
> impression on him. But its impact is completely
> absorbed by his more superficial emotions, and it
> never reaches the finer, loftier elements within his
> soul. Therefore, we relive the Exodus from Egypt
> with stories, symbols and allusions rather than with
> dramatic presentations, for that is the way to create
> lasting impressions that will not be easily forgotten
> (*Shiurei Da'as, Nishmas HaTorah*).

In other words, the more subtle the approach, the deeper it
penetrates. Rabbi Bloch sees this as inherent in human nature;
the passions that play on the surface dull the effect upon the
deeper emotions within. It is also true on another level. We all
have some resistance to things that accuse us of falling short, or
that demand from us increased effort and energy. Thus, when
something addresses our overt feelings, it also arouses our
inner defenses. "What does he mean: I'm not good enough?"
Or, "How can I possibly try any harder?" In many cases, we
find excuses to negate the effect of that which moved us — in
order to protect ourselves from their implications. The subtler
influences, however, make no demands or accusations. They
merely plant seeds of awareness — awareness of our obligations and our capabilities that steadily rise to the surface of our
psyche and urge us forward.

✦ Maintaining a Balance
of the Overt and the Subtle

Don't get me wrong. We surely need to learn, and to teach, clear moral lessons — to define the lines between right and wrong and between good and evil in no uncertain terms. But we must also maintain a balance of the overt and the subtle if we want our messages to penetrate. We need to create a general atmosphere where our children can internalize the Torah's values — naturally, comfortably and effectively. We need, in other words, to foster the "cultural osmosis" of *Yiddishkeit* without the ceaseless drum roll of overstated moralization.

Teaching, for example, *can* be done with subtlety. We *can* get our points across in ways that give breathing space to their recipients. One of today's outstanding yeshivah *rebbe'im* uses this approach: "I begin every class with a story, but I never explain its moral. That I leave for the students to figure out themselves." This is not just intellectually challenging. It also enables his students to plug into the story at their level of devotion — and to thereby increase that level.

The same applies to creative activities. A play or a story that depicts *mesiras nefesh* (self sacrifice) does not need an accompanying speech to drive the point home. The medium itself gets the message across much more effectively. And it enables the children to relate to the concept on *their* terms, in ways that are meaningful to *them*. This allows them to embrace the moral wholeheartedly, without resistance from any feeling of doubt or inadequacy that may fester within.

✦ The Jellybean Approach

With a bit of imagination, this concept of subtlety opens up whole new worlds of opportunity in *chinuch*. Here, for example, is an idea that has been used by teachers in the classroom, but is equally applicable at home. Bring home a jar of jellybeans — or of any other item of minimal value — and introduce the following arrangement: Every time a child does something that is difficult for him, he gets a jellybean. This will vary from one child to the next. For the "absent-minded professor," remembering to clear his place or hang up his coat may be an achievement. One who is highly competitive deserves a reward if he accepts a smaller portion (of dessert, not spinach) or a less expensive present without complaining. Kindness and cleanliness, making a careful *berachah*, keeping one's bedtime — these accomplishments and many others are all worth jellybeans for those to whom they present a challenge. When the jellybean jar is emptied, the entire family is rewarded with a special trip, treat or activity.

However, a child earns a jellybean only if someone else recommends him for one. It can be a parent or one of his siblings, but he cannot endorse himself. (Obviously, the parents must decide if the deed qualifies for a reward.) Since the ultimate goal is far more valuable than the immediate prize, each child will recommend the others as often as possible. Thus, the cry of "It's not fair" that fills many homes is replaced with an atmosphere of mutual support, everyone rooting for each other to earn jellybeans. At the same time, the children learn to appreciate each other's diverse strengths and weaknesses. This fosters the awareness that true achievement is measured in terms of personal effort, and that fair treatment must always take that into consideration. And, most important, this is all done smoothly and naturally, without the speeches and lectures that make a child feel like doing something wicked just to get the sour taste of preaching out of his mouth.

→ The Unmistakable Message

These are but a few applications; the essential point is the principle itself. It is a principle that is clearly expressed in the Torah: *And behold Hashem passed by, and a great and mighty wind was shattering the mountains and breaking rocks before Hashem — Hashem is not in the wind. And after the wind, a quaking — Hashem is not in the quaking. And after the quaking, fire — Hashem is not in*

the fire. And after the fire, a still, subtle voice (Melachim I 19:11-12).
The Gemara (Chagigah 16a) concludes: And behold Hashem passed by,
i.e., within that still, subtle voice.

The message here is unmistakable. Fire and brimstone can proclaim G-d's presence, but they cannot be Its carrier. True spirituality is found within the still, subtle voice — the voice that penetrates to the core of the human soul.

Teaching Moral Sensitivity — and Truth

Rabbi Heshy Grossman

"Sheker Ein Lo Raglayim"

✦ The Kohlberg Attraction

M oral development has become a major factor in educational theory. *Mussar* and *middos* have received renewed attention and emphasis in recent years, in recognition that good character traits do not merely happen on their own, but must be inculcated into children by parents and teachers.

The non-Jewish world, in its own way, has also become keenly aware of the need for developing proper ethics and morals, with the theories of Harvard's Lawrence Kohlberg receiving much attention in the academic world. Kohlberg's teachings have had such a major impact on recent trends in educational psychology and methodology, that attempts have been made to use his findings in Jewish education, as well. In fact, for the past number of years, a group of Jewish educators has met on campuses of prestigious universities to study Kohlberg's "Six

Stages of Moral Development" and their specific application to Hebrew Day Schools.

Though the debates at Harvard and U.C.L.A. are not always within the purview of interest of the Torah Jew, a short synopsis of Kohlberg's ideas will demonstrate why they hold such mesmerizing influence over many Jewish educators.

Kohlberg has studied various cultures and suggests that there are six stages of development (with a possible seventh) that incorporate universal moral principles shared by all societies. These stages range from the most childish self-involved stage to the most abstract and altruistic. The six stages as delineated by Kohlberg are:

- The Stage of Punishment and Obedience,
- The Stage of Individual Instrumental Purpose and Exchange,
- The Stage of Mutual Interpersonal Expectations, Relationships and Conformity,
- The Stage of Social System and Conscience Maintenance,
- The Stage of Prior Rights and Social Contract, and
- The Stage of Universal Ethical Principles.

A cursory glance at their titles indicates how Kohlberg's system aims at guiding a person into full flowering as an ideal moral human being, for at the final, highest stage, specific laws or social agreements are valid only to the extent that they are in accord with principles of justice and equality. Purity of motive is a given at this stage, and man does what is right because he has accepted the validity of certain principles and has become committed to them.

Virtue is taught through the Socratic method of creating dissatisfaction in students regarding their inadequate knowledge of the good. The teacher facilitates their development by presenting ethical dilemmas, for which the students have no ready solution. In the ensuing discussion, the students become exposed to the opinions of others, and are most likely to prefer arguments based on a moral stage one level above their own. Moral action is strongly correlated with moral thinking, so it is assumed that the person's actions will rise to the level of his thoughts, and a more moral human being will eventually emerge from the process.

Substitute "Torah and *Halachah*" for "Justice and Equality," and one begins to understand the tantalizing appeal this theory holds for many Orthodox educators. Since our goal is to produce Torah-observant, ethical Jews, the promise of Kohlberg to direct behavior is indeed attractive.

Take, for example, Jerry Friedman, who serves on the National Council of Jewish Federations as well as on the Los Angeles Federation Council, heads the Institute on Cognitive Moral Education, based on the Kohlberg approach, and has become a nationally recognized expert in the field.

He lectures on ethical sensitizing across the country and has been praised for his work by Rabbi Alvin I. Schiff, executive vice president of Greater New York's Board of Jewish Education. His work in the Sinai Akiba Academy in Los Angeles was praised in the L.A. *Jewish Journal* as a more successful replacement of the "traditional reliance on the study of Torah and *halachah* (Jewish law) and the teacher or *rebbe* as a role model to instill ethical behavior."

A closer analysis of the philosophic moorings that anchor Kohlberg's system, however, should give pause to those who would rush to embrace concepts without questioning the foundations that may belie their surface attraction.

✦ Morality: by Man's Reasoning or G-d's Guidance?

The stages of moral development, delineated by Kohlberg, are meant only to set the framework for defining conflicting claims and choosing between them. They do not attempt to answer the question, "Is there such a thing as an objective moral standard?" — which is essentially a religious question.

On the heels of Socrates, who rejected the idea that "x is just" or "ought to be done" because "x is a command of G-d" or "x is in the Bible," Kohlberg distinguishes between moral and religious forms of thinking and discourse. Morality is a *decision-making process*, and moral principles are exercised by making choices in resolving moral conflicts. Moral development, in his view, occurs regardless of whether the individual has any particular religious beliefs.

Torah Judaism takes a different approach, for we believe that "virtue" is synonymous with conforming with G-d's Will or command. As opposed to Kohlberg, we believe that *moral* judgment and consciousness are singularly derived from *religious* judgment and consciousness and not from human insight or understanding. Though this difference in approach should be obvious, the headlong rush towards Kohlberg and his friends on the part of some Jewish educators does demonstrate that they recognize a desperate need to guide our children in their moral development. In addition, however, it shows that the pervasive influence of secular culture filters down to the Torah community more than we care to admit.

First, then, let us clarify the Torah view on the subject: On what basis do we determine what is and is not *moral*?

To be sure, every society has its criteria for what is moral and what is not, what is good and what is evil. In the Torah frame of reference, the operative terms of moral thinking are not limited to good and evil, nor to right and wrong, but actually extend to the realm of *emes* and *sheker*, truth and falsehood. That is, a course prescribed by Torah is consistent with the Creator's designs for the world, and one forbidden by Torah runs contrary to His will — which is the essence of all existence.

With this in mind, we can understand that the moral decisions and conflicts facing a Jew are not a choice between two valid alternatives, or even between two options of varying degrees of acceptability, but the realization that there is only one viable possibility. It is here that it becomes obvious that we and society at large are on divergent paths, and it is precisely this point that non-Orthodox groups cannot grasp. An approach contrary to Torah is a path of falsehood, essentially illusory — not only without value, but without substance. The Torah Jew cannot grant it legitimacy by acknowledging it as a path to be considered; he surely would not teach his children to deal with falsehood as one of several viable alternatives.

✦ Beginning at an Early Age

At a very early age, we begin creating an awareness in our children of the awesome responsibility that awaits them — that they realize their fullest potential as people of the Torah. In the struggles that await them, they should choose good not only for its material benefit or because it is intellectually gratifying, but because one has no other choice if he wishes to be a Torah Jew. To be sure, this is achieved by exercising freedom of choice, but in this context it refers to the ability to acknowledge one's functional imperatives and to act accordingly. Man touches eternity through submission to G-d's Will, eschewing submission to the self, or in the words of the Brisker Rav, *"Bechirah chofshis*/free will means choosing to do what you may not wish to do."* At every level of maturity, man will confront new manifestations of the same moral conflict: the battle between *emes* and *sheker*. "Falsehood" is a matter of responding to material want and physical desire. "Truth" is humbling one's own will before the Will of G-d. The resolution of this dilemma is always the same: To determine what the Torah's directives are, and to do one's utmost to live by them.

✦ Where Kohlberg's System Fails

From a Torah perspective, there is no essential difference between Kohlberg's stage one and six, or any other such plateau of awareness, conflict and resolution, no matter how valid they may be in their own terms.

Kohlberg's moral standards are man-oriented, with conflicts resolved through the presentation of moral dilemmas. This method, which utilizes a rational process, cannot be reconciled with Torah's approach to education, which sees human opinion as an irrelevant factor in determining correct behavior. Moral conflicts are not resolved through use of broad principles, admirable though they may be; to the contrary, any decision that is self-centered, without reference to the Divine Will, cannot be moral.

Though a person may agree that every word of the Torah is true, and conform to its teachings, that alone is insufficient. We are guided by the clear declaration of *Rashi* (*Sanhedrin* 90a), regarding the person who believes in *techiyas hameisim* (resurrection of the dead), but does not accept its Torah origins: "*Mah lanu u'l'emunaso? V'chi meheichan hu yode'a shekein hu?* What [value does] his belief [have] to us? And from whence does he know that it is so?" One cannot accept the mitzvos in a sequence of "*nishma v'naaseh* — we will understand them and then perform them," for the directives of the Torah are an imperative of nature, not the end product of a host of enlightened choices.

→ *Some Practical Considerations*

In our open society, we are subject daily to a myriad of words that aim to entice us and attract us towards whatever product is currently offered, be it a new car or a recycled idea. Such is the characteristic of Eisav — "*tzayid befiv* — he has game in his mouth" — i.e., powers of entrapment. And though his advances are often rejected, we frequently forget that this confrontational framework, within which human beings are rendered vulnerable to persuasive seductions, is inimical to Torah, where truth is paramount, self-evident and should not be forced to compete with alternative "truths."

Torah is not to be "sold" as a commodity to our students, who will then weigh and measure its words in light of what they currently hold true. Such an approach holds the Torah accountable to human standards, and despite its shining luminescence, its words become subject to questioning and scrutiny, risking weakened commitment and even rejection.

The words of our Sages must be understood not as "interpretation," but as "revelation" — every nuance opening vistas of understanding into both the depths of the human psyche and the secrets of creation.

While we certainly wish to encourage children to probe and analyze, the process is a quest to uncover hidden gateways rather than a struggle to accept convincing argumentation. The

Sages are not merely men of superior reasoning, whose words are open to discussion. Rather, they are standard bearers of an image once revealed, whose teachings stand as witness: A faithful rendition of Sinai for subsequent generations. It is not *divrei Chazal* (the words of the rabbis of Talmud) that need scrutiny, but rather, the outlook of the recipient, who upon recognizing a discordant note strives to re-adjust his *Weltanschauung* accordingly.

It is precisely at this point that the weakness of Kohlberg becomes apparent. Take for example "Sharon's Dilemma" — a classic example of the Kohlberg approach. [Ed. Note: See the end of this article.]

This dilemma is designed to create genuine conflict in the individual participant, and to provoke a lively class discussion of the issues involved. Students are encouraged to take a position and defend it, but at the same time to empathize with and tolerate contrasting views.

Observers of a class discussion following the presentation of such dilemmas have described the classroom atmosphere as "student-oriented" — "debate-like" — "frustrating — no clear answer," while the teacher's facilitative role has been characterized as "open to all ideas" — "did not have the answer" — "quiet much of the time."

Clearly, the utilization of this and similar dilemmas, and the manner in which it is presented, should pose almost insurmountable problems for those of us who view ethical behavior and sensitivity as functions of *limud haTorah* and *mussar* — the source material where one carries out his and her quest for eternal truth. The "Dilemma" story is designed to arouse feelings of personal loyalty and friendship, and to direct students to focus upon and clarify their own opinions.

In contrast, the Torah Jew is certainly obliged to be aware of these feelings, but they are to be viewed as pitfalls, rather than as a source for decision making. *Ki hashochad ye'aver einei chachamim* — one's personal view can only be viewed as a hindrance from a perspective that envisions absolute truth as an objective reality. The mere hint of friendship would disqualify a judge from legal proceedings, all the more so the lay individual, who must eliminate any personal bias if there is to be any hope of moral development.

→ *A Traditional Alternative*

Perhaps a fresh look at a more traditional approach would bear fruitful results as we strive to preserve our own moral system in the hearts and minds of our children.

Rabbi Shlomo Wolbe, writing of the necessity for *shimush talmidei chachamim* (apprenticing Torah scholars), points in amazement to the diligence with which our sages attached themselves to their teachers, even to the extent of entering their private quarters to observe firsthand how a Jew should behave. *"Torah hi v'lilmod ani tzarich* — it is Torah and I must learn" (*Berachos* 62a).

And what of the students of today, many of whom rarely have the opportunity to even see a flesh-and-blood *talmid chacham*, much less come in contact with the truly great sages of yesteryear? What are they to do?

> How does one know that when one hears [Torah] from a Jew of modest stature that it should be received as though he hears it from a person wise in Torah? The passage says, "[Let these matters] that I command you today ...." And not just from a wise man, but as though it were from the *Sanhedrin* .... And not ... just from the *Sanhedrin*, but as though it were from Moshe. And not ... just from Moshe, but as though from the "one shepherd" — G-d Himself (*Koheles Rabbah* 12:11).

Rabbi Wolbe highlights this passage as illustrating that the value and impact of a message is not dependent upon the greatness of the teacher. To the contrary, one who listens properly can find the words of the most modest of individuals as illuminating as if they were uttered by G-d Himself!

Shemias ha'ozen — proper listening, the second of the forty-eight qualities by which Torah is acquired — is the key ingredient of *shimush talmidei chachamim*. Teaching our students to listen properly to the words of our Sages,

> to abandon the urge to speak on one's own and develop new modes of thought, but rather find sustenance and support in listening to the words of the *Rav* with precision and exactitude.
>
> To be sure, we are not speaking of blind acceptance, but a deep and all-encompassing comprehension, to the greatest extent possible.
>
> … not to surrender in any way a direct understanding; to the extent a student serves his Rav, he will increase his knowledge, strengthen his wisdom, and purify his independent approach to an understanding of the Torah (Rabbi Shlomo Wolbe, in *Alei Shur*, p. 76).

✣ *The Role of the Teacher*

Challenging students to grow beyond themselves — beyond their limited perceptions — is *our* definition of moral development. The proper role of the teacher in this setting should be to inspire his students to broaden their horizons. This cannot be accomplished by merely exposing them to different ideas, but rather, by demonstrating through word and deed how an individual can subsume and submerge his own identity to the directives of the Torah. In short, he must recreate *Maamad Har Sinai* — the assembly at Mount Sinai — where the entire nation was reborn. His position is never neutral, for he must act as guide, to measure the students' responses on the scales of truth and falsehood; to locate the *sheker* inherent in every difficulty; and to bring his charges closer to *emes*.

Moral growth will never be achieved by an approach that demands less, for unless change is expected from our students, they will merely co-opt whatever information they acquire to their preexistent mindset. Only minor adjustments will be made to satisfy any conflict, rather than the complete transformation that *emes* sometimes requires.

Though the teacher need not be a world class scholar, he must be true to the Torah he teaches. A disembodied understanding of the lesson he is teaching is not Truth. Only if he fulfills the task set out by *Mesillas Yesharim* — "*she'yisbarer v'yisames eitzel ha'adam...* that [these teachings] be clear and truthful to him" — can he be portrayed as a living manifestation of an *emes* worthy of emulation. The truth will speak for itself — "*Chochmos bachutz tarona birchovos titein kolah* — wisdom will resound in the streets, and give voice in the avenues." To adduce support from external sources can only detract from its glistening perfection.

The one dilemma for which we *should* prepare our students is the conflict wherein man is obliged to "choose life": the battle between his personal inclination and G-d's command. This conflict is always with us, and within the same parameters; but unlike the Kohlberg approach, its resolution is consistent at every level of development: to be determined by "*What is G-d's Will in this situation?*" What changes in the process of growing is the amount of truth we have accepted to date, and how much more knowledgeable we have become, how much of a *maamin* we have become.

Torah is not merely one more product in the marketplace of ideas. From our vantage point, all manmade theories suffer from one basic shortcoming: they lack the Divine perspective that defines morality. Torah Judaism is not one more niche in an expansive continuum but a means of existence that transcends time and space. We may cajole and entice our students to enter our world, but human constructs of morality will never suffice if we are to make a lasting impact on our children and students — "*V'im ani l'atzmi mah ani*? And if I am for myself, what am I?"

True moral elevation can only progress from a commitment to keeping G-d's commandments. Without this initial commitment, the philosopher at stage six is no closer to G-d than the innocent of stage one. While Kohlberg aims to transform a selfish brute into a sensitive human being who reflects upon his actions, Judaism's goal is the perfect man, G-d's partner in creation, whose life is sanctified by every deed, following a precisely delineated code of conduct.

✦ Sharon's Dilemma

Sharon and her best friend Jill walked into a department store to shop. As they browsed, Jill saw a blouse she really liked and told Sharon she wanted to try the blouse on. While Jill went to the dressing room, Sharon continued to shop.

Soon Jill came out of the dressing room wearing her coat. She caught Sharon's attention with her eyes and glanced down at the blouse under her coat. Without a word, Jill turned and walked out of the store.

Moments later the store security officer, a salesclerk and the store manager approached Sharon. "That's her, that's one of the girls. Check her bags," blurted the clerk. The security officer pointed to a sign over the door saying that the store reserved the right to inspect bags and packages. Sharon gave him her bag. "No blouse in here," he told the manager. "Then I know the other girl has it," the clerk said. "I saw them just as plain as anything. They were together on this." The security officer then asked the manager if he wanted to follow through on the case. "Absolutely," he insisted. "Shoplifting is getting to be a major expense in running this store. I can't let shoplifters off the hook and expect to run a successful business."

The security officer turned to Sharon. "What's the name of the girl you were with?" he asked. Sharon looked up at him silently. "Come on now; come clean," said the security officer. "If you don't tell us, you can be charged with the crime or with aiding the person who committed the crime."

Question: Should Sharon tell Jill's name to the security officer? Why or why not?

Teacher/Facilitator Probe Questions on Sharon's Dilemma

- Would it make any difference if Sharon and Jill did not know each other very well? Why or why not?
- Is it ever all right to lie? To break the law? If it is, under what circumstances?

- *Would it make a difference if Jill had recently reported Sharon for cheating on a test at school? Why or why not?*
- *What would happen to society if everybody were to lie, steal or disobey laws whenever they felt like it or to protect friends?*
- *What would the store-owner want Sharon to do? Why? The security officer? Why? Her parents? Why? The police? Why? What obligation does she have to each of these people?*

News Clippings

Rabbi Nisson Wolpin

→ *"Indict Rabbi for ..."*
"Rabbi Accused of ..."

T he headlines scream it and the TV reporters intone it with all the gravity of a judge pronouncing an irrevocable verdict.

I am not aware of any mechanism for nullifying someone's *semichah*. Nor am I convinced that we should want to do so, on the basis of a news story, for indictments and accusations in and of themselves are not grounds for condemnation. But the pain and the *chillul Hashem* that emanate from these headline-making stories are unmistakable. They bring to mind an incident of some 35 years ago that deserves to be forgotten ... except for its nagging relevance.

Rabbi Yehonasan Z., scion of a well-known chassidic rabbinical family, was indicted as the key figure in a gem smuggling operation. Rather than free himself by fingering the true culprit, Reb Yehonasan — in fact, an unwitting participant — took the rap and went to prison .... Well, not exactly. Reb

Yehonasan "disappeared," to be replaced by a clean-shaven fellow, sans *payos*, in a business suit, "Johnny" Z.

When a shocked chassid reported Reb Yehonasan's transformation to the late Satmar Rav, he allegedly commented, "Reb Yehonasan earned himself *Olam Haba* with that clipping."

Now, there's nothing necessarily wrong with Jews in traditional or chassidic garb engaging in the professions or business. Nor are matters made worse by the fact that they were once ordained as rabbis. But so much pain and unfavorable publicity could be avoided if all people who devote their major efforts to pursuits outside of the religious arena would be content with the pride they derive from their proud *semichah* certificates on the walls of our studies, while they head their business/professional letterhead and telephone listings as "Mister."

Honesty and integrity are everybody's obligation, but titles should be the exclusive domain of the practicing clergy.

When the Penny Vanishes From the Purse ...

Avrohom Chaim Feuer

The key to the Temple's ruin and its
future reconstruction

On the 17th of Tammuz, the wall of Jerusalem was broken through.

During the summer months of Tammuz and Av we painfully review the events which caused the *Beis HaMikdash,* the House of G–d, to be destroyed. We are told that the furious flame of senseless hate, *sinas chinom,* burned our second Sanctuary and turned its splendor into ashes. One might fail to comprehend what could have stoked the flames of hatred to such destructive force. *Chazal,* our Sages who penetrate the surface of events with their Torah vision, offer: *"For their love for money, they came to hate one another"* (*Yerushalmi Yoma*).

This answer touches on man's basic nature — for man, compared to most lesser creatures, is almost totally lacking in natural defenses and thus desperately craves for a sense of safety and security. Men are powerfully drawn to whatever seems to promise them this protection and insurance. In the time of the First *Beis HaMikdash* pagan forces impressed many Jews as being their guardian angels, and they placed their confidence in *avo-dah zarah*. The sun, the moon, the wind, the trees and other natural phenomena provided security in a panic-filled present and against the perils of an unforseeable future.

→ *Deflected Desire*

The destruction of the First Temple and the Babylonian *galus* shook the people back to their senses, and they came to recognize that the Creator is the supreme and exclusive protector. Thus, they merited their return to Zion. But the attraction of *avodah zarah* continued to taunt them and they felt too weak to withstand it. So the leaders of the time, under the guidance of the Prophet Zachariah, took drastic and extraordinary action: They prayed that this *yetzer hara* be eradicated from their passions and their hearts. Their unusual request was granted (*Yoma* 69b). But the *yetzer hara* of *avodah zarah* could not be removed without a different temptation taking its place, for the balance between the attractions of good and evil must be maintained to present man with free choice. The Ari Hakodosh, Rabbeinu Chaim (the brother of the Maharal), and the Chida, among others, tell us that desire for money took its place. This desire for possessing money proved insatiable — an appetite impossible to still. Even if a man's needs be few, his possessions — no matter how vast — never seem sufficient.

> "He who loves silver will never be content with silver" (*Koheles* 5:9).
> "He who possesses one hundred, desires two. He who possesses two hundred, desires four" (*Koheles Rabbah* 1:34).

An endless, vicious, frustrating cycle. When one owns nothing, he has nothing to lose and nothing to protect. But he who has tasted the sweetness of having one hundred is concerned that his hundred remain with him. The only way he can ascertain that is to prove that he can duplicate this amount. Once he has demonstrated this ability to his satisfaction, he has also experienced the incomparable thrill of possessing two hundred, and he cannot be secure with perpetuating this sensation until he duplicates this sum again....and again....

As a wise and audacious beggar once said to a king: "Your Highness is really needier than I am, for I need so little to be comfortable and secure, and you need so very much to be at ease." Insecurity is without limits and so is greed.

→ *True Security*

Man's true source of security, his *bitachon,* should be with his Creator. G–d is boundless and so is His protection boundless. No security can compare with this. But man, in his foolishness, has transferred his account; he has withdrawn from G–d and has deposited his faith with his funds and his finances. It follows that to replace a boundless, protective Creator he must forever seek endless, unlimited supplies of money. Thus did the Sages comment: "Man does not die with even half of his desires in his grasp."

As long as man seeks his security in tangible possessions, he will never realize complete security until he has every last cent in the world in his grasp. And more. As long as his neighbor has any possessions of his own he is reduced to a ruthless rival, a competitor who jeopardizes his security and must be quashed. It is not difficult to see how, "Because they loved money, they despised one another."

→ *"On Account of Kamtza and Bar Kamtza Jerusalem Was destroyed"*

While this tragic tale of intense hatred is well known, it is interesting to note that Kamtza — or *kamtzan* — literally means a miser whose fist is clamped over his coins. It was this obsession with money that aroused men to horrible feuds and bitter vendettas.

→ The Ultimate Defilement

The fate of the Second *Beis HaMikdash* was irrevocably sealed when the gold rush entered the Temple grounds. This was the ultimate defilement. For this House had been set aside as a spiritual haven, a refuge from worldly pursuits and greed: "One may not enter the *Har HaBayis* (the Temple Mount) while wearing his money belt" (*Berachos* 62b).

In the administration of the Sanctuary, a cost-consciousness had no place: "Poverty is not befitting an abode of wealth" (*Menachos* 89b).

The Kohanim themselves were personally divorced from the pursuit of personal profit, for they possessed no real estate or farms. The priestly gifts they received were not even considered "dividends" or tokens of gratitude from the people. "The priests eat from the table of G–d."

In the Second Temple this changed. The post of Kohen Gadol — the High Priest — was sold annually to the highest bidder. The High Priest in turn misused his power to enhance his personal standing (*Yoma* 8b-9a).

> *Rav Yosef said: I discern a conspiracy here. Marsa bas Baysas brought King Yannai three pots of dinarim in order that he appoint her husband, Yehoshua ben Gamla, Kohen Gadol* (*Yevamos* 61a).

Religion became profit-oriented, and the Temple as its focal point had to be destroyed.

Is there any hope for reconstruction? Is there anything we can do to speed its advent? Listen to the prophetic voices of old as they describe a new order which will someday reign:

Rabbi Michel of Zlotchov would point to the prophetic vision of *parshas Ha'azinu*: "And there is no strange god with Him" (*Devorim* 32:12). "This is an assurance that there will be no idolators in your midst. Another explanation: There will be no one engaged in merchantry in your midst" (*Sifre*, ibid.).

If one invests all his trust in merchandise and commerce,

this too can become an object of worship: *"As for the merchant, the balances of deceit are in his hands; he loves to extort"* (Hoshea 12:8).

"They rely on dishonest profits for they are dealers in fraud. Therefore do they proclaim: I have waxed rich, what need have I for G–d?" (*Rashi*, ibid.)

The very last words of one of the three last prophets, Zachariah, predict a new era in the Temple. (It was he who was responsible for eradicating the *yetzer hara* for *avodah zarah*.)

> And on that day there will no longer be a merchant in the House of the L–rd of Hosts (*Zachariah* 14:21).
> No longer will there be traders in the Beis HaMikdash (*Targum*).

The Temple will be rebuilt when we become like the Kohanim — who depend on G–d's table, rather than on their own.

✣ *Footfalls of Mashiach*

There is an old *tzaddik* residing today in the Holy Land, whose words of *mussar* discipline thousands from far and wide, and whose personal life exemplifies this trait of utter dependence on G–d's table. He is a gravely serious man, earnest and composed. One day his students observed that their master was extraordinarily light-hearted, and they who dared inquired: "Rebbe, why the unusual gaiety?"

The *tzaddik* replied, "All of my years I have depended on a meager income and even this was erratic in coming. I knew full well that I could not depend on those irregular payments for my subsistence, and I came to realize that I existed only by the grace and direct generosity of G–d. I lived from His open hand. Some time ago, however, I began to prosper, my income increased and became more regular — I began to count on the constant unfailing payments. This became my security, my support, and I slowly slipped out of the arms of G–d. But now, *baruch Hashem*, I have slipped behind and I have not received any income in months. How wonderful it is to be back at G–d's table — and you wonder why I rejoice?"

It is just such men who can hear the *ikvesa d'Meshicha* — the footfalls of *Mashiach* — drawing near in our time. The rest of us are deaf to these steps, for the coins jingling in our pockets are drowning out this long-awaited sound. But G–d wants us to pay attention and hear.

As the entire world was plunged into the Great Depression of 1929, the Chofetz Chaim observed that this economic crisis did not result from a shortage of money or food or goods. This was evident because all nations, both rich and poor, industrialized and primitive, suffered alike.

The *tzaddik* of Radin explained that a stable, thriving economy is not based solely on money. Credit is the cornerstone of world finances, and credit is based on mutual faith and trust. In 1929, there was no shortage of money — only a breakdown in the confidence that businesses and banks ordinarily place in one another. This abnormal crisis situation, this hostile climate of suspicion and doubt, was an act of Heaven punishing the world, measure for measure: When men abandon faith in Hashem and place all of their security in cash and credit, then G–d eventually destroys this false depository of trust. Men questioned the integrity and endurance of once-sacred contracts. Panic ensued, with the long, dark Depression in its wake.

We witness this in everyday life. Men who put their lives in G–d's hands know that no other man can do them harm, and so their thoughts and acts are not clouded by fears and suspicion of their neighbors. Those who lack this belief are bundles of jagged quivering nerves, for every man is a potential threat to their security.

In the time of *Mashiach*, international peace, understanding, cooperation and trust will be universal. As faith in G–d is restored, men will eventually regain faith in one another. When men will cease to be anamoured with their money, they will cease to hate one another.

→ *Rude Awakening for Mashiach's Arrival*

Ideally, we should recognize our utter dependence on G–d and — whether penniless or endowed with a generous abundance of resources — we should conceive of every cent we possess as bread from His table. Any measure of affluence should be understood as a Divine trust for us to execute with responsibility and fealty to His wishes. Failing this, G–d resorts to tactics of shock to awaken us to the bankruptcy of the faith we have invested in our own powers of self-support. He then shakes the confidence we have placed in our bulging coffers and fat bank accounts. *Depression ... recession ... inflation ... devaluation ... price freeze ... profit squeeze ... wage slash ... stock market slips ... unemployment rise ... soaring taxes* — all of these elements of economic instability have a definite purpose and are part of a Divine plan. *Chazal* tell us with great emphasis that the confusion, the anarchy, and the audacity that mark the era preceding *Mashiach's* arrival are designed to shake our self-confidence and to make us realize that *"...we have no one to lean upon except our Father in Heaven"* (*Sotah* 49b).

Moshiach himself will come empty-handed, *"a pauper riding on a donkey"* (*Zachariah* 9:9).

"The Son of David will not come until the penny vanishes from the purse" (*Sanhedrin* 97a).

Only then will we hear the footfalls. Only then will our mourning turn to joy and will the ruins of the Temple will be rebuilt.

Tzedakah:
A Matter of Justice

Eliezer Cohen

"... as for me, if I haven't any money to give the needy,
I pine away from distress."
— Reb Chaim of Sanz

→ *Tzedakah vs. "Charity"*

*T*zedakah — its mere mention strikes a responsive chord in a Torah Jew's heart. Though compassion and benevolence are traits characteristic of *all* descendants of Avraham Avinu, there is no doubt that the Torah community is unique in both the quantity and the quality of its *tzedakah* giving. Who but a Torah Jew could fathom the kind of outpouring of funds that we witness on Purim, when rich and poor, old and young give until their pockets are literally empty? Where but in the Torah community are hundreds of thousands of dollars raised each year to pay for weddings, furniture and clothing for poor brides and grooms?

It seems obvious that there is a very basic distinction between the Torah Jew's concept of *tzedakah* and the universal concept of charity. The latter is seen as a manifestation of one's desire to help those less fortunate than himself. Webster's Unabridged Dictionary defines philanthropy in exactly this way, as "a desire to help mankind as indicated by acts of charity." Such a desire is certainly commendable, but if this is the sole drive behind one's benevolence, then the giving will usually cease as soon as it seems to be interfering with one's own personal needs. It does not take long for one to feel that this is actually happening. A Torah Jew, on the other hand, gives *tzedakah* with both compassion and a sense of obligation.

Yet each of us must still ask himself if his *tzedakah*-giving truly earns him the title of "*baal tzedakah*." The term "*baal*" denotes mastery in a specific area. (See *Malbim* to *II Samuel* 11:26.) A *baal tzedakah*, then, is one who has mastered this mitzvah in both approach and deed. If we will but begin to delve into the words of our sages on this subject, we will see that the title of "*baal tzedakah*" is not easily earned.

✦ *A Unique Commandment*

The giving of *tzedakah* as an obligation is based on the Torah's requirement that we assist those in need, as is written, "You shall not close your hand against your destitute brother" (*Devarim* 15:7). The obligation to give *tzedakah* may seem no different from any of the Torah's 613 mitzvos, but this is not so. Whereas with other mitzvos, "obligation" merely indicates that the commandment is incumbent upon one and is not a matter of choice, in regard to *tzedakah* it defines the very essence of the mitzvah.

We can see this by examining the word צדקה, which comes from the root צדק, justice. While giving *tzedakah* expresses a Jew's compassion for those in need, it is truly more — it is also an act of justice.

As Rabbi Samson Raphael Hirsch writes:

"Why should G-d give you more than you need unless He intended to make you the administrator of this blessing for the benefit of others, the treasurer of His treasures? Every penny you can spare is not yours, but should be used as a tool for bringing blessing to others .... This is why our sages prefer to give the beautiful name of צדקה to this act of charity by means of material goods. For צדק is the justice which gives to every creature that which G–d allots to it."[1]

→ *Attitude and Act*

Certainly one's approach toward any venture involving money will have a marked effect on his conduct in that venture.

> *A relative of Rabbi Shlomo Heyman (who served as Rosh Yeshivah of Mesivta Torah Vodaath in the late 30's and early 40's) once offered him one of the apartments in his summer home, where the two couples would share a kitchen and eating area. Reb Shlomo, totally involved in other-worldly pursuits, asked his wife to figure out if their modest income would cover the expenses of such a venture. She made the computations and announced that the apartment would be within their means, and Reb Shlomo asked to see the figures — an unusual request for him. He checked them over and then told his wife, "You forgot to add in one expense — 'Shalom Bayis Gelt.'"*
>
> *"Shalom Bayis Gelt?" his wife asked incredulously.*
>
> *Reb Shlomo explained, "When two parties share living facilities there are bound to be some questions as to how much each side should contribute to the expenses: Who used more electricity, who used the telephone more, and so on. When those questions come up, each party often finds it difficult to part with their hard-earned money, and that is where arguments begin. To avoid this, one should set aside some money from the start, in the event such problems arise. Then he will have no difficulty in surrendering the money."*

This observation of Reb Shlomo can also be applied to the giving of *tzedakah*, for, similarly, giving up one's hard-earned

---

1. *Horeb*, cited in ArtScroll *Bereishis*/Genesis I, p. 200.

money for charity may sometimes prove difficult. If, however, one sees this mitzvah as an "act of justice," and in this light, always sees a proper portion of his earnings as being "off-limits" to himself, the giving of *tzedakah* will be a test easily passed.

✦ *Compassion — a Vital Component*

Defining *tzedakah* as an act of justice does not mean that compassion cannot figure prominently in the performance of this mitzvah. There are, of course, times when it is the Jew's role as a *rachmon* (compassionate one) that will bring him to perform unusual charitable deeds.

> *Mr. Harry Hershkowitz, who during his lifetime was a pillar of many charitable causes, celebrated the wedding of his daughter. Judges, lawyers and members of New York's social elite were in attendance. (Besides serving as a member of the board of directors of Mesivta Torah Vodaath, Mr. Hershkowitz was director of Internal Revenue for the Southern District of Manhattan.) Suddenly the music stopped; Mr. Herskowitz was requesting silence. He then spoke: "Friends, though I have married off a child tonight, my happiness is not complete. How can my heart be filled with joy when I know that there are dedicated teachers of Torah, living in this very city, who cannot properly feed their families? I am speaking of one specific yeshivah where there is no money with which to pay the teachers ... "Mr. Herskowitz ended his words with a plea for contributions.*

A sense of justice, too, can lead a person to the highest levels of *tzedakah* performance.

> *Mr. Avraham Meyers was a supporter of Beth Medrash Govoha of Lakewood, N.J. in its formative years. Mr. Meyer's son became engaged at the height of World War II, when word of the extermination in Nazi concentration*

camps had already reached the West. Mr. Meyers said to Rabbi Aharon Kotler, "How can I spend money on a wedding when Jewish blood is being spilled on the other side of the ocean?" Mr. Meyers told Reb Aharon that if the Rosh Yeshivah would allow his son's wedding to take place on the lawn of the yeshivah, he would donate all the money saved to tzedakah.

After Reb Aharon gave his consent, Mr. Meyers consulted with a catering hall, band and all the other necessities, drew up a guest list and figured out to the penny what the wedding would have cost. He then gave the total — $7,500 — to tzedakah.

✦ The Need to Pursue the Mitzvah

Our Sages exhort the *baal tzedakah* to actively search out those in need of his charity. This idea is actually inherent in the very letters of the Hebrew alphabet: "Why is the foot of the *gimmel* stretched out toward the *dalet*? In order to teach us that the *gomel* (provider) should always try to seek out the *dal* (poor man) and offer help without delay" (*Shabbos* 104a).

Whether one is assertive or reactive in his *tzedakah*-giving will surely be influenced by his attitude towards giving. This is clearly illustrated in a *mishnah* (*Avos D'Rabbi Nosson*, Ch. 7) which speaks of the more general mitzvah of *gemillas chesed*.

> G-d said to Iyov, "Your level (of *chesed*) is not even half that of Avraham's. You sit in your house and guests enter, he who is accustomed to eating meat is served meat, he who is accustomed to drinking wine is served wine. But Avraham did not act this way; he actively searched the world [for guests]. And when he found guests — he who was not accustomed to eating meat was served meat ..."
>
> Rabbi Eliyahu Eliezer Dessler[2] clarifies the difference

---

2. *Michtav MeEliyahu* Vol. 2, p. 178.

between Iyov and Avraham. Iyov's acts of kindness were motivated by compassion and, as the *Chovas HaLevavos* states, compassion is a manifestation of a desire to satisfy one's own discomfort at seeing someone else in distress. Once that discomfort has been assuaged, the compassionate one no longer feels a need to benefit others. On the other hand, as the classic *baal chesed*, Avraham's acts of kindness stemmed from an insatiable desire to benefit his fellow man in any way possible. (This is borne out by the fact that Avraham was grieved when, on the third day following his circumcision, no travelers appeared.) As such, Avraham could never be satisfied that he had "done his share" for others. His "share" was limitless.

As we shall see, *chesed* should be an integral part of the *baal tzedakah*'s acts of charity. In truth, though, the sense of justice in giving *tzedakah* should be enough to motivate one to pursue those in need — when a borrower of money has the necessary funds to repay his loan, is it proper for him to delay payment until the lender comes knocking on his door? Similarly, the person who sees himself as a custodian of funds entrusted to him from Above, *specifically* intended for *tzedakah* purposes, will not wait for the poor man or the yeshivah fundraiser to come asking for a donation.

> One evening, the executive director of a well-known yeshivah came to the home of Mr. R to request a donation on behalf of the yeshivah. Mr. R immediately interrupted what he was doing, warmly received his visitor, and responded generously to his request. The visitor wished Mr. R well and, as he rose to leave, apologized for having intruded at an obviously busy time.
>
> Mr. R told him, "You know, Rav Hutner [Rabbi Yitzchok Hutner, late Rosh Yeshivah of Yeshivah Rabbi Chaim Berlin] calls me at times for donations for his yeshivah. Before I hang up, I always thank him for the call, and I once explained to the Rosh Yeshivah why he deserves my thanks. I am very

organized in my tzedakah. I set aside a certain share of my earnings and distribute it to worthy causes. My donation would be the same without a call, but I want my children to see that giving tzedakah is not (l'havdil) like paying the electric bill. I don't interrupt my dinner to pay bills, but I do when I get a call for tzedakah. If the request is made in person, I ask my son to fetch my checkbook for me. So I say the same to you — thanks for coming by."

☞ The Pursuer of Tzedakah Will Find Tzedakah

The reward for actively seeking to give *tzedakah* is the enhanced fulfillment of this very mitzvah.

"... He who pursues [acts of] *tzedakah*, the Holy One, Blessed is He, will extend to him coins with which to perform *tzedakah*." R' Nachman bar Yitzchak says, "The Holy One, Blessed is He, will extend to him upright people through whom to perform *tzedakah*, so that he will receive reward [for his act]" (*Bava Basra* 9b). As the *Gemara* goes on to relate, the prophet Yirmiyahu requested of Hashem that when the people of Anasos (who sought to kill the prophet) would be inspired to perform acts of charity, their money should fall into the hands of undeserving individuals. A person must merit having his *tzedakah* go to proper recipients.

Rabbi Avraham Kahaneman, son of the late Ponovezher Rav, approached an aged widow of means for a donation for the Ponovezh Yeshivah. The woman readily acceded to his request and remarked that she contributed to many such worthy causes. Rav Kahaneman knew that the woman, widowed for 15 years, was without someone to advise her where to contribute her money, and she could hardly be very familiar with the makeup of the many organizations and yeshivos that existed. Curious, he asked her which other causes she contributed to. The woman listed a dozen or more "sterling" causes to which she donated handsomely. Rabbi Kahaneman asked in surprise, "May I ask who advised you to contribute to these very worthy charities?"

"No one," the woman replied. "The money my husband left me is 'kosher money' — all of it was earned honestly and none of it came to us through chillul Shabbos. I am constantly praying that in this merit, my tzedakah should end up in the right hands, and my request is always granted."

✦ Infusing Justice With Kindness

As we have seen, the attribute of *chesed* should figure prominently in the *baal tzedakah*'s acts of charity. Rabbi Elazar (*Succah* 49b) teaches that the reward for the giving of *tzedakah* increases in proportion to the giver's efforts in making the donation achieve its end as meaningfully and as kindly as possible. As *Rashi* (ibid) explains, rather than give money to the poor, the *baal chesed* will instead deliver food or clothing to them to enable them to utilize their time toward earning a livelihood.

Additionally, there is an added reward simply for giving them something of immediate benefit. The classic illustration of this idea is the story of Mar Ukva and his wife (*Kesubos* 67b), who, not wishing to be discovered by the beneficiary of their *tzedakah*, ran and hid in a large oven that had not completely cooled from its last baking. Mar Ukva suffered great discomfort from the heat, but his wife did not. She later explained to her husband why her merits were greater than his. "I give poor people cooked food, which they can enjoy immediately. You give them money with which they must go out and purchase food, thus delaying their enjoyment of your benevolence."

And so the classic *baal tzedakah* is one who is at the same time a pursuer of charitable deeds and a pursuer of loving-kindness.

> The principal of a high school for girls was impressed by the request of the woman who stood before him. She had asked him for a list of the ten neediest girls in the school. The Yomim Tovim were approaching and these girls would surely be needing new clothing for the holidays.

"And you're going to leave money so each of these girls can buy something?" the principal asked admiringly.

"No," the woman replied. "I'd like permission for them to leave school for a couple of hours so that I can take them shopping."

✦ The Baal Tzedakah — a Recipient

Tzedakah, then, is unique among mitzvos. While it is a *mitzvah bein adam l'chaveiro* (between man and his fellow man) of the highest degree, it also serves as an expression of faith that "everything is from You and from Your own we have given You" (*Divrei HaYamim I* 29:14). The Midrashic dictum (*Ruth Rabbah* 5:9), "More than the benefactor does for the poor man, the poor man does for the benefactor" would then seem simple enough. The poor man's gain in receiving *tzedakah* is merely physical; in no way does it compare with his benefactor's spiritual reward. It is possible, however, to explain this teaching in an entirely temporal sense, for the *baal tzedakah*'s dividends in *this* world are, of themselves, substantial.

> *One night Rabbi Yochanan ben Zakkai dreamt that his orphaned nephews would suffer a loss of 700 dinarim in the coming year. Throughout that year, Rabbi Yochanan coaxed his nephews into contributing to the poor. By year's end, they had contributed a total of 683 dinarim. On Erev Yom Kippur the Roman government demanded of them a tax of 17 dinarim. Rabbi Yochanan said to them, "Do not fear; [but] 17 dinarim have they taken from you," meaning that there would be no further tax. Rabbi Yochanan then informed his nephews of his dream. They asked, "Why didn't you inform us of this [so that we would have given you the full amount]?" Rabbi Yochanan replied, "I said to myself, [better] that you should do it for the sake of the mitzvah.'"*

As stated, a Jew is merely a custodian of funds entrusted to him from Above. That portion of his income that should be set aside for *tzedakah* will inevitably leave his possession one way or another. Fortunate is the one who willingly gives his share of *tzedakah*, rather than having the money snatched away from him, sometimes through unpleasant circumstances; as our Sages say, "The Omnipresent has many emissaries."[3] Conversely, the Rambam[4] writes, "One can never become impoverished from [giving] *tzedakah* nor can any harm or damage come about because of [giving] *tzedakah*. Whoever is merciful will have mercy bestowed upon him ..." Thus, the beneficiary, in accepting charity, has helped his benefactor immeasurably, in this world as well as in the next.

⤳ *The Multi-Faceted Benefits of Giving*

Even this, writes Rabbi Dessler, does not fully elucidate the relationship between the benefactor and beneficiary. An understanding of an exchange found in the *Gemara* sheds new light on our subject.

The evil Turnus Rufus asked Rabbi Akiva, "If your G-d loves the needy, why does He not properly sustain them?" Rabbi Akiva replied, "In order that we be saved from the judgment of *Gehinnom*" (*Bava Basra* 10a).

Every Jew, whatever his station in life, has been put in this world to fulfill a particular mission. While poverty can be seen as a test of the poor man's resolve to resist the temptation to resort to dishonesty, or at the very least to quash the desire to complain about his lot, it can also be viewed in a different light. The poor man will *gain* from his plight if he will serve as a vehicle through which others will perform the mitzvah of *tzedakah*. "It is worthwhile for a man to live his entire life destitute and in need, and have his lot be one of sickness and affliction, if only for the purpose of causing others to do good."[5]

This perspective, while uplifting to those in need, magnifies the responsibility of those who are blessed to be on the giving

---

3. Ibid., vol. 3, p. 324.

4. *Hilchos Matnos Aniyim* 10:2.

5. Ibid.

end. As Rabbi Dessler puts it, one who has the means to give charity but fails to do so, stands to lose much more than he might imagine. Not only will he have denied himself reward in the World to Come, not only will this money be lost to him through some other means; but worse — he will have to account for having denied the poor man the fulfillment of his purpose in being poor, namely, to serve as a cause for others to give *tzedakah*.

✦ Giving With Consideration

Our Sages place great importance on making the poor man feel as comfortable as possible in accepting charity. This too, is implicit in the shapes of the letters of the Hebrew alphabet. "Why is the *dalet's* face turned away from the *gimmel*? Because [the rich person] should give [to the poor person] discreetly so he should not feel ashamed before him" (*Shabbos* 104a). (In this respect, a loan is superior to an outright donation. See *Shabbos* 63a.)[6]

On the surface, this would seem to be part of the *chessed* aspect of *tzedakah* giving, that is — benefit others, but do not make them *feel* that their survival is dependent upon you. In light of what has been said thus far, however, we can see this as an attitude most basic to the proper performance of the mitzvah. What right does one have to make a poor man feel uncomfortable or indebted when he has been designated by G-d as the means through which we "justly" distribute our share of *tzedakah*? Need a sick man feel guilty for having allowed us the opportunity to perform the mitzvah of *bikur cholim*?

It is thus clear why the Rambam[7] codifies the following *halachah*:

> Whoever gives *tzedakah* to a poor man with an
> unpleasant face and a vexed expression, even if he

---

6. The reader is referred to the late Rabbi Michael Munk's *The Wisdom in the Hebrew Alphabet*, "Letter Dalet" for a fuller, fascinating discussion.

7. *Hilchos Matnos Aniyim* 10:4, based on *Bava Basra* 9b.

gives him a thousand gold pieces, has lost his merit and ruined [the mitzvah]. Rather, he should give it to him with a cheerful face and with joy.

→ *Torah Institutions — a Give and Take*

Whatever has been said thus far with regard to the needy can certainly be applied to Torah institutions, as well. In addition to their primary function of inculcating the next generation with the word of G-d, these institutions serve another important, although subtle, function — they allow all Jews to share in the reward for Torah study through their support of those who toil in it.

Supporting Torah institutions is not an option — it is an obligation. The prophet Yechezkel (*Ezekiel* 11:16) described the *beis hamidrash* as a "miniature sanctuary." The Chofetz Chaim declared that just as all Jews were required to take part in the building of the *Beis HaMikdash,* so, too are they all obligated to support the Torah institutions of every generation. In this context, the Chofetz Chaim would apply the dictum, "Every generation in whose time the *Beis HaMikdash* is not rebuilt is considered as thought it had demolished it" (*Yerushalmi Yoma* 1).

> The Chofetz Chaim's yeshivah in Radin was originally housed in the local *beis midrash*. Eventually the yeshivah outgrew its quarters and the Chofetz Chaim sought to erect a building for the yeshivah. A wealthy admirer of the Chofetz Chaim offered to contribute the entire sum needed. The Chofetz Chaim told him, "I am sorry, but I cannot accept this. A yeshivah belongs to *Klal Yisrael,* all Jews have the right to have a share in it. I will allow you to donate the cost of the erection of one wall — and no more."

Seen from this perspective, those who seek our contributions for Torah causes can be likened to the Temple administrators who saw to it that every Jew fulfilled his obligation toward the building and upkeep of the *Beis HaMikdash*. These people should not be made to feel as though they are at our mercy, shamed and humbled, when they bring us reward in the next world, sparing us potential tribulation in this world, and saving us from judgment for not having "built a sanctuary" in our day.

> *A yeshivah received a substantial loan from one of its loyal supporters, to be repaid in installments. One of the yeshivah's post-dated checks for partial payment was returned by the bank for lack of funds. A few days later, the yeshivah office received a call from the lender. The office staffers were reluctant to accept the call, fearful of what the man, who was surely irate, would have to say. Finally someone picked up the phone. "I want to apologize," the man said. "My secretary erred in depositing that check. I realize that the yeshivah is in financial straits, and in such a case, my policy is never to deposit a check without first clearing it with the yeshivah. I'm sorry for whatever trouble it caused."*

✦ Redemption Through Tzedakah — a Challenge of Our Time

We are witnessing an ever-increasing need for *tzedakah*. There is a positive aspect to this phenomenon — new organizations are constantly springing up to serve the needs of *baalei teshuvah*, to help those with special educational needs, and so on. However, there is certainly the negative aspect — such as the swelled ranks of the Jewish poor, especially in *Eretz Yisrael*, and the financial precariousness of virtually every Torah institution in the world.

One might be inclined to dismiss this observation as lacking real significance, for our financial difficulties are merely a reflection of the generally unstable world situation. However, our sages make it clear that world events revolve around *Klal Yisrael* and not vice-versa; we are the cause, not the effect (see *Yevamos* 63a). An explanation can, perhaps, be suggested for the situation.

"Great is *tzedakah* for it brings near the redemption" (*Bava Basra* 10a). *Tzedakah* hastens the time when the Jewish Nation will be returned to its once exalted status, for *tzedakah*-giving has the power to exalt (*Maharal*), as the Psalmist said: "He gave distribution to the destitute; his charity endures forever; his pride is exalted with glory" (*Tehillim* 112:9). As *Sforno* writes, the *baal tzedakah* will see his sojourn both in this world and the next blessed with Divine favor.

As we who are living in *ikvesa d'Meshichah* (the period immediately preceding *Mashiach's* arrival) draw ever closer to that awesome day, the need for *zechusim* (merits) becomes even more crucial. How much better to accrue these *zechusim* through good deeds rather than, G-d forbid, through tribulations. "What should a person do to be spared [the terrible conditions of] the birth-pangs of *Mashiach*? Let him occupy himself with Torah [study] and acts of loving-kindness" (*Sanhedrin* 98b). Hashem, in His infinite mercy, has presented us with an abundance of opportunities to earn these merits. People in need come our way, awaiting our assistance, which in turn will justify their plight. Representatives of worthy institutions implore us to save them from financial collapse — no, imploring us to enhance ourselves as supporters of Torah. In general, the situation can be seen as one of opportunity rather than havoc, if only *we* see it as opportunity.

The Rambam writes:

> We are obligated to be meticulous with regard to the mitzvah of *tzedakah*, more so than all other positive commandments for *tzedakah* is a mark of the righteous seed of Avraham Avinu ... and the throne of Israel is not established, nor can the statutes of truth endure, but through *tzedakah* ... and Israel will not be redeemed but through *tzedakah*, as it is written, *"Zion shall be redeemed with justice and her captives through tzedakah"* (*Isaiah* 1:27).

Let us strive to become better *baalei tzedakah* and in so doing merit the time when G-d alone will reign over us "with kindness and compassion and justify us with judgment."

Learning From a Computer

David Schaps

I t is said that the Chofetz Chaim was asked what we can learn from a railroad train. "Because of one minute," he replied, "all can be lost." What is there to be learned from a telephone? "What is said here can be heard there." From a telegraph? "Every word is counted and paid for."[1] It has fallen to my portion to expend more of the last few years than I would have wished working with computers. What is there to be learned from a computer?

The Computer and the Attribute of Justice. *Rashi*[2] tells us that G-d originally planned to create the world with *middas hadin,* the attribute of justice, but "He saw that it could not stand," and so made *middas harachamim,* the attribute of mercy, a partner with it.

We know that no man can measure up to the *middas hadin;* in a very touching *piyyut*[3] that is often left out on Rosh Hashanah,

---

1. I do not know the source of this story; although I have seen it in print, I quote it from memory.

2. On *Bereishis* 1:1.

3. *Ometz adirei kol chefetz,* before the *Kedushah* of Mussaf on the first day.

the poet describes how even the greatest of men were found lacking. "Adam, formed of dust from the earth, comparable to the mighty ones on high ... transgressed His commandment, and He banished him. When Avraham rose up from the darkness, the world had been chaos, base and degraded for twenty generations; he showed the stubborn the straight pathway — and for saying, 'How shall I know (that I shall inherit the land)?' he was judged straight to the line: 'You shall surely know (that your children will be strangers for four hundred years)'...Yitzchak, who agreed to be bound as a sacrifice, found no rest in his old age, and his eyes grew dim from the smoke of Eisav's idolatry..."

Granted, then, that nobody is perfect; we tend not to think that we are that far off. In fact, I have been told by a practicing rabbi that, "People like you and me don't violate *d'Oreisos* (commandments of Torah origin)." Americans, in particular, are fond of the idea that as long as a person is "a law-abiding citizen," he is as righteous as he need be. Working with a computer has taught me otherwise.

Programming a computer can be complicated, but it is not deep. The commands to be given to the computer are exceedingly simple:

"Take the number in place 'B' and add seven to it."

"Do whatever it says in instruction 100."

"Do the next few steps five times."

The language, too, is simple; in BASIC, one popular language, the commands above would read:

"B=B7"

"GO to 100"

"FOR 1= TO 5"

How many such commands can a professional programmer write in a day? I was astounded to find out: approximately thirty. That is to say, if he works from nine to five with a half-hour off for lunch, a single statement every 15 minutes.

Of course, the work is not really a matter of writing a statement every 15 minutes. The programmer writes about three hundred statements the first or second day; the next ten days are devoted to getting the mistakes out of the program.

It is not that he cannot write more than four statements like the above in an hour. It is just that, on the average, he cannot get more than four of them *right* per hour.

The problem is the computer; and the problem is that it does exactly what it is told. If the programmer put a zero instead of the letter "O" — the computer sees a zero and uses a zero. When the program does not run, the programmer will have to examine it again and again until he — or, more embarrassing, his boss or his friend — notices the mistake and corrects it. Beginners find their first encounter with the machine terribly frustrating: no matter how many times you try the program, it will not run until you have found the error and corrected it.

What the computer is lacking is a *middas harachamim*, for as it presently operates whatever is done wrong is simply wrong — it is never ignored, never forgiven. How often can I succeed in doing it right? If the task is extremely simple, I am professionally trained, and I have no *yeitzer* that urges me to do it wrong? On the average — about once every 15 minutes.

With this paradigm for functioning under *middas hadin*, I wonder: How dare I *daven*, talking in front of the King of Kings for an hour at a stretch without full involvement of heart and mind? How do I risk talking freely for hours, when every word must be weighed for *lashon hara*? How do I embark on marriage, taking the responsibility of raising children? Praised be Hashem for dealing with us with mercy![4]

The unobserved flaw. There is more that an observant programmer can learn. The humility he has gotten from being judged by *midas hadin* is good, but it is not enough. The computer does not accept apologies; it requires *tikkun*. How many times checking over the program are enough? The computer's answer is always the same: until you get it right. So the programmer checks and checks, and finally finds it — very often a simple error in a place that he has examined ten times.

---

4. The experience of the programmer shows that it is not only the *yetzer* that makes us imperfect; it is in the nature of being finite. The *Ohr HaChaim* (on *Bereishis* 1:1) explains on this basis those passages of *Chazal* that describe "sins" of angels and of inanimate objects.

Cheshbon hanefesh, spiritual accounting, is not an easier matter. Although a Jew may check over the actions of the day every evening, of the week on *erev* Shabbos, of the month on *erev* Rosh Chodesh, of the year on the *Yamim Noraim* — a flaw, even a fatal flaw, can still slip through. A person who has worked with computers knows: never be sure it is all right just before you've checked it over once, or even many times.

Looking in the wrong place. No computer program is anywhere near as complex as a single day in the life of a Jew; but it is rare that a person can "take in" the whole of the program without knowing where to focus. As he goes through the program searching for the flaw that caused it to fail, he centers his attention on the place where the fault occurred — where, usually, the computer stopped executing the program and sent a message that the program contained an error. Alas, the error is often else where. The real error is buried in an entirely different area; it simply did not cause trouble until, when the program reached this point, everything stopped because the structure it had built up was mistaken in the first place.

This, too, is a common problem in *cheshbon hanefesh.* Why did I fail in this matter? Where was my behavior wrong in this situation? Sometimes the problem centers on what I did in the particular situation; sometimes — much more often than I generally think — the problem lies elsewhere entirely, in the ways of thinking and behaving that caused me "naturally," even "inevitably," to fail in the situation that came up now. In life, we tend not to probe past the surface. Yet, the Talmud instructs us otherwise, when faced with a problem: *Pishpesh v'lo matza, yisleh b'vitul Torah*[5] — if he has checked into his behavior and found nothing wrong, he should presume that the problem stemmed from wasting time from Torah. Perhaps, indeed, his problem is a punishment for wasting time from Torah; or perhaps (as some explain this advice) his puzzlement is a natural result of the wasted time: Not having learned enough Torah, the Jew doesn't realize the deeper faults that must be corrected before his efforts can be crowned with success. Study as you

---

5. *Berachos* 5a.

should, and you will find your shortcoming that generated your problem.[6]

The program that runs wrong. And a final stage that is well-known to programmers: the program finally runs from start to finish, and yet that does not necessarily mean that all is well. On the contrary; the normal situation is that once the programmer has eliminated all the flaws that prevented the computer from executing it, the program runs nicely, and produces ... well, at first, just nonsense; then later, a plausible-looking but wrong result. Each of these stages represents progress: first we have eliminated all the errors that *the computer* could recognize, then all of those that *we* could recognize. Progress. But in another sense, each stage is more perilous than the previous one. A program that does not run does no more than waste a bit of computer time and paper; a program that produces the wrong answer may cost millions of dollars, even lives. A good deal of the work of a programmer goes into devising tests to make sure that the answers being produced are really the right answers. The results are often disappointing ... and illuminating.

The Jew, like the programmer, can make deep errors that do not show up at the surface. A person may easily mistake his wordly success — seeing that "his program runs" — for spiritual well-being. It can be a dangerous illusion; my own experience shows that time and again, the successful person is in more spiritual danger precisely because he thinks he is well-off and feels no need to change, and refrains from any self-criticism. If you have risen, with the help of Heaven, to success, beware: when you do well enough to satisfy those around you, that is exactly when you have to spend a lot of effort in checking and re-checking, immersed in Torah and *mussar*, so that you can be sure that you are still on the right path — because the others will no longer notice if you are not.

The swift simpleton. Popular mythology once described the computer as an "electronic brain" that could "think"; in fact, it is only a glorified adding machine. It can add two numbers, or compare them to see whether or not they are equal; and that is about all it can do, although the modern machines have built in

6. The first is the explanation of most commentators, the second of the *Olelos Ephraim.*

some slightly more complicated things that the old ones did by repeated additions. It is hard to imagine an adding machine having so great an impact on our lives. But the computer has one extraordinary trait: it does what it does at the speed of light. A simpleton it is; its "thinking" powers are not as great as those of a five-year-old (who, unlike the most advanced computer yet built, can understand what his mother says). But by virtue of its enormous *zerizus*, its swift and accurate performance of its very limited task, it has brought the whole world to its doorstep, with dozens or hundreds of people spending years to reduce social, economic, scientific and even literary problems to questions of adding numbers and comparing numbers. We cannot be as swift as a computer; but we can learn from it what a difference *zerizus* can make!

➔ Who Needs Demonstrations?

If, as the Chofetz Chaim said, each machine teaches us a lesson, why did our fathers not require the dramatic presentation of these lessons that the telephone, the telegraph, and now the computer offer? Apparently, centuries ago, Jews did not have to be told that "what is said here is heard over there," or that "every word is counted and paid for." Only when the scientific revolution had given the illusion of explaining everything in physical terms did we begin to lose touch with reality. A sound, people came to think, was only a vibration of air; no air, no vibration, no sound. Our prayers cannot go up to Heaven, they posited, for the air is just a thin envelope around the earth.

Such an idea was always shallow, confusing Heaven with a place and Hashem with His creation, and did not have much currency with thinking people. But in the last century, some people became sufficiently dazzled by natural science to believe that there was nothing else. This was the generation that needed a telephone, so that they could be reminded that, indeed, what is said here can be heard there, with no vibration, even with no air. In a similar fashion, Rabban Gamliel, faced with a literal-minded student who laughed at the idea that in the time of *Mashiach* a woman would give birth every day, took him outside and showed him a hen.[7] A simple-minded demonstration? Perhaps; for a simple-minded student who could understand nothing deeper.

Our fathers — the best of them — understood the depth of the accounting that a person will owe before G-d. We — successful as we are in this world — begin to think that surely all is well in the next world, as well. But our spiritual accounts are sloppy and neglected, our character traits below standard. We need, perhaps, a simpleminded demonstration.

We are not computers; G-d created us *b'middas harachamim*, so that we would be able to endure. — How long could one last under the exacting demands of *middas hadin*? But He did create us to choose good and reject evil, and we are required, no less than the programmer, to continue working until, as far as is in our power, we get it right. The programmer has one great advantage over us: except in the very latest stages, he can usually tell whether his program runs properly or not. We, too, will eventually know that *cheshbon* — but not in this world. Here, where our decisions must be made, there is something to be learned from what people do when they really must correct the faults, and not just go through the motions.

---

7. *Shabbos* 30b.

The Invasive Spirit
of Modern Values
Finding Eternity in Every Breath of Life

Rabbi Yissocher Frand

✦ *When Eyes and Hearts are Sealed*

We live in an era of constant change. This may be exciting, but it also involves great risk. There are many emerging issues, many innovative concepts, that at first blush seem to be innocuous, and no threat to Torah at all. But on further reflection, these same concepts can be an antithesis to all that Torah stands for. That is our problem — not knowing which of the novel and intriguing modern concepts and values are consonant with the eternity of Torah, and which are inimical to Torah.

Our problem is well expressed by a well-known *Chazal*, quoted by *Rashi* in the beginning of *parshas Vayechi*. "*Parsha zu stumma* — This portion of the Torah is sealed" — that is, the customary blank space that separates one *parshah* from the next is not there. The reason for this, says *Rashi*, is that when Yaakov Avinu was *niftar* (passed away), as recorded in the chapter that follows, "the hearts and eyes of the Jews were sealed," so to speak, as a result of the oppressive enslavement. Ask the commentaries: The enslavement did not begin until all twelve of Yaakov's sons had died, many years later. Why ascribe this condition to the time of Yaakov's passing?

The *Sfas Emes* answered by saying that, true, the physical subjugation did not begin as long as any one of the brothers was alive. But with Yaakov Avinu's absence from the scene, *Klal Yisrael* underwent a profound change, affecting the eyes and hearts of Jewry. There is a phenomenon known as a *Yiddishe oig* and a *Yiddishe hartz*. A Jew who is totally committed to G–d has a unique way of viewing situations. His *Weltanschauung* is unlike that of any others. And so is the way he feels and responds to various situations unique. With the *petirah* of Yaakov Avinu, that *Yiddishe hartz* and that *Yiddishe oig* were blunted, clouded, dulled. The singular sensitivities and sensibilities that define *Klal Yisrael* became diminished.

If that generation of spiritual giants suffered such marked diminution at that time, how are we — so distant from such towering figures — to view our own stature? We, who are so fortunate to live in America, are welcome as citizens with full equality. As a result, it can be difficult for us to distinguish between ideas that are part of our sacred tradition, and those that are foreign to Torah, even though they may have a Jewish ring to them. As Americans, we are comfortable with them; as Jews, we identify with them.

✦ The Do's and Be's of Self-Esteem

For example: We hear so much today about the problems and ills associated with low self-esteem. Such a lack can be serious — to the extent that California has established a State Commission on Self-Esteem and Health Care Reform. Indeed, the media have crowned self-esteem "The elixir of the 90's; the panacea for all ills, from poor grades to bad management."

As for our perspective, what could be more Jewish than self-esteem? How often I heard my *Rosh Yeshivah*, Rabbi Yaakov Weinberg, quote Rabbeinu Yonah (circa 1250 C.E.) in his Introduction to *Shaar Avodah*: "Beyond the first portal into being an *oved Hashem* — a true servant of G-d — is *ha'yeida ha'ish ha'oveid erech atzmo* — a person must recognize his own full worth." Knowing who I am — achieving self-esteem — is very much a Jewish value, it would seem.

Upon further reflection, however, we find a huge chasm separating Rabbeinu Yonah's concept of self-worth and the modern concept of self-esteem. The latter is an expression of worth based on external success. And in the contemporary scene, which is so productivity-oriented, worthiness is determined solely by one factor: one's capacity to perform and to produce. In the Torah-based value system, however, worthiness is not so much determined by *what you do* as by *who you are*. This crucial difference is borne out by an insight from the Dubner Maggid:

> *The Torah tells us that Yitzchak loved — vaye'ehav — Eisav because game was in his mouth, but Rivkah loves — oheves — Yaakov (Bereishis 25:28). The commentaries are troubled as to why the pasuk refers to the relationship between Yitzchak and Eisav in the past tense, while Rivkah's love for Yaakov is voiced in the present, as an ongoing condition. The Dubner Maggid explains that when dealing with an Eisav, his worthiness is determined by the game he has trapped and served to his father. Material achievement is always a matter of productivity. (As the expression goes, "What have you done for me lately?") But Rivkah's love for Yaakov is determined by Yaakov's spiritual stature — by his person, which, in turn, is a function of what he is...What he is and who he is are constant.*

Ask a child, "What do you want to be when you grow up?" Invariably, the answer is, "I want to be a doctor." "I want to be a lawyer." "I want to be an executive officer." But that does not answer the question. "What you want to *be*" is not the same as "What you want to *do*." In Western society, however, being is doing. One's personal identity is a function of what one does. That is why, in contemporary society, after the initial two minutes, a conversation between two strangers inevitably wanders into, "So what do you do for a living?" Because what you *are* is the equivalent of what you *do*.

⤳ *Of Quality and Sanctity*

This phenomenon is highly significant, for a society that determines worthiness by productivity will spawn new terms, such as "quality of life." The phrase and the concept it conveys demonstrate how modernity can be an assault to eternity. In the lexicon of Torah, there is no such terminology as "quality of life." The only terminology akin to that is "sanctity of life," because by the standards of the Eternal Torah, all life has value, as a *cheilek Elokah mi'maal* — a portion, so to speak, of G–d Himself. On this basis, *halachah* calls for violating the Sabbath to save even the most tenuous of lives. In sum, contemporary society, where self-esteem depends upon worthiness, and worthiness is determined by productivity, the very young, the old, and the terminally ill are viewed as intolerable burdens that compromise our quality of life. And consequently, these are the people against whom we lash out in anger. We consign them to the fringe of existence where they are obliterated from our view, and left to die.

Every day, our society tells us in diverse ways that there are certain lives that are just not worth living. That explains why, since 1973, over 23 million babies have been disposed of through abortion. And it explains how the former governor of Colorado, Richard Lamm, could say that which others only think: "The elderly have a duty to die, and get out of the way." Such are the attitudes that modernity has spawned. Such are the values created by a self-esteem dependent upon worthiness, which is based on productivity in terms of tangible results ... a quality of life that says *Get out of the way and die.*

As a result, our society is so thoroughly indoctrinated with the concept of "the quality of life," that it has become exceedingly difficult to explain to others the value of suffering. Seeing a dying patient in a hospital enduring suffering, one asks, *How could this life have meaning*? To our Eternal Torah, however, there is an intrinsic value to life. Every *neshamah* has reason to be here for just as long as Divine wisdom decrees. That alone provides life with purpose.

Dr. Abraham J. Twerski tells how he visited a young mother of two who, suffering from multiple sclerosis, ע״ל, was completely blind. She felt herself a total burden to her family. Instead of mothering her children, they had to administer to *her* needs. The woman was, understandably, depressed. Dr. Twerski visited her in the hospital, and from a non-theological point of view, had nothing to offer this woman. But he did relate to her the following *Gemara* from the end of *Sanhedrin*.

> When Rabbi Eliezer became ill, four talmidim visited him: Rabbi Tarfon, Rabbi Yehoshua, Rabbi Elazar ben Azaria and Rabbi Akiva. Each of the first three praised their ailing rabbi in metaphorical terms, likening his powers to those of the rains, the sun, and one's parents — only more so, because his influence extends beyond This World, to Olam Haba — the World to Come. None of their words brought him comfort. Then spoke Rabbi Akiva, saying, "Chavivin yesurim — How precious are your sufferings!" Rabbi Eliezer responded, "My disciples, bring me closer, let me hear what Rabbi Akiva has to tell me."

One may wonder, what did Rabbi Akiva say, that brought Rabbi Eliezer greater comfort than the words of the others? Perhaps it is because Rabbi Eliezer was on his death-bed, and could no longer teach Torah. He did not see what he could do for his *talmidim* now, what he could do for *Klal Yisrael* in such a condition. When the other *talmidim* employed all sorts of metaphors to tell him, in effect: "You are a *gevaldike rebbe!*" Rabbi Eliezer said to himself, "I *was* a *gevaldike rebbe*. But what am I now, lying here on my death-bed?"

Rabbi Akiva, however, told him, "Chavivin yesurim." You can lie there in your bed and be *mekabel yesurim b'emunah* ... and *b'ahavah*. Accept your lot with faith and love. Even now, in a diminished state, Rabbi Eliezer, you have a *tachlis* — a purpose in this world. There is no standard of productivity. All the

Ribbono Shel Olam wants from a *mensch* is that he be His *eved*, His willing servant, to the maximum of his ability at any given moment. And if that capacity is merely to lie in a bed, then that's sufficient. What you are at that moment is the only criterion.

→ *Tears ... and an Answer*

A *talmid* of mine in Yeshivah Ner Israel, Baltimore, is a *baal teshuvah*, formerly a student in Columbia University.... He recently returned to Columbia University for a *Shabbaton*, in hope of reaching a few more souls. That Friday night, with the best and the brightest of Columbia University, were some children from Yachad, an OU-sponsored group that reaches out to developmentally disabled children, ל״ע. This young man was saying a *dvar Torah* describing how every Jew has an individual role to play; just as there are many *osios* (letters) in the Torah, and yet no two *osios* touch each other, so too does every *Yid* have an individual role, a special *tafkid* in life. A 17-year-old mentally handicapped boy from Yachad raised his hand. "I have a question. What's my role? I'm mentally disabled! What's *my* role? I can't do anything." And the boy started to cry. *What's my role?* The kids from Columbia joined him in his tears, wondering, *What's his role?* This *talmid*, thinking quickly on his feet, said, "What's your role? You asked a question! You made people think! You made people cry! You touched people! That's your role."

A week after the *bachur* had returned to the yeshivah, he heard that this 17-year-old boy from Yachad got up one morning, and told his mother, "I'm not feeling well." Later that day he was *niftar*.

The *talmid* decided to travel to New York to be *menachem ovel* the family. As he sat dawn in their living room, he wondered, *What am I going to tell the bereaved parents?* While trying to formulate his thoughts, the parents told him, "Our son fulfilled his task in life. He asked his question. Maybe that was his role."

Sometimes, that's all one has to do in one's life: Ask a question ... Lie in a bed ... It may not be a life of obvious quality, but it will be a life of sanctity.

→ Health Care Reform vs. the Sanctity Criterion

The discussion thus far brings us to the doorstep of an extremely relevant topic: health care reform. If — when? — universal health care is going to be instituted, cost-control will be of top priority. There is a word for what is going to be happening, but everyone is loathe to use it: *rationing*. And the first people whose health care will be denied are those whose quality of life is deemed inadequate. If 40 percent of a person's health-care costs are incurred during the last year of his or her life, do you have any doubts as to where the government is going to cut costs?

There are experts who are assigned the formidable task of assessing these factors. And they deal with treatment costs in tenns of "qualies" — an acronym: Qu-A-L-Y=Quality Adjusted Life Years. The people who are charged with this responsibility will be answering such questions as: Is it worth $40,000 to equip an old person who has bad lungs and bad kidneys with a cardiac defibrillator? How many "qualies" can he have? The Washington official who will be making this decision does not know about the comment of *Me'iri* in *Yoma*. The *mishnah* in *Yoma* discusses the obligation to attempt to dig out a person buried under a caved-in building on Shabbos, which would constitute a violation of the Sabbath, even though the possibility of saving his life is far from certain. The *Me'iri* says that even after the person is found, the digging is carried on to completion even though it is certain that the victim is going to die within the hour. Explains the *Me'iri*: It is worth violating the Shabbos for the sake of gaining these few minutes, for it is possible that in the bit of time the man has left on this earth, he may do *teshuvah*.

It is quite unlikely that the Washington expert dealing with "qualies" will take the *teshuvah* factor into account. When he thinks of a comatose person, he is convinced that the patient has no Quality Adjustment Life Years ahead. But from a perspective of Eternity, the sanctity of life looms larger than all mundane considerations. (May I emphasize that this is not a halachic paper and I am not suggesting that one rule applies to every person in every situation, ר״ל. When one has responsibility for a relative who is on the outer brink of life, one must consult an authority on such *halachos*, as to whether one must keep the patient alive regardless of cost, regardless of perceived benefit.) When the doctor, however, informs the family, "But there's no quality of life...," one must recognize that the well-meaning doctor is approaching the situation from the vantage point of modernity. He does not know about the *Me'iri*, nor has he ever heard that the *neshamah* has to be here for a specific period of time.

Nor has the National Task Force on Health-Care Reform have the ability, unfortunately, to relate to the following anecdote, written by Rabbi David Bleich in one of his *sefarim* on medical ethics.

> *Rabbi Bleich's grandmother-in-law had suffered renal failure, and was comatose for 36 hours. He came into her hospital room, looked at her chart, and saw that no treatment had been prescribed for her. The rabbi called the attending physician and asked him, "Why aren't you doing anything for her?"*
>
> *The doctor responded, "Listen, she's an old lady. Let her go in peace."*
>
> *Rabbi Bleich said that he then made a decision that he recognized as intellectually correct, but emotionally, very difficult. He ordered the doctor, "You treat her. Try to keep her alive as long as you can." They started treating her, and after davening Minchah — it was Shabbos — Rabbi Bleich returned to the hospital room and said, "Gut Shabbos, Bobbeh!"*
>
> *This woman who had been comatose for 36 hours opened half an eye and whispered, "Gut Shabbos."*

Rabbi Akiva Eiger (the great sage of Posen, 1761-1837), in his glosses on *Shulchan Aruch* (*Orach Chaim* 271), says that if a person says the words *"Gut Shabbos,"* he fulfills the positive command of *Kiddush*, *"Zachor es yom haShabbos l'kadsho —*

Remember the Sabbath day to keep it holy." Rabbi Bleich's grandmother, on that last Shabbos of her life, fullfilled the mitzvah of *Kiddush*.

The rabbis tell us that a moment of good deeds in this world is greater than all of *Olam Haba* — The World to Come, and the *Bobbeh* is now reaping her reward for that *"Gut Shabbos,"* of which the doctor would have deprived her ... because in his view, those final hours lacked Quality Of Life.... Such has been the eternal clash between modernity and eternity.

Torah Study and Its Support: The Many Faces of Their Rewards

Shlomo Kohn

→ *The Reciprocal Relationship*

Zevulun was to be endowed with monetary wealth, to be a tribe that would flourish through its commerce on the seas, while Yissachar was destined to be immersed in uninterrupted Torah study. Should not Yissachar, the older son, have been blessed first, putting the blessing of Torah before the one of monetary wealth? Yet Yaakov blessed Zevulun first (*Bereishis* 49:11-13).

The *Midrash* notes that because Zevulun's support made his older brother Yissachar's Torah study possible, his blessing gained priority; for without Zevulun, there could not have been a Yissachar.

According to the *Midrash*, Zevulun would provide for his brother, placing the food in his mouth — that is to say, Yissachar would not have to ask Zevulun for support. Zevulun would come on his own initiative, anxious to gain a share in his brother's Torah study.

→ The Many Ways of Torah Support

The Chofetz Chaim lists many forms of Torah support: paying tuition for children of poor families, strengthening yeshivos, maintaining Torah scholars, supporting teachers of Torah, or providing some means of livelihood for a Torah scholar. According to the *Rambam* (*Hilchos Shekalim*), supporting the family of a Torah scholar is also included in this mitzvah.

In his work *Eitz Pri*, Rabbi Yitzchok Elchonon Spector, famed *Rav* of Kovno (from 1864 to 1896), describes some of the benefits accrued to those who support Torah. We paraphrase his comments:

Whether a man is a congregational rabbi or a computer programmer, whether he sells groceries or flips mortgages in real estate programs, if his intention is to apportion a specific amount of his earnings towards the sustenance of Torah in any of its multifaceted areas, he is rewarded both in this world and the next. Moreover, as a supporter of Torah, he is given control over his *yetzer hora* (evil inclination), i.e. he is not ruled by his desires. Also, *Chazal* say, his sins are forgiven without suffering afflictions, for he has already chosen to deny himself some of life's pleasures by assuming the burden of supporting Torah and its scholars. While the true reward awaits him in the next world, whoever supports Torah study is assured of financial success in this world as well: "Rejoice, Zevulun, as you leave (to conduct business), and Yissachar, in your tents" (*Devarim* 33:18). Both experience joy in their respective tasks.

When considering a new business venture, it is natural to feel apprehensive: Will my transactions be profitable, or will my efforts be in vain?

Zevulun, who supports Yissachar, can work with a tranquil mind, for he is assured that his business dealings will prosper. Hence, "rejoice Zevulun as you leave," because a great source of merit is already protecting you: "Yissachar in your tents [of Torah]."

✦ Filling the Boss's Barrels

We are aware that reward for mitzvos awaits us in the Next World. Why, then, does one receive benefits in *Olam Hazeh* — this world — for mitzvos of *tzedakah* and support of needy Torah scholars? The late Satmar Rav, Rabbi Yoel Teitelbaum, offered an explanation based on the passage: "When you enter the vineyard of your friend, you may eat grapes as you desire, until you are satisfied. But do not store any in your vessels" (*Devarim* 23:25).

This carte blanche is extended by the Torah during the harvest season, when workers fill the vessels of the vintner (see *Rashi* ibid). During any other time of the year, it is forbidden for a laborer to eat so much as a single grape from the vineyard, even if he labors diligently for the benefit of the master of the vineyard. When the laborer is placing the fruit into the vessels of the vineyard's owner, only then can he eat as much as he desires.

In the same vein, when we perform the mitzvah of *tzedakah*, giving to the needy, we are filling "G–d's vessels." In such times the contributors, like the laborers in the vineyard, receive extra "on-the-job" benefits. Thus, G–d rewards the Torah supporter in this world as well as in the next.

✦ Rewards of a Different Sort — Sharing in the Scholar's Growth

Other rewards are given to those who support Torah study — rewards identical to those apportioned to Torah scholars themselves.

The Talmud states: "Whoever has in his hand the light of Torah (that is, a Torah scholar), the light of Torah will give him life (a reference to *techiyas hameisim* — resurrection). And whoever does not have in his hand the light of Torah, the light of Torah will not give him life" (*Kesubos* 111a). The *Gemara* concludes that those who support Torah scholars are linked to them and will also merit *techiyas hameisim*.

Furthermore, whoever supports Torah scholars, even though he may be very unlearned in this life, will possess a wealth of Torah knowledge in the World to Come. At first glance, this might seem odd, but closer examination makes it clear that the reward is very much in order.

The Chofetz Chaim relates: A rather ignorant man gave huge sums of money to the yeshivah in Volozhin. Just before his passing, he asked Reb Chaim of Volozhin to study *Mishnayos* on his behalf, to which Reb Chaim readily agreed. During the *shivah* period (week of mourning), the *gaon* Reb Chaim had difficulty with a particular *mishnah* in *Maseches Keilim*. That night, the deceased man appeared to him in a dream and explained the *mishnah* brilliantly. Said Reb Chaim, "I know that the dead who are worthy are taught in the next world, but I never realized that they are taught so much so quickly."

"The explanation for this phenomenon," said the Chofetz Chaim, "is really quite simple. Someone who supports Torah deserves a portion of the reward reserved for the Torah scholar. After all, he enabled the scholar to study. We also know that the greatest pleasures of the Next World are formed from the spirituality of the Torah. To receive its just reward, the soul would, of necessity, have to understand the Torah upon its arrival in *Olam Haba.* Thus that supporter of Torah in Volozhin knew so much, so quickly."'

Along this line, the *Yalkut* says that "G–d will spread a canopy over the contributors of *tzedakah,* alongside those who labor in Torah." The inference here is that the supporter will have Torah knowledge. For what greater anguish could there be for that soul, than to hear a scholar speaking in Torah and not understand him! The protective canopy is the knowledge that will protect him from the anguish of ignorance.

✦ *Extending the Privilege*

There are a multitude of ways, then, in which the supporter of Torah is equal to the scholar of Torah. Thus, many have recognized that it is a privilege, rather than a burden, to support Torah scholars. Notable among them was a Reb Banish, an extremely wealthy man who lived in Poland some 50 years ago.

One rainy day, Rabbi Elchonon Bunim Wasserman, revered head of the yeshivah of Baranowitz, Poland, approached the home of Reb Banish to solicit some funds. Not wishing to track up the polished floors of the wealthy man's home, Rabbi Wasserman knocked on a door at the side of the house, where he planned to clean the mud from his boots before entering.

"HaRav Wasserman," called Reb Banish, hurrying to him, "I beg of you, come into my home through the main entrance! I want to teach my family an important lesson: The mud on the boots of Rav Wasserman is worth more than all the luxurious furnishings of my home!"

→ *Priorities in Torah Support*

"My three sons-in-law study in a Kollel, and I have two single sons in other yeshivos as well. A good portion of my salary goes towards their support. Am I still obligated to send donations to the numerous yeshivos that are constantly petitioning me?"

When this not-uncommon problem was presented to the late Satmar Rav, he opened a *Chumash Devarim* and read the following *pasuk*: "And you will rejoice before Hashem, your G–d — you, your son, your daughter, servant and maidservant; the Levi who dwells within your gates, the proselyte, orphan and widow."

The Satmar Rav went on: "*Rashi* categorizes the first four as belonging to the owner: son, daughter, servant and maidservant; the second four are G–d's people: Levi, proselyte, orphan and widow. 'My four,' says G–d, 'are parallel to your four. If you cause Mine to rejoice, I will cause yours to rejoice.'

"Here Rashi teaches us a crucial lesson. If a man rejoices on the holiday solely by providing for his family and household, it is possible that he is not doing so because it is a mitzvah. Rather, it may be devotion to his family and servants which prompts him to provide for them. Perhaps his expenditure cannot be considered the mitzvah of 'rejoicing on the holiday' at all: — If, however, one brings joy to those in the second category — to G–d's four — He considers that sufficient proof that the person's effort to bring rejoicing to 'his' four is also motivated by the mitzvah involved. G–d's four, in effect, elevate the four belonging to the father / owner.

"It is certainly true," said the Satmar Rav, "that it is a great mitzvah to support one's own sons and sons-in-law in yeshivah. Perhaps, though, the father is motivated by filial devotion rather than by the mitzvah of supporting Torah. When a father supports other yeshivos and scholars as well, then no such accusation can be leveled at him, and he is worthy of reward for all that he does."

⤑ Up to the Limit … and Beyond

To be sure, there are limits as to how far one need extend oneself in supporting Torah, but as with all mitzvos, every extra effort and hardship endured enhances the mitzvah; G–d assesses the self-sacrifice that each man undergoes and rewards him accordingly. The Sanzer Rav, Rabbi Chaim Halberstam (known by the name of his *sefer*, the *Divrei Chaim*), related an extraordinary episode concerning the humiliation and ridicule endured by one man — Reb Pesach, by name — to help an impoverished Torah scholar.

One day a learned but penniless and dejected man approached Reb Pesach, begging him to help him raise money for his family. The situation looked bleak, for Reb Pesach had already asked the wealthy men of his village three times that very day to assist three separate needy cases. He felt he could not approach them again that day.

A group of rowdy youths in the village learned of Reb Pesach's predicament and devised a way to make sport of him. They challenged Reb Pesach to parade through the streets dressed in an old monk's tunic. In exchange for providing them with moments of merriment, they would readily contribute 50 rubles for the poor scholar.

Lacking any other avenue, Reb Pesach hesitantly agreed. Dressed in the monk's robe, but trembling inwardly, Reb Pesach — known to all as a devout Jew — strolled nonchalantly through the streets of the *shtetl*, which had never seen the likes of a monk in his habit. The townspeople stared unbelievingly at Reb Pesach and were convinced that he had lost his mind. Adults began to mock and jeer at him and children chased after him, singing and shouting. Without faltering one step, Reb Pesach walked the whole route and earned the 50 rubles. Joyfully, he handed them over to the grateful Torah scholar.

Years later, the *Divrei Chaim* visited Reb Pesach. He chanced upon the monk's tunic, hanging in a closet in Reb Pesach's home, and later commented that he had detected the fragrance of *Gan Eden* wafting from the old clothing.

Why, wondered the *Divrei Chaim*, did the pious Reb Pesach possess a monk's tunic? And more perplexing still, why did it have the fragrance of *Gan Eden*?

When the *Divrei Chaim* questioned him, Reb Pesach related the entire episode. The *Divrei Chaim* listened spellbound.

"Reb Pesach," said the great man earnestly, "when you leave this existence after 120 years, demand that the townspeople bury you in this very same garment. Not a single evil angel will dare come near you!"

→ *Other Avenues*

The Chofetz Chaim states that those who cannot afford to give funds themselves should encourage others to support Torah study (as did Reb Pesach in the anecdote above). There are various means of such indirect assistance as well.

"She is a tree of life for those who cling to her and those who support her are praised" (*Mishlei* 3:18). "Cling" refers to those who aid Torah scholars financially, while "support" refers to those who attend to the physical needs of a Torah scholar. "Personally serving Torah scholars is too time-consuming," one might argue. "I have many other pressing needs, including my own obligation to study Torah."

The words of the Chazon Ish can help place matters in a proper perspective:

A man famous for his acts of *chesed* to *bnei Torah* asked the Chazon Ish if he should continue this practice with his usual devotion as it required considerable time. Might it not be more worthwhile to spend that time in study?

"On the contrary," replied the Chazon Ish. "When you are occupied with *chesed*, your soul is elevated and your Torah is of a different caliber. The understanding that you will acquire when you do learn is automatically uplifted and broadened."

The *Divrei Chaim* once said in a similar vein, "If a man feels that he cannot close his *Gemara* to help a fellow Jew, then even when his *Gemara* is open, it is closed.' The opposite is also true. If a man closes his *Gemara* to do a *chesed*, then even while his *Gemara* is closed — it remains open."

→ *The Topmost Priority: Survival*

Supporting Torah must take precedence over indulging in one's own material desires, because supporting Torah scholars and maintaining Torah study is absolutely vital for our people's continuity, and survival is undeniably of greater importance than good living.

Rabbi Aaron Kotler, the revered leader of Bais Medrash Govoha in Lakewood, wrote, "Torah study is the life-force of *Klal Yisrael* ... It is well known that with the weakening of Torah study in different countries, the very foundations of *Klal Yisrael* were weakened. Slowly but surely, the reservoir from which flowed the enthusiasm for upholding the Torah and performing its mitzvos, dried up completely... The result was complete assimilation.

"Only with true Torah scholars who can transmit the unadulterated Torah to the next generation, will the chain of *mesorah* continue."

An Open Letter to
My Friend on the Slide

D ear Friend, עמו"ש

I know you well, though you may not be able to identify me. You've passed me by quite a few times in *shul* on your way to *Shacharis*, when your eyes were only half-open. I'm usually there before you, finishing my *seder* before *davening*, but I wasn't always there so early. I knew I could relate to you when I saw you fall asleep during *Kabbalas Shabbos*. I did that, too, for the first six months after leaving the *"koslei beis hamidrash"* to enter the workforce.

Many of us have gone through the same thing — schedules that have suddenly grown hectic, and adjustments to new responsibilities which throw people off the patterns of life they have so carefully cultivated. Rubbing shoulders with a very mundane world creates many new *nisyonos*. Now that you're working, maybe the "keeping up with the Joneses" syndrome has also set in. It must be very hard for you; I can see evidence of the frustrations you are experiencing. Your entire self-esteem as a *ben Torah* who toils in *avodas Hashem* may just have evaporated. It may seem impossible, at this point, to establish a respectable *k'vias ittim l'Torah* (schedule for regular Torah-study). It is for this reason that I write to you through this very public forum — because I know that you are by no means alone in this difficulty.

Let me share with you some suggestions that you may find useful:

Firstly, realize that though your learning, in whatever quantity, will not be of the same depth as during your yeshivah years, it is equally, if not more, beloved to Hashem, because of the sacrifice entailed in its acquisition — ripping yourself away from pressing responsibilities, desperately trying to clear your head, at a time when you may be both physically and emotionally exhausted.

I have found that keeping a *Daf Yomi* schedule on a simple *Gemara/Rashi* level sets a good minimum base of *k'vias ittim*, especially for *mesechtos* that I learned in yeshivah. Joining in a *shiur* is helpful in another way — being connected to a *maggid shiur* or *rebbi* can provide vital encouragement in difficult times.

Picking one *mesechta*, even a small one, to review again, again, and again, on a simple *Gemara/Rashi* level has allowed me the comfort necessary to progress and expand to *Tosafos* and more, reviewing again and again. In the sixth *perek* of the Chofetz Chaim's *Toras HaBayis,* you will find encouraging, even eye-opening, words for undertaking such a project.

I hope that this letter will serve as an encouragement to you, and perhaps spawn further discussion within these pages regarding the many difficulties of entering the workforce, along with possible solutions.

Sincerely yours,
Bar Nisayon

More Strategies
for the Baal Nisayon

The writer of "An Open Letter to My Friend on the Slide" highlighted two major problems that face so many *bnei Torah* on leaving full-time learning:

1. How to maintain the standard of learning you acquired over many years of effort and dedication, in the time-frame now available to you. The drop in the quality of learning experienced by many in your position is, in the words of *Chazal*, equivalent to a free fall from a multi-story building into a deep crater.

2. In what way can you strengthen yourself on an ongoing basis, to ensure that you will be able to stand up to the many difficult *nisyonos* that you now have to face — *nisyonos* that are relevant to every *chelek* of *Shulchan Aruch*?

The author of that letter gives valuable advice to the *ben Torah who finds himself alone* in the turmoil of the world. But he does not have to remain alone!

May I suggest the solution that experience has shown to be the most effective. Join a *chaburah*! In other words, the time you have available to learn should not be spent alone, nor even just with a *chavrusa*, but as part of a group learning together.

Everyone knows that due to intrusive commitments even a *chavrusah* relationship is very hard to maintain. Meetings, *simchos*, etc. all chip away at the number of planned sessions, and even when the partners do get together, they are often too tired or preoccupied to tackle the subject matter. The first difficult *Tosafos* will often prove to be the *"makeh b'patish"* (or coup de grâce)!

→ *Enter the Chaburah ...*

Enter the *chaburah* with its manifold advantages. There are a number of such "mini-*kollelim*" currently in action, providing tremendous opportunity for their members. Allow me to outline the general principle together with a few details from our own *kollel* — *Kollel Erev/Boker* of Boro Park and Flatbush. Firstly, being part of a group enables one to learn with greater depth and increased clarity. The involvement of a *rosh chaburah* and the valuable element of *pilpul chaveirim* ensure that rather than coming to occasional standstill, the learning always flows, and each *sugya* can be tackled with very successful results. Furthermore, the occasional absence of a *chavrusa* does not have to result in a wasted session for his partner. In fact, a number of *chavrusos* in our *kollel* have agreed — mutually — not to inform one another of an impending absence, so that the learning goes on as usual, the missing *chavrusah* being well compensated for by the *dibuk chaveirim* available.

The tremendous gains achieved with this method are felt by all. Frequently, one hears from new members that they have not learnt so well since leaving *koslei beis hamidrash*, in one case referring to a lapse of 14 years!

Special notice should be given to the advantage of learning early in the morning before *davening*. At this time of day one can learn with a clear head and reinvigorated body, affording full concentration on the *Gemara*. Obviously, the remainder of the day runs very differently after such a start. It is interesting that most current members had considered themselves as "night people" and were not accustomed to such a schedule; however, all were able to make a successful adjustment. The biological clock changes to the extent that some now enjoy a *seder* of learning on Shabbos at the newly established regular time. Of course, it does require an amount of *mesiras nefesh* to start the day this early, but remember that the "formula" is proven and the gain is immeasurable. The encouragement of the *eizer k'negdo* (wife) is of particular importance.

In general, this type of *kollel* is all-encompassing, bringing together alumni from many yeshivos and *kollelim*, catering to different age groups.

→ *Time, Place, and People as Spiritual Anchors*

Here we come to your second point. We know well that a *kesher* formed through *limud haTorah* is stronger than any other. The mere feeling of belonging to such a *chaburah* provides *chizuk* for each member. Particularly in a large community, a *ben Torah* can often feel that he has no *mokom*, with the result that he is in a spiritual free fall. Here the person gains a "*ruchniyos* base," which serves to strengthen him for his daily *nisyonos*. In many cases, a close personal relationship is gained with the *rosh kollel* (the *kesher* you refer to in your letter), further fortifying the *ben Torah* for the day ahead — both at work and on the domestic scene.

In short, my dear *Baal Nisayon*, what is missing is some simple organization. We are currently planning to open a new *Kollel Erev* in Flatbush for those whose schedule does not allow for the morning *seder*. Furthermore, we hope to offer a choice of *sidrei limud* to maximize the gains and to allow each person to realize his full learning potential. Other *chaburos* are also on the drawing board. We hope that this successful form of *kvi'us ittim* will continue to grow and many other *chaburos* will be formed to add to those already in existence, so that the "working *ben Torah*" will be able to live up to his name!

Rabbi Shmuel Halberstadt,
Rosh Chaburah — *Kollel Boker of Flatbush*
Brooklyn, NY

↷ Outreach on the Job

The One-Minute *Kiruv* Person

Our Mandate to Generate *Kiddush Shem Shamayim*:
A Private Matter

The One-Minute Kiruv Person

Yaakov Astor

T he One-Minute Manager was a New York Times national best-seller with millions of copies sold. It purported to present a system whereby any manager in any business could vastly improve the performance of those he managed with a few simple, pointed techniques that on the average took no more than one minute to implement. The book became such a success that it produced spin-offs: The One-Minute Salesman, The One-Minute Father, The One-Minute Mother, The One-Minute Teacher, etc. All in all, there have been now over 10 million "One-Minute" books sold!

Only in America.

The truth is that, unlike fast food, instant lottery and presidential promises, there really is substance to the "one-minute" approach. Based on the 20/80 rule in business, which states that 20 percent of a company's salespeople produce 80 percent of its sales revenues, the operant dynamic is quality. Often taking even one minute just to think about what we are doing or what to tell another person produces more than the hours we spend doing a task or speaking to others without thinking.

It sounds logical enough and many people have apparently

benefited from these books. The question is: Is it a Jewish idea? More to the point: Is the title of this article misleading? In *kiruv*, is there really such a thing as a "one-minute" approach? Isn't *kiruv* — bringing an estranged Jew "close" to Torah and mitzvos — a long, arduous process for the individual(s) doing the *kiruv*?

✈ *One-Minute Kiruv ... As It Was*

As strange as it sounds, the "one-minute" approach can be a Jewish idea, one that applies to *kiruv* as well as parenting, education and everything else we do. The source is a very famous *Chazal* (discussion by rabbis of the Talmud).

> A non-Jew approached Shammai. "Convert me on the condition that you teach me the entire Torah while I stand on one foot," he said. [Shammai] pushed him away with the rod that was in his hand.
> [The gentile] came before Hillel. "Convert me."
> [Hillel] said, "'That which is hateful to you, do not do to others.' That is the entire Torah. The rest is commentary. [Now] go and learn" (*Shabbos* 31a).

How long can a person stand on one foot? One minute? Two minutes? After a while, it gets uncomfortable. Shammai and Hillel, then, were debating the value of the one-minute approach. Shammai saw no advantage to it. If the gentile was not ready to undergo the hard work of turning himself into a Jew, there was no reason to lead him on. So he pushed him away. Hillel, on the other hand, drew him close. He felt he could accomplish something of far-reaching effects, while not underselling Torah, even in one-minute's time.[1]

---

1. The *Ben Yehoyada* points out that, in reality, Shammai and Hillel acted as a team. Together they fulfilled the exhortation to "push away with the left hand while drawing close with the right." Apparently, according to the *Ben Yehoyada*, had the gentile received only Hillel's "drawing close with the right hand" approach, he would not have become a true Jew in the end. According to this, then, even Shammai was utilizing a one-minute approach. He was performing something similar to what the "One-Minute" books call a "one-minute reprimand."

The same passage (*Shabbos* 31a) tells us the stories of two other potential converts approaching Shammai and Hillel. Taken all together, I believe that these three stories correspond to the teaching in *Avos* (4:28) that "*Kinah* (jealousy), *taavah* (pleasure seeking), and *kavod* (egotism or *gaavah*[2]) drive a person from this world." Analyzing each story will not only offer insight into how Hillel employed the one-minute technique to draw three types of typically estranged people "close" to the ways of Torah, but will also give us basic insight into human nature (others' and our own).

→ The Baal Taavah/ The Pleasure Seeker

To Hillel, the essence of life itself was "*V'ahavta l'rei'acha kamocha* — Love your neighbor as yourself." He translated that love into the very practical and easy-to-do dictum: "That which is hateful to you, do not do to others." Just as you would not want to be shunned by another, so should you not shun others who seek you out, even if they have ulterior motives or are off-base in one way or another.

It does not take great analytic powers to determine how the gentile who wanted Hillel to teach him the entire Torah on one foot was off base. He was not exactly a "*hineni*" personality type — an Avraham Avinu saying: "Here I am" — ready and willing to answer G-d's call on a moment's notice, no matter what or how long the effort involved. He wanted it all done in less than a minute.

A sound-system technology hit the market not long ago that made everything before it seem obsolete. No need to strain yourself with that remote-control CD-changer any longer. Now all one has to do is tell the stereo what he wants. Say "Track five," and the CD switches to five; say "louder" and the volume increases; say "off" and the system turns off. Remote control is

---

2. Although "*kavod*" is usually translated as "honor," the Vilna Gaon in *Even Sheleimah* (2:1) equates *kavod* with *gaavah*, or egotism. I have assumed that meaning here, as will become evident below.

Neanderthal. It requires too much work. Your finger may get strained flicking the buttons as you lean back in your padded lounge chair.

Only in America.

From the condition the gentile made (to hear everything while standing on one foot), we can discern that he was the typically lazy person. Laziness, generally, is a function of *taavah*, "desire" or pleasure seeking. The body's pleasure is to be slothful, to "take it easy." It does not want to work too hard. It does not want to hear a long *shmuess* or concentrate too hard. This gentile did not want to study or learn. He wanted to be fed facts, preferably in an amusing way, in the shortest amount of time possible.

OK, Hillel said. I will give you what you want, an answer to life, the universe and everything while standing on one foot: Love (which, behavioristically speaking, translates into not doing hateful things to others) is the secret behind everything in the Torah. That was a concept the gentile could relate to. Hillel was able to show him the proverbial forest amidst the trees.

That is an important point to understand. Often a lazy person is lazy because he has no real meaning in his life; he has no goal other than fulfilling his own drive for pleasure. If you have no goal, then everything you do is a burden. A donkey does not understand what it does, either. So, too, an outsider looking at the *avodah*, the Divine service of a Jew, without knowing why or what-for sees Judaism as nothing but drudgery. However, show him the larger picture — a meaning, a goal, a purpose — and the same drudgery becomes pleasure.

The gentile could relate to loving your neighbor as yourself. Indeed, once convinced that this was the simple, basic truth of Torah life, Hillel was able to tell him: "[Now] go and learn." He was able to convince him to undertake the very thing he did not want to do: the hard work of learning!

A pleasure seeker (*baal taavah*) only understands the pleasure of the moment. If you can broaden his perspective and show him the pleasure of eternity, then he is more likely to work to overcome his nature. He is more likely to make that effort, and make it willingly.

530 ☐ THE ETHICAL IMPERATIVE

In another case mentioned in the same passage, a gentile approached Shammai and wanted him to teach him only the Written Torah because, he admitted, he believed only in it, not the Oral Torah. This gentile is the typical egocentric person. As the Vilna Gaon writes, *kavod* is in essence the same as *gaavah*,[3] egocentricity: the need to domineer or feel haughty. (The desire for honor or *kavod* is rooted in the need to feel superior.) This egocentric person was his own man. Nobody was going to tell him how to read a book, or how to interpret the Torah.

Shammai abruptly brushed him away. When the gentile came before Hillel, however, the sage offered to teach him the first few letters in the *Alef-Beis*, a normal way for a gentile interested in becoming a Jew to begin. After the lesson was over Hillel told him to absorb what he had learned and to come back for another lesson the next day. The next day arrived, the gentile returned, and Hillel taught him the same letters, but with different names and sounds.

"Are you playing games with me?" the gentile said.

"No," Hillel responded. "But if you need a teacher of consistency and reliability for something as elementary as the *Alef-Beis*, then how can you expect to understand the entire Torah without such a teacher?"

In less than one minute, Hillel taught him perhaps the first lesson of Torah Judaism: the absolute necessity of *mesorah*, of an oral tradition.

Yet, the information Hillel conveyed was only part of the work. At least as vital was the way he conveyed it. Hillel sensed the man's thirst for ego fulfillment. Had he argued with him and conveyed even the most flawless proofs supporting the necessity for *mesorah*, he probably would have failed. He would never have gotten around the man's ego. It might have sounded nice and made a good book, but it would not have done the job. Hillel taught the man in such a way that he was

---

3. See *Even Sheleimah* 2:1 and the note above.

able to conclude on his own that one needed to depend on others even for the rudimentary understanding, i.e., how to read the *Alef-Beis*. Thus, he painlessly bypassed the *baal gaavah*'s *gaavah* and still taught the essential principle that one must have a rabbi with a clear understanding of the *mesorah* to truly interpret the written Torah.

→ *Kinah/Envy*

The third case involved a non-Jew who wanted to convert on the condition of being made the Kohen Gadol. However, the only thing he knew then about the Kohen Gadol was that he wore majestic clothes, the *bigdei kehunah*. We see, therefore, that he did not want the position in order to lord over others (as the *baal gaavah* laden with desires for *kavod* would). He merely desired nice clothes; indeed, the nicest clothes. If he could wear such clothes, he would never be envious of anyone — they would be envious of him. Thus, he was essentially driven by *kinah*, jealousy, the need to possess the best of what others have … merely because others possess it; to keep up with the Joneses (or the Weisbergs), if you will.

Naturally, when this potential convert, obviously motivated by base desires, approached Shammai, the sage pushed him away with his stick again. Hillel, however, converted the gentile then and there. (Below we will attempt to explain why.) Later, Hillel guided the convert to the verse that said that a "stranger" could never become even a simple Kohen. Curious to know who the word "stranger" included, Hillel told the gentile that it even applied to King David. On his own, the convert then drew the conclusion that if King David could not be Kohen Gadol, his dream to be a Kohen Gadol was impossible. He was not heartbroken, though, because if even one as great as King David could never become Kohen Gadol then he had nothing to feel envious about. He was in good company.

Interestingly, unlike with the other two, Hillel converted this gentile before even seemingly addressing his character flaw. He intuited that this gentile's path to becoming truly

Torah observant was not the same as the previous two. Perhaps we can explain the reason by suggesting that jealousy at its root is the lack of a sense of self-worth. It is selflessness not based on humility, which is the recognition of the greatness of Hashem. It is rather a selflessness born from weakness, from the inability to recognize one's intrinsic worth. Hillel himself was famous for saying, "If I will not be me (If there is no essential *"ani"* to me), who will be me?" A person who feels he has no intrinsic worth (who has no *"ani"*) will probably seek relativistic worth, i.e., he will feel good about himself only when he compares himself to others who are equal to or less than him. And that is exactly what jealousy is: comparing oneself to another.[4]

And that is perhaps why Hillel converted him on the spot. The root of this non-Jew's character flaw was that he simply lacked self-worth. So Hillel gave it to him — he made him a Jew. Once he was a Jew, a member of the people chosen by Hashem to bring light to the world, he possessed the tool necessary to eventually overcome his lack of self-worth. He possessed intrinsic identity. He possessed a Jewish soul.

The bottom line is that Hillel once more showed that *kiruv* can be a one-minute affair. One minute, indeed, is sometimes all that is needed to change another's life and ultimately bring that person closer to the ways of Torah.

❧ One-Minute Kiruv ... in Today's Scene

Not long ago, I asked Rabbi Meir Shuster the secret of his success. As you probably know, Rabbi Shuster is that very quiet, unassuming man in the black suit, tie and hat, who has successfully approached tens of thousands of Jews at the *Kosel* and all around Jerusalem, asking them if they would like a class to attend, or a place to stay, or a family to eat with on

---

4. Jealousy, then, is the opposite of *gaavah*. *Gaavah* is an inflated or misplaced sense of self while jealousy is a missing sense of self. The cure for *gaavah* is seeing that there is more to the world than you. The cure for *kinah* is recognizing that *bishvili nivra ha'olam*, "For my sake the universe was created."

Shabbos. Rabbi Shuster told me what I already knew, what we already knew: The main thing is that one has to care about the other.

That was Hillel's success. Time and again he tuned into the need of the person standing before him and used what can be called an "other-centered" approach. He did not discount the potential convert's personality. He quickly surmised it and gave each of them a path to come to the truth on his own. Torah has an answer for everyone. However, not everyone is satisfied with the same answer. We have the responsibility to find out which answer will satisfy the need of the other and supply that answer in a way that is sensitive to that person's needs. If you understand that, then you may be able to move mountains in minutes. If you do not, then you may never budge them an inch, no matter how long you try and how well you argue your position.

The applications of one-minute *kiruv* extend far beyond the bringing close of assimilated strangers, and refers to much more than the fundamentals taught in an outreach professional's workshop. It is a powerful and useful tool for fulfilling nothing less than the "Great Principle of the Torah: Love your neighbor as yourself." It reflects the essence of the Torah ideal of *chessed*, the empowering of another soul to exploit its greatest gift: *bechirah*, choice.

And G-d knows we need more of it. A *baal(as) teshuvah*, even long after outwardly and even inwardly committing to Torah, has special needs more of us have to be sensitive to. And, of course, the always-observant need *kiruv*, too. A friend or acquaintance at work, observant or non-observant, whom you have been dealing with routinely may benefit from you changing your routine and taking a minute to think how you can fulfill their need, physical or spiritual, and then acting upon that thought.

Perhaps more than any others, your own children and students are in need of your undivided attention, and hopefully you can give them more than just the one-minute variety. On the other hand, a good minute or two of quality listening and caring usually goes a lot further than hours of merely occupying the same space together.

One-minute *kiruv* (I like better to think of it as one-minute *"V'ahavta l'rei'acha kamocha* — Love you neighbor as yourself") may be efficient, but it is not necessarily easy. It may only take a minute — but it takes a minute. It requires real time to turn your focus away from your daily preoccupations. It does not produce if you do not take that quality minute. But you will find that when you do take the short minute to really tune into others (sometimes that other can be yourself), you improve the quality of life, theirs and yours, immeasurably. That one minute is a great investment. Why not take a minute right now and start thinking about where to invest it?

Our Mandate to Generate Kiddush Shem Shamayim: A Private Matter

Rabbi Yisroel Reisman

✦ *A Matter of Perspective*

S hlomo HaMelech provides an insight regarding human relations: *"Al kol pesha'im techaseh ahavah* — all inequities can be overcome by love," whereby nagging faults become viewed as inconveniences of life. Where there is no love and caring, however, even minor faults become major problems. And worse, when there is animosity and hatred, faults are sought out, they are amplified and enlarged, until they become major problems which take over a relationship.

As this is true in relationships between individuals, so is it true regarding relationships between peoples. And certainly, this is the most telling factor regarding the relationship of *Yisrael bein ha'umos,* the Jews among the nations. Yes, the nations complain about us; they always fault us for this or that perceived shortcoming.

We certainly realize that some criticisms are correct, but let us not lose focus of the whole picture. Indeed, we have much to be proud of.

At the national conventions of Agudath Israel of America, as well as at various inspirational gatherings, we have the privilege of hearing *gedolei Torah* implore us to rectify our shortcomings. I cannot help but think: "What a wonderful people we are! In a society where elementary school children are taught birth control, we agonize over the proper length of hemlines and the correct height of a *mechitzah*. In a society steeped in vulgarisms and profanity, our problems involve talking in *shul* and *lashon hara*. In a society that suffers from deviant excesses, we study the finite laws of *tzenius*. In society where 60 percent of 10-year-olds have been exposed to drugs, we criticize lax *kashrus* supervision. In a society steeped in greed and avarice, we have *Tomchei Shabbos, Bikur Cholim* and the selfless volunteers of *Hatzalah*. Today, more than ever before, we should hold our heads high and proclaim, *"Mi k'amcha Yisrael, goy echad ba'aretz* — Where in the world is there a people like *Klal Yisrael*?"

✧ Catching the Disease

The secular world, however, does not quite see it this way. They do not compliment our community for our accomplishments. They choose to highlight our shortcomings. And it hurts. Ever since the second grade, our *rebbe'im* have impressed on us that our behavior is constantly being judged by those around us, and that our mission is to see to it *she'yehei Shem Shamayim mis-ahev al yadecha* — that our behavior should cause others to admire our dedication to moral values and proper conduct. We call this *kiddush Hashem*, sanctifying the Name of Heaven, and we are taught that this is one of the most important obligations that we carry.

But carrying this obligation is frustrating indeed. We follow the rules, but the gentiles never seem to admire us. In fact, they deride us whenever they spot an opportunity. And yes, it hurts.

Unfortunately, in responding to this disappointment, too many of us begin to show symptoms of The Smelly Jew Syndrome. Those of us who might dress in a more modern fashion start to criticize those who still wear European *shtetl* garb. Those of us who are articulate in English are tempted to criticize those who still speak with the "old-fashioned" accents. Those of us who are fortunate enough to have been taught proper etiquette, respond harshly to those who have not.

All too often, when non-Jews criticize us, many of us — precisely because we are a people of conscience — tend to jump on the bandwagon and join the chorus of abuse. It is bad enough that we must suffer as victims of The Smelly Jew Syndrome; it would be terrible, however, if we caught that disease.

→ *Projecting Kiddush Hashem*

What exactly is the obligation of *kiddush Hashem*? Is it primarily a matter of inspiring admiration from the gentiles?

In the third volume of *Michtav MeEliyahu*, Rabbi Eliyahu Eliezer Dessler explores "*Kiddush Hashem — HaAmiti VeHaMedumah* (Genuine and Imaginary)." The essay quotes Rabbi Yisrael Salanter, as defining *kiddush Hashem* in a manner quite different from that which we were taught in elementary school: *kiddush Hashem* does not necessarily involve the presence or observation of gentiles, nor even of other Jews. It does not require that one's actions be admired by others. In fact, true *kiddush Hashem* often takes place in private, when one is alone. This is because *kiddush Hashem* occurs whenever a person acknowledges that the *Ribbono Shel Olam* is in his presence, wherever he might be — whether he is home alone or out among people.

When a person is home eating breakfast with an open *sefer* on his table, he has created a *kiddush Hashem*. Nobody has seen him, no one is praising him.

Conversely, *chillul Hashem* occurs when one fails to sense the presence of Hashem in his life. The Hebrew word *chillul* is related to *challal* — a vacuum. One who lives in a spiritual vacuum, one who does not sense that the Creator is nearby ... such a person lives a life of *chillul Hashem*, regardless of whether his secular neighbors criticize him for it, or admire him for it.

The *Gemara* (*Sotah* 36b) tells us that Yosef HaTzaddik was rewarded for sanctifying the Name of Hashem. The *Gemara* questions, "*Mai Yosef?* — Where did Yosef sanctify the Name of Heaven?" The response is that this took place during the incident of Yosef and the wife of Potiphar, when Yosef was tempted to sin, but refrained from so doing at the last moment. Yosef HaTzaddik sensed his accountability to the *Ribbono Shel Olam* as a member of Yaakov Avinu's family — one of the *Shivtei Kah* (Holy Tribes) — and therefore resisted the temptation to sin. This is *kiddush Hashem*.

Anyone familiar with the incident of Yosef and Potiphar's wife knows that this incident did not endear Yosef to his gentile hosts. In fact, the Egyptians — totally unaware of Yosef's innocence — viewed his behavior as scandalous, and had him imprisoned. Clearly, the *Gemara's* explanation of *kiddush Hashem* supports the explanation of Rav Yisrael Salanter.

Rambam (*Hilchos Yesodei HaTorah* 5:10), in codifying this *Gemara*, writes:

> Anyone who turns away from sin or performs a mitzvah, for no [ulterior] motive in the world, not because he is frightened or fearful or because he hopes to be respected but only because of [the will of] the Creator, as when Yosef restrained himself from his master's wife, this is one who sanctifies the Name.

✦ Sanctifying Whose Name?

Why is it then, that the popular interpretation of *kiddush Hashem* requires that the behavior of a Jew be admired by the secular world?

Michtav MeEliyahu explains this as well. Every human being wants to be liked by others. A Jew who desires to be admired by non-Jews can be driven by two different factors: by a desire to sanctify the Name of Heaven, or by his own innate, personal desire to be liked. All too often our wires get crossed and we fail to distinguish between the two.

Take, as an example, the Orthodox Jew who travels away from home on a business trip. If, when among gentiles, he acts as they do, dresses as they do, talks as they do and eats as they do, he may find that they accept him warmly. But this does not necessarily qualify as *kiddush Hashem*. And if he steps over the limits of *halachah*, and discusses what he is prohibited from discussing, eats what he is prohibited from eating, or goes where he is not permitted to go, that constitutes *chillul Hashem*. His gentile companions may truly appreciate him for his conduct, but this is a "beautification" of his own person, not a sanctification of our Creator. His companions may admire his personality, but G-d has been left out of the relationship.

When we live our lives in the manner prescribed by the Torah, those gentiles who are seeking spirituality will indeed admire us. *Shem Shamayim [yihiyeh] misaheiv al yadeinu* — the Name of our Creator will indeed be admired by those who examine us in their pursuit of ethical behavior and G-dliness.

Sadly, in our day and age, the secularists who seek to find spirituality in the Jewish People are few and far between. When they do look at us, it is through lenses that operate by totally different criteria. Our loyalty to ancient values and to an unchanging G-d is strange to their sensibilities. Even when they are not burdened by prejudice and hatred, they cannot identify with our unflinching loyalty to centuries-old traditions that affect our every waking hour. They see as queer our fidelity to "old-fashioned" laws of modesty, our failure to participate in the telling of off-color jokes, our aversion to entering a movie theater, and our reluctance to socialize with them. Is this *chillul Hashem*? Certainly not.

We have many true *mekadshei Shem Shamayim* among us, and we should be proud of them. On the other hand, we cannot ignore the stories of dishonesty or rudeness in our midst. G-d forbid! But we must respond to these stories in a manner that deals foremost with our relationship with Hashem, rather than with our neighbor's response.

✦ In the Presence of ... Rav Moshe

When we hear of a shameful incident in our own ranks, we must deal with it as a symptom, not as the disease. Our primary concern should be with developing a stronger sense of the presence of the *Ribbono Shel Olam* in our homes. If we were to succeed in this, we would subsequently find Him accompanying us when we step outside, as well. This point can be made clear with a *mashal* drawn from my own experience:

As an American boy, I enjoy getting behind the wheel of a car. Once there, my aggressive, hurried style often gets the better of me, and puts me in a position where my actions may, G-d forbid, cause unpleasant things to be said about Orthodox Jews. I don't condone this, and I accept criticism of my behavior, which my wife is often kind enough to provide.

In my *beis hamidrash* days, I had the *zechus* of attending Rabbi Moshe Feinstein's Friday *shiurim* at Mesifta Tiferes Yerushalayim, for almost two years. Very often, my *chaveirim* and I had the opportunity to drive Reb Moshe from the yeshivah to his home on FDR Drive. I can assure you that when Reb Moshe was in the car, my wife would have loved my driving. There was no danger of *chillul Hashem*.

Why? Because Reb Moshe was looking.

Ask yourselves: How would *you* drive if Reb Moshe were looking? How would you talk to others if Reb Moshe were listening? How would you conduct your business affairs if Reb Moshe were in the office?

We must learn to take this a step further and ask ourselves: How do we drive when the *Ribbono Shel Olam* is looking? How do we talk when He is listening? How do we conduct our business dealings with Him in the office?

As you can see, the problem is *not* that we must worry about the gentiles who are watching. We would be far better off worrying about our Creator watching. The problem of *chillul Hashem* is not that the gentile is spitting at us; he's been collecting saliva for a long time, waiting for the opportunity to find fault. The core of our problem is in our relationship with

Hashem; that we do not always sense His presence as we should. If we were to succeed in being aware of His presence, we would avoid *chillul Hashem* without once wondering, "But what are they saying about us?"

→ *On a Higher Level*

Kiddush Hashem, by its most common interpretation, occurs when a gentile admires the moral and ethical behavior of an Orthodox Jew. Does this fit into our explanation of *kiddush Hashem*?

Michtav M'Eliyahu explains that it does. Most of us might understand this as a starting point in *kiddush Hashem*. In truth, this is a higher level of *kiddush Hashem*, which should come as a consequence of one's being aware that he stands in the presence of the *Ribbono Shel Olam*.

> To quote *Michtav MeEliyahu*:
> The basic *kiddush Hashem* is to correct the *chillul Hashem* within ourselves (by being cognizant of *Hashem*'s constant presence). Only after this, can a person rise to the level of sanctifying the name of Heaven in public, in the proper, pure manner; primarily to glorify G-d in the presence of (at least) ten other Jews.... An individual who is on a still higher level, is one to whom the honor of Heaven is so great, that he strives with all his might and all his resources to sanctify the Name of Heaven among the other peoples of the world. So great is his love for G-d that he wishes that He be recognized by all humanity.

This is our challenge: to raise our level of awareness and responsibility so that our every action gives a sense of G-dliness to our surroundings. When we do so, we impart an aura of holiness to our own homes and we can then seek to extend that glow to our fellow Jews, and, ultimately, to gentiles as well.

→ The "K'Goan Anna" Rule

When I told a friend that I would address the topic of "Why Are They Saying Those Things About Us?" he presented me with a long list of problems besetting the Orthodox Jewish community, which he suggested I attack. I pointed out that not one of the problems that he considered of paramount importance to our community was a fault of which he was personally guilty. Weren't there other problems, applicable to him, which also belonged on the list?

I am afraid that this friend suffers, to a degree, from The Smelly Jew Syndrome. He hears negative things about Orthodox Jews, and feels that he has to agree with some of the stereotypes. His motivation is *not* to rectify the problem: it is purely to assess the blame. In seeking a guilty party, he naturally looks elsewhere. Finding the faults of others is hardly the method of combating the problem of *chillul Hashem*.

A discussion of *chillul Hashem* must seek to resolve the problem. Criticizing others for being different, even where faults truly exist, does not remedy the situation. People enjoy finding fault in others. I doubt that this causes anyone to become a better person.

The *Gemara* (*Yoma* 86a) discusses the concept of *kiddush Hashem* and the obligation of *she'yehei Shem Shamayim misahev al yadecha* — that the Name of Heaven be praised because of us. What was the response of our greatest *Amora'im* to this lesson?

The *Gemara* tells us that Rav responded with the statement, "*K'Goan Anna* ... For someone like me (whom the community holds to the highest standards of conduct) purchasing meat on credit is an issue of *chillul Hashem* (because people may suspect that I hope to avoid paying)." Rebbe Yochanan said, "*K'Goan Anna* ... For someone like me ...," and he too outlined the parameters for proper behavior that pertained to himself. The response of these people was "*K'Goan Anna* ...." this is what *I* have to do. Their response to the problems of *chillul Hashem* was not to find the faults of others, nor was it to analyze the critique of the gentile world around them.

We should reject the feeling that the problem of *chillul Hashem* is the problem of "What are they saying about us?" We must see it as a problem of our failure to sense that Hashem is there with us at all times, if we can begin sensing the presence of the *Ribbono Shel Olam* among us, our everyday conduct will improve. The secular world will not start loving us for it, but we will be living a life of *kiddush Hashem*. And those who seek spirituality, who seek morals and values, will indeed find it in *Klal Yisrael*. The Name of Heaven will indeed be loved because of us.

✣ Of Role Models and Giants of Impeccable Integrity

The *Ish Ha'Emes*: Rabbi Shimon Schwab

Rabbi Moshe Sherer (excerpt)

A Day in the Life of a
"*Tzaddik Nistar*": Dr. Shimon Askovitz

Kiddush Hashem in the House of Lords

The Ish HaEmes:
The Man of Unimpeachable
Integrity, Rabbi Shimon Schwab

Rabbi Eliyahu Meir Klugman

Frankfurt, 1915: A six-year-old boy is sent by his mother to the store to buy groceries. With the change he buys himself some chocolate, which he eats on the way. When he arrives home, his mother asks him for the change. "Here it is," the boy answers.

"But where is the rest?" his mother asks.

"I must have lost it," the boy replies. But his mother notices a chocolate wrapper in his pocket.

"Oh," she says, with a look that he will remember for the rest of his life, "you didn't tell the *emes*."

Later that day his father comes home. He does not hit him or send him to his room. "What is this I hear that you didn't tell the *emes*? Your punishment will be that tonight, Friday night, I will not *bentsch* you. No, I won't *bentsch* you tonight." The young boy never forgot that lesson.

Radin, 1930: The young Frankfurt boy, now a Mirrer Yeshivah *bachur*, comes to visit the Chofetz Chaim. When the elderly sage is told that he is "a Frankfurter *bachur*," he takes his hand in his own and caresses it gently. "A yeshivah *bachur*! How fortunate! So many are drowning today. Only through Torah can one survive. How fortunate that you are learning!"

Marienbad, 1934: The Mirrer Yeshivah *bachur*, by now a *Rav* in Germany, pays a visit to the saintly Gerrer Rebbe. The *Rebbe* tells him, "Remember, *yungerman*! One must be very careful to safeguard the honor of Rav Hirsch, the *tzaddik* of Frankfurt, for he was a living *mussar sefer*."

Washington Heights, 1994: In the last winter of his life, the young Frankfurt lad, now *Rav* of the largest German Jewish *kehillah* in the world and a leader of Torah Jewry, calls in a wealthy benefactor of the *kehillah*. "I don't have much time left on this world," he said, "and I will be going to *Gehinnom*. The yeshivah's deficit is close to a million dollars and most of it is in the unpaid salaries of its *melamdim*. I am *Rav* of the *kehillah* that teaches *Torah im Derech Eretz*. Where is the *derech eretz* if we haven't paid our teachers for months? It will not be long before I will be called to give a *din v'cheshbon* for my actions and I will be going to *Gehinnom* for this. I'm begging you. Please take me out of *Gehinnom*."

The man is shaken. After giving the matter some thought, he agrees to cover the entire deficit in teachers' salaries, in weekly installments to be completed before the yeshivah's annual dinner. The last payment is made on the Friday before the dinner. The yeshivah's dinner is on Sunday night.

The following evening, Rabbi Schwab passed away.

Who was this man who lived a life of such adherence to honesty and integrity? What is this potent combination of the ideals of Rabbi Samson Raphael Hirsch, architect of Torah Orthodoxy in the Western world, and the intense commitment to *limud haTorah* that is the legacy of the great Lithuanian yeshivos? What can we learn from his life to enable us to make this heady blend the reality of authentic Torah life in America? Specifically, what example did he set for the American *ben Torah*, whether engaged in full-time Torah study or as a working man?

1. GEOGRAPHY OF A LIFE

Boyhood in Frankfurt-am-Main

Shimon Schwab was born in Frankfurt on 7 Teves, 5569 (1908), to an old German Jewish family. In the 1850's, his great-grandfather moved from a small Bavarian village to Frankfurt, soon after Rabbi S.R. Hirsch had become rabbi, so his children could study in Rav Hirsch's *Realschule*. Like his father and grandfather, Shimon Schwab studied in the *Realschule*, which went only until the ninth grade. There he received his only formal secular education.

His parents, Leopold and Chana (Erlanger) Schwab, were *erliche*, respected *baalei batim*, who were active in the life of the Frankfurt *Kehillah*. They produced five sons, each of them a man of note in his own right. Three of them were world famous—in addition to Reb Shimon, there was Reb Mordechai, renowned as a *tzaddik*, and Reb Moshe, *mashgiach* of the Gateshead Yeshivah.

What explains their success in child-rearing? The Schwab brothers were fond of telling of the *Seder* night when their father asked his children which of the four sons they would like to be. Most of them answered "the *chacham*," as could be expected; young Mordechai responded that he would like to be the *"tam."* The father then addressed his children in a stern voice: "If any of my sons becomes a *rasha*, even if only deviating from a single *din* or a *minhag*, I say to him '*Li, velo lo*, I will have nothing to do with him.' I love my children more than anything in the world, but I love the *Ribbono Shel Olam* even more." His father's *yiras Shamayim*, Rabbi Schwab said decades later, chilled his bones.

He grew up in Frankfurt as a normal child, with no hint of the greatness he would attain. He often stressed that many *gedolim* were not accomplished *talmidei chachamim* at age 13 or geniuses in their youth. Many who were *amei ha'aretz* at that age, later became Torah leaders. This awareness, he felt, should be an encouragement to many lads who are nothing special at their bar mitzvah, yet have the potential to become great *talmidei chachamim* and Torah leaders.

After completing the *Realschule*, Shimon learned for 2 years under the Frankfurter Rav and *Rosh Yeshivah*, Rabbi Shlomo Zalman Breuer, son-in-law of Rabbi S.R. Hirsch. There he absorbed the joys of *yegias haTorah*, the delight of intense effort in trying to ascertain the correct *pshat*, and an absolute commitment to finding the *emes* in the *dvar Hashem*. This strong commitment of Reb Shlomo Breuer to unadulterated *emes* as the guiding light of his life obtained in communal matters as well as in Torah study. For the rest of his life, Rabbi Schwab always saw himself, in his words, as "*talmid talmido*" of Rabbi S. R. Hirsch—his disciple's pupil — and, indeed, he was suffused with Rav Hirsch's spirit.

In 1926, the Ponevezher Rav, Rabbi Yosef Shlomo Kahaneman, visited Frankfurt and delivered a *shiur* in Rav Breuer's yeshivah. The young Frankfurter boy was entranced both by the *shiur* and by the *derech halimud*. He wanted more. The Ponevezher Rav suggested Telshe, with its emphasis on *seder* and its approach to education, as most appropriate.

Shimon Schwab was among the first German *bachurim* in his time to study in a Lithuanian yeshivah, and a considerable number followed his lead. But many who had left Germany to study in the East ceased to appreciate their *mesores avos*, the hallowed traditions of *minhag Ashkenaz*, when they beheld the sublime grandeur and tasted the intoxicating sweetness of the *blatt Gemara*. Rabbi Schwab clung to every detail of his *mesorah*, the continuation of close to two millennia of Torah life in Germany, channeled into the post-ghetto world by Rabbi S.R. Hirsch and his colleagues.

A Yeshivah Bachur in Lithuania

During the three years he spent in Telshe, he was awed by the regal dignity, the iron will, the sublime mind, and the singing *neshamah* (as he described it) of the Telzer Rav, Rabbi Yosef Leib Bloch. In Telshe he learned about *malchus haTorah*, seeing the *Rosh Yeshivah* as a *nesi Elokim*. Whereas his relationship with the Telzer Rav was a mixture of awe and fear, for his *rebbi*, Reb Avrohom Yitzchok Bloch, there was only the adoring enthusiasm of a 17-year-old yeshivah *bachur* for the *rebbi's* sweet personality. In Telshe, he also learned a lifelong lesson: the meaning of "*shteigen*" — steady, sustained growth in Torah, *yiras Shamayim* and character development.

Rabbi Schwab spent six weeks in the summer of 1929 teaching in Montreux, Switzerland. There, he also served as the personal attendant of Rabbi Chaim Ozer Grodzenski. Those weeks of intimate daily contact with the *gadol hador* left an indelible imprint on him. Reb Chaim Ozer suggested that he go to study in the Mirrer yeshivah in Poland, whose *mashgiach*, Rabbi Yeruchem Levovitz, would be the perfect mentor for the Frankfurter *bachur*.

So in Elul, 1929, he went to the Mir, where he developed an unusually close relationship with Reb Yeruchem. There too he was a trendsetter for the many German *bachurim* who followed. Several years later, Reb Yeruchem delivered a regular *Chumash shiur* exclusively for these "*oislanders*," as they were called. Reb Yeruchem's *Daas Torah* on *Chumash* contains much from those *shiurim*. Reb Shimon stayed in the Mir for two years, and received *semichah* from the *Rosh Yeshivah*, Reb Lazer Yudel Finkel, as well as from Reb Chaim Ozer Grodzenski.

His visit to the Chofetz Chaim in 1930 is part of the public consciousness. Although he spent no more than a weekend in Radin — from Friday morning to Sunday morning — *Klal Yisrael* has learned more from those few days than from many who spent years in Radin.

A Rav in Germany

In 1931, Rabbi Schwab was appointed assistant to Rabbi Yonah Merzbach of Darmstadt, who later joined Rabbi Yechiel Schlesinger to found yeshivah Kol Torah in Jerusalem. The same year, he married Recha Froelich of Gelsenkirchen, who was his devoted and cheerful companion for life, and with whom he had five children. Two years later he was appointed District Rabbi of Ichenhausen in Bavaria. Noting a lack of the spirit of the Lithuanian yeshivah in German Jewry, he attempted to establish a yeshivah there, but the local Nazis closed it on the day it opened.

He was under constant pressure from the local Gestapo. As the situation deteriorated, he began to sleep at night with his clothes on. He later explained that one of his acquaintances who had been outspoken in his criticism of the regime was taken away in the middle of the night and was found the next morning hanging. Should the same fate await him, he wanted to meet it fully clothed, as befits a rabbi. Matters in Germany reached a point where it was only a matter of time before his arrest, and he decided to seek a rabbinical position overseas.

Refugee Rabbi in Baltimore

Upon the suggestion of Rabbi Leo Jung, a leading Orthodox rabbi in New York, he was accepted as the rabbi of the German Jewish Shearith Israel Congregation of Baltimore. He arrived in the U.S. with his family on 10 Teves, 1936.

Soon after his arrival, he was faced with his first crisis. He insisted that the by-laws of the congregation, which conferred voting rights only on *shomrei Shabbos*, be upheld. As a result, two hundred members, the overwhelming majority of the membership, who considered themselves Orthodox but were unable to resist the pressure to work on Shabbos, left the *shul* and established their own congregation. Shearith Israel was left with a skeleton of a congregation of barely two dozen members, sometimes without a *minyan* during the week, and almost no wherewithal to cover his salary. He was forced to borrow and scrape to make ends meet; there were times when he did not receive his salary for months. It was not the only time in his life when he was willing to sacrifice position and livelihood for principle. It was, in fact, one of the Hirschian tenets upon which he was weaned: "Learn how to withstand animosity and to weather unpopularity, and to carry on the struggle to uphold Hashem's ideals." Despite his poverty, in 1943 he auctioned off his only possession of value, a *sefer Torah* that he had brought with him from Germany, and gave the proceeds of $2,000 — a substantial sum at the time — to the Va'ad Hatzalah for saving Jewish lives in Europe. He was active in securing affidavits to facilitate the entry of Jewish refugees into the United States, and the Schwab home in Baltimore became a way station for many poor, newly-arrived refugees from the European inferno.

Baltimore of those years was hardly a spiritual oasis.

The kashrus situation was a mess. Rabbi Schwab told of the time, soon after he had arrived in Baltimore, when he received a request to provide a hashgachah for chickens. When he informed the owner that he would visit his plant, the man replied, "That's OK, Rabbi, we'll bring the check to you."

The *Rebbitzen* was one of only a handful of women in the city who covered her hair. Even yeshivah Chofetz Chaim, headed by the illustrious Rabbi Chaim Samson, had almost no *shomer Shabbos* students. One of the Schwab boys had only one *shomer Shabbos* friend. He pleaded with his mother not to give him sandwiches for lunch in school because the boys laughed at him when he washed his hands before eating.

Before the establishment of the Bais Yaakov, Rabbi Schwab would gather the few *shomer Shabbos* girls in his home for a weekly *shiur*. "*Ess past nisht,*" he was told by a local rabbi, "for a *rav* to teach girls." Rabbi Schwab replied that the *Gemara* says that a *chassid shoteh*, a pious idiot, is one who refuses to save a woman who is drowning because she is a woman. "I don't want to be a *chassid shoteh*." Together with a few local *baalei batim* he founded the Bais Yaakov of Baltimore, despite the derision of local rabbis who considered the undertaking a waste of time, effort, and especially resources. "Why," one Orthodox rabbi asked him, "are you bothering with these insignificant mitzvos?" This "insignificant mitzvah" is today the largest such institution outside the New York area.

The Frankfurt Kehillah in New York

In 1958, Rabbi Schwab's Rebbi from Frankfurt, Rabbi Joseph Breuer, then 75-years old, decided that K'hal Adath Jeshurun of Washington Heights needed a vigorous presence on the rabbinate, and he invited his *talmid* to serve alongside him. It is testimony to the greatness of these two men that for the next 23 years they served the *kehillah* side by side with hardly an uncomfortable moment. Although many of the *kehillah* institutions were in place when he arrived, he was instrumental in founding the *Mesivta* and the Bais Yaakov High School, the *beis hamidrash* and the world-renowned Rivka Breuer Teacher's Seminary. It was during these years in Washington Heights that Rabbi Schwab's leadership and influence in the affairs of American Torah Jewry reached their peak.

2. THE EMBODIMENT OF MALACHI'S PROPHECY

A Kingdom of Priests

The Jewish People, the *Rav* never tired of declaring, must he a *Mamleches Kohanim v'goy kadosh*, a nation of priests and a holy nation. A Kohen, he explained, is one who by word and example spreads the knowledge of the Almighty. The Kohen imperative of the Jew, which he epitomized, was the constant theme in his life.

Living in *galus* America, a *malchus shel chesed*, only strengthened this obligation. Every form of *chillul Hashem*, he taught, lowers the awareness of the Divine presence in this world. If the perpetrator is a supposedly observant Jew — or worse, a so-called Torah scholar — then the offense is even greater. The *chillul Hashem* strengthens the hand of the non-observer, gives ammunition to the scoffers, and fosters yet more rejection of religion; and it is responsible, directly or indirectly, for the increase of frivolity, heresy and licentiousness in the world. How can one who cheated his neighbor or defrauded the government, he asked, have the audacity to stand in front of the congregation and recite *Kaddish*, a prayer for sanctifying G–d's Name in the world? There can be no whitewashing, no condoning and no apologizing on behalf of the desecrators. It must be made clear that he who besmirches the Divine Name has defected from our ranks and joined our opponents. And the more prominent a person is, the more scrupulous and painstaking he must be in his business dealings to avoid even the slightest hint of a *chillul*

Hashem. When the *Rav* was asked to assist in efforts to secure the release of a "religious" Jew who was incarcerated for fraud, he refused. "Help him be released? He's a *rodeif* of *Klal Yisrael.* Because of him, *frumme Yidden* will suffer. Let him sit!"

Traveling once with his son on the subway, the boy found fifty cents on the floor in front of the change booth, which he intended to pocket, thinking that there was no obligation to return it. "Give it to the attendant," his father insisted, "and I will stick my beard in his window so that he sees that religious Jews do not want other people's money."

The prophet Malachi, speaking of the End of Days, described the attributes of the Kohen, and these qualities are perhaps the most accurate description of Rabbi Schwab, his life and his teachings:

> *"Toras emes haysa befihu, ve'avla lo nimtza bi'sfasav;*
> *beshalom vemishor halach itti, v'rabbim heishiv me'avon.* The
> teaching of truth was in his mouth and no injustice was
> found on his lips; in peace and in straightforwardness
> he walked with Me and he turned many away from sin"
> (*Malachi* 2:6-7).

"Toras Emes ...."

He viewed his mission in life as being a *marbitz Torah,* giving *shiurim* to those of all ages and backgrounds in his *kehillah* — men, women and children. He had a unique approach to *Aggadah* and shared with his *talmidim* and congregants countless original insights into *Chazal.* A lengthy series of *shiurim* on the *Siddur Tefillah* presenting invaluable insights were recorded for posterity. Many of his *chiddushim* on *Chumash* and *Midrash* were recently published in his magnum opus, *Maayan Bais Hashoeva* (Mesorah Publications, New York, 1994). Some of his public addresses of the last decade, and many essays of the last half century, have been published in three volumes of his collected works (CIS Publishers).

He exhorted his followers to learn "with an inner glow and persistence, with ardor and single minded passion, with noble joy and a serene spirit," and he put great effort into inspiring the youth of his *kehillah* to continue on in advanced yeshivos. The thousands of *bnei Torah* at his funeral and the overwhelming majority of *bnei Torah* at a *hesped* in his memory in Jerusalem — children and grandchildren of his congregants — are eloquent testimony to his success in this realm.

Besides serving for many years as the *Av Beis Din* of the justly respected *beis din* of K'hal Adath Jeshurun, and the *beis din* of Torah Umesorah, he was frequently called upon to decide crucial *dinei Torah* dealing with major Torah institutions.

Rabbi Schwab was not a bridge between two worlds, between East and West — bridges are not for living on. He was rather the embodiment of the *eilu v'eilu divrei Elokim Chaim* ("these and those are the words of the living G–d") of two sacred traditions. He embodied in one person two diverse Torah cultures: the glorious Frankfurt tradition of Rabbi Hirsch, with its emphasis on adherence to the *emes* and insistence on putting the stamp of Torah on every area of public and private endeavor... combined with unwavering devotion to intense Torah study, which was the hallmark of the great yeshivos of Lithuania. On the one hand, he absorbed the Chofetz Chaim's caress; on the other, he observed the admonishment of the *alter* Gerrer Rebbe who characterized Rabbi Hirsch as "*a lebedike mussar sefer.*" That combination was the reason why he was the inspiration and source of guidance to so many in the Torah community of America.

Rabbi Schwab was convinced that *Torah im Derech Eretz* offers a vision of Judaism "in a way that can be accepted... by the five-and-a-half-million uncommitted Jews in the vast spiritual wasteland that is today's America, in a language they can understand."

He exemplified the "*Torah im Derech Eretz-ben Torah.*" *Torah im Derech Eretz* means "the subjugation and control of all mundane affairs by the royal sovereignty of the Torah." It is the call to take the Torah out into the world in order to sanctify the Divine Name on earth by our every action. It demands the Torah's conquest of life and not its flight from life. *The Torah im Derech Eretz-ben Torah* is well aware of what happens in the world that surrounds him, "for he is constantly called upon to apply the yardstick of *halachah* and the searchlight of *hashkafah* to the realities that confront him." He also knows that *Torah im Derech Eretz* cannot be separated from Rav Hirsch's *Austritt* (secession) principle, which requires absolute separation from institutionalized heresy or any view of Judaism based on anything other than Torah. Without *Austritt, Torah im Derech Eretz* is merely a cover for a convenient lifestyle, and a rejection of its essence, which is the total domination by Torah of all of life.

Torah im Derech Eretz means honesty and integrity in the business world and in the professions. It means seeing G–d in the wonders of Creation, in the magnificence of nature, in the breathtaking discoveries of science and in the grandeur of plant and animal life. It means an awareness of the fact that everything in the physical world is a manifestation of the *Shechinah*.

Rabbi Schwab himself attended neither high-school nor college; knowledge of the world and the wonders of Creation were self-taught. On nature walks with his children, he would tell them the names and nature of the flora and fauna. But the greatest revelation of G–d is the Torah, and without that, man will not know what to do with the awareness of His existence. Whereas nature shows the wonders of the Creator, Torah reveals, as it were, the Creator Himself.

Rabbi Chaim Ozer Grodzenski once put it all in perspective. While taking a walk in Switzerland, young Shimon Schwab pointed out the awesome Divine beauty of the Alps. "*S'iz shain,*" Reb Chaim Ozer agreed, "*ober a Yid mit a bord iz noch shenner.*" It would seem to this writer that the message was clear. One can perceive the Divine in nature as it performs G–d's will instinctively. That, however, can never match the beauty of the Jew who performs the Divine imperative in free-willed volition.

"Torah of Truth"

Early in life, his father taught him the importance of not only speaking the truth, but of living the truth. This writer recalls visiting the *Rav* as a young boy on the last day of Pesach, when the *Rav* told the following story:

As a young boy around the age of bar mitzvah, I decided to stand for the entire tefillos on the night and day of Yom Kippur, a custom cited in the Shulchan Aruch (O.C. 619). My father, who was not one to ignore things like that, made no comment. On Motza'ei Yom Kippur, one of my younger brothers did something that was not to my liking, and I let him have it physically. My father slapped my face. "I thought that you had perhaps attained the madreigah of observing even a custom brought as yesh omdim (some stand) in the Shulchan Aruch," he said. "But your behavior immediately following Yom Kippur indicates that you reached no such level at all, and were just showing off. For that you got the potsch."

His insistence on *emes* extended to things which usually go unnoticed. His stationery said: "*Head of the Beis Din* of the Kehilla Adath Jeshurun." When Rabbi Gelley joined the rabbinate, Rabbi Schwab began to cross out those words on the stationery, even though he was still the *Rav* of the *kehillah,* since he no longer sat on *dinei Torah.*

His first exposure to the insistence on *emes* in public life was from his revered *rebbi,* the Frankfurter Rav, Rabbi Shlomo Breuer, who followed in the footsteps of his father-in-law, Rabbi S.R. Hirsch. Reb Shlomo Breuer refused to recognize any Jewish community not absolutely governed by Torah, firmly opposed cooperation between Jewish communities and organizations based on Torah with those opposed to it. "He hated the untruth," Rabbi Schwab wrote of his *rebbi,* "but he despised even more the easy compromise between *emes* and *shekker,* the political double talk which in the name of unity would relegate the Torah Nation to a modest niche, to a mere 'branch' within the superstructure of a nondescript 'Jewish People.'"

The Kehillah as an Instrument of Truth

> The kehillah, Rabbi Schwab taught, is a microcosm of *Klal Yisrael* and as such, "is not beholden to any non-Torah authority, not associated with any board,
> federation, council, roof organization — local, national, or international — that is not absolutely and exclusively

identified with the Law of Torah. The true *kehillah* will not subscribe to or encourage any Jewish orientation or philosophy which is not based on the truth of the Torah."

This was not mere talk. The *kehillah* that he headed suffered great financial difficulty for its principled stand in this matter. yeshivah Rabbi S.R. Hirsch is one of very few in the New York area that has refused on principle to accept funding from the Federation's Board of Jewish Education, even from special "funds" that only used the Federation as a conduit. It was unthinkable to take money from an organization created for Jewish purposes, yet not based on allegiance to Torah as the supreme authority in Jewish life. The *Rav* was also certain that a yeshivah that derives part of its income from such sources cannot fulfill its potential in producing *talmidei chachamim*. He once told this writer that he was convinced that the yeshivos in *Eretz Yisrael* would be able to produce many more *gedolei Torah* if they were not constrained to rely on Israeli government funding for their existence. (See *Bava Metzia* 85b.)

Surely tolerance is important. Judaism has different *shitos* and philosophies. Chassidim, Litvaks, Sephardim — all must live together in peace and harmony, and can and should work together as components of one grand symphony. But all must be within the parameters of *emes*. This commitment to *emes* in organizational life was expressed in his allegiance to Agudath Israel of America, as well as in the fact that an overwhelming proportion of his congregants are members of the Agudah.

Commitment to *emes* means that there can be no tolerance for the statement that two and two are five. If the one making such an absurd statement never learned arithmetic, we can be tolerant of him, but not of his views. One must distinguish between Reform and Conservative rabbis and leaders, who are *meisisim umeidichim* (indoctrinators of non-truth), and their adherents, who are *tinokos shenishbu* (innocent victims), to whom we must reach out.

The insistence of the absolute standard of *emes* in public life is impossible unless it is the outgrowth of unshakable honesty in one's private affairs. And it is not enough, he never tired of saying, to be *l'Shem Shamayim*. One must constantly make sure that one's *l'Shem Shamayim* is *l'Shem Shamayim*. *Kanaus* (zealousness) must be driven by the purest of motives. And it must be without anger or invective. The *kana'i* must always bear in mind that those whom he criticizes are fellow Jews, whom he must rebuke with love. Only the one who leads others astray must be hated.

Revision, for the Sake of Truth

His adherence to *emes* was such that he was willing to revise long held views, even if that meant a reassessment of publicly stated positions. His views on the relevance of *Torah im Derech Eretz* are a case in point. With the rise of Nazism in the 1930's, Rabbi Schwab was convinced that *Torah im Derech Eretz* as expounded by Rabbi S.R. Hirsch was no longer relevant, not as an educational program and certainly not as a *Weltanschauung*. The barbarity of the Nazi beast (even before World War II), the virulent anti-Semitism in Germany, and the total failure of the ideals of enlightened humanism and Western culture to change the essential nature of gentile society led him to conclude that the only path for the Torah-observant German Jew was to return to the "Torah Only" approach, and to shun Western culture and the world at large as much as possible. Rabbi Hirsch's *Torah im Derech Eretz* ideal, he averred, was only a *horaas shaah*, a temporary measure for a temporary situation. In 1934, he aired these views in a slim volume entitled *Heimkehr ins Judentum* (Homecoming into Judaism), which caused a sensation in German Orthodoxy.

But after coming to America, he concluded that the realities of the ghetto and the *shtetl* where one could spend all one's life in the local *beis hamidrash*, with its total dissociation from the rest of society, was a way of life that had also been consumed in the flames of the Holocaust. The realities of life in the United States and other Western countries, where the Jew traveled in non-Jewish circles and could not live totally apart from the society around him, were not essentially different from the situation in the Western Europe of Rabbi Hirsch. Furthermore, a careful study of all of Rabbi Hirsch's writings led him to the inevitable conclusion that he had never meant *Torah im Derech Eretz* as a *horaas shaah* at all. It was not a compromise, a *kula*, or a *heter*. Although Rav Hirsch did not insist that it was for everyone, he certainly did not see it as time bound. Rabbi Schwab then publicly retracted his earlier insistence on "Torah Only" as the sole way of life for the Torah Jew in Western society. (Rabbi Schwab always viewed the situation in *Eretz Yisrael* as essentially unique, but that is beyond the purview of this article.) To that end he published in 1966 a booklet entitled *These and Those (Eilu v'Eilu)*, wherein he set forth the arguments and counter-arguments for both positions, with the conclusion, as the title indicates, that both, in their proper time and place, are legitimate ways of life for the Torah Jew in Western society.

There is an old Ashkenazi custom to call out "emes" in the Aleinu prayer recited during the Chazaras HaShatz of Mussaf on the Yamim Noraim. He retained this custom even in America where others had ceased to observe it. His last words to a disciple were, "Remember, you must always tell the emes. I have many failings," he continued, "but one thing I never did was chanfah (flatter) people."

"... Was in His Mouth"

He taught himself to speak and write eloquent, polished English, for that was the medium to reach the hearts and minds of American Jewry. Even the best of speakers sometimes have an off day, but of him it was said that he never spoke less than perfectly. He was always inspiring, stimulating, never humdrum. At the *Siyumei Hashas* of the *Daf Yomi*, at Agudath Israel and Torah Umesorah conventions, his carefully crafted addresses set the tone and inspired the audience. He could admonish and suggest areas in need of improvement without alienating his listeners. Why? Because he respected his audiences and never took them for granted. Because of that respect, he was always well prepared. His listeners knew that whatever he said derived from a sense of heartfelt concern. And he spoke of nothing to which he himself did not adhere.

He viewed his ability to influence others in a totally different way. He felt that it was because he was a *dachil rabbanan*, one who feared the Sages. The *Gemara* says that such a person will either become a *tzurva m'rabbanan*, a sage in his own right, or, if incapable of that, will be listened to as if he were a sage. He put himself in the latter category.

His son once found his father standing and talking on the telephone, at a time when he suffered terrible arthritis in his knees, which made it exruciatingly painful to stand. When asked why he was standing, he explained that he was talking to Rabbi Moshe Feinstein. "But you're not obligated to, if it's only on the phone," his son protested. "Surely, I have no chiyuv to stand," the Rav replied, "but how can I sit when talking to Reb Moshe?"

His influence was not limited to the spoken word. His articles and his *seforim* influenced many. In addition, he was a poet. At the request of Rabbi Breuer he authored a *Kinna* (lamentation) in memory of the Six Million. This eloquent and moving elegy for the *kedoshim* is now recited on *Tisha B'Av* in congregations throughout the world.

"Injustice Was Not on His Lips"

He was scrupulous to a fault in financial matters. He hated even a suggestion of crooked dealings. "I don't want to be a *bedi'eved Yid*," he would say, "I want to be a *lechat'chilah Yid*." He often wondered why people who were so stringent in regard to a *yeish omrim* (alternative opinion) in *Orach Chaim* and *Yoreh Deah* (ritual *halachah*) simply ignore the *yeish omrim* in *Choshen Mishpat* that prohibits *gezel akum*. His tax form was exact, recording even gifts from friends. He was once called in by the IRS for an audit, as they could not believe that a man with such modest income could give so much charity. He sent an accountant, a member of the *kehillah*, to represent him. At the conclusion, the IRS agent declared that never, in all his years as an auditor, had he met anyone who was so forthcoming and meticulous in reporting income and in documenting all contributions. He followed that with a letter to Rabbi Schwab saying that the latter's scrupulous honesty "had restored my faith in humanity."

Someone once undertook to publish the writings of a certain Torah luminary of a previous generation. Knowing that the editor of the work was having difficulty raising the necessary funds to cover the publication costs, the *Rav* called him on his own initiative and offered him a loan of $10,000 to cover the initial costs. Several weeks later, he notified the editor that since the publisher of the work had been sending him books from time to time, he was afraid that those complimentary books might be construed as *ribbis* (interest). He thus decided to give the entire sum, which constituted a good portion of his life savings, as a gift, so that there would be no hint of a *she'eilah*, even though halachically there was no problem whatsoever.

Kashrus, he always stressed, refers not only to food but to money as well.

"While those who resort to cheating, trickery, dishonesty and fraud may at times have the outward appearance of being G–d-fearing Jews, they are, in fact, irreligious. They may well be strict in their observance of certain mitzvos, but in their business dealings they reveal that they are kofrim (infidels) in regard to Hashgachah pratis, Divine Providence. Since they certainly do not believe that G–d wants them to take what is not rightfully theirs, they are conducting their business as though He does not exist. 'Glatt yosher,' as Rabbi Breuer once wrote, 'is no less important than glatt kosher.'"

He was the ultimate *sonei betza*. He refused to accept compensation for any rabbinic function, including weddings, funerals, *dinei Torah* and *kashrus* supervision. "Rabbi," he was often asked, "what do I owe you?"

"Owe me? This is not a business. It is my responsibility to *Klal Yisrael*." He refused to accept money even for *mechiras chometz*. He did not, however, wish to hurt the income of other rabbis, so he established a *tzedakah* fund to which anyone who insisted on paying for *mechiras chametz* could contribute.

In his six decades as a Rav, he never once asked for a raise. When, in his advanced years, the kehillah engaged Rabbi Zechariah Gelley to serve alongside him, he requested the Board of Trustees to reduce his own salary since he would have less responsibilities. They replied that, as it was, his salary was so low that it constituted no more than a retirement wage.

"In Peace and Straightforwardness He Walked With Me"

He was princely in his relations with others. He treated young and old with warmth, and greeted everyone *b'seiver panim yafos*, the hallmark of all the Schwab brothers. His smile warmed as it shone, his sparkling eyes and his shining countenance put his visitors at ease, no matter what their station in life.

"*Ha'emes v'hashalom ehavu,*" the prophet says. Both peace and truth are important, but one must always bear in mind that peace is a virtue when dealing with one's personal affairs, where one must bend and give in for the sake of peace. Judaism, however, is not one's to compromise. In matters touching upon Torah issues, it must be *emes* first and then *shalom*. Peace, Rabbi S.R. Hirsch often said, is the child of truth; not the reverse.

He personified the imperative of the prophet Michah to be a *hatzne'a leches im Elokecha*, to walk humbly with G–d. Although requested at various times to serve on the *Moetzes Gedolei HaTorah* of Agudath Israel, he refused, saying that he was not worthy of being a member of this august body.

The *tzenius* referred to by the prophet Michah means not only humility, but more importantly, a lack of ostentation. He despised conspicuous consumption. He pleaded incessantly for *tzenius* and simplicity in *simchos*, in manner of dress, and comportment, in lifestyles and vacations.

Tzenius, lack of ostentation, is no less important in spiritual matters. How does one walk with Hashem inconspicuously? For a person who truly walks with G–d, being in the public eye is no reason to manifest one's devoutness. *Le'olam yehei adam yerei Shamayim b'seiser u'vagaluy*. One must always fear G–d, in private and in public. The question is obvious: One who does not fear G–d in private does not fear G–d at all. What does it mean to fear G–d in private? *Hatzne'a leches*, the *Rav* explained, requires that one's *yiras Shamayim* be something one has no need to show off. True *yiras Shamayim* is between you and G–d, and the more *yiras Shamayim* one has, the less should others be aware of it. The *Gemara* tells us that the *Ishah HaShunamis* (Shunamite woman) knew that Elisha the Prophet was a holy man because flies did not disturb him, among other private indications.

Couldn't she tell that he was a *kadosh* by just looking at him and watching his behavior? The answer is that true *kedushah*, true *yiras Shamayim*, is not readily apparent to the casual observer. One sees nothing extraordinary on the externals of the true *tzaddik*. He learned this, he said, from the Chofetz Chaim. If one was *zocheh*, one could see the *Shechinah* on his visage, but otherwise, he looked like a plain man dressed in the clothes of a simple laborer with an ordinary cap pulled low over his forehead. The greater the *gadol*, the more simple the comportment. Real *kedushah* is within; as soon as it becomes manifested outwardly, it is diminished.

The *Rav* personified this in his daily life and in his davening, which was without noise or fuss. From his early youth, when no one watched or cared, the first *pesukim* of *Krias Shema* took him an inordinate amount of time to recite. Only his family knew that he began *davening* at home, much before he came to *shul*, and when the congregation was at *Borchu*, he was already holding by the second *berachah* of *Krias Shema*. In his later years, or when illness prevented him from *davening* with a *minyan* in *shul*, his *tefillos* at home were wrenching in their intensity — but never when anyone was watching.

For years he would buy two *esrogim* for *Succos*. The exquisite one, for which he spent a large sum of money, he kept at home. He took the simpler one to *shul*. The *hiddur mitzvah* was pure, with no element of public display. *Kavanah* in mitzvos was not limited to the more glamorous ones. One must have no less *kavanah* in one's daily *benching*, he used to say, than one has when eating the first *k'zayis* of matzah on Pesach.

One who walks with G-d feels that he is always in the Divine presence. Rabbi Schwab's regal bearing reflected that. He was his children's best friend, yet his son testified that until his father was 83 years old and in the hospital, he never saw him in bed. He spared himself little time for rest, citing Rav Hirsch on the verse, "*Vayikatz Yaakov mishnaso: Ehr hat sich ge'ekelt fun sein shluf* — He was revolted by his sleep." Yet for all his busy schedule and his dignified demeanor, he always had time for his children. His Shabbos and Yom Tov table were occasions of sheer delight.

When one walks with G–d, it is insufficient merely to start the journey with his Creator. Every step of the way must reflect that reality. The prophet Isaiah criticized the Jewish People, "*Vatehi yirasam osei mitzvas anashim melumadah* — they did their mitzvos as if by rote." Rabbi Schwab explained that not only one's mitzvah performance, but even one's *yiras Shamayim* can become mechanical. Even a person's *kanaus* and path in life must be under constant scrutiny so that it not become stale.

Walking with Hashem means constant awareness of His presence. He always stressed that the prime necessity of the Jew was *emunah peshutah*, an uncomplicated awareness of G–d's closeness and *Hashgachah pratis*. *Emunah* (which Rav Hirsch relates to *omein*, nurse) is the feeling of security and well-being one must have, sensing the protective and caring presence of G–d — as a nursing child feels in his mother's arms. In this manner Rabbi Schwab lived for 86 years, and when the time came for him to leave this world, it was in the same calm and trusting manner.

On Rosh Chodesh Adar I, 5755, he was hospitalized after a heart attack. On the eve of Purim Katan, he suffered another severe attack. Now that his teachers were paid, he could leave the world. His family gathered around his bed and he calmly recited *Viduy, Shema Yisrael, Baruch Shem* and the sevenfold *Hashem Hu HaElokim*. With the seventh *Hashem Hu HaElokim*, he returned his soul to his Maker, moving on to the *Olam HaEmes* as he lived, declaring "*Hashem Hu HaElokim,*" the fundamental truth of the universe.

Integrity: HaRav Moshe Sherer

(excerpt)
Rabbi Eliyahu Meir Klugman

"Neki chapayim u'var leivav asher lo nasa lashav nafshi v'lo nishba l'mirmah — Only one with clean hands and pure heart who has not lifted up his soul in vain, and one who does not use his word for purposes of deception [can ascend Hashem's holy mountain]"
(Tehillim 24:4).

Rabbi Sherer's absolute integrity explains much of his ability to be *mekadesh Shem Shamayim*, and is the reason for the great esteem he and the Agudah enjoyed in the eyes of the general public, from presidents on down.

Rabbi Sherer bent over backwards to stay clear of even the slightest appearance of impropriety. In an age where public scandals and financial malfeasance are a too frequent occurrence, Agudath Israel was always beyond reproach, even as millions of dollars of government funding were being administered annually by various public agencies of the Agudah. And as Under Secretary of State Stuart Eizenstadt told this writer, that absolute rectitude was recognized in government circles.

If a government contract for social or educational services could not be followed to the letter, Rabbi Sherer insisted that the

Agudah contact the relevant agency explaining that it could not comply with the guidelines. If the regulations could not be amended, the money was returned.

Public scandals, especially those involving Torah institutions, tore him apart. He had no tolerance whatsoever for those whose involvement in corrupt schemes brought about *chillul Hashem*. "*Harchek min hakiyur v'hadomeh lo* — Distance yourself from anything even resembling repulsive behavior," he frequently said. For all his loathing of corruption, he invested monumental behind-the-scenes efforts to prevent those scandals from bringing about even greater *chillul Hashem*. The fingerprints of Agudath Israel never appeared in connection with any case involving possible *chillul Hashem*, but Rabbi Sherer did intervene personally on behalf of the families of Orthodox Jews who had run afoul of the law.

Rabbi Sherer was instrumental in establishing AARTS, the accrediting agency for *yeshivos gedolos* receiving government funding for students of institutions of higher education, to ensure that the pipeline of government funding was absolutely clean. He placed in charge people of unimpeachable integrity to make the process as fraud proof as possible.

Rabbi Sherer's interest in career training and employment services stemmed from his desire to help *bnei Torah* without college educations earn respectable livings without being dependent on government largesse.

"Clean hands" betokens much more than not stealing or cheating. In those two words lies an entire *Weltanschauung*, a conviction that *Klal* work must never be undertaken for personal or institutional benefit. A businessman once needed a contact in Washington for an export license from a foreign country. Rabbi Sherer put him in touch with the proper State Department official. When the recipient thanked Rabbi Sherer and asked him how he could repay the favor, Rabbi Sherer told him there was nothing to repay, and added: "I will check the books of the Agudah, and if I find that this year you gave more than last year, I will return it."

One of the divisions of Agudath Israel provides assistance to yeshivos in dealing with the government regulatory agencies.

Its operating expenses are high, and its services are of great value to the yeshivos that avail themselves of its services. Rabbi Sherer adamantly rejected suggestions that the yeshivos be charged a fee for those services. "We exist to service the yeshivos, period," he said. The most he would permit was that Agudath Israel send these yeshivos ad blanks at dinner time. Some yeshivos participated; many did not.

From the early 60's, when Rabbi Sherer assumed full financial responsibility for the Agudah, the organization stopped borrowing money to cover operations. From then on, Agudath Israel rarely missed a payroll, and he was always the last to be paid. He realized that no staff member could give his full efforts if he had to borrow money to support a family. And although he was responsible for raising the budget, he insisted that he have no authority to sign checks.

"*V'lo nishba l'mirmah* — he does not use his word for purposes of deception" (*Tehillim* ibid.). Politicians and organizational leaders live day-to-day by making promises they have no intention of keeping. No one expects otherwise. Rabbi Sherer, says a colleague who worked at his side for the last 50 years, never made a promise unless he was sure he could keep it.

A Day in the Life of a "Tzaddik Nistar": Dr. Shimon Askovitz

Rabbi Yisroel Greenwald

❖ The Tzaddik's Time Frame

What marks a person as a *tzaddik*? A special awareness — and then some. Everyone "knows" that life is transitory and elusive. Didn't Shakespeare say that man struts and frets upon the stage of life, and passes like a shadow soon to be forgotten? In contrast to Shakespeare, a *tzaddik lives* with this concept. He is deeply aware that life is a journey and not a destination, and that every step on the way must proclaim the honor of Hashem. "And even if he has an occupation, he can be on the same level as one for whom the words of the Torah never cease from his lips" (end of *Mesillas Yesharim*).

A *tzaddik* lives not by years or decades, but rather by moments and days. While small men do great things on occasion, great men constantly deal with small things. To the great, each day is laden with meaning and importance (see Hirsch,

Bereishis 47:8), with new goals to accomplish and obstacles to hurdle. That is why we ask G-d to "teach us to count our days."

I was fortunate to know a person who lived by this credo. His name was Reb Shimon Yitzchak ben Reb Yecheskel Dov, more commonly known as Dr. Askovitz, a highly regarded, world-famous opthalmologist.

✢ *A Typical Day*

It was a balmy Nissan morning in 5740 as the doctor left his house to join the Philadelphia Yeshivah's *Shacharis minyan*. The pain in his chest was increasing and he began to emit a sigh, which he quickly cut short: G-d is a *Rofei Chinom* ... He heals without charge — but it also means that G-d heals for nothing, even if we do not deserve it.

> *His house was only minutes away from the yeshivah, which was one of the reasons he selected it. It was a large structure with the office on the ground floor, next to living quarters.*
>
> *The house was equipped with an extra floor for use by poor people, guests and meshulachim who were always staying at his house. Piles of seforim were permanent residents in his house — on tables and shelves in every available room, each with one or several markers indicating where he was up to.*

Once inside the yeshivah, he paused at the bulletin board in front of the *beis hamidrash* and posted his annual sign: "The apple tree (on the corner of 59th and Overbrook) is in full bloom. Everyone is welcome to make a *berachah*! (see *Orach Chaim* Ch. 55 Par. 3)." He respectfully paused before setting foot inside the *beis midrash*, and then walked to his seat in the back row. Dr. Askovitz was a welcome *mispallel* there. Through personal example, he instructed generations of *talmidim* in the way the *Chazal* meant *"Omein yehei Shmei Rabbah"* to be said .... He *davened* as though having a personal conversation with Hashem, the tone and inflection of his voice practically translating the *tefillos*.

It was a Monday, so as usual he passed around the *Chumashim* — his own private *Chumashim,* which he had bought for this expressed purpose — handing them to those near him before the reading of the Torah. After *davening,* he closed his *Siddur HaGra* and carefully replaced the several IBM cards he used as bookmarks. Some of these cards contained long lists of names of deceased, with no one else to say *Kaddish* for them. Others listed names of ailing individuals, some for whom he had been *davening* for years on end.

He sat down to learn, but he expected frequent interruptions. He had been collecting for the Philadelphia Agudath Israel's Annual *Ma'os Chittim* campaign, and boys would be coming over every few minutes to offer their contributions. He did not feel less dignity in collecting *tzedakah* than in giving it; in fact he relished the former as a far greater *mitzvah.*

His study was interruped by a *bachur* who came over to discuss a *halachah* with him:

"Do we still say the *'Birchas Shehecheyanu'* upon seeing a close friend after 30 days?" (see *Orach Chaim* Ch. 225). Dr. Askovitz consulted a *Mishnah Berurah* for a while, and then replied in his smooth melodious voice, "Since the *berachah* is dependent on feeling happy upon the sight of your friend, if you're happy why shouldn't you make a *berachah*? I used to make a *berachah* when I was in the army, and I saw my parents when on furlough. I recall seeing a commentary on the *pasuk* vsav og usev hf (For man is like the tree of the field), who translated the *pasuk*: 'Is a person any worse than a tree?' Everyone makes a *Shehecheyanu* on a new fruit — shouldn't a human being have the same value? But probably the reason it came into disuse is because if Reuven sees Shimon and makes a *berachah,* and the following time they meet, Shimon doesn't make a *berachah* on Reuven, Reuven would get very insulted."

The *bachur* hemmed and hawed for a moment and then asked the doctor to look at a rash on his arm. Talk unrelated to Torah and mitzvos (even for one's livelihood) is prohibited in *shul* (see *Mishnah Berurah* 151, minor Par. 2). So, as he had done time and again over the decades, Dr. Askovitz slowly stepped outside the study hall while respectfully facing the *Aron*

HaKodesh, examined the rash, and asked the boy to come back the next day. (The following day he would bring medication free of charge. An opthalmologist, he stored general medication in his house only for this type of occasion.)

He continued studying for another hour, and then took leave of the *beis midrash.*

→ *Home for Breakfast*

At home, he opened the daily mail lying on his kitchen table. He recognized the handwriting of the topmost letter to be that of a sick, heartbroken invalid. From the many letters pouring into his office on a regular basis, he learned to discern the telltale signs of worry and depression from handwritings.

> *Dear President of Agudath Israel of Philadelphia:*
> *I am writing you this letter asking your organization to help me out with some clothing. I have a bad heart and I am a diabetic. I have to go to a nursing home for medical care and I have no money. I thank you, G-d bless you and yours.*

He put down the letter, jotted down name and address on a slip of paper, and picked up the phone. He placed an order of clothing with a local merchant to be sent to the man's address, to be billed to the local Agudah. For Yom Tov the man would also receive a food parcel of matzah, wine, meat and fish, together with a warm, friendly note, inviting further inquiries.

The next letter was from Rabbi Moshe Sherer thanking Dr. Askovitz for sending him a clipping on autopsies, which he found to be of great interest. He also asked Dr. Askovitz to accelerate activity on stopping the State of Pennsylvania from ratifying the ERA. The letter concluded with a recommendation for a New York representative to the local Agudah's yearly *teshuvah* gathering. He placed the two letters in their respective files, cleared away the rest of the mail and entered his office.

The secretary looked up from her typewriter to exchange greetings with the doctor and then returned to her work. She often told her friends how grateful she was to have a boss who was proficient in *mussar;* in her 20 years on the job, the doctor never showed irritability or made her feel bad in any way.

Behind the secretary were the card files, which took up the entire wall. All patients were treated equally: same type of card, same time offered to them, same treatment — regardless if they paid full price or nothing at all. Rabbis were free of charge; and so were yeshivah *bachurim* — until, at the *Rosh Yeshivah's* insistence, this was changed to a discounted fee. *Yungeleit* from Lakewood paid half the regular fee, to allow for their travel expenses. There were also the sick and elderly throughout the city to whom he travelled, to give them eye examinations.

✦ *"Lunch," Supper, and More Learning*

He had no lunch hour since he had no lunch, as he saw mentioned in certain *seforim* (for *halachah,* see *Mishnah Berurah* 157, minor Par. 4). His hours stretched till before sunset when he would rush out to catch the *Mincha-Maariv minyan.* He would drive to *shul* if only to hear the final *Kaddish,* and even held a key to the *shul,* to daven in the *beis haknesses* should he have missed the *minyan.*

After *Maariv* he would return home for supper. He never ate supper before *Maariv,* which was often a great difficulty since he was fatigued after a hard working day without having eaten in over eight hours.

After supper he would continue his Torah studies. "Continue" because his life revolved around Torah, his work being only his secondary occupation. He would often tell his wife how he could not wait until he'd retire so he could learn the entire day. His learning was sometimes interrupted by phone calls all hours of the night. Searching individuals would call to ask philosophical questions, patients would call for medical advice. One patient worried excessively, and would often "drop in" at 11:30 P.M. to pickup some eye wash. Never did the doctor show irritability, and would always respond with a cheerful, "That's what we're here for." He would then continue to learn with great joy and fervor.

His *sefarim* library contained thousands of *sefarim* — not as a collection, for they were in constant use. The hundreds of *mussar seforim* he learned made him into a living *mussar sefer;* the *halachah sefarim* he studied cover to cover made him an expert in the field, and it was not infrequent that yeshivah *bachurim* would ask him their difficult *she'eilos.* (Rabbi Yaakov Yitzchak Ruderman of Ner Israel testified that he knew the entire *Mishnah Berurah* by heart.) And the hundreds of obscure *seforim*, which were full of asterisks, underlined sentences and glosses, made him into the *talmid chacham* that he was .... The lights in his study burned until 2:30 in the morning, leaving him less than five hours of sleep.

→ *The Focal Point of His Day*

A doctor once asked the Chofetz Chaim in what way people like himself could merit a share in the World to Come. The Chofetz Chaim replied that the *Chumash* describes the *Eitz Chaim,* the Tree of Life, as being "in the garden." The *Targum* translated this, "in the *center* of the garden." What significance is there if the tree is in the center or in the far end of the garden? However, the Torah is indicating that the *Eitz Chaim,* like any item found in the center, is equally accessible from all sides. No matter what occupation he holds — whether in Torah or in a profession — he has equal access to the Tree of Life (*Writings of the Chofetz Chaim,* p. 56; see also *Taanis* 21a).

Dr. Askovitz never had the opportunity to learn in a yeshiva and all alone set out on his long journey to Torah knowledge. He sought to find mentors to provide him with guidance and direction, and clung dearly to them his entire life. His *rabbe'im* included *Rashi,* the *Rambam, Chayei Adam* and especially the Chofetz Chaim.

Dr. Askovitz made his daily life conform to the Torah: He didn't particularly enjoy lukewarm tea, yet he always drank it that way, as he saw written in *halachah,* to require an after-*berachah* ... He had never cared for gefilte fish, but after learning the importance of Shabbos fish he developed a taste for it. Even during his final days in the hospital, unable to eat for an entire week, he forced himself on Shabbos to eat a little fish and meat, and then feebly sang some Shabbos *zemiros* .... The *halachah* does not permit a person to force himself to eat something he does not like on Shabbos. So if he ate it, he must have enjoyed it — probably because his greatest enjoyment in life was fulfilling the will of Hashem.

Dr. Askovitz would not merely say a *berachah*. He would make a loud, ear-ringing declaration of Hashem's glory and kindness. The refreshments at the Agudah executive meetings were chosen by their *berachah* variety, so that one could say as many *berachos* as possible. He would encourage guests to make *berachos* out loud to enable the whole family to "*chap arein* some extra *Ameins*." He would pick up a bunch of raisins or peanuts, lift it up in his right hand, and with a look of utter joy and concentration pronounce the appropriate *berachah*. He did not reach for a second helping of peanuts because he did not make the *berachah* to eat. He ate in order to make the *berachah*.

✦ *No More Days*

When Dr. Askovitz passed away, he was mourned by all. The poor, the sick, the senile, the alcoholic, the ex-convict, the invalid — all had known that he was a friend who bore their burdens with an unburdened feeling. He would receive their calls from bars, prisons and institutions, and would always open his home to them, some for even a long duration.

> *A poor man who often visited the yeshivah contracted an illness that gave him an extremely offensive odor. Most bachurim found it difficult to even breathe in his presence, let alone carry on a conversation with him... A rebbe in the yeshivah once went to Dr. Askovitz after Shacharis to pick up his eyeglasses, and he found Dr. Askovitz serving the poor fellow breakfast as though he were a royal guest.*

Doctor ... Man of *chesed* ... *Tzaddik nistar* — a man of unknown greatness.

Kiddush Hashem in the House of Lords

Dr. Yoel Jakobovits

✥ A "Jewish" Approach to Social Issues

The recent elevation of my father, Rabbi Immanuel Jakobovits, to the House of Lords has prompted much comment. As a son, there well within me a profusion of emotions and thoughts. In addition to the purely personal aspects, many of these are of universal Jewish concern, and it is regarding these that I devote these lines.

Reaction in the general press, and especially in the British press, has been almost hyperbolic. "Unique," "momentous," "singular," are just a few adjectives used to describe this event, unparalleled in the annals of British history. In Britain, the first Jew to be elevated as a peer to the Upper House of Parliament was Nathaniel Meyer de Rothschild, in 1885. Thereafter the elevation of English Jews for social or political reasons was not uncommon. Indeed, today there are many Jews among the 1200 or so Lords in the "Mother of Parliaments."

What is exceptional about this appointment, however, is this: whereas previous Jews have been elevated in recognition of secular services, this elevation is clearly in acknowledgment and admiration of religious and spiritual contributions. This may explain the remarkable analysis, which appeared in one of England's most prestigious newspapers, *The Sunday Telegraph,* January 10, 1988 editorial bearing the title "Judaism is the new creed of Thatcherite Britain":

> Rightly affronted by this Government's attitude to Israel, British Jewry can, however, take consolation from Mrs. Thatcher's evident determination to give Judaism a much more prominent say in the life of this nation than it has ever enjoyed before. For months the Chief Rabbi has, in effect, been the spiritual leader of Thatcherite Britain. By putting him in the House of Lords the Prime Minister has publicly and formally recognized the enormously important role he has come to play, more than amply filling the vacuum created by the blank refusal of the Christian Churches to make any constructive contribution towards her crusade for the regeneration of Britain ... Only the Chief Rabbi, in his pronouncements, makes any attempts to suggest that what she is frying to do might be pleasing to G–d.
>
> ... Judaism has a much sterner approach to life than that of contemporary Christian denominations. The emphasis is more on justice for all, including the rich, than on compassion for the poor, more on duties than on rights ... Modern Christianity tends to fall into sentimentality when it considers social problems. The temptation for Judaism might be an excessive legalism. But it must also be remembered that Jews are noted for their charity. Many of the most notable donations to charities come from Jews.
>
> ... The attitude of Judaism towards individual achievement reflects the experience of a people who, because they were precluded from other occupations, formed a class of merchants and financiers during their diaspora.

... The Judaic lessons of the Old Testament seem to be that we live in a harsh world where only our own efforts and trust in G–d and obedience to His commandments will carry us through .... This is a far more appropriate message than the Sermon on the Mount.

... It could be that the elevation of the Chief Rabbi to the House of Lords — following and transcending the elevation of so many Jews to the Cabinet — will prove a far more significant event for British Jewry, and indeed for Jewry the world over, than anything that happened last week in the West Bank or Gaza Strip.

❧ Lessons to be Learned

How should this affect the Jewish community in general, and the Torah-true community in particular? Are there any lessons of wider application which can be learnt?

Rabbi Chanoch Ehrentreu, the *Rosh Beis Din* of the London *Beis Din*, speaking at a communal reception marking the occasion, pointed out that since Jewish teachings are timeless, it is our obligation to try to make the times conform with the Torah's spirit and standards, not the reverse. By doing so we can augment the spiritual dimensions of our vexing times, elevating it beyond the mundane, bringing the whole of society closer to Hashem.

The doctrine of *kiddush Hashem* comprises several facets. The requirement to sanctify the name of Hashem before a group of ten Jews, even by martyrdom, if necessary, is well established.[1] This has characterized the Jews' response in times of crises throughout the centuries of our incomparably bitter history. In the wake of these brutal ordeals of the *galus*, it is perhaps not surprising that a second aspect of *kiddush Hashem* is today not so widely recognized, namely our obligations in being *mekadesh Hashem* in the eyes of the gentile world as well. As Rabbi Shimon

---

1. *Rambam, Yad HaChazakah, Hil. Yesodei HaTorah,* 5:1-2.

Schwab so eloquently expressed it, who can be blamed for rejecting the nations and their attitudes, when they have dealt so treacherously with us?

Particularly in the decades since the atrocities of World War II the Torah-true community, in particular, has been more occupied with internal self-betterment than with exporting our principles to the "outside" world. This concentration on internal needs has borne extraordinarily abundant fruits. Hence the enormous expansion of Torah learning and living in communities all over the world. Through the inspired guidance of a few Torah giants who were spared from the crematoria of Europe we have been privileged to witness the new rise of Torah life, an authentic phoenix arising from the ashes.

✦ Nations to be Taught

Nevertheless, we cannot ignore the *kiddush Hashem l'einei hagoyim* aspect.[2] Clearly, this constitutes a critical mission in the unfolding of our destiny. Moshe Rabbeinu's argument to Hashem to exculpate *Klal Yisrael* after the failing of the Golden Calf was precisely this: "Why should the Egyptians say that with bad intentions (You) took them out?" (*Shemos* 32:12). To which Rabbi S.R. Hirsch comments, "It was not only to educate this people to be Thy people; the enlightenment and instruction of the other nations was also an essential objective of this whole miraculous redemption." Evidently, the motivation for our delivery from bondage was not only to establish us as a nation. It was also supposed to inspire the gentiles with our message and our G–d.

Our prophets, of course, abound with examples of admonition directed towards the gentile society, as well as our own. Yonah's charge to reprimand Ninveh is one such example. That our national prototype is supposed to be a beacon to the world, and that this is our collective responsibility, is manifest from the following verses in *Yechezkel*, 36:20, and on:

2. An important discussion of this aspect of *kiddush Hashem* can be found in *Maharal's Nesivos Olam, Nesiv Yiras Hashem* 5 and *Nesiv Ahavas Hashem* 2.

As one unit did (Klal Yisrael) come into the nations, and they pro-
faned My Holy Name, inasmuch as it was said of them: "These are the
people of G–d and they have come out of His land." But I had pity for
My Holy Name which as the House of Israel they had profaned among
the nations. Therefore say unto the House of Israel: "Thus says ... G–d:
Not for your sakes do I do this ... but for My Holy Name which you have
profaned among the nation to which you have come. And I will sancti-
fy My Holy Name ... and the nations will know that I am G–d, ... inas-
much as I will show My Holiness through you before their eyes."

The indisputable message of these passages — as interpreted by *Rashi*[3] — is that we as Jews have been placed on the stage
of world history, and have been spared from the disintegration
which terminated numerous other peoples, for one distinctive
reason: to be *mekadesh Hashem* in the eyes of the world.
Ultimately, then, all the dedication and efforts in refining ourselves, in living lives of spiritual goals and aspiring to noble
heights, must also find articulation in how we enlighten the
world at large. Indeed, by now most of the Western world does
accept as standard the basic principles of social justice and
moral equity which our Torah and *Neviim* first proclaimed. In a
striking, though (therefore?) censored, passage at the culmina-
tion of his *Yad HaChazakah,*[4] Rambam says:

For it is beyond the human mind to fathom the designs of the
Creator; for our ways are not His ways, neither are our thoughts His
thoughts. All these matters relating to Jesus of Nazereth and the
Ishmaelite (Mohammed) who came after him, only served to clear the
way for King Messiah, to prepare the whole world to worship G–d with
one accord.

... Thus the Messianic hope, the Torah, and the commandments have
become familiar topics — topics of conversation among the inhabitants
of the far isles (sic!) and many peoples, uncircumcised of heart and flesh.
They are discussing these matters and the commands of the Torah.

Mindful of these comments, it is clear that tributes from the
gentile world for the Torah and its principles are desirable and

---

3. More, especially *Rashi* on *Yoma* 86a, the Talmud's key text defining *chillul Hashem.*

4. *Hil. Melachim*, Ch. 11. See Isadore Twersky's "Maimonides Reader."

significant. That this is so on this specific event is quite evident from many of the remarkable favorable press reports the world over occasioned by the elevation of an Orthodox, uncompromising spokesman.

The London Daily Mail, December 31, 1987, in a commentary entitled: "A Life Peerage for the Great Moral Crusader," contends:

> ... Undoubtedly his firm stance at a time when the Church of England is wracked by moral doubts, has been welcomed in high circles. He takes the view that adultery, homosexuality and [promiscuity] are wrong under all circumstances, and he would like to see homosexuality and adultery made illegal. He has argued that only a moral revolution can contain the scourage of AIDS.

✦ *Curbing Unlimited License*

This leads us to a brief consideration of some of the factors which have occurred, allowing such a remarkably forthright recognition of our value system. In truth, it is hard to envision that such an endorsement could have occurred 20, or even 10, years ago. But the last decade has seen some hithertofore quite unimagined transformations take place, which I believe may be as germane in America as they are in Britain. Most especially, the emergence of AIDS, perhaps more than any other single incentive, has stymied the very foundations of the indulgent society, which preached unlimited license coupled with negligible liability. People can no longer expect to act irresponsibly, without constraint, and not have to face the repercussions in a very immediate and often fatal way.[5] The subculture spawned by permissiveness has had its day.

Many thoughtful people are now searching for a relevant

---

5. Compare *Rashi, Bereishis,* 6:13: "Wherever you find lewdness and idolatry, punishment of an indiscriminate nature comes upon the world, killing good and bad alike."

value system to fill the vacuum. That the persuasive and stead-fast representation of our heritage should now receive such welcome and praise is a significant recognition of the pertinence of our timeless teachings in today's modern world.

The lesson to be taken from this fulfillment of our role as moral pacesetters for the world is that ultimately living truthfully to our own traditions and teachings will, when expressed with sincerity and conviction, help speed the day when it will be said that "the world is filled with the knowledge of G–d as the waters cover the seas." In emphasizing this concept, *The New York Times*, February 10, 1988, elected to publish the following quote from an interview with my father:

> Nobody today thinks that, by dropping their
> Jewishness, they will find it easier to be accepted in
> society. My elevation is the best example of that. I have
> been elevated not because I renounced my Jewish
> beliefs or modified them or made concessions, but on
> the contrary, because I held strictly to them and pro-
> claimed them without adulteration and
> without concessions.

Some might be uneasy, thinking that the price for such recognition must be excessive. They may assume that in order to be comfortable with the non-Jewish world, it is necessary to compromise our own values and distinctiveness. It is therefore significant that the celebrated *Times of London* saw it this way in an article on December 31, 1987:

> Sir Immanuel is regarded as the chief spokesman for
> Jewry in Britain — (even) by the other non-Orthodox
> Jewish communities, in spite of sometimes being
> involved in religious controversy .... He is a strong
> supporter of Israel, though sometimes willing to
> criticize Israeli government policies .... The warmth of
> the relationships he has developed with Christian
> leaders in Britain has no equal, and he has been
> universally recognized by the churches as a man of

deep and attractive spiritual wisdom. But he does not believe in inter-faith theological dialogue and has not seen eye to eye with other faiths on everything. He rather upstaged senior churchmen in 1987 with a statement on AIDS and homosexuality which was more forthright and uncompromising than any they had made.

There are few among us who are likely to have occasion to reach such open societal acclaim. However, this patent *kiddush Hashem* should fortify us in committing ourselves to our distinctive role *l'einei hagoyim.* Hopefully it will act as a catalyst for all of us — shopkeepers and entrepreneurs, professionals and housewives — to remain conscious at all times of our distinguishing assignment and exceptional opportunity in the realization of our destiny so that it will be said of us "you, my servant Yisrael, in whom I — Hashem — will be glorified."[6]

---

6. *Isaiah* 49:3. This verse is quoted by the *Rambam* in his concluding statement on *kiddush Hashem, Hil. Yesodei HaTorah* 5:11. The context here, as in its Talmudic source, *Yoma* 86a, relates to our obligations in being *mekadesh Hashem* in our world at large. Of note too is *Isaiah* 49:6 in the same expression: "*ohr lagoyim.*"